Migration, Remittances, and Sustainable Development in Africa

This book provides a strong multidisciplinary examination of the links between migration, remittances and sustainable development in Africa. It makes evidence-based policy recommendations on migration to help achieve the Sustainable Development Goals.

The key themes examined are migration and remittances, and their relations with the following issues: economic transformation, education and knowledge, corruption and conflict. Cross-cutting issues such as gender equality and youth are weaved throughout the chapters, and a rich range of country contexts are presented. The volume also discusses challenges in managing migration flows.

It will be of interest to advanced students, academics and policy makers in development economics and sustainable development.

Maty Konte is Research Fellow and lecturer in economics at UNU–MERIT and Maastricht University in the Netherlands, and Research Scholar at Columbia University in New York City. She is also an affiliated faculty at the African School of Economics in Benin and expert advisor for INCLUDE (the Dutch Ministry of Foreign Affairs knowledge platform on inclusive policies for development), and Research Fellow at the Global Labor Organisation.

Linguère Mously Mbaye is a Senior Research Economist at the African Development Bank in Côte d'Ivoire. She is also Research Affiliate at the Institute of Labor Economics, Germany, and Research Fellow at the Global Labor Organisation.

Routledge Studies in Development Economics

For more information about this series, please visit: www.routledge.com/series/SE0266

Migration, Remittances, and Sustainable Development in Africa

Edited by
Maty Konte and
Linguère Mously Mbaye

LONDON AND NEW YORK

First published 2021
by Routledge
2 Park Square, Milton Park, Abingdon, Oxon OX14 4RN

and by Routledge
52 Vanderbilt Avenue, New York, NY 10017

Routledge is an imprint of the Taylor & Francis Group, an informa business

British Library Cataloguing-in-Publication Data
A catalogue record for this book is available from the British Library

Library of Congress Cataloging-in-Publication Data
A catalog record has been requested for this book

ISBN: 978-0-367-25647-0 (hbk)
ISBN: 978-0-429-28881-4 (ebk)

Typeset in Bembo
by codeMantra

Contents

Contributors

Editors

Maty Konte is Research Fellow and Lecturer in economics and governance at the United Nations University in Maastricht, the Netherlands, and Research Scholar at Columbia University in New York City. She is also an expert advisor for INCLUDE (the Dutch Ministry of Foreign Affairs knowledge platform on inclusive policies for development) and an affiliated faculty at the African School of Economics in Benin. She is interested in policy-relevant research on political economy, productivity and economic growth, and gender. She obtains her PhD in economics from the University of Aix Marseille in France. Maty Konte may be reached at konte@merit.unu.edu.

Linguère Mously Mbaye is Senior Research Economist at the Macroeconomics Policy, Forecasting and Research Department of the African Development Bank in Abidjan, Côte d'Ivoire. She is also Research Affiliate at the Institute of Labor Economics (IZA), Bonn, Germany and a Research Fellow at the Global Labor Organization (GLO). Her main fields of interest are Development Economics, Migration, Labor Economics, Gender, and Economic and Policy analysis. She received her PhD in economics from the University of Auvergne in France. Linguère Mously Mbaye may be reached at l.mbaye@afdb.org.

Contributors

Kwaku Arhin-Sam is a PhD fellow from the Bremen International Graduate School of Social Sciences, University of Bremen, Germany. His research interest is on transnational migration, return migration, policy analysis, identity and belonging politics, migration governance, migration economics

Victor Cebotari is Strategic Advisor for Academic Affairs at the University of Luxembourg and an affiliated Researcher at Maastricht University (MGSoG). He holds a PhD in social protection from Maastricht University. His research interests span social policy, education, migration, gender, child wellbeing, and multidimensional deprivation.

Macoura Doumbia is a PhD Student at Université Clermont-Auvergne, CERDI (Centre d'Etudes et de Recherches sur le Développement International) in Clermont Ferrand, France.

Romain Fourmy is a Junior Expert in Impact Evaluation for ADE (Belgium). He holds two master's degrees in economic development, from UC3M and Maastricht University. His research interests focus on migration and emerging technologies in developing countries.

Paul Gbahabo is a PhD candidate of Development Finance at the University of Stellenbosch Business School in Cape Town, South Africa. His research interests are in the areas of financial sector development, project finance, structural economic change, socioeconomic welfare, and blockchain technology. He has also co-authored several instructional materials that are currently in use in junior secondary schools in Nigeria.

Ortrun Merkle is a post-doctoral researcher working on corruption, gender, and migration. Her research focuses on the relationship between corruption and migration, and pays particular attention to gendered forms of corruption such as sextortion. She holds a PhD from Maastricht University.

Fouzi Mourji is Professor of Applied Econometrics at the Faculty of Legal, Economic and Social Sciences at Hassan II-Ain Chock-Casablanca University and Visiting Professor at various universities (Auvergne / CERDI, Rouen, Paris 12 in France and Montreal in Canada, and occasionally other universities / Geneva). He received his PhD from the University of Sorbonne in Paris, France.

Charlotte Mueller is a PhD candidate in the Migration and Development research group at UNU-MERIT/Maastricht University. The aim of her PhD project is to explore diaspora knowledge transfer and factors that enable and inhibit knowledge transfer in the case of a temporary return programme.

Lwanga Elizabeth Nanziri is Senior Lecturer of Development Finance at the University of Stellenbosch Business School in Cape Town – South Africa. She also served as the Chief Executive Officer of the South African Savings Institute, founded by the Ministry of Finance in South Africa and the Industrial Development Corporation. She is also the director of the Association for the Advancement of African Women Economists in Southern Africa. Her research field is development economics focussing on financial sector development, financial inclusion for households and firms, behavioural economics, gender and welfare, and public policy analysis.

Gideon Ndubuisi is a PhD Candidate at Maastricht University and UNU-MERIT. His research interests include economics and management of innovation, intellectual property rights (IPR), international trade, knowledge and technology transfers, and industrial policy. His doctoral thesis focuses on understanding whether the global trajectory towards stringent IPR protection offers any prospect for economic development.

Linda Adhiambo Oucho is currently the Executive Director of Research of the African Migration and Development Policy Centre (AMADPOC), based in Nairobi Kenya. The independent think tank organization undertakes policy-based research in East Africa and beyond on migration and development as well as other related subjects with the aim of influencing policy processes. She conducts research on irregular migration, displacement, labour migration and understanding the African diaspora. She holds a PhD in ethnic relations (2012) from the University of Warwick.

Rasmane Ouedraogo is an economist at the International Monetary Fund in Washington DC, United States. He holds a PhD in economics from the University of Auvergne in France.

Julia Reinold is a PhD candidate at Maastricht University's Institute for Transnational and Euregional Cross border cooperation and Mobility / ITEM and part of the Migration Group at UNU-MERIT.

Claire Ricard is a PhD Student at Université Clermont-Auvergne CERDI (Centre d'Etudes et de Recherches sur le Développement International) in Clermont Ferrand, France. She is affiliated to ERECA (Equipe de Recherche en Econométrie Appliquée) based at the Hassan II-Ain Chock-Casablanca University.

Mary Boatemaa Setrana is Lecturer at the Centre for Migration Studies, University of Ghana, and affiliated to Radboud University of Nijmegen, the Netherlands. She holds a PhD in migration studies at the Centre for Migration Studies, University of Ghana, under the Netherlands Organizations for International Cooperation in Higher Education Fellowship (Nuffic).

Melissa Siegel is Professor of Migration Studies and Head of Migration Studies at the Maastricht Graduate School of Governance and UNU-MERIT in Maastricht, where she manages several migration research projects, coordinates the Migration Studies Specialisation as part of the Master's Programme in Public Policy and Human Development, and heads the Migration Management Diploma Programme. She also heads the Migration and Development research theme of the Maastricht Center for Citizenship, Migration and Development (MACIMIDE). She holds a PhD in public policy from Maastricht University in the Netherlands.

Windemanegda Sandrine Sourouema is Lecturer at the University Ouaga II in Burkina Faso.

Massimiliano Tani is a Professor of Finance and Economics at the University of New South Wales, Australia. He is also Research Fellow at the Institute of Labor Economics, Germany, and a Research Fellow at the Global Labor Organization. He researches issues related to human capital and its transfer across borders, higher education, and productivity. He obtained at PhD in Economics from the Australian National University.

Michaella Vanore is Research Fellow at the Maastricht Graduate School of Governance, where she has worked for the past six years as a researcher and lecturer on migration and development. She holds a PhD in public policy from Maastricht University. Michaella has addressed topics such as defining and analysing poverty among migrant children, assessing the consequences of family-member migration for children and the elderly who remain in the home country, diaspora engagement and contributions in conflict and post-conflict settings, and remittances.

Acknowledgements

The editors thank and commend the authors of the chapters for their commitment to conducting policy-relevant research to extend our knowledge on the role of migration and remittances on the Sustainable Development Goals for Africa. This project would not be possible without their expertise and patience when writing, revising, and editing their individual chapters.

We would also like to thank Valentina Mazzucato and Sam Wong and anonymous reviewers for their constructive comments and suggestions. We express our deepest gratitude to Romain Fourmy and Rumbidzai Ndoro for their excellent research assistance funded by UNU-MERIT.

1 Introduction

Maty Konte and Linguère Mously Mbaye

Over the past decade, migration has become a critical humanitarian and development issue in the world, including in Africa. Moreover, remittances sent by migrants to their home countries provide substantial funds that have been increasing, surpassing official development aid.[1] Research has shown that migrants act as agents of change through their financial contributions that improve the living standards of those left behind. Through the transmission of norms and knowledge, migrants stimulate social and political changes in their home countries. However, migrants also face several challenges and barriers during their journey to their transit and host countries. Such challenges violate migrants' rights and reduce their potential contribution to development in their home countries.

Surprisingly, the previous development agenda (the UN's Millennium Development Goals) did not pay attention to the importance of migration and remittances in transforming the societies in migrants' home countries, nor did it tackle the challenges migrants face in their transit and host countries. Thanks to the Sustainable Development Goals (SDGs), migration has been formally recognised as an important factor that should be considered for poverty reduction, human rights protection, and inclusive development by 2030.

Cutting-edge research is needed to better understand the role of migration and remittances within the SDG context in addition to an examination of the potential repercussions that nonresponsive migration policies may have on the achievement of SDGs in Africa. Therefore, this book's main goal is to research, document, and discuss the role of migration in transforming the economic, social, and political aspects necessary for the success of SDGs. It also contributes to the discourse on the characteristics of migration decisions and challenges faced by migrants from Africa and analyse how some policies in the SDG context may help alleviate the conditions of African migrants. The book offers timely and comprehensive evidence to inform policymakers, researchers, and students who are interested in the links between population movements and the SDGs in Africa.

Unlike other books on migration and remittances, this book examines the links between the evidence and the goals and targets of the Sustainable Development Agenda, and how failure to undertake responsive migration policies may affect the success of some of the SDGs. The findings in each of the chapters identify SDGs' goals or targets that have informative implications. It is worth noting that few reports exist on migration and the SDGs that have discussed why migration is important to the success of the SDGs. We go beyond anecdotal evidence and conduct accurate quantitative and qualitative research and use the findings to recommend policies for specific SDG goals. The authors of the chapters have adopted quantitative, qualitative, and explorative approaches in the book, which allows students and teachers to use it as supplementary or complementary material. This book is also a useful tool for policymakers interested in rigorous policy-based evidence with regard to migration issues. The experts writing the book chapters have a diverse range of experiences, backgrounds, origins, and genders. They have enriching experiences in conducting research and field work in Africa.

The book's scope is related to the following issues: (1) migration, remittances, and the transformation of economies in Africa; (2) migration, remittances and education, and knowledge; (3) migration, remittances, and corruption and conflict; and (4) challenges in the management of migration flows. Cross-cutting issues such as gender equality and women's empowerment and youth are also examined in the book.

Migration and remittances in Africa

Even though migration across countries represents a significant share of global human mobility, a much greater number of people migrate within their country's borders. Based on the latest estimates, more than 700 million people in the world have been reported as having migrated within their country (IOM, 2018). Furthermore, recent environmental changes, as well as the over-exploitation of resources, are significant causes driving rural–urban and cyclical migration in Africa.[2] Four out of five of African migrants, or 19 million, originate from another African country. Put differently, migration in Africa is predominantly an intracontinental phenomenon, with nearly 80% of African immigrants coming from elsewhere in the region. Moreover, it is important to recall that Africa is also an attractive destination, as in 2017, 22% of immigrants were coming from outside the continent (AfDB, 2019). These figures are helpful to put into perspective the narrative around African migration, which often focusses on the flows outside the continent, or the phenomenon of irregular migration. Without underestimating the challenges posed by those types of flows, the picture of migration in Africa is more complex and nuanced than one might think. Migration patterns have thus been evolving across years and influenced by a set of different factors (UNCTAD, 2018).

Within the continent, Western Africa is characterised as the region with the highest share of migrants coming from other African countries and, more precisely, from neighbouring countries (Adepoju, 2017; AfDB, 2019). For instance, this flow largely comprises migrants originating from Mali and Niger moving to prominent migration hubs in the region, such as Cote d'Ivoire and Ghana (IOM, 2018). This migration pattern is strongly driven by seasonal, temporary, and permanent workers, for which labour mobility across the region has been facilitated by the visa-free movement instituted within the Economic Community of West African States. Southern Africa has also experienced an increasing level of intraregional migration. This flow has primarily been shaped by growing economic opportunities such as those emerging from the mining industry in South Africa (UNCTAD, 2018). In addition to economic reasons, conflicts and political instability have significantly influenced migration patterns in Africa over recent years, especially in Central and Eastern Africa.

Moreover, these regions are characterised not only by a high number of outgoing migrants and refugees, but also by an increasing number of incoming migrants and refugees. For example, the Democratic Republic of Congo and Ethiopia are origin countries of a large refugee population and host countries for this population coming from other countries (UNHCR, 2016). In contrast to Western African, migrants moving across Southern, Eastern, and Central Africa often use irregular channels to migrate, and they are frequently facilitated with the help of smugglers to reach their intended destinations (Carling, 2016; Frouws & Horwood, 2017; Majidi & Oucho, 2016). Unlike the other regions, Northern Africa does not feature high intraregional migration. Instead, the region has principally been recognised as a transit area for migrants and refugees going to Europe, due to its proximity to the Mediterranean Sea. Libya is the country that has hosted the most international migrants since 2010, originating mainly from Eastern and Western Africa (UNCTAD, 2018). However, the story is slightly different in Morocco. While this country was previously used mainly as a transit channel for migration, it is progressively converting into a destination country for migrants coming from other African regions (Berriane et al., 2015). This is also well documented in Chapter 14 of this book.

While the number of African migrants residing outside the continent has remained low compared to the number of internal migrants, extracontinental migration experienced a faster growth over recent years compared to intracontinental migration (UNCTAD, 2018). Between 2000 and 2017, the number of international migrants increased by 49% across the globe, from 173 to 258 million. African migrants contribute to 14% of the international migration flow, being 36 million across the world (UNDESA, 2017). This migration flow is characterised by a higher share of Northern African migrants, for whom the propensity to migrate outside the continent is higher than for migrants from other regions in Africa.

High levels of unemployment, as well as high income disparities between the origin and destination countries, are recognised as important drivers of this migration. In terms of destination, Europe and the Middle East are the main extracontinental destinations for African migrants (IOM, 2018). A number of migrants from North and West Africa are, for instance, hosted in Europe (European Commission Joint Research Centre, 2018).

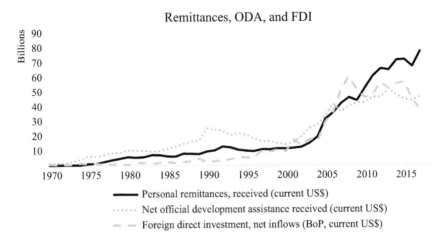

Figure 1.1 Remittances, official development assistance, and foreign direct investment in Africa.
Source: World Development Indicators, The World Bank.

The importance of these flows highlights the potential benefits associated with migration, which has been recognised as a potential source of development. In the context of labour migration, migrants contribute not only to filling labour and skill shortage in destination countries but also to the development in their country of origin, through remittances. For instance, the flow of financial remittances to Africa has been increasing constantly over recent decades. By 2018, remittance inflow in Africa reached $86 billion. In addition to being more stable than official development assistance and foreign direct investment, remittances have recently exceeded these other inflows (see Figure 1.1). Some countries in Africa are highly dependent on remittances, such as Liberia and Lesotho, for which 27% and 18% of their GDPs, respectively, are composed of remittances (UNCTAD, 2018).

Migrants as agents of change in their home countries: a brief literature review

Remittances are recognised as a powerful factor in poverty reduction for families staying in their communities of origin (Hagen-Zanker et al., 2017). For instance, evidence from Ghana and Ethiopia show that households receiving remittances are significantly less likely to be poor (Adams & Cuecuecha, 2013; Beyene, 2014). In addition to alleviating poverty, remittances have been found to reduce inequality in Sub-Saharan Africa (Akobeng, 2016). Using household surveys from Kenya, Bang et al. (2016) provide evidence that remittances increase expenditures at all levels of the distribution, though poorest households tend to benefit the most.

Due to the presence of imperfect insurance markets in developing countries, remittances can also be viewed as an informal insurance, which acts as a safety net for households in the event of negative shocks (Lucas & Stark, 1985; Yang, 2011). As a consequence, this mechanism has been found to lessen household consumption instability for a range of different adverse events, such as unfavourable weather, natural disasters, and conflicts (Bettin & Zazzaro, 2017; Combes & Ebeke, 2011; Fransen & Mazzucato, 2014; Wouterse & Taylor, 2008).

Additionally, remittances can be pro-cyclical and used as a means to accumulate assets and physical capital investment, leading to an improvement in the wealth of households and long-term welfare (Yang, 2011). For instance, household surveys from Burkina Faso, Kenya, Nigeria, Senegal, and Uganda show that 20% of international remittances are used for investment in buying land or equipment, starting a business, or improving a farm (Boly et al., 2014). More recent reports on Ethiopia show the same tendency, yet with an increased share of 40% of international remittances that are used for physical capital investment (UNCTAD, 2018). Besides the accumulation of physical capital, remittances can have a positive impact on education (Nicolai et al., 2016). Based on a household survey from Ghana, Adams and Cuecuecha (2013) provide empirical evidence that households that are the recipients of international and internal remittances tend to spend 1.9% and 3.6% more at the margin on education, respectively.

In terms of educational outcomes, remittances have been found to increase school enrolment, school completion rate, and private school enrolment in developing countries; for these outcomes girls tend to benefit more from remittances than boys (Azizi, 2018). Consequently, the absence of the migrant does not necessarily have a disruptive effect by increasing child labour. Using the case of Burkina Faso, Bargain and Boutin (2015) demonstrate that child labour decreases when remittances increase. Regarding another dimension of human capital, remittances can positively affect health outcomes for recipient households (Tulloch et al., 2016). For instance, studies have demonstrated that remittances play a significant role in reducing both child and infant mortality in developing countries (Chauvet et al., 2013; Terrelonge, 2014). Furthermore, life expectancy tends to be positively affected by remittance inflows. More precisely, Zhunio et al. (2012) provide evidence that a 1% increase in real remittances per capita translates into a 0.03% increase in life expectancy in developing countries.

Through these different channels, remittances have been advanced to foster economic growth, and particularly for countries with low levels of financial development (Sobiech, 2019). However, this effect may be mitigated by the institutional quality present in the origin country. For instance, Adams and Klobodu (2016) find that regime durability and democracy are necessary factors for remittances to have a significant and positive impact on economic growth in Sub-Saharan African countries.

Moreover, these findings are supported by Chitambara (2019), who shows a stronger impact of remittances in Africa when associated with other instructional quality measures. However, institutions in origin countries may themselves be affected by migration, through another type of remittances, which are often referred to as social remittances. Social remittances are defined as the norms, beliefs, and practices that migrants accumulate in the host country, which they transfer to the country of origin either during their stay or when they return (Levitt & Lamba-Nieves, 2011). In the case that there is a positive difference in institutional quality experienced by the migrants in the host country, these social remittances have been found to positively affect institutional development, such as democratic changes in developing countries including Sub-Saharan Africa (Docquier et al., 2016; Williams, 2017).

Moreover, these findings are supported and complemented by other studies based on the African context, which find that political accountability and participation, as well as electoral competitiveness, are improved through the transfer of political norms emitted by migrants, both during their stay in the host country and upon their return (Batista et al., 2019; Batista & Vicente, 2011; Chauvet & Mercier, 2014). In addition to affecting institutional quality in origin countries, social remittances can be used as a means of skills, knowledge, and technology diffusion, which could subsequently contribute to economic growth in developing countries (Hübler, 2016; Rapoport, 2018).

Migration, remittances, and the Sustainable Development Goals

Although migration and remittances were not included in the previous development agenda (the UN's Millennium Development Goals), they play an important role in the development process and as such may have implications for several Sustainable Development Goals such as SDGs 4 (quality education), 5 (gender equality), 8 (decent work and economic growth), 10 (reduced inequalities), 16 (peace, justice, and strong institutions), and 17 (partnerships for the goals). Nevertheless, migration and remittances can have further implications for many SDGs due to their cross-cutting nature (IOM, 2017). For instance, migration, through remittances, can contribute to alleviating poverty in origin countries, which reflects progress towards SDG 1 (no poverty), and can act as a powerful instrument to secure consumption levels of recipient households, thus contributing to progress on SDG 2 (zero hunger). SDGs 3 (good health and well-being) and 4 can be supported through the use of remittances in human capital accumulation, which can subsequently have implications for target 16.2 on child labour. In addition, the allocation of remittances towards the investment in physical capital, such as new businesses, can enhance employment opportunities, which supports SDG 8. Additionally, SDG 9 (industry, innovation, and infrastructure) can be supported by the skills and technological transfers spurred by migrants and returnees. Moreover, migration can contribute to SDG 10 by reducing global inequality across countries through the transfer of remittances from high-income to low-income countries, and it can diminish inequality within countries. Last but not least, social remittances can provide support for the improvement of institutional quality in origin countries, thus contributing to SGD 16, which can, in turn, be favourable to the environment in which economic growth takes place, supporting, again, SDG 8 (ODI, 2018).

However, the positive effects of migration and remittances on welfare can be attenuated by several challenges and barriers that migrants face throughout their journeys, which may violate migrants' rights and reduce their potential contribution to development in their home countries. Although irregular migration is difficult to quantify, it remains a real issue preventing safe and orderly migration, as recommended by the Global Compact for Safe, Orderly, and Regular Migration (GCM). Such migrants often utilise smugglers as a means to facilitate their transit to their destination. However, these practices tend to lead to vulnerabilities for these persons, such as extortion, violence, trafficking, and often inhumane conditions during transit (Metcalfe-Hough, 2015). Women are in a particularly vulnerable situation when transiting through irregular channels (IOM, 2018).

After their arrival in the destination country, migrants may face barriers in transferring money to their community of origin due to the high costs of remitting channels. In comparison to other regions in the world, Africa has the highest costs of sending remittances (equalling 9% in transfer fees to send $200; UNCTAD, 2018). As a consequence, the net value of remittances received by recipient households decreases, impeding the money's potential positive impact on welfare (The World Bank, 2018). In addition to challenges faced by migrants, poor institutional settings in the country of origin can lead to an adverse welfare impact of remittances. Because remittances increase household income, receiving them may indicate a higher ability to pay bribes in exchange for provision of public goods and services in the presence of poor institutional quality (Abdih et al., 2012; Berdiev et al., 2013). Even though no empirical evidence exists for the case of Africa, it has been suggested that diaspora remittances could, in some cases, be diverted to fuel conflicts in origin countries (Mariani et al., 2018; Van Hear, 2003). As a result, remittances could indirectly hinder the welfare impact in migrants' home countries, by increasing the level of corruption and conflict.

In addition to impeding the welfare impact of migration and remittances, these challenges and barriers can be detrimental to the accomplishment of particular SDGs. For instance, the extortion faced by migrants transiting with the help of smugglers can stand in the way of the achievement of SDG 1 (no poverty). Furthermore, the violence and inhumane conditions experienced through this type of transit jeopardise several health-related SDGs, such as SDG 2 (zero hunger), 3 (good health and well-being), and 6 (clean water and sanitation). Women's irregular-channel transit can have a negative impact on SDG 5 (gender equality). Additionally, financial remittances could lead to unfavourable consequences such as an increase in corruption and conflict in origin countries, thus reducing the progress towards SDG 16 (peace, justice, and strong institutions). Based on these challenges and barriers, nonresponsive migration policies could thus have negative consequences for the achievement of the SDGs in Africa. Accordingly, appropriate policies should be considered regarding these issues, which could consequently lead to maximising the impact of migration on poverty reduction and development.

Structure of the book

This book is a collection of reviews of the literature, empirical evidence, and policy discussions, which is intended to inform academics, policymakers and advanced students who are interested in the relationship between migration and its implications for the achievement of SDGs in Africa. There are 13 chapters structured into four parts, in addition to the introduction and the conclusion.

Part I addresses the contribution of migration and remittances to economic transformation in Africa. In Chapter 2, Vanore provides a literature review on the conceptual and empirical linkages between migration and trade. Moreover, this chapter explores how policies can help to foster this relationship. Mbaye and Tani, in Chapter 3, investigate the relationship between short-term migration and innovation, by particularly identifying how short-term forms of people's interactions may intensify the introduction of new processes, products, and services. In Chapter 4, Oucho discusses the youth-employment-migration nexus, with a focus on the linkages between labour market challenges and internal migration in Kenya. This chapter explores the drivers of internal migration, as well as the link between urbanisation and migration, using mixed methods including survey responses of both migrants and non-migrants, qualitative interviews, and focus group discussions with youth groups. In Chapter 5, Nanziri and Gbahabo examine the effect of the cost of remittance transactions on welfare in Sub-Saharan Africa using Remittances Prices Worldwide data from the World Bank that cover 17 countries in Sub-Saharan Africa over the period 2011–2018.

Part II focusses on the human capital accumulation that can be positively influenced by migration through remittances invested in education and the transfer of knowledge. In Chapter 6, Cebotari analyses the relationship between migration and educational development of children using panel data collected in two Ghanaian regions, Kumasi and Sunyani, by comparing children whose parents migrated and children living with both parents in the country. Additionally, the author contrasts the findings based on the gender of both migrants and children. Chapter 7, by Mueller, examines how diaspora members involved in the programme Connecting Diaspora for Development (CD4D) transfer both explicit and tacit knowledge to institutions in their origin countries. This chapter adopts a comparative case analysis, which relies on data collected in Sierra Leone and Somaliland. In Chapter 8, Setrana and

Arhin-Sam investigate social and political remittances in the context of the return of skilled migrants in Ghana. Moreover, the authors examine how these migrants sustain their return and mobilise themselves for the development of the country of origin. In Chapter 9, Fourmy studies the effect of mobile money on remittance recipients' household welfare using longitudinal data from Kenya. By providing transfer records for each recipient household, this data set allows investigators to precisely identify the actual use of mobile money in remittance transfers.

Part III covers the political implications with regard to migration and remittances. In Chapter 10, Konte and Ndubuisi empirically evaluate the effects of remittances on corruption levels using Afrobarometer surveys across 36 African countries. In this chapter, the authors investigate this relationship not only through the financial remittances channel but also through the transfer of norms. Merkle, Reinold, and Siegel, in Chapter 11, address the role of corruption in shaping the migration path and how it continues to be important throughout the journey. Based on desk research and semistructured interviews, the authors also conclude that for irregular and forced migrants in Africa the experiences with corruption are gendered. Ouedraogo and Soureouema, in Chapter 12, also employ Afrobarometer surveys to explore how remittances affect electoral violence in Africa, which remains a major issue that threatens the development and consolidation of democracy within the continent.

Part IV explores the challenges in the management of migration flows in Africa, which are important to consider because they may interfere with how migration contributes to development. Chapter 13, by Oucho, provides insights on the mainstreaming of the principles outlined in the GCM with regard to irregular migration in Eastern Africa. Because migration policies are addressed differently across countries, the implementation of the GCM framework may involve further challenges for some countries compared to others. This chapter also advances some solutions based on best practices across the world that can be contextualised in the African environment. In Chapter 14, Mourji, Ricard, and Doumbia examine how Morocco has recently become a country of destination for African migrants. More particularly, the authors use survey data from two migration hubs in the country, Casablanca-Mohammedia and Rabat-Salé, to study the profile of migrants and their social and professional integration in Morocco. Furthermore, this chapter is complemented by a comparison of the socio-economic and behavioural characteristics of migrants, as well as an analysis of their perception of social integration compared to that of the native population.

The final part of the book summarises the findings of each chapter and more particularly discusses the contributions to the accomplishment of specific SDG targets. Furthermore, recommendations for policymakers are advanced, and research gaps that need to be further investigated by researchers interested in migration and remittances in Africa are identified.

Notes

1 World Development Indicators. http://datatopics.worldbank.org/world-development-indicators/.
2 However, this migration taking place within country borders in Africa is not as measurable as for the case of migration taking place across countries (IOM, 2018; UNCTAD, 2018).

References

Abdih, Y., Chami, R., Dagher, J., & Montiel, P. (2012). Remittances and institutions: Are remittances a curse? *World Development, 40*(4), 657–666.

Adams, R. H., & Cuecuecha, A. (2013). The impact of remittances on investment and poverty in Ghana. *World Development, 50*, 24–40.

Adams, S., & Klobodu, E. K. M. (2016). Remittances, regime durability and economic growth in Sub-Saharan Africa (SSA). *Economic Analysis and Policy, 50*, 1–8.

Adepoju, A. (2017). Migration dynamics, refugees and internally displaced persons in Africa. Human Resources Development Centre, Lagos, Nigeria. United Nations. https://academicimpact.un.org/content/migration-dynamics-refugees-and-internally-displacedpersons-africa.

African Development Bank group (AfDB). (2019). African economic outlook. https://www.afdb.org/en/knowledge/publications/african-economic-outlook.

Akobeng, E. (2016). Out of inequality and poverty: Evidence for the effectiveness of remittances in Sub-Saharan Africa. *The Quarterly Review of Economics and Finance, 60*, 207–223.

Azizi, S. (2018). The impacts of workers' remittances on human capital and labor supply in developing countries. *Economic Modelling, 75*, 377–396.

Bang, J. T., Mitra, A., & Wunnava, P. V. (2016). Do remittances improve income inequality? An instrumental variable quantile analysis of the Kenyan case. *Economic Modelling, 58*, 394–402.

Bargain, O., & Boutin, D. (2015). Remittance effects on child labour: Evidence from Burkina Faso. *The Journal of Development Studies, 51*(7), 922–938.

Batista, C., Seither, J., & Vicente, P. C. (2019). Do migrant social networks shape political attitudes and behavior at home? *World Development, 117*, 328–343.

Batista, C., & Vicente, P. C. (2011). Do migrants improve governance at home? Evidence from a voting experiment. *The World Bank Economic Review, 25*(1), 77–104.

Berdiev, A. N., Kim, Y., & Chang, C.-P. (2013). Remittances and corruption. *Economics Letters, 118*(1), 182–185.

Berriane, M., de Haas, H., & Natter, K. (2015). Introduction: Revisiting Moroccan migrations. *Journal of North African Studies, 20*(4), 503–521.

Bettin, G., & Zazzaro, A. (2017). The impact of natural disasters on remittances to low- and middle-income countries. *The Journal of Development Studies, 54*(3), 481–500.

Beyene, B. M. (2014). The effects of international remittances on poverty and inequality in Ethiopia. *The Journal of Development Studies, 50*(10), 1380–1396.

Boly, A., Coniglio, N. D., Prota, F., & Seric, A. (2014). Diaspora investments and firm export performance in selected Sub-Saharan African countries. *World Development, 59*, 422–433.

Carling, J. (2016). West and Central Africa. *Migrant Smuggling Data and Research*, 25. Retrieved from http://www.cestim.it/argomenti/14irregolari/2013-oim-migrant-smuggling_report.pdf#page=39

Chauvet, L., Gubert, F., & Mesplé-Somps, S. (2013). Aid, remittances, medical brain drain and child mortality: evidence using inter and intra-country data. *Journal of Development Studies, 49*(6), 801–818.

Chauvet, L., & Mercier, M. (2014). Do return migrants transfer political norms to their origin country? Evidence from Mali. *Journal of Comparative Economics, 42*(3), 630–651.

Chitambara, P. (2019). Remittances, Institutions and Growth in Africa. *International Migration*, 57.5: 56–70.

Combes, J.-L., & Ebeke, C. (2011). Remittances and household consumption instability in developing countries. *World Development, 39*(7), 1076–1089.

Docquier, F., Lodigiani, E., Rapoport, H., & Schiff, M. (2016). Emigration and democracy. *Journal of Development Economics, 120*, 209–223.

European Commission Joint Research Centre. (2018). *Many More to Come? Migration from and within Africa*. Retrieved from https://ec.europa.eu/jrc/en/publication/eur-scientific-and-technical-research-reports/many-more-come-migration-and-within-africa.

Fransen, S., & Mazzucato, V. (2014). Remittances and household wealth after conflict: a case study on urban Burundi. *World Development, 60*, 57–68.

Frouws, B., & Horwood, C. (2017). *Smuggled South*. Retrieved from https://reliefweb.int/sites/reliefweb.int/files/resources/Smuggled_South.pdf.

Hagen-Zanker, J., Postel, H., & Vidal, E. M. (2017). Poverty, migration and the 2030 agenda for sustainable development. *Briefing Paper*. London: Overseas Development Institute.

Hübler, M. (2016). Does migration support technology diffusion in developing countries? *World Development, 83*, 148–162.

IOM. (2017). *Migration in the 2030 Agenda*. Retrieved from https://publications.iom.int/system/files/pdf/migration_in_the_2030_agenda.pdf.

IOM. (2018). *World Migration Report 2018*. Retrieved from https://www.iom.int/sites/default/files/country/docs/china/r5_world_migration_report_2018_en.pdf.

Levitt, P., & Lamba-Nieves, D. (2011). Social remittances revisited. *Journal of Ethnic and Migration Studies, 37*(1), 1–22.

Lucas, R. E., & Stark, O. (1985). Motivations to remit: evidence from Botswana. *Journal of Political Economy, 93*(5), 901–918.

Majidi, N., & Oucho, L. (2016). East Africa. In McAuliffe M.L. and F. Laczko (eds.) (2016), *Migrant Smuggling Data and Research: A global review of the emerging evidence base*, IOM: Geneva.

Mariani, F., Mercier, M., & Verdier, T. (2018). Diasporas and conflict. *Journal of Economic Geography, 18*(4), 761–793.

Metcalfe-Hough, V. (2015). The migration crisis? Facts, challenges and possible solutions. Retrieved from https://www.odi.org/sites/odi.org.uk/files/odi-assets/publicationsopinion-files/9913.pdf.

Nicolai, S., Wales, J., & Aiazzi, E. (2016). Education, migration and the 2030 agenda for sustainable development.

ODI. (2018). *Migration and the 2030 Agenda for Sustainable Development*. Retrieved from https://doc.rero.ch/record/308985/files/28-6._ODI_Education.pdf.

Rapoport, H. (2018). Diaspora externalities: a view from the South. *WIDER Working Paper 2018/25* https://www.odi.org/projects/2849-migration-and-2030-agenda-sustainable-development.

Sobiech, I. (2019). Remittances, finance and growth: does financial development foster the impact of remittances on economic growth? *World Development, 113*, 44–59.

Terrelonge, S. C. (2014). For health, strength, and daily food: the dual impact of remittances and public health expenditure on household health spending and child health outcomes. *The Journal of Development Studies, 50*(10), 1397–1410.

The World Bank. (2018). *Migration and Remittances, April 2018: Recent Developments and Outlook.* Washington.

Tulloch, O., Machingura, F., & Melamed, C. (2016). Health, migration and the 2030 agenda for sustainable development Retreived from https://doc.rero.ch/record/308984/files/27-7._ODI_Health.pdf.

UNCTAD. (2018). *Economic Development in Africa Report 2018: Migration for Structural Transformation.* Retrieved from https://unctad.org/en/pages/PublicationWebflyer.aspx?publicationid=2118.

UNDESA. (2017). *International Migration Report 2017.* Retrieved from https://www.un.org/en/development/desa/population/migration/publications/migrationreport/docs/MigrationReport2017_Highlights.pdf.

UNHCR. (2016). *Global Trends: Forced Displacement in 2016.* Retrieved from Retrieved from https://www.unhcr.org/5943e8a34.pdf.

Van Hear, N. (2003). Refugee diasporas, remittances, development, and conflict. *Migration Information Source, 1.* Retrieved from https://www.migrationpolicy.org/article/refugee-diasporas-remittances-development-and-conflict.

Williams, K. (2017). Do remittances improve political institutions? Evidence from Sub-Saharan Africa. *Economic Modelling, 61,* 65–75.

Wouterse, F., & Taylor, J. E. (2008). Migration and income diversification. *World Development, 36*(4), 625–640.

Yang, D. (2011). Migrant remittances. *Journal of Economic Perspectives, 25*(3), 129–152.

Zhunio, M. C., Vishwasrao, S., & Chiang, E. P. (2012). The influence of remittances on education and health outcomes: a cross country study. *Applied Economics, 44*(35), 4605–4616.

Part I

Migration, remittances, and economic transformation in Africa

2 Migration, trade, and development in Africa

Conceptual and empirical links

Michaella Vanore

Introduction

As in many other world regions, Africa is facing multiple transitions, three of which are deeply interconnected: those related to mobility, demography, and economic growth. Changing fertility patterns and residential mobility have already begun to shift the age structures of populations across the continent and the places in which those populations mature. These shifts have been accompanied by a growing middle class in many African countries, which, in turn, increase demand for specialized goods and services that require skilled- and semi-skilled professionals to supply them (Mburu-Ndoria, 2016) – highlighting the role of mobile traders in both goods and services who can stimulate and sustain economic growth. Such transitions are also embedded within a context of growing regional integration, where sub-regional communities have developed and encouraged free movement to further stimulate regional integration and, ideally, regional growth.

These transitions provide unique opportunities for – and build upon long-standing histories of – cross-border trade. The story of cross-border trade in Africa is intimately tied to mobility. Intra-continental migration – movement from one country to another within the same continent – has been an important trend within the recent past for much of the African region. While it is beyond the scope of this chapter to meaningfully describe historical and contemporary migration patterns for the entire continent, it is important to recognize the interactions between regional economic systems and regional migration patterns. Regions like East Africa have been shaped by trade systems that extended beyond African borders to include countries in the wider Indian Ocean coastal region. With technological shifts in the 1750s related to manufacturing capabilities and shipping that facilitated greater trade in goods and services, the East African coast became more entrenched in a regional system of exchange. Within this system, a growing number of migrants from Central Africa, Arabia, and Western India arrived in East Africa, many as part of trade enterprises (Gilbert, 2002). Similarly, countries in West Africa have been part of long-standing systems of exchange in which a variety of migrants, including semi-skilled short-term workers and petty traders, routinely cross state borders to provide services and goods. According to Adepoju (2007), West Africa functions as a single socioeconomic zone where social and ethno-cultural ties support continuous cross-border movement and exchange. In Southern Africa, historical integration of countries into what can be described as a 'regional labour market' under colonial rule entailed frequent cross-border moves of service providers. While the motivations for migration and the policy frameworks under which migration occurs have changed markedly over time, trade remains an important reason for mobility within the Southern Africa region. Informal and small-scale cross-border trade is particularly important between South Africa and its neighbouring countries, with surveys conducted in the early 2000s indicating a strong presence of informal cross-border traders among those making daily crossings between countries like Zimbabwe and South Africa (Peberdy & Crush, 2007).

Historical and contemporary migration trends are often interpreted from a development lens, and discussions of migration and trade in the African context are often connected to *under*development. African migration is often framed as a symptom of development failure, with poverty and desperation driving people away from a 'home' that they would otherwise not leave given adequate levels of development (Bakewell, 2008). Governments and civil society voices from countries of origin and destination alike support this discourse. Throughout the last decade, the European Union's engagement with Africa on migration has reflected what is termed the 'root causes' doctrine. The doctrine draws a simple line between migration outcomes – actual mobility – and social, political, and economic contexts in the place of origin that inspire movement. The doctrine emphasizes the logic that migration would not occur if the 'root causes' are fixed – that migration can be prevented by addressing systematic underdevelopment (Carling & Talleraas, 2016). Within this doctrine – and other development paradigms that equate mobility with development failure – trade has been framed as a tool to suppress migration by boosting employment and increasing wages in communities of origin. The underlying logic is that trade liberalization, including through policy frameworks such as the Euro-Mediterranean Partnership, will increase exports from migrant countries of origin to 'more developed' regions, which, in turn, will support employment and economic growth in origin countries, and incline would-be migrants to remain in countries of origin (Campaniello, 2014).

Despite the 'root causes' discourse that typically views migration as a result of underdevelopment, increasing mobility within and beyond Africa likely reflects economic growth, social transformation, and the changes in mobility aspirations and the resources needed to realize them (Flahaux & de Haas, 2016). As this chapter argues, migration is itself an important contributor to economic growth, and its pro-trade potential supports the inclusive development agenda envisioned in the Sustainable Development Goals (SDGs). Trade is an explicit element of the SDGs, which frames increased participation in international trade regimes as one means to increase economic growth in developing countries and regions. By supporting the development of networks and offering market-specific knowledge that can lower the transaction costs associated with entering new markets, migrants can stimulate trade. They can also encourage businesses to innovate in processes and products by offering scarce skills and services, which can enable businesses to produce products demanded on international markets. For these effects to materialize, however, restrictions on intra-African mobility should be eased.

Migration, trade, and development are deeply connected in the African context, yet their interlinkages have not been fully conceptualized or modelled. This chapter explores the relationships among trade, migration, and development in the African context. It is framed around three broad questions: (1) what is specific about the relationship between migration and trade in the African context?, (2) how are trade and migration linked, and what may this imply for African trade flows?, and (3) what policies can support the relationships among trade, migration, and development in Africa? This chapter is exploratory in nature, as there is relatively limited scholarship and data on the interconnections among migration, trade, and the policy regimes that affect both. The first section of this chapter provides an in-depth assessment of how demography, mobility, and trade are evolving across African countries. The second section then explores the conceptual links between migration and trade, and identifies potential impacts of migration on trade flows on both the global and the African level. The third section briefly reviews policy initiatives that stimulate both migration and trade.

What is specific about migration and trade in the African context?

Migration and trade are embedded within specific contexts, where both regional and local processes and dynamics shape contemporary trends. To properly embed discussions among migration, trade, and development within the African context, this section explores how transitions related to mobility and demography relate to economic growth and the role of trade in stimulating and sustaining growth.

Contemporary migration trends

Over the course of the past 30 years, migration patterns within and beyond Africa have shifted, as too have continental and regional governance frameworks that (explicitly) encourage intraregional mobility as a step to greater regional integration. Compared to 1990 when the total stock of African migrants residing outside of their country of citizenship was approximately 20.3 million, by 2017 that number had reached 36.2 million. While in absolute numbers the difference may seem stark, the share of African emigrants within the total global migration stock has remained fairly consistent over

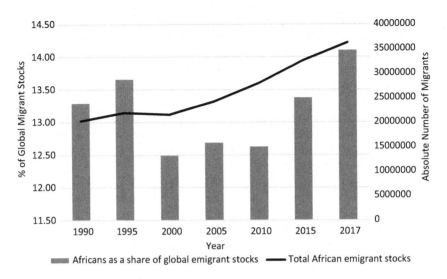

Figure 2.1 African emigrant stocks, 1990–2017, in absolute numbers and as a share
of global stocks.
Source: Own calculations based on data from UNDESA (2017a).

time, representing 13.2% of the share of emigrants residing outside of their
country of citizenship in 1990 and 14.1% in 2017 (see Figure 2.1).

Over the past 30 years, migration patterns have more markedly shifted in
terms of destination, with growing shares of African emigrants residing outside of the African region. Compared to 1990 when over 85% of the emigrant
stock in Africa was a citizen of another African country, the share in 2017
had dropped to 78.5%. In line with this shift, the share of African emigrants
residing within Africa dropped, from a high of 65.9% in 1990 to 53.3% in
2017 (own calculations based on UNDESA, 2015). The geography of African migration has thus gradually changed, and the share of African migrants
residing particularly in Asia and Europe has generally increased – although
the share of Africans residing in Europe has declined in recent years. The
regional distribution of the African emigrant stock is visualized in Figure 2.2.

The expansion of migrant populations outside of Africa has been mirrored by
changes in intra-African migration dynamics. As other authors (e.g., Flahaux &
de Haas, 2016) have noted, much intra-African migration in the post-colonial
period has been characterized by rural-to-urban migration and the movement
of populations from marginal, inland areas to more fertile agricultural areas
and (peri-)urban areas along the coast. Intra-African mobility is thus strongly
regional in nature. Since 1990, Eastern and Western Africa have consistently
hosted the largest stocks of migrants from other African countries, although the
share of the African emigrant stock residing in each sub-region has shifted substantially. In 1990, Eastern Africa was home to over 26% of the total global stock

of Africans, a share that shrunk to 18.5% by 2017. The region has also hosted a dwindling share of intra-African migrants: whereas over 40% of all African emigrants residing in another Africa country lived in the Eastern Africa region in 1990, by 2017 that share had decreased to 34.7% (see Figure 2.3 below).

During the same time period, Western Africa emerged as a more important regional destination, with over 30% of the African emigrant stock residing in that region between 1990 and 2005. While the share of the total African emigrant stock residing in Western Africa dipped between 2010 and 2015, it remained an important regional destination: by 2017 over 31% of all

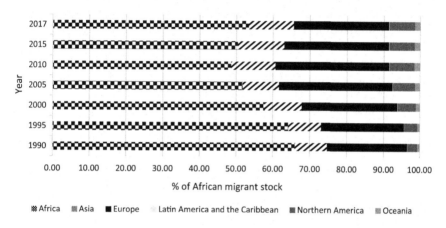

Figure 2.2 Share of African emigrant stock by world region, 1990–2017.
Source: Own calculations based on data from UNDESA (2017a).

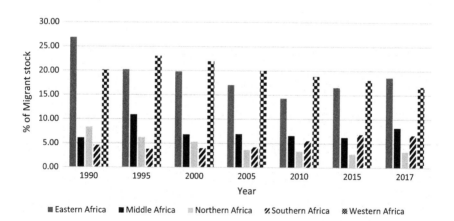

Figure 2.3 Share of total African emigrant stock residing in Africa by region, 1990–2017.
Source: Own calculations based on data from UNDESA (2017a).

intra-African migrants resided in Western Africa. Compared to Eastern and Western Africa, the other regions of Africa appeared to be relatively moderate players in intra-African mobility trends, yet increasing movements have occurred to the Southern Africa region. Following the end of apartheid and the gradual transition of the South African economy, greater mobility in the sub-region emerged around 2005; while Southern Africa hosted only 6.9% of intra-African migrants in 1990, by 2017 that share was 12.5% (own calculations based on data from UNDESA, 2015) (see Figure 2.4 below).

Observing migration trends on sub-regional level disguises local-level migration dynamics and underplays the importance of migration between neighbouring states. Much intra-African migration is among citizens of countries in the same sub-region and often involves movement across shared borders from landlocked to coastal countries (e.g., Burkina Faso-Côte d'Ivoire). Countries and cities may also act as migration magnets given their specialization in specific activities or industries, such as the oil industries in countries like Gabon and Libya (Flahaux & de Haas, 2016). Governance frameworks may also stimulate intra-regional mobility, particularly within regional economic communities (RECs), where free movement of persons protocols have been developed to further support regional integration. All but one of Africa's RECs have developed free movement of persons protocols to ease intraregional mobility, but their success in doing so has been stymied by limited convergence in national laws and in differences across members states in ratification and implementation of the protocol. For example, intraregional migration within the Economic Community of West African States (ECOWAS) increased following the body's adoption of the free movement protocol and its supplementary protocols, which the African Development Bank (2018) attributes to the ratification and implementation of the first phase of the protocol by all 15 member states. In contrast, the Southern African Development Community (SADC) experienced limited

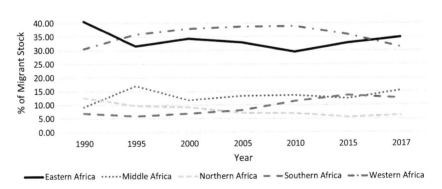

Figure 2.4 Share of intra-African emigrant stock by destination region, 1990–2017.
Source: Own calculations based on data from UNDESA (2017a).

changes in mobility following ratification of the free movement protocol due to limited domestic implementation among its member states. Intraregional migration dynamics should therefore be understood within the context of regional integration, but limited data on stocks and flows of migrants within sub-regions challenges further study (AFDB, 2019).

The given statistics are likely to underrepresent the true scale of intra-African mobility, as they are collected through population censuses, population registries, and nationally representative surveys that generally require an individual to be present in a foreign territory for three or more months consecutively to be considered a migrant. The statistics would also likely exclude irregular migrants or migrants who are not required to register their residence. Systematic estimates of short-term cross-border moves are unfortunately absent, which makes it challenging to understand the true scale of intra-African mobility, particularly among traders in goods and services who may be temporary movers.

Demographic changes, mobility, and trade

Migration and demography are intimately linked, as migration – in combination with fertility and mortality – is one of the prime phenomena that shapes the demographic profile of a population. Demographic shifts may also precipitate or accelerate migration, particularly given the intersection between demographic profiles and livelihood opportunities.

According to UN estimates, the population of Africa is expected to rise from approximately 1.2 billion people in 2015 to 1.7 billion by 2030, yet the annual rate of population expansion is expected to slow over time. Whereas the number of live births per African woman in the early 2000s was around 5, this number is expected to drop to 3.9 between 2025 and 2030 (UNDESA, 2017b). This seemingly modest change may translate into significant changes to the total dependency ratio. The ratio of the working-age population (aged 15–64) to the population aged 0–14 and 65 and over has shifted rapidly over time. As indicated in Figure 2.5, the dependency ratios of Middle, Eastern, and Western African countries have demonstrated similar trends for much of the observed period, whereas Southern and Northern Africa have strongly divergent dependency ratios starting in the mid-1980s. Dependency ratios across most of Africa's regions are expected to converge around 2055, at which point the dependency ratio is predicted to be below 65 for all regions.

Across much of Africa, changes in fertility have also been accompanied by changes in population distribution between rural and urban areas. With an annual urban growth rate of 3.5% over the past 20 years, Africa has experienced an acute growth of urban areas, and by 2025, it is estimated that more than 50% of the continent's population will live in urban areas. Much of the growth of (peri-)urban areas is likely to occur through migration, which may continue to contribute to rapid urbanization in countries like Ghana (Awumbila, 2014).

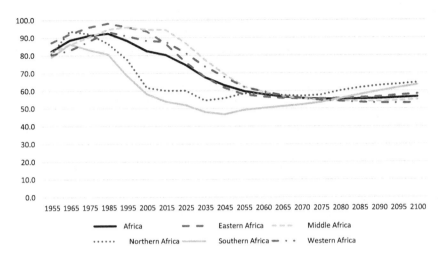

Figure 2.5 Total dependency ratio per African sub-region, 1955–2100.
Source: Own visualization based on UNDESA (2017c).

The combination of demographic shifts – particularly given the predicted effects on the dependency ratio – in combination with urban growth may create a unique opportunity for Africa to exploit a so-called 'demographic dividend'. As the population of prime working-age individuals increases relative to the population of people who are less able to contribute to economic systems (e.g., children and the elderly), the labour force, its productivity capacity, and savings tend to rise. Simulations of the potential impacts of decreasing total fertility rates on per capital income and GDP growth suggest significant economic gains with decreasing fertility. For example, estimations by Bloom et al. (2014 as reported in Bloom, Kuhn, & Prettner, 2017) suggest that lowering fertility by meeting one-third of the unmet contraceptive need in Kenya, Nigeria, and Senegal would correspond to increased per capita income of 16%, 9%, and 12%, respectively, by 2030. Similarly, per capita GDP growth would be expected to rise with decreasing fertility. An increase of the ratio of the working-age population to the total population by 1% has been estimated to correspond to a 1.39% increase in the per capita GDP growth rate (Bloom & Canning, 2008, as reported in Bloom, Kuhn, & Prettner, 2017), an impressive elasticity in a region like Africa where total fertility is expected to decline so markedly.

Africa's demographic transition may generate sizeable economic gains, contributing to an increase in the share of Africans considered to be 'middle class' and who can provide predictable sources of income for states to invest in public infrastructure and services like education. If rising incomes are used to support policies that encourage greater human capital gains, a likely outcome is that a higher share of Africans will receive specialized education and training in medium- and high-skilled functions. While some authors (e.g., Bloom, Kuhn, & Prettner, 2017) have identified education-support policies as one of the important ways African governments can generate a substantial demographic dividend, there is a risk that the functions and services for which the skilled are trained are absent in some local labour markets. Growing education levels and the absence of local labour markets that can absorb those skills are likely to increase emigration pressures in specific countries (Hatton & Williamson, 2011). Structural mismatches in the available supply of skills and economic sectors to employ skilled persons may be offset, at least temporarily, through greater mobility, specifically of service providers, which emphasizes the importance of developing trade policies that can facilitate such cross-border flows.

The transitions many Africa countries face are deeply intertwined, as shifts in population age structure influence the places people choose to settle and the activities they engage in. The growing population of young people in cities with greater disposable income are likely to demand a range of goods and services – some of which are not readily available in local markets. The growing demand for specialized and leisure goods and services is likely to stimulate cross-border trade (Mburu-Ndoria, 2016).

Trade and economic growth

Trade is deeply implicated in Africa's economic growth, and if the predicted demographic dividend comes to fruition, the support of cross-border trade may become even more key to ensure continued growth. While figures of formal trade are readily available, assessing the complete scale of African trade is challenged by limited data on informal trade flows.

Across many countries of Africa, trade in goods and services is an important contributor to gross domestic product (GDP). According to World Bank (2017) data, trade (the sum of exports and imports in goods and services) constituted a significant share of GDP for many countries, from a low of 21% in Sudan to a high of 174% in the Seychelles. For most countries, trade in services constitutes a much smaller share of GDP, ranging from 2.58% in Sudan to 103% in the Seychelles. While the Seychelles stands out for the role of trade in its GDP, trade in services has an important role in many other countries, including large economies like Ghana, Morocco, and Rwanda, where the contribution to GDP is well above 20%. The net contribution of trade flows to GDP is considerable in many countries, but across the continent, the export of goods and services is much more important to GDP in some countries over others. For example, while the export of goods and services constituted 7.7% of Ethiopia's GDP in 2017, it constituted a much larger share to the GDP of smaller economies such as the Republic of the Congo (94% of GDP), the Seychelles (81.2% of GDP), and Equatorial Guinea (57.4% of GDP). Among Africa's largest economies, trade export nevertheless contributed an important share of GDP, such as 13.1% in Nigeria, 29.7% in

South Africa, and 15.8% in Egypt (World Bank, 2017). In contrast to migration flows, which are still strongly intra-African in direction, the greatest share of African exports is destined for countries outside of the continent. As of 2017, only 17% of all African exports were destined for another African country, yet intra-African trade flows involve more complex, added-value goods. As of 2014, around 41.9% of intra-African trade was in manufactured and processed goods, whereas only 14.8% of exports beyond Africa were manufactured goods (Songwe, 2018).

The reported trade volumes are likely to capture only formal trade, and the figures are likely to under-represent the contributions of trade to GDP. In general, informal work is much more prevalent in Africa than in other world regions, with over 85% of all employment (and 71.9% of non-agricultural employment) across the continent considered informal in 2016. The proportion of informal work varies considerably across the continent, however, with 40.2% of work (including agriculture) considered informal in South Africa compared to 92.4% in Western Africa. In all regions except Northern Africa, a greater share of women than men are considered to work informally (ILO, 2018). High rates of informal work in general correspond to high rates of informal cross-border trade (ICBT), which may be of equivalent volume as formal flows for certain products (e.g., food staples, livestock) in specific African countries. Measuring these flows is challenging given their nature: ICBT can involve informal traders who function outside the formal economy, formal firms that do not comply with trade regulations and duties, and formal firms that partially comply with trade regulations and duties but evade part of their obligations. Recent estimations of the volume of ICBT are generally restricted to specific trade corridors or border-crossing points and generally capture only specific dimensions of ICBT (e.g., trade from informal traders functioning outside the formal economy). Nevertheless, they signal the important volume and value of goods exchanged through ICBT. In Uganda, for example, ICBT was estimated to account for approximately 15% of total exports in 2015, and in Rwanda, 59% of exports in 2014 were classified as ICBT (Bouet, Pace, & Glauber, 2018).

Trade – whether occurring formally or informally – may contribute to GDP and to future economic resilience and the attainment of the SDGs. Trade in the context of global development is certainly not uncontested, and the SDGs in particular have received critique from states, civil society, and academia (see, e.g., Spangenberg, 2016) for unbalanced framing of trade as a positive development force despite its potential impacts on environmental sustainability and inequality. Despite this critique, trade has been identified as a force that can support more equitable and inclusive development in the African context, particularly if it stimulates investment in export diversification, vertically integrated industries on regional level, and further value chain development (Songwe, 2018). Trade, specifically ICBT, is also an important contributor to food security: many informal cross-border traders specialize in staple foods (Awumbila, 2014), and in West Africa, ICBT in staple foods was estimated to account for around one-third of total trade in the region in the mid-aughts (Bouet, Pace, & Glauber, 2018).

Increasing the volume of trade, particularly intra-African trade, has been an explicit strategy within the African Economic Community (AEC) as a way to support sustainable regional growth. While reducing barriers to trade through channels such as customs unions and free trade areas have been key elements of this strategy, promotion of free movement of persons within RECs has also been emphasized as a mechanism that can foster regional integration and economic growth. This emphasizes that migration can indeed strengthen both economic growth and trade, but it is important to more carefully identify the channels through which migration and trade are tied.

How are trade and migration linked?

Understanding more about how migration, demography, and trade are evolving in the African context is important in answering the question of how trade and migration are linked and what the implication of this relationship is for African trade. Both theoretical and empirical literature provide some preliminary answers. The movement of people and goods between any two given places is likely to be mutually reinforcing, and it is likely to be supported by some common factors (e.g., colonial ties) that stimulate exchange between two regions or countries. The channels through which trade affects migration – and vice versa – can therefore be conceptualized as direct or indirect. Trade may *cause* migration in the sense that people move for the purpose of trading, which may be considered a direct channel of influence. Indirectly, trade may *mediate* migration choices by affecting the context in which mobility decisions are made, including by influencing production sectors and wages. Similarly, migration may directly *cause* trade through investment in businesses that allow exchange of goods between countries of origin and destination. Indirectly, there are a range of ways in which migrants can *mediate* trade relationships: for example, by lowering transactions costs of trade, by promoting the concentration or reach of trade networks, or by having preferences for goods that are novel to the market in a country of destination or origin. This section surveys the theoretical and empirical literature that suggests either direct or indirect channels by which migration and trade may influence each other.

Ties between migration and trade: theoretical assumptions and empirical evidence

The relationship between migration and trade has been theorized in neo-classical economic theory, most notably from Mundell (1957), who proposed that labour and capital may be substitutes and that labour (as a factor of production) may be a substitute for trade. The premise is that countries will have an incentive to trade with one another when there is a difference in the relative cost of production between countries, which reflect underlying differences in each country's endowment of resources that shape factors of production (including labour). If goods could be exchanged without restrictions between countries with almost identical profiles (in terms of the goods they produce, the factors of production, technology, and infrastructure), commodity-price equalization and eventually factor-price equalization would occur. Constraints on trade would stimulate factors of production (including labour) to move instead, and restrictions on factor mobility would conversely stimulate trade (Mundell, 1957) – implying that international trade and labour mobility may act as substitutes and that trade – or lack thereof – could stimulate migration.

Given the strict theoretical assumptions under which trade and migration would be expected to act as substitutes, the theory has been contested and has inspired competing models of the conditions under which trade and migration act as substitutes or complements. Del Rio and Thorwarth (2009), for example, suggest that differences in technologies, differences in return to scale for production of differentiated goods, and heterogeneity of labour skills across countries, among other factors, can shift the complementarity/substitution effect between trade and migration. Under some circumstances, trade would be expected to stimulate migration – for example, in circumstances when one country produces a homogenous good with constant returns to scale, and another produces differentiated goods with increased returns to scale. Given free trade, a country may specialize in the sector with increasing returns to scale, supporting wage growth that then results in wage differentials between the two countries and motivates labour (as a factor of production) to move (Del Rio & Thorwarth, 2009). Alternatively, Anukoonwattaka and Heal (2014) argue that migration and trade may act as substitutes when countries differ only in factor endowments, which may lead to countries substituting both finished goods and low-skilled, labour-intensive goods from countries with lower factor costs (e.g., wages) in place of importing labour. Countries with higher factor costs may try to suppress the cost of factors of production by outsourcing services, indicating substitution between trade and migration. Trade and migration may instead act as complements when trade and the mobility of factors of production increase simultaneously. Further, while trade and migration may not be fully complementary, migration may nevertheless stimulate trade when migrant workers are complementary to local workers qua skill profiles and occupational choices, which may accelerate growth of export-related industries and therefore promote trade (Anukoonwattaka & Heal, 2014).

The advancement of theory on the relationship between migration and trade has been accompanied by a growth in empirical studies that model the impact of trade on migration flows and the impact of migration on bilateral import and export flows. As noted by Campaniello (2014), empirical studies on causal relationships between trade and migration are relatively scarce; of the small number of studies that have modelled this relationship, most have been limited to establishing correlation. Within such studies, trade is generally found to positively correlate with migration, at least in the short- and medium-term. A study on the impacts of trade on migration between Mexico and the United States between 1968 and 2004 found strong, positive correlations between trade volume and irregular migration (as proxied by number or border apprehensions). One estimation suggested that an increase of volume of trade between Mexico and the United States of US$1 billion would correspond to an increase in irregular migration of up to 71,000 people per year (Del Rio & Thorwarth, 2009). Campaniello (2014) similarly estimated the causal effect of trade on migration from the so-called 'Mediterranean third countries' (non-EU countries included in the Euro-Mediterranean partnership) to EU destination countries between 1970 and 2000. The results of different model specifications consistently predicted an elasticity between trade and migration exceeding 40%, which suggests that additional trade flows between the Mediterranean third countries and the EU would substantially accelerate migration to EU countries.

A larger number of studies have modelled the opposite relationship: that between migration and trade. Several empirical studies have calculated what can be termed the 'immigrant elasticity of trade' – essentially the percent change in import/export volumes given a 1% change in the stock of migrants in a given country of residence. A quantitative meta-review of 48 studies investigating the immigrant elasticity of trade in goods conducted by Genç (2014) concluded that a 10% increase of the migrant stock from a particular origin country increased the volume of exports between the destination and origin country by 2.4% (on average) and the volume of imports between the origin and destination country by 2.9% on average. The average values disguise some important variations: elasticities appeared to decrease as migrant populations matured, tended to be smallest for homogenous goods (goods that are indistinguishable in quality and appearance between manufacturers in countries of origin and residence), and increased among higher-skilled migrants (Genç, 2014).

Few of the studies reviewed by Genç (2014) specifically modelled the *emigrant* elasticity of trade or trade elasticities for migration corridors beyond the high-income OECD region. A small number of past studies have estimated emigrant elasticities of trade and for non-OECD country sets, however. For example, Parsons (2012) estimated the influence of both immigrant and emigrant stocks on bilateral trade using panel data for the period between 1960 and 2000. The study found that emigration and immigration were both positively correlated with bilateral trade flows, and the emigrant elasticity of trade was generally higher than the immigrant elasticity. Any positive effect of either immigration or emigration on trade flows generally disappeared in panel regressions, however, suggesting that time-invariant factors related to specific trade partners that may not be captured in cross-sectional data drive the positive impacts of migration on trade flows. The association between migration and bilateral trade flows was found to vary significantly across regional partners, however, with both immigrants and emigrants found to exert statistically significant influence on aggregate bilateral trade flows of exports moving from countries in the global north to those in the global south (Parsons, 2012). Other scholarship focussed specifically on the role of *emigrants* in shaping African trade flows suggest other patterns. A 2012 study by Ehrhart et al. explored the immigrant elasticity of trade among 52 African origin countries and their 195 global commercial partners. Their estimations suggest that a 1% increase in the global stock of African migrants corresponded to an increase of exports from their countries of origin by 0.178% on average. The authors estimated that in the year 2010, such an elasticity would imply that every African emigrant would generate approximately US$2100 in additional exports per year for the origin country (Ehrhart et al., 2014).

Despite relatively consistent findings between studies on the positive association between migration and trade flows, several important questions remain open about the relationship between migration and trade in the African context given the focus and framing of previous studies. First, in modelling the influence of trade on migration, few studies have been able to establish causal links, and even among those that have, the specific channels that support the impact of trade and migration have not been rigorously examined – in part given the specific information required on the ties between specific pairs of trade partners. Second, in terms of modelling the influence of migration on trade, few empirical studies have explicitly modelled the immigrant or emigrant elasticity of trade between pairs of non-high-income OECD countries, and the role of intra-African migration on import and export volumes between African trading partners have not been extensively explored. Most studies have also focussed exclusively on the migrant elasticity of trade in *goods* only, and the impact of migration on service trade remains unclear. The studies also highlight that factors such as maturity of the immigrant stock, skill structure of the migrant population, and nature of trade goods mediate the effect of migration on trade. These factors suggest that migration can affect trade through different channels, the function of which may differ in the African context.

Channels of influence between migration and trade

Both theoretical and empirical literature have identified different channels through which migration and bilateral trade flows may influence each other. The channels through which trade may influence migration include: (1) increasing incomes, which can be used to fund migration, and (2) widening differences in labour conditions between countries of destination and origin.

One mechanism by which trade could stimulate migration relates to relaxation of capital constraints that would frustrate migration. Migration can be a costly process, particularly in the absence of transparent or regulated migration channels. A growing body of migration and development literature has addressed how economic growth and trade liberalization may spur rather than stymie migration because of their impacts on the human and financial capital resources that inform migration aspirations and enable migration journeys (see, e.g., de Haas, 2007). In a study among a sample of countries in the Euro-Mediterranean region, Faini and Venturini (2010) modelled the impact of increasing incomes on migration propensity, finding that migration propensities spiked with increasing incomes – at least until incomes approached convergence between countries of origin and destination.

The issue of relative differences between conditions in countries of origin and destination is central in neo-classical economic theories of migration (such as the Harris-Todaro model related to expected wage differentials), and indeed differences in labour market conditions between countries of origin and destination may affect migration choices – suggesting another channel through which trade can shape migration. Trade may encourage countries to specialize in specific sectors where factors of production, such as labour, are relatively more productive, which can support expansion of industry; higher demand for labour; and, in some cases, more competitive wages. Such conditions may attract migrant workers – a familiar scenario in the United States, where trade-related sector expansion corresponded to increased volumes of Mexican workers (Del Rio & Thorwarth, 2009). A third channel by which trade could stimulate migration is through *worsening* labour conditions in origin countries, which could increase pressures to migrate. For example, differences in production technologies between trading partners may increase the relative efficiency of production in one country at the expense of another. Based again on the relationship between the United States and Mexico, Del Rio and Thorwarth (2009) suggested that Mexico, with its labour-intensive agricultural production, could not compete with the United States, which is characterized by capital-intensive production. As a consequence, trade between the two countries compounded losses to the Mexican agricultural industry, which resulted in reduction of agricultural employment in Mexico and increased pressures to migrate for work to the United States. In how far these mechanisms apply to countries with more similar economies is uncertain, as these channels of influence between trade and migration have been observed primarily in contexts of global south to global north migration.

The channels through which migration may affect trade have received greater examination in the literature and include: (1) lowering of transaction costs, (2) facilitating nostalgia trade (the so-called immigrant-preference effect), (3) direct capital investment in businesses in the country of origin or ancestry, and (4) the development of migrant- or diaspora-owned enterprises. The extent to which these different channels support the growth of trade remains ambiguous, particularly in contexts where migrants move between countries in the same region.

Migrants and their descendants may support trade between their countries of destination and origin by leveraging their knowledge of market conditions, language skills, cultural norms, and business contacts/networks that facilitate the exchange of privileged information and business resources, which in turn lower transaction costs (Gould, 1994; White, 2007; Lewer & van den Berg, 2009). Gould (1994) proposed in his seminal contribution to the literature that 'human-capital-type externalities' (p. 302) generated by migrants could improve bilateral trade opportunities. He proposed that migrants are uniquely positioned to provide information on foreign markets to aspiring exporters and may act as network builders between contacts in countries of origin and residence, which helps businesses and investors overcome information asymmetries that increase the risks associated with new trade routes. These proposed mechanisms were tested using bilateral import/export flow data collected between 1970 and 1989 for the United States and 47 of its trade partners, and the analysis revealed that migrant information had a significant, positive influence on trade flows between the United States and migrant origin countries (Gould, 1994).

Specifically within the African context, networks may play a particularly pivotal role in supporting trade given the absence of strong, formal institutions that support and protect businesses engaging in trade. Networks, particularly those convened among co-ethnics or co-nationals, are often based on trust and a commitment of the community to enforce (implicit) agreements within that community. In settings where contracts are difficult to enforce given the absence of legal bodies with the mandate to do or so or where corruption can lead to opportunistic, selective enforcement, such informal networks may stand in for formal institutions by promoting adherence and cooperation (Rauch, 2001). The role of networks in facilitating African trade flows in weak institutional environments was modelled econometrically by Ehrhart et al. (2012). While the African emigrant stock in a particular destination country was generally found to increase trade flows between the destination and origin country, the effect was especially pronounced for countries with low-quality institutions (Ehrhart et al., 2012) – suggesting that migrants can have a pro-trade effect by substituting for formal, protective institutions.

Migrants may also stimulate trade by generating demand for new products and services, called the 'immigrant preference effect'. This effect occurs when migrants retain preferences for goods/services that are more readily available in the origin country, eventually stimulating the importation of preferred goods from countries of origin to the residence country (Gould, 1994). If such an effect occurs, flows of imports from the origin to destination country would be expected to increase, but only when such goods are strongly differentiated between the two places. There is empirical evidence that such preference effects exist, particularly linked to migrants from lower-income countries. White (2007) modelled bilateral trade flows between the United States and 73 trading partners between 1980 and 2001, revealing that the influence of migrant stocks on bilateral import/export flows was most marked for specific countries. The strongest annual increases in trade flows were between the United States and China, Bangladesh, and Nigeria. The analysis revealed that migrants from lower-income countries supported greater growth in imports than exports, generating an average annual value of US$910 in exports to and up to US$2,967 in imports from the origin country.

While less directly related to trade as such, migrants may also strengthen trade flows by directly investing in businesses or by starting businesses that may eventually engage in trade activities. The investments made by migrants and their descendants – who are often referred to as *diaspora* regardless of their self-identification or felt ties – have been increasingly addressed in literature, with the term *diaspora direct investments* (DDIs) used to identify investments made from expatriate populations in enterprises (foreign direct investment) and in capital markets (e.g., stock and bond sales) in countries of origin or ancestry (Newland & Tanaka, 2010). Investments made from abroad may support businesses to enter trade systems, particularly if those investments enable scaling up and professionalization of products, processes, and services in such a way that would enable a business to meet complex regulatory requirements tied to trade. Tracking DDI and its influence on business growth is difficult, as many countries do not discern the national origin or ancestral ties of investors in businesses. There is some limited evidence that businesses that receive DDIs, particularly small and medium-size enterprises traditionally shut out of trade systems because of regulatory complexity and cost, are better able to engage in trade given their ties to the diaspora. A recent assessment of firms started by migrants and diaspora members (or supported by DDI from abroad) in 19 sub-Saharan African countries found that diaspora-linked firms were more likely to be involved in export than domestic firms without diaspora ties. Such businesses also signalled a higher export intensity, the share of exports in total sales, and were connected to a greater number and diversity of export markets. The study also found that diaspora-linked firms had a higher probability of exporting to countries in the global south – namely other African countries, South Asia, India, and China – but no higher probabilities of exporting to OECD countries than non-diaspora-linked firms. The finding may signal that diaspora investors or investors with a previous migration experience may be better able to leverage their knowledge of destination countries in the global south (Boly et al., 2014).

Taken together, the different strands of literature signal that migrants can have a pro-trade effect by stimulating businesses to offer goods to new markets, supporting networks that can assist businesses in entering international markets, and providing the capital businesses need to compete in new trade spaces. How well migration supports trade is likely to be conditioned by policy, however.

How can policy foster migration, trade, and development in the African context?

While the relationship is by no means linear, literature suggests compelling links among demography, migration, trade, and eventually economic growth and development. If indeed the demographic transition in Africa will support the growth of a young, economically active population, a potential demographic dividend may emerge that also enables greater expenditure in education; growing wages; and, in turn, growing supply of and demand for specialized goods and services. Higher incomes and education levels combined with potential mismatches in the supply and demand of (semi-)skilled youth in local labour markets may incentivize greater migration. Greater migration may increase trade flows, which, in turn, may support greater food security, stimulate product and process innovation, encourage the development of regional and global value chains, and eventually stimulate more inclusive economic growth.

In how far migration, demography, and trade converge in the ways sketched to support economic growth in Africa is likely to depend on the development of supportive policy regimes. The role of policy in supporting migration-related trade merits an individual chapter; this section therefore only shortly addresses some of the ways in which policies related to migration and trade can foster their mutual advantages.

Enhancing the pro-trade potential of migration

As addressed in 'How are trade and migration linked?', the pro-trade effect of migration is likely to reflect migrants' capacities to leverage knowledge and networks to lower transaction costs, their demand for nostalgia goods and services, and their investments in enterprises that engage in international trade. Policies that aim to enhance the pro-trade potential of migration could address these mechanisms specifically or could facilitate mobility more generally by lowering barriers to migration – particularly among traders involved in ICBT and service provision.

Facilitating intra-African migration has been prioritized within the African policy agenda. The African Union's *Protocol to the Treaty Establishing the African Economic Community Relating to Free Movement of Persons, Rights of Residence and Right of Establishment* (Free Movement of Persons Protocol), adopted in January 2018, reflects the centrality of free movement and labour migration in continental policy strategies. Enabling continental free movement has been a goal since 1991, and while the protocol's adoption represents an important step forward in eliminating barriers to intra-African migration, its impacts remain uncertain (Dick & Schraven, 2019). As of July 2018, 32 of 55 AU member states had signed the Free Movement of Persons Protocol, but only one (Rwanda) had domestically ratified it. Signatories are clustered regionally: whereas 8 of 9 Middle African states, 11 of 17 in Western Africa, and 11 of 20 in East Africa have signed the protocol, only one country each in Northern and Southern Africa has signed (AU, 2018).

The Free Movement of Persons Protocol could have a significant impact on trade, as cross-border traders may face unclear visa requirements and stringent entry rules that make it challenging to access new markets. Firms could also benefit from more relaxed movement and stay regimes by making it easier for skilled and semi-skilled labourers to enter and be hired by businesses, particularly those in need of skill sets that are scarce locally. As noted above, however, there remain substantial challenges in harmonizing domestic regulation and legislation related to issues such as admission of workers, which diffuses potential positive impacts of both continent-wide and REC-specific free movement protocols on economic integration and trade.

Following the intuition that migration can support trade, the African Continental Free Trade Area Agreement (AfCFTA) was adopted in March 2018. The aim of the AfCFTA is to create a single African market – ultimately the largest free trade area in the world – through a 90% reduction of trade tariffs, elimination of non-tariff barriers (e.g., subsidies, import tariffs, technical barriers), and liberalization of service trade (Songwe, 2018). Liberalization of trade in services is an especially novel element of AfCFTA, which will likely create greater modalities for cross-border labour flows and channels for movement of services related to finance, distribution, and transport, which would be necessary to support greater regional integration and intra-African trade in goods (Mburu-Ndoria, 2016). The AfCFTA has inspired greater commitment from AU member states, with 44 of 55 countries signatory and 22 countries ratifying it, which is the minimum number needed to bring the agreement into effect. In addition to AU-level initiatives, regional co-operation bodies like the Common Market for Eastern and Southern Africa (COMESA), East Africa Community (EAC), ECOWAS, the West African Economic and Monetary Union (WAEMU), Economic Community of Central African Countries (ECCAS), and SADC have agreed to support services liberalization as part of regional integration efforts (Mburu-Ndoria, 2016), and the near-universal acceptance of free movement of persons protocols within RECs may also support trade in services. Such efforts reflect proactive commitments on sub-region level to increase mobility and circulation, which in some cases – such as ECOWAS, which concluded its own free movement protocol in 1979 – have been explicit strategies for economic integration (Dick & Schraven, 2019).

The extent to which regional integration efforts – particularly in the form of free movement protocols and the reduction of barriers to trade – have succeeded in supporting greater mobility and exchange among participating members is ambiguous. Given the recent acceptance of AfCFTA, there is limited evidence of its efficacy – particularly in terms of impacts on mobility of traders and service providers. Some research has suggested that other efforts to promote trade more generally (and by extension mobility of traders) through RECs have been underwhelming. For example, within the AEC, under which most RECs constitute 'pillars', strategic aims include supporting economic growth through greater regional economic cooperation, which entailed creation of free trade areas and customs unions. The creation of RECs within the AEC has appeared to have modest impacts on intra-African trade, however. One study of intra-African trade intensity, which compared intensity two years prior and five years after the implementation of RECs, suggested that most regions experienced minimal intra-regional trade gains through the creation of an REC. In the EAC region, the intensity of intra-regional trade had increased substantially five years after conclusion of the REC agreement, but the intra-regional intensity actually decreased within COMESA, suggesting mixed impacts of lower trade barriers through RECs on intra-regional trade intensity (de Melo & Tskikata, 2015, as cited in ADB, 2018).

Policies that support free movement and service trade liberalization – if effectively implemented – should accelerate intra-African trade and stimulate the production of added-value goods, but other types of policies can support the pro-trade potential of migration. Policies that encourage or facilitate migrants/diaspora members to invest in businesses that engage in trade by improving investment environments are one example. Countries such as Benin, Sierra Leone, and Uganda have developed diaspora institutions specifically to channel migrant and diaspora investments (Gamlen, 2014). Others, such as Nigeria and Ethiopia, have developed diaspora bonds to attract capital from their expatriate communities, which can be used to finance infrastructure improvements (e.g., transportation, energy networks, telecommunication) that, in turn, support manufacturing and enable trade. Other policies may indirectly support migrant investments by improving the private sector ecosystem. A recent assessment among Sierra Leonean emigrants in the United States, the UK, and Canada found that significant shares of the sampled population wanted to invest in enterprises and projects in Sierra Leone but did not do so due to limited infrastructure, difficulties in identifying supply chain partners, and difficulties in needed human capital resources in Sierra Leone capable of performing necessary functions for business growth (World Bank, 2015). Policies that support infrastructure development, stimulate the growth of business networks, and encourage skill mobility could play an instrumental role in diffusing such investment barriers.

Conclusions and ways forward

Migration, trade, and development are inherently tied, and, as this review suggests, better supporting their integration is necessary for Africa to meet the inclusive growth envisioned by the SDGs. Migration and trade are implied in a number of SDGs, most notably goal 8 (decent work and economic growth), goal 9 (industry, innovation, and infrastructure), and goal 17 (partnerships for the goals). Eased intra-African movement can play an important role in supporting businesses to acquire the knowledge and skills they need to innovate in products in processes, engage in technological upgrading, and boost productivity through diversification (target 8.2) by allowing greater mobility of workers and service providers. Easing cross-border movements and encouraging circularity may also stimulate the development of business and scientific networks among migrants and non-migrants, which can support businesses to acquire the knowledge and resources needed to innovate, professionalize, and enter international trade systems (ideas linked to targets 9.3, 9.4, and 9.a). Migrant resources – including social, human, and financial capital – can support development within the private sector through both investment and philanthropy (target 17.3), which can also increase export and import flows within and beyond Africa (target 17.11). For these benefits to materialize, however, trade and migration policies must be designed to be mutually complementary and forward-looking. From this perspective, demographic shifts must be taken into account, as the availability of the human capital needed to sustain business transitions will shift along with the structure of the population.

While this chapter suggests that there are compelling ties among migration, demography, trade, and inclusive development, there remain important gaps in knowledge regarding how these intersections function within Africa. In order to develop more sensitive policies and programmes that enhance these links, future research should provide more nuanced analysis of how intra-African migration affects intra-African trade, particularly trade in services. Research could also further disentangle the channels through which African migrants stimulate trade in goods and services between sets of African countries, and it could also explore whether the sophistication of exports, indicating innovation, increases with migration. The adoption of recent policy initiatives (e.g., the AU Free Movement in Persons Protocol, AfCFTA) that can intensify the intra-African mobility of traders in goods and services also invites future research that explores the impacts of these policies on intra-African trade flows and the implications of those flows for equitable economic growth.

References

Adepoju, A. (2007). "Creating a borderless West Africa: Constraints and prospects for intra-regional migration" in A. Pecaud and P. de Guchteneire (eds.). *Migration without Borders: Essays on the Free Movement of People* (pp. 161–174). New York: UNESCO & Berghahn Books.

African Development Bank group (AfDB). (2019). African economic outlook.

African Union. (2018). List of countries which have signed, ratified/acceded to the *Protocol to the Treaty Establishing the African Economic Community Relating to Free Movement of Persons, Rights of Residence and Right of Establishment.* https://au.int/sites/default/files/treaties/36403-sl-PROTOCOL%20TO%20THE%20TREATY%20ESTABLISHING%20THE%20AFRICAN%20ECONOMIC%20COMMUNITY%20RELAT....pdf

Anukoonwattaka, W. & Heal, A. (2014). "Regional integration and labour mobility: Linking trade, migration and development." *Studies in Trade and Investment No. 81,* United Nations Economic and Social Commissions for Asia and the Pacific (ESCAP): New York.

Awumbila, M. (2014). "Linkages between urbanization, rural-urban migration and poverty outcomes in Africa." Background paper for the *World Migration Report 2015.* International Organisation for Migration: Geneva.

Bakewell, O. (2008). "'Keeping them in their place': The ambivalent relationship between development and migration in Africa." *Third World Quarterly*, 29(7): 1341–1358. DOI: 10.1080/01436590802386492.

Bloom, D.E., Kuhn, M., & Prettner, K. (2017). "Africa's prospects for enjoying a demographic dividend." *Journal of Demographic Economics*, 83: 63–76.

Boly, A., Coniglio, N.D., Prota, F., & Seric, A. (2014). "Diaspora investments and firm export performance in selected sub-Saharan African countries." *World Development*, 59: 422–433.

Bouet, A., Pace, K., & Glauber, J. (2018). "Informal cross-border trade in Africa: How much? Why? And what impact?" International Food Policy Research Institute Discussion Paper No. 01783, Washington DC.

Campaniello, N. (2014). "The causal effect of trade on migration: Evidence from countries of the Euro-Mediterranean partnership." *Labour Economics*, 30: 223–233.

Carling, J. & Talleraas, C. (2016). "Root Causes and Drivers of Migration." *Oslo: Peace Research Institute Oslo (PRIO)* 2016: 1–44.
Paper.

Del Rio, A.M. & Thorwarthe, S. (2009). "Tomatoes or tomato pickers? Free trade and migration between Mexico and the United States." *Journal of Applied Econometrics*, 12(1): 109–135.

Dick, E. & Schraven, B. (2019). "Towards a borderless Africa? Regional organisations and free movement of persons in west and north-east Africa." German Development Institute briefing paper 1/2019. DOI: 10.23661/bp1.2019.

Ehrhart, H., Le Goff, M., Rocher, E., & Singh, R.J. (2014). "Does migration foster exports? Evidence from Africa." *World Bank Policy Research Working Papers*. DOI: 10.1596/1813-9450-6739.

Faini, R. & Venturini, A. (2010). "Development and migration: lessons from Southern Europe." *Migration and Culture*. Emerald Group Publishing Limited. DOI: 10.1108/S1574-8715(2010)0000008011

Flahaux, M.-L. & de Haas, H. (2016). "African migration: Trends, patterns, drivers." *Comparative Migration Studies*, 4(1): 1–25. DOI: 10.1186/s40878-015-0015-6.

Gamlen, A. (2014). "Diaspora institutions and diaspora governance." *International Migration Review*, 48(1): 180–217. DOI: 10.1111/imre.12136.

Genç, M. (2014). "The impact of migration on trade." *IZA World of Labour*: 82. DOI: 10.15185/izawol.82.

Gilbert, E. (2002). "Coastal east Africa and the western Indian Ocean: Long-distance trade, empire, migration, and regional unity, 1750–1970." *The History Teacher*, 36(1): 7–34.

Gould, D.M. (1994). "Immigrant links to the home country: Empirical implications for U.S. bilateral trade flows." *The Review of Economics and Statistics*, 76(2): 302–316.

de Haas, H. (2007). "Turning the tide? Why development will not stop migration." *Development and Change*, 38(5): 819–841.

International Labour Organisation (ILO). (2018). *Women and Men in the Informal Economy: A Statistical Picture*, 3rd edition. ILO: Geneva.

Lewer, J.J. & van den Verg, H. (2009). "Does immigration stimulate international trade? Measuring the channels of influence." *The International Trade Journal*, 23(2): 187–230.

Mburu-Ndoria, E. (2016). "Africa continental free trade area: Liberalizing trade in services for trade facilitation." UNCTAD report on project "Strengthening Capacities of African Countries in Boosting Intra-African Trade." Retrieved from https://

unctad.org/meetings/en/SessionalDocuments/ditc-ted-Nairobi-24082015-mburu.pdf

Mundell, R.A. (1957). "International trade and factor mobility." *The American Economic Review*, 47(3): 321–335.

Newland, K. & Tanaka, H. (2010). *Mobilizing diaspora entrepreneurship for development.* Migration Policy Institute: Washington, DC.

Parsons, C.R. (2012). "Do migrants really foster trade? The trade-migration nexus, a panel approach 1960–2000". *World Bank Policy Research Working Paper No. 6034.* The World Bank: Washington, DC.

Peberdy, S. & Crush, J. (2007). "Histories, realities and negotiating free movement in southern Africa" in A. Pecaud and P. de Guchteneire (eds.). *Migration without Borders: Essays on the Free Movement of People* (pp. 175–198). New York: UNESCO & Berghahn Books.

Rauch, J.E. (2001). "Business and social networks in international trade." *Journal of Economic Literature*, 39: 1177–1203.

Songwe, V. (2018). "Intra-African trade: A path to economic diversification and inclusion." *Boosting Trade and Investment: A New Agenda for Regional and International Engagement.* Brookings Institution report. Retrieved from https://www.brookings.edu/wp-content/uploads/2019/01/BLS18234_BRO_book_006.1_CH6.pdf

Spangenberg, J.H. (2016). "Hot air or comprehensive progress? A critical assessment of the SDGs." *Sustainable Development*, 25(4): 311–321.

United Nations, Department of Economic and Social Affairs (UNDESA). (2017a). *Trends in International Migrant Stock: Migrants by Destination and Origin.* United Nations database, POP/DB/MIG/Stock/Rev.2017.

United Nations, Department of Economic and Social Affairs (UNDESA). (2017b). *World Population Prospects: The 2017 Revision. Volume II: Demographic Profiles.* UNDESA Population Division, document number ST/ESA/SER.A/400.

United Nations, Department of Economic and Social Affairs (UNDESA). (2017c). *World Population Prospects: The 2017 Revision.* Custom data acquired via website.

White, R. (2007). "Immigrant-trade links, transplanted home bias and network effects." *Applied Economics*, 39(7): 839–852. DOI: 10.1080/00036840500447849.

World Bank. (2015). "Sierra Leone diaspora investment and trade study: Executive summary." World Bank document number 99768. World Bank: Washington, DC.

World Bank. (2017). Databank macroeconomic indicators, trade as % of GDP. Retrieved from https://data.worldbank.org/indicator/ne.trd.gnfs.zs (accessed March 2019).

3 Migration, innovation, and growth

An African story?

Linguère Mously Mbaye and Massimiliano Tani

Introduction

Research on the sources of economic growth has traditionally highlighted the positive contribution of elements that are somewhat 'disembodied' like technological advances, investments in Research and Development (R&D), patents, and routines at the core of firms' comparative advantage, institutional factors like openness to international trade, foreign direct investments (FDI), and financial capital. Embodied explanations, which instead centre on individual capabilities and activities, have received comparatively less attention. As an example, the relationship between peoples' interactions and the creation of new productivity-improving knowledge has been systematically investigated only in recent times.

Yet embodied sources of growth could have a special place in research and policymaking in countries that are predominantly labour abundant, as they may offer complementary, or even alternative, paths to generate productivity and technological advances. In the context of Africa, several countries are relatively well endowed with young people, labour mobility is relatively common, and income levels are low, though fast growing, vis-à-vis other parts of the world. This makes the continent an ideal case study as a place in which the relationship between labour mobility and innovation may be at work. Furthermore, as the Fourth Industrial Revolution is heralded with migration at the core of global governance issues, the nature of the relationship between peoples' movements and productivity and innovation calls for more analyses and understanding of its possible effects on, and potential uses in, the achievements of the Sustainable Development Goals (SDGs).

In this chapter, we study the link between migration and innovation in Africa. In particular, we focus on the relationship between short-term labour movements, as proxied by international tourist arrivals per capita, and the introduction of new products, services, or processes, as collected by innovation surveys. Tourism flows have been used as a proxy of short-term work-related visits (Andersen and Dalgaard, 2011) because movements lasting for less than a year are recorded in 'tourism' rather than 'migration' statistics, following a recommendation by the United Nations.[1]

This chapter aims to make three specific contributions. First, we wish to add to existing work, which focusses on the link between long-term or permanent migration and innovation, by extending the analysis to short-term movements. These have been shown to be substantive channels through which new ideas and productive knowledge flow across borders in high-income countries, but there is no such research in the case of Africa. Labour movements are common throughout Africa, consisting mainly of circular and labour migration (Adepoju, 2008; Oucho, 1990) and intra-African movements (AfDB, 2019).

Second, we explore the importance of peoples' interactions for introducing innovation as measured by new products, services, and processes rather than patents, which tend to represent only a fraction of new knowledge generated (Agrawal et al., 2006; Hovhannisyan and Keller, 2015; Kerr, 2008). This approach reflects current standards to measure innovation (OECD and Eurostat, 2005).

Third, we investigate innovation activities in Africa using recent and comprehensive firm-level data gathered by the World Bank's Enterprises Survey (WBES). In doing so we not only present novel results arising from this rich dataset but also complement existing analyses carried out in OECD and other high-income countries.

Our analysis provides support to the hypothesis that short-term labour movements have a substantial positive effect on the innovation activity of African firms, with a point estimate almost as large as that of R&D investments, in line with recent literature (Piva et al., 2018). This result is robust to various econometric approaches and model specifications.

The structure of the chapter is as follows. 'Migration, mobility, and innovation' reviews the literature exploring the relationship between migration and innovation. 'Innovation in Africa' presents some facts and figures about R&D and innovation in Africa. 'Data and descriptive statistics' introduces the data. 'Migration, innovation and growth in Africa' presents the results. 'Discussion: migration, innovation and the SDGs in Africa' concludes by discussing the link between migration, innovation, and their policy implications for the SDGs.

Migration, mobility, and innovation

Defining innovation

Schumpeter's (1934) definition of 'innovation' as a cause of economic development and underlying force underpinning 'creative destruction' (a dynamic process where new technologies replace what is currently used) remains a fundamental reference in today's research. Schumpeter identifies innovation with the introduction of new products or new methods of production, the opening of new markets, the development of new sources of supply for raw materials or other inputs, and the creation of new market structures in an industry. This approach is still at the base of the Oslo Manual (2005), the benchmark for innovation data collection developed by the OECD, which defines innovation as the implementation of a new or significantly improved product (good or service), or new process, a new marketing method, or a new organizational method in business practices, workplace organization, or external relations.

Despite the existence of an internationally agreed definition, measuring innovation is not a straightforward empirical exercise due to the broad nature and scope of the activities involved. The literature measures innovation using variables related to its *outputs*, like enhanced firm profitability; number of new products (e.g. SPRU database); creation of patents, designs, and trademarks; and improvements in total factor productivity, or its *inputs*, like the amount of resources devoted to R&D (see, for example, Acs et al., 2002; Bloom et al., 2016; Hovhannisyan and Keller, 2015; Rogers, 1998).

However, as pointed out in the Oslo Manual (2005), while input and output variables *relate* to innovation, they only measure it imperfectly. First and foremost, they do not account for the essential activities that may have led to the innovation. For example, trials and failures in developing a new product generate skills, knowledge, and experience, which may be essential to a later technological breakthrough. Yet such interim learning process is not at all recognized by existing metrics due to the practical challenge of observing and reporting it.

Output measures such as patents are useful but they are only the observed tip of a large unmeasured 'iceberg' of intermediate efforts and attempts. In addition, many innovations are not patented because of complicated and lengthy registration processes involved. Protection then comes in the form of indirect barriers such as continuous product updates, trade secrets, or other constraints to competition like the prohibition for some key workers to join a competitor firm for a minimum period after leaving the innovative firm.

Input measures, like expenditure in R&D or the number of R&D employees, are useful when institutional settings like accounting principles and taxation regimes are established, as they affect firms' internal organization and reporting requirements. In addition, when the economy includes a large informal sector escaping official data collection, R&D statistics may overly distort the actual level of innovation activity. This may be particularly problematic in the case of Africa, where the share of informal employment is 72% of non-agricultural employment, the highest in the world (AfDB, 2019).

As an alternative to both patents and R&D data, knowledge diffusion is regarded as a suitable proxy of knowledge production. This approach relies on the assumption that knowledge exchanges lead eventually to the adoption of new or more productive technology, products, or processes (Rapoport, 2018). Under this framework, international trade flows and peoples' mobility or interactions are valid indicators of knowledge transfers and exchanges.[2] These are incorporated either in products and services when knowledge is disembodied (Bahar and Rapoport, 2018; Breschi and Lissoni, 2009;

Hovhannisyan and Keller, 2015; Jaffe et al., 1993; Keller, 2010); in peoples' skills when knowledge is embodied, especially in the case of temporary cross-border flows (Andersen and Dalgaard, 2011; Hovhannisyan and Keller, 2015; Piva et al., 2018); or through permanent movements of highly trained individuals like engineers or scientists (Bahar and Rapoport, 2018; Choudhury, 2016; Dos Santos and Postel-Vinay, 2003; Hunt and Gauthier-Loiselle, 2010).

Migration and innovation

Migration, a priori, can positively or negatively affect innovation activity. The negative effect arises in theory when the migration of high-skilled people generates a 'brain drain' in the country of origin depleting its stock of knowledge producing assets. However, empirical evidence suggests that migration has a positive impact on innovation, as labour movements establish the circulation of knowledge between sending and receiving countries through 'diaspora' networks (Rapoport, 2018). The link between those moving in a new country and family and friends or former colleagues remaining in the place of origin is seldom lost. As a result, attributing the gains and losses of migration on the basis of migrant headcounts is overly simplistic.

Using data from 135 countries and 781 products from 1990 to 2010, Bahar and Rapoport (2018) show that the increase in the number of immigrants from a country exporting a certain product raises the likelihood of the receiving country to begin exporting that product in the next ten years. A 10% increase in the immigrant stock from a country exporting a good is associated with a 2% increase in the probability of the receiving country to export the same good.[3] It has also been shown that compared to domestic firms, diaspora firms have a higher likelihood to be exporters, to export more and towards more destinations (Boly et al., 2014).

This positive effect between migration and innovation has also been documented in the case of returning migrants (Dos Santos and Postel-Vinay, 2003), as they tend to be more innovative, having learnt across various places, relative to local hires. Migrants in fact play the role of bridge from transferring knowledge from multinational enterprise headquarters to local employees (Choudhury, 2016).

Business visits and innovation

Migration, however, represents only one of the ways in which people move nowadays. Several movements last for less than a year (the convention used to separate migrants from visitors) and are not necessarily associated with employment rights in the country of destination, as is the case for business visits. Business travel involves a trip motivated by work purposes, but it is not necessarily associated with the permit to work in the host country: as this trip cannot be classified as 'employment' it tends to be unregulated.

Yet, partly because of the challenge of measuring such short-term work-related movements and partly because of the difficulties in measuring innovation (see later in this section), research about the effect of short-term labour movements on innovation remains limited. Notwithstanding the status quo, there is concordant support that short-term labour movements have a positive effect. Hovhannisyan and Keller (2015) show that business travel has a positive impact on countries' rate of innovation, as measured by the number of patents. Using data from the United States on patenting from 37 sectors in 34 developed and developing countries over the period 1993–2003, they find that a 10% increase in visits in the United States raises patenting in the places of origin by 0.2%. The technological content exchanged through visits is also important. Anderson (2007) shows that the inflows of business and professional visits have a positive effect on levels of per capita income in developing countries.

Channels of transmission

The mechanism through which visits affect knowledge is the direct human interaction, as these foster mutual trust and thus the exchange of ideas and productive knowledge (Gambetta, 1988; Storper and Venables, 2004). These exchanges reduce information asymmetries between what the interacting parties already know, leading to productivity shifts, especially when the interaction is carried out by highly educated individuals. This is well illustrated by Bahar and Rapoport (2018), who show that the positive relationship between migration and knowledge diffusion increases good specific productivity shift at a sectoral level.

Labour movements can also increase the circulation and diffusion of knowledge through co-inventorship and R&D outsourcing, allowing collaboration between applicants of developed countries and inventors of developing countries (Agrawal et al., 2011; Kerr, 2008; Miguélez, 2018). This is particularly so in the case of tacit knowledge (Howells, 1996).

Productivity shift and the level of skills of workers also explain the positive effect of visits of shorter duration on innovation since significant knowledge flows occur during short-term visits, such as conferences and academic visits (Bathelt and Schuldt, 2008; Hamermesh, 2006). Another example from the art domain shows that travel enhances the value of painting of modern artists through human capital investment, knowledge spill-overs, and inspiration acquired in the places visited (Hellmanzik, 2013).

Evidence also exists about a positive relationship between business visits and productivity (Andersen and Dalgaard, 2011; Dowrick and Tani, 2011). Business visits make a substantive contribution to productivity relative to other determinants. For instance, comparing the productivity impact of business visits to R&D expenditures using a panel of 16 sectors in 10 countries over the period 1998–2011, Piva et al. (2018) show that labour mobility through business visits raises productivity by half as much as investing in R&D, a well-known and researched determinant of productivity and innovation.

Innovation in Africa

Africa has witnessed an unsteady but slow upward trend in R&D, as measured by expenditure as a proportion of GDP and in PPP dollars, and the number of researchers in absolute terms and per million inhabitants (Figure 3.1a and b). UNESCO statistics show that the sub–Saharan Africa region's overall expenditure in R&D as a percentage of GDP rose from 0.23% in the 1990s[4] to 0.35% in the 2010s[5] (Figure 3.1a). Over the last decade, the highest average expenditure as a percentage of GDP was recorded in Kenya (0.79%), South Africa (0.75%), Senegal (0.65%), Tanzania (0.46%), and Ethiopia (0.42%).[6] Only Kenya and South Africa are close to the 1% expenditure target (by 2020) set by the African Union.

In contrast, the countries with the lowest share of R&D expenditure are Cabo Verde, Lesotho, and Madagascar with values estimated at less than 0.08%. Sub-Saharan Africa's performances in R&D have been very distant from other regions such as North America, East Asia & Pacific, and Europe & Central Asia. For instance, since 2010, Africa has spent on average only a quarter as much as North America and East Asia & Pacific (Figure 3.1a). However, in terms of expenditure over the last period, Africa's achievements have not been significantly different from those observed in South Asia, and Latin America & Caribbean. The average expenditure of each of these three regions ranges between 0.33% and 0.36% of GDP (Figure 3.1a).

Since the work of Jaffe et al. (1993), one common way to measure innovation has been to use patenting activities. A patent grant implies that the idea embodied in the patent represents a novel and useful contribution (an innovation) over the previous state of knowledge. Data on total patent grants by applicant's place of origin sourced from the World International Property Organization (WIPO) show that the average number of patents granted to Africa's residents has been quite unstable (Figure 3.2).

Over the period considered, Africa's inventors were granted on average 163 patents, with a peak in 2002 (509 patent grants). Patent grants are mainly driven by South Africa's resident inventors, which from 2010 to 2016 accounted for 1275 patents on average, far ahead of Cote d'Ivoire, which comes second with only 306. With regard to patenting activities, Africa is lagging behind other regions of the world such as North America, East Asia & Pacific, and Europe & Central Asia – the most innovative regions. Sub-Saharan Africa has witnessed the least patenting activities over the period 1990–2010.

Data and descriptive statistics

Data

To study the relationship between short-term migration and innovation we combine data from various sources. Innovation data are sourced from the WBES,[7] a firm-level survey focussing on topics related to the business

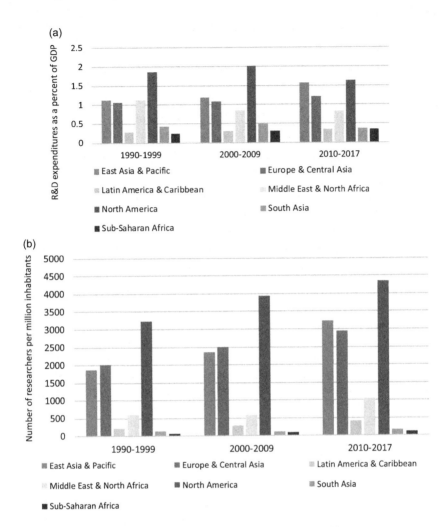

Figure 3.1 Research and development statistics in Africa and other regions.
Source: Authors' computation using data from the UNESCO statistics.

environment in which a country's private sector is evolving. It surveys business owners and top managers by sector, mainly focussing on cities and/or regions of major economic activities. We use a pooled cross-section covering 34 African countries during the period 2011 to 2016 from the aggregated WBES dataset, which does not include the country-specific questions, allowing us to make firm-level comparisons across a large number of nations. The initial sample includes more than 37,000 firms. Questions cover, among others, innovation activities, R&D expenditures, personnel, location, ownership structure, relationship with institutions and suppliers, and whether the firm holds an internationally recognized quality certification.

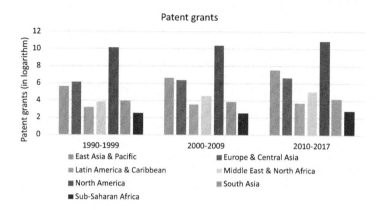

Figure 3.2 Patent grants by region.
Source: Authors' computation using data from the WIPO statistics.

We combine the WBES with country-level variables sourced from various data repositories. In particular we use information on the GDP growth rate, trade, population, migration, and tourism from the World Bank Development Indicators (WDI), FDI stock data from the United Nations Conference on Trade and Development (UNCTAD), informal employment statistics from the International Labor Organization (ILO), and institutional quality indicators about the rule of law from the World Governance Indicators database.[8]

Descriptive statistics

Within-firm determinants of innovation

Table 3.1[9] describes the share of innovative firms across Africa, by country, based on our initial WBES sample. Innovation is sourced from two questions: 'Have you introduced a new product or service in the past 3 years?' (Question h1) and 'During the last 3 years, has the establishment introduced a new or a significantly improved process?' (Question h5). Unfortunately the WBES does not ask these questions in each country over the period covered, and some, like South Africa, are notable omissions in the table.[10]
Notwithstanding this restriction, which reduces the number of responding firms to about 20,000, WBES data show that the average share of firms introducing new products or services, or either over the past three years, is 53.5% – that is more than half of the sample.[11] In most cases, and this is noteworthy, innovation emerges from the introduction of both products and processes (column labelled C).

Table 3.1 ranks countries according to the share of innovative firms from highest to lowest. It is worth noting that the total share of innovative firms

Table 3.1 Share of innovating firms across Africa from highest to lowest share

Country	Innovating firms				Did not innovate	N
	Total (A + B + C)	Product only (A)	Process only (B)	Both (C)		
	(%)	(%)	(%)	(%)	(%)	
Rwanda	87.6	5.8	26.1	55.6	12.4	241
Kenya	85.1	6.2	16.6	61.8	15.4	759
Namibia	81.8	2.3	17.3	62.2	18.2	556
Uganda	76.9	4.0	11.9	61.0	23.1	748
Mauritania	75.8	6.7	20.1	49.0	24.2	149
Zambia	74.2	8.5	20.9	44.8	25.8	698
Malawi	74.0	7.9	19.5	46.5	26.0	507
Central African R	73.3	10.0	25.3	38.0	26.7	150
Burundi	73.2	5.7	26.8	40.8	26.8	157
Ghana	71.7	4.6	20.6	46.5	28.3	710
Nigeria	67.6	4.2	17.5	45.6	32.7	2,571
Tanzania	67.1	7.4	14.9	44.8	32.9	784
South Sudan	66.0	24.4	16.9	24.8	34.0	718
Senegal	65.3	8.4	17.9	39.2	34.5	592
Sudan	59.0	14.4	5.0	39.6	41.0	637
Ethiopia	54.2	8.6	14.6	31.0	45.8	1,481
Dem Rep Congo	53.2	9.1	11.2	32.8	46.9	525
Zimbabwe	53.1	11.1	9.7	31.7	47.4	1,195
Djibouti	51.0	3.9	16.9	30.2	49.0	255
Morocco	50.9	5.9	18.6	25.7	49.9	393
Gambia	50.0	29.3	2.7	18.0	50.0	150
Mali	47.8	15.2	12.0	20.7	52.2	184
Liberia	47.0	22.5	2.0	22.5	53.0	151
Cameroon	43.8	28.1	3.4	11.5	57.0	349
Chad	42.8	27.0	5.9	9.9	57.2	152
Cote d'Ivoire	41.4	23.7	5.7	12.0	58.6	350
Togo	39.3	24.0	2.7	12.7	60.7	150
Niger	38.3	20.1	4.7	13.4	61.7	149
Sierra Leone	34.9	15.8	0.7	18.4	65.1	152
Guinea	32.9	18.6	3.6	10.7	67.1	140
Benin	30.9	16.8	4.7	9.4	69.1	149
Swaziland	27.1	20.0	1.4	5.7	72.9	140
Egypt	24.2	7.7	7.1	8.7	76.6	4,678
Lesotho	9.0	2.8	3.4	2.8	91.0	145
Total	53.5	9.4	12.6	31.4	46.5	20,865

Source: World Bank – Enterprise Survey. A: question h1 ('Have you introduced a new product or service in the past 3 years?'). B: question h5 ('During the last 3 years, has the establishment introduced a new or a significantly improved process?').

(first column) is highest in East African countries. The case of Rwanda is compelling: according to the Global Innovation Index, out of 126 countries, Rwanda went from 112th in 2013 to 99th in 2017, making it the best performing low-income country in the world. Similarly, the 2017–2018 Global competitiveness ranked Rwanda 44th out of 137 countries in terms of innovation before many Asian and Latin American countries (Schwab, 2017; World Bank, 2019). Other East African countries are also experiencing a rapid economic and digital transformation. For example Africa is now the world leader in 'mobile money', and East African countries are leading this trend. In Kenya, Rwanda, Tanzania, Uganda, and Ghana, the only West African country of the list, there are more than 1,000 mobile money accounts per 1,000 adults, suggesting that money transfers are a common commodity and, probably, a substantive contributor to help funding private consumption and investments. In Kenya alone, M-Pesa, a financial services provider, earns more than $550 million annually in financial services revenues,[12] a non-negligible amount for a country whose GDP reached $75 billion in 2017.

Table 3.1 also shows that the countries with the least innovative firms tend to be small in population and size, with the exception of one (Egypt). Innovation in these countries is predominantly due to the introduction of a new product or service (column labelled A) rather than process, supporting the hypothesis that small domestic market size and limited transport infrastructure may hinder the emergence of such countries as centres of production for a wider region.

Short-term mobility and innovation

The relationship between short-term mobility and innovation at country level is initially explored in Figure 3.3, where the share of visitor arrivals per capita (horizontal axis) is juxtaposed to that of innovating firms (vertical axis). In particular, two graphs are presented, broadly splitting the share of tourist arrivals per capita in two groups of equal size, labelled as low- and high-mobility countries, respectively, to limit the influence of outliers of this variable, which include countries hosting world-famous historical or natural sites and wildlife sanctuaries, or having a small population. The graphs reflect country-year observations, so countries with multiple WBES appear more than once. The data in Figure 3.3 are unconditional means and therefore do not take into account the effect of other covariates. However, they support *a priori* the hypothesis of a positive relationship between short-term mobility and the share of innovating firms. The fitted lines have a positive slope, which becomes more pronounced for higher shares of visitors per capita. The underlying correlation coefficients are 0.5093 and 0.3218, respectively, for the graphs on the left and right in Figure 3.3.

The possible existence of a positive relation between short-term mobility and the introduction of new products or services arises also when innovation is restricted to new processes, as depicted in Figure 3.4 (share of innovating firms on the vertical axis): the relationship is positive and more pronounced for higher shares of visitors per capita, while the underlying correlation coefficients of the graphs on the left and right of Figure 3.3 are 0.3536 and 0.2949, respectively.

The relationship between mobility and innovation also arises when the analysis is carried out at a sectoral level, as shown in Figure 3.5. Here the vertical axis reports the average share of innovating firms by industries using the WBES variable *stra_sector* (39 industries) while the horizontal axis reports

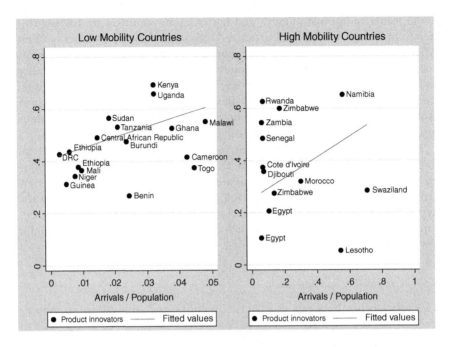

Figure 3.3 The link between short-term mobility and new products and services.
Source: WBES (various years): Question h1 'Have you introduced a new product or service in the past 3 years?' and WB indicators database (tourist arrivals, population). The vertical axis reports the share of innovating firms.

the national average inflow of tourists per capita. Each plot in the scatter therefore represents a national industry/short-term arrivals combination. Figure 3.5 groups such combinations within the aggregate sector defined by the WBES variable *d1a1a*.

Figure 3.5 suggests that the positive relationship between mobility and innovation is not specific to an industry but seems to span across all sectors of the economy, with some variation. The link between mobility and innovation is more pronounced in industries that are more 'strategic' such as manufacturing (especially machinery within this sector) and services (particularly IT), as reflected by steeper fitted lines.

These results support using a more formal approach to test the link between mobility and innovation, so that the influence of other relevant covariates can be properly taken into account. Doing so also enables us to quantify the strength of the relationship of interest.

Towards a quantitative analysis

As a prelude to the quantitative analysis, Table 3.2 shows the data trimming occurring as a result of information not being available for each

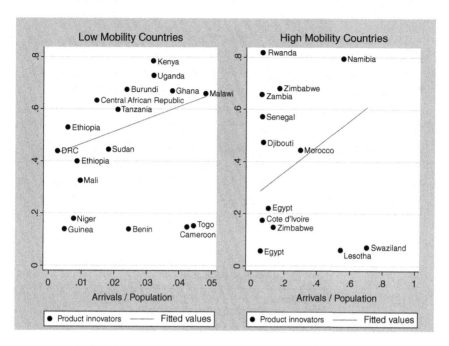

Figure 3.4 The link between short-term mobility and new processes.
Source: Authors' computation using data from WBES (various years): Question h5 'During the last 3 years, has the establishment introduced a new or a significantly improved process?' and WB indicators database (tourist arrivals, population). The vertical axis reports the share of innovating firms.

country. The initial sample reduces to a working sample consisting of 12,147 firms, with employment data causing the largest drop in the number of usable observations. Within the working sample, Table 3.3 shows that on average, 75% of the firms have innovated over the past three years, equally split between those introducing a new product (37%) or process (38%). Since the number of observations in the working sample (Table 3.2) is smaller than the number of observations for all countries for which the innovation data is available (Table 3.1), we prefer being conservative in our preliminary discussion by considering the 53.5% of firms which have been innovative over the past three years. In both cases, these shares are likely to underestimate the true degree of innovation in Africa, as the working sample does not cover large and advanced economies like South Africa.

Table 3.3 shows that 17% of the firms in the working sample have invested in R&D during the year before the survey. The equivalent share for Israel, a well-known high-R&D country, is 30%, less than double, though Israel's GDP per capita is more than double the GDP per capita of the African countries considered. Table 3.3 also shows that 39% of the firms in the working sample are located in the capital city, where infrastructure is

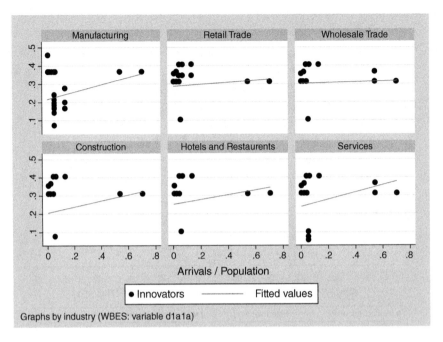

Figure 3.5 The link between short-term mobility and innovation, by industry.

Source: Authors' computation using data from WBES (various years): new variables combining questions h1 ('Have you introduced a new product or service in the past 3 years?') and h5 ('During the last 3 years, has the establishment introduced a new or a significantly improved process?') by industry (variable stra_sector), and WB indicators database (tourist arrivals, population). The six aggregate industries presented correspond to the WBES variable d1a1a (Establishment's main product or service in the last year). The vertical axis reports the share of innovating firms.

Table 3.2 Data trimming

Item	N
Number of firms in enterprise survey	37,107
With valid responses on innovation of either product or process	20,865
With valid controls at firm level	20,214
With valid governance for rule of law [+]	19,920
With valid GDP growth data [++]	19,672
With valid informal employment data [+++]	12,297
With valid tourist arrival data [++]	12,147

Source: [+] Worldwide Governance Indicators, [++] World Development Indicators, [+++] ILO.

likely to be most advanced relatively to the rest of the country. Only 17% of them have an internationally recognized quality certification, partly because they are the domestic arms of a multinational company. More than half of the firm in the working sample are small ones, having less than 20 employees; 31% are medium size (21–99 employees); and 16% of firms are

Table 3.3 Data summary – working sample

Variable	Mean	Standard deviation
Has innovated in past three years	0.75	0.86
Has innovated product or service	0.37	0.48
Has innovated process	0.38	0.49
Firm-level controls		
Has invested in R&D in last year	0.17	0.37
Is located in capital city	0.39	0.49
Has internationally recognized quality certification	0.17	0.38
Firm is medium size (20–99 employees)	0.31	0.46
Firm is large size (100+ employees)	0.16	0.37
Country-level controls		
GDP growth (lagged) [+]	.052	.039
Governance indicator – rule of law [++]	-0.59	0.45
Informal employment as % of employment [+++]	0.76	0.16
Tourist arrivals as % of population [+]	.095	.122
N	**12,147**	

Source: World Bank – Enterprise Survey, [+] Worldwide Governance Indicators, [++] World Development Indicators, [+++] ILO.

large-size firms (100+ employees). This perhaps reflects the importance of the informal sector, where firms tend to be small, and which accounts for 76% of employment in the countries covered in the working sample (Table 3.3). With reference to peoples' interactions, annual tourist arrivals represent on average about 1% of the population. For comparative purposes, the corresponding figure for the United States in 2017 is 21% (World Tourism Organisation – World Bank[13]).

Migration, innovation, and growth in Africa

Empirical framework

The relationship between innovation and short-term labour movements is estimated using a linear probability model, hence applying Ordinary Least Squares (OLS) to the model:

$$Innov_{ijt} = a_0 + X_{ijt}\beta + C_{jt}a_1 + a_2 ARR_{jt} + T_t a_3 + \varepsilon_{ijt} \tag{1}$$

where $Innov_{ijt}$ is an innovation indicator of whether firm i in country j at time t has innovated a product, a process or both in the previous three years. The vector of explanatory variables X_{ijt} contains a set of firm-specific parameters that include whether the firm has invested in R&D in the previous 12 months, its location in a capital city, its holding of an internationally recognized quality certification, and its size, as measured by the number of employees. Information on whether the firm has invested in R&D last year aims to capture efforts in improving services and processes. The location of the firm allows us to control for the differences that could exist in terms of availability of infrastructures, access to opportunities, and disparities in level of development within a country. The ownership of international quality certification and the size of the firm typically affect the productivity level of the firm and its capacity to innovate.

The vector of explanatory variables C_{jt} includes a set of country-specific controls that include GDP growth, lagged one year, a measure of institutional quality (the rule of law), and the share of informal employment in the economy. Including GDP growth aims to control for the changes in economic conditions of the country such as infrastructure creation. The lagged growth rate is more exogenous than the contemporaneous one. Indeed if economic growth at time t-1 can affect innovation at time t, it is very unlikely that innovation at time t affects GDP growth in the previous period. The level of governance in a country provides the legal setting to carry out transactions and is therefore a fundamental determinant of both economic activity and incentives to introduce new products or processes.

The single variable ARR_{jt} is the key explanatory variable, the number of tourist arrivals per person in the country's population, which we use as a proxy for the intensity of interactions between those living in the destination country and the rest of the world. This data is from the World Development Indicators but is initially collected from the World Tourism Organization (WTO). We choose this variable as a proxy for short-term migration and temporary arrivals following the literature (e.g. Andersen and Dalgaard, 2011; Gambardella et al., 2009). As highlighted by Andersen and Dalgaard (2011), the label *tourist arrivals* covers a wider reality since tourism is a subset of the arrivals. This variable considered arrivals of people coming for no more than one consecutive year for business, leisure, and other purposes not related to an activity remunerated from within the place visited. We only consider arrivals since we are interested in the effect of the people flows in the innovation of the receiving countries, thereby considering only one aspect of the ways in which interactions can be actually carried out.

T_t is a vector of year dummy variables. The error term, ε_{ijt}, is clustered by industry at country level, allowing observations to be correlated within industry-country combinations across Africa.

Results

Table 3.4 presents the results. The table includes four specifications to identify the baseline model and single out the contribution when additional channels of innovation-related interactions are included. The four sub-specifications differ in the measurement of the dependent variables, as representing only the introduction of a new product (model I) or a process (II) or both depending on whether innovation is still quantified as a dummy variable equal to zero if

Table 3.4 Results

Model	I	II	III	IV
Dependent variable	New product	New process	Innovation	Innovation
	OLS	OLS	OLS	ML (oprobit)[+]
Explanatory variables				
Invested in R&D last year	.331★★★	.315★★★	.647★★★	.054★★★
	(.014)	(.016)	(.027)	(.004)
Located in capital city	.052★★	.038★★★	.090★★★	.009★★★
	(.014)	(.013)	(.025)	(.002)
Recognized certification	.076★★★	.080★★★	.156★★★	.015★★★
	(.014)	(.012)	(.022)	(.002)
Medium–size firm	.038★★★	.050★★★	.088★★★	.008★★★
	(.011)	(.013)	(.020)	(.002)
Large firm	.057★★★	.034★★★	.092★★★	.010★★★
	(.014)	(.013)	(.022)	(.002)
Country controls				
GDP growth lagged	.418	.846★★★	1.26★★	.075★
	(.299)	(.282)	(.512)	(.045)
Rule of law	.059★★★	.188★★★	.246★★★	.015★★★
	(.019)	(.015)	(.029)	(.002)
Informal employment	.806★★★	.771★★★	1.58★★★	.158★★★
	(.054)	(.053)	(.096)	(.013)
Tourist arrivals / population	.421★★★	.357★★★	.779★★★	.092★★★
	(.063)	(.069)	(.119)	(.011)
Constant	−.515★★★	−.563★★★	−1.07★★★	
	(.055)	(.053)	(.093)	
Year dummies	Yes	Yes	Yes	Yes
Nr clusters (country*industry)	452	452	452	452
Adjusted R^2 (pseudo R^2 for ML)	.2129	.3247	.3310	.1866
Wald chi2				2,056.94
N	12,146	12,146	12,146	12,146

Note: [+]Marginal effects for innovation of either product or process relative to no innovation. The reference group for the firm size is small firm. Robust standard errors in parentheses. The symbols ★★★, ★★, ★ indicate significance level at the 1%, 5%, 10% level, respectively.

the firm did not innovate and 1 if the firm introduced either a new product or process (III) or a variable containing three categories: zero for no innovation, 1 for either new product or process, and 2 for both new product and process (IV). While models I–III are estimated by OLS, model IV is estimated by maximum likelihood (ordered probit), which is more efficient in catering for the non-linearity of the dependent variable.

All the estimates in Table 3.4 are marginal effects. Namely they indicate the change in the dependent variable from 'no innovation' to 'innovation in either product or process' (i.e. from 0 to 1) when the independent variable increases by a unit, maintaining unchanged the value of the other variables. Overall, the models explain about 20–30% of the variation in innovation activity. This order of magnitude is comparable to existing innovation studies.

With reference to firm-level variables, specifications I–IV support that innovation for African firms responds to the same determinants as found in other parts of the world. New products (I) and processes (II), as well as innovation more broadly (III and IV), respond mostly to investments in R&D, a direct knowledge-producing activity. The coefficient of R&D is by far the most important in terms of both magnitude, accounting for over 30% of the probability of innovating in the following year, and statistical significance (p-value < .01). Innovation also positively relates to being located in a capital city, holding an internationally recognized quality certification, and being a medium-size or large-size firm.

With reference to the country-level controls, innovation positively correlates with lagged GDP growth and more certainty in the applications of laws. This coefficient is always positive and statistically significant (p-value < .01). The size of the estimate in the case of new process is three times as high as in the case of new product and services, suggesting that new processes may involve technological and knowledge transfers that require adequate protection, as measured by the level of institutional quality in the country of destination. This explanatory variable is also the only one where the coefficient estimates for new product (model I) and processes (model II) differ substantively.

Another noteworthy result is the relevance of the informal sector in positively contributing to innovation activity: this result does not imply that informal activities ought to be incentivized because they lead to more innovation, but it suggests that informality is not a black box with no or negative value for the hosting economy. On the contrary, it may have a place in the formation of productive knowledge and in the introduction of new products and processes. This may be specific to Africa and other regions where informality accounts for such a high share of employment. More research on this topic is needed to understand the mechanisms through which such a result arises.

These results are broadly consistent in highlighting that short-term mobility in Africa may act as a potential channel for knowledge exchanges and the generation of new productive knowledge. The results hold even when we expand vector C_{jt} in model (1) to include additional country-specific explanatory variables controlling for other factor and commodity movements. We show this in Table 3.5, where we augment model (III) with country-specific variables capturing the openness to trade, as measured by imports plus exports as a share of GDP, the stock of FDI as a share of GDP, and the share of migrants in the population.[14] The results confirm that innovation significantly benefits from previous investments in R&D, locational and firm-size advantages, and holding an internationally recognized certification. Innovation seems also more likely when the quality of the domestic institution is higher, regardless of the size of the informal sector.

Table 3.5 Robustness tests

MODEL	Baseline III in Table 3.4	Baseline + Trade	Baseline + Trade + FDI	Baseline + Trade + FDI + Migration
Dependent variable	Innovation OLS	Innovation OLS	Innovation OLS	Innovation OLS
Explanatory variables				
Invested in R&D last year	.647***	.647***	.639***	.635***
	(.027)	(.028)	(.027)	(.028)
Located in capital city	.090***	.088***	.079***	.074***
	(.025)	(.025)	(.025)	(.025)
Recognized certification	.156***	.156***	.149***	.152***
	(.022)	(.022)	(.022)	(.022)
Medium-size firm	.088***	.088***	.091***	.090***
	(.020)	(.020)	(.020)	(.020)
Large firm	.092***	.092***	.098***	.100***
	(.022)	(.022)	(.022)	(.022)
Country controls				
GDP growth lagged	1.26**	.980*	−.141	.868
	(.512)	(.590)	(.659)	(.851)
Rule of law	.246***	.239***	.214***	.165***
	(.029)	(.030)	(.029)	(.037)
Informal employment	1.58***	1.52***	1.70***	1.62***
	(.096)	(.131)	(.138)	(.148)
Tourist arrivals/ population	.779***	.638***	.792***	.906***
	(.119)	(.232)	(.229)	(.233)
Trade as % GDP		.100	.120	.045
		(.130)	(.128)	(.132)
FDI as % GDP			.745***	.851***
			(.221)	(.243)
Migrant share				.552**
				(.279)
Constant	−1.07***	−1.06***	−1.77***	−1.86***
	(.093)	(.099)	(.241)	(.255)
Year dummies	Yes	Yes	Yes	Yes
Nr clusters (country*industry)	452	452	452	452
Adjustted R²	.3310	.3311	.3327	.3334
N	12,146	12,146	12,146	12,146

Notes: regression based on model (1) augmented by additional international channels of interactions influencing the innovation activities of domestic firms.

With reference to factor movements, the results in Table 3.5 confirm what already found by previous studies: innovation is higher when economies are opened to FDI and migrants, while the coefficient associated with commodity trade is positive but statistically no different from zero, perhaps due to opposite effects on innovation from imports and exports. With reference to short-term labour mobility, its relevance and effect on innovation are unchanged, strengthening the hypothesis that it may be viewed as a distinct source of productive knowledge. In fact, its point estimate increases as more factor movements are controlled for (fourth column, labelled Baseline + Trade + FDI + Migration).

The magnitude of the coefficients is quite large. One possible influencing factor is the small number of countries included in the working sample, which tends to inflate the size of the coefficients. At the same time, mixing individual- and group-level variables may be problematic if the 'large sample size' assumption required for consistent and efficient estimates is not met (Bryan and Jenkins, 2015). If the ideal solution of collecting new firm-level data on interactions with the external environment is not possible, as in our case, the suggestion is to apply a two-step regression technique and produce a graphic representation of the relationship of interest. To verify the robustness of the results discussed we hence regress firm-level data on firm-level explanatory variables and a vector of country dummies (step 1), and then regress the estimated average country effects on other country-level explanatory variables (step 2).[15] In other words, we apply OLS to model (1) with vector C_{jt} containing only country dummies. Then, the estimated coefficients $\widehat{C_{j-1}}$ (the average country effects on firms' innovation activity) are graphically linked to arrivals per capita.[16] The result, graphed in Figure 3.6, illustrates a positive

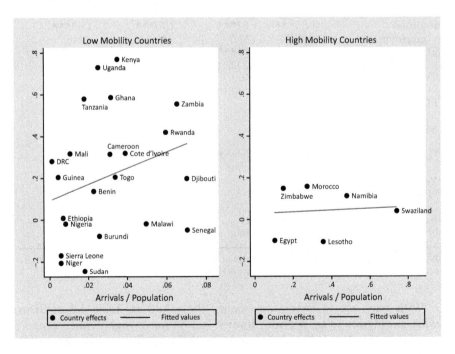

Figure 3.6 Estimated country effects and peoples' interactions.
Source: Authors' computation using data from WBES (various years) and WB indicators database (tourist arrivals, population).

relationship between average country effects on innovation and short-term mobility, especially for countries where arrivals per capita are not distorted by visits to world-known historical and natural attractions, as in the case of Egypt and Zimbabwe, or by the small population size, as in the case of Swaziland, Lesotho, and Namibia.

The outliers (graph on the right) receive a much higher share of tourist per capita, making it more difficult to detect a clear relationship between country effects and mobility.

Discussion: migration, innovation, and the SDGs in Africa

The results provide support to the hypothesis that short-term mobility, as proxied by tourist arrivals per capita, is associated with higher innovation activity. This result adds support to one of mobility's established fundamental benefits: the exchange and formation of productive knowledge. As stated by Goal 10.7 of the SDGs, within the goal of inequality reduction and aiming to facilitate safe, orderly, and regular migration through better migration policies, labour movements matter, and our results show that both short- and long-term forms of movement carry important economic consequences. Their realization across countries could hence be viewed as a way to further enhance economic growth. According to the African Visa Openness Index report (AfDB and AU, 2018), the free movement of people has still a way to go within the continent. In 2018, Africans needed a visa to travel to 51% of other African countries. This figure was only marginally higher in the previous years (54% in 2017 and 55% in 2016).

These figures should be put in a context where the Free Movement of persons is critical to facilitate knowledge exchanges across borders. This is all the more important with the African Free Trade Area (AfCFTA), aiming at 'creating a single continental market for goods and services, with free movement of business persons and investments' and the Single African Air Transport Market launched in 2018. As mobility does neither require a permanent relocation of people nor equips visitors with employment rights in the host country, its encouragement can be used to overcome a small domestic market size or lacklustre innovation. Mobility could be increased via the promotion of trade fairs or international conferences as activities generating opportunities for intense knowledge exchanges in a short period of time. Our results support the view that short-term labour mobility, as the one carried out through international business visits, can contribute to achieve Goal 9 of the SDGs to 'build resilience, promote inclusive and sustainable industrialization and foster innovation'.

There are other objectives that can also be linked indirectly to the relationship between short-term labour mobility and innovation. These are poverty reduction (Goal 1); ensuring quality education (Goal 4); promoting productive employment and decent work (Goal 8); and the promotion of peace, justice and strong institutions (Goal 16). The link to the goal of poverty reduction is quite straightforward since innovation is one of the motor of economic growth and short-term visits seem to act as a channel to new productive knowledge in Africa too, as found for other countries.

This chapter also provides some support to the hypothesis that innovation can occur even when the informal sector is the predominant sector of employment, and the proportion of high-skilled workers is much lower than other parts of the world. However, as the informal sector typically does not provide good jobs or jobs that are safe, attached to decent salaries and working conditions, there are substantial benefits to be gained at the national level if workers transit from the informal to the formal sector, perhaps via larger firms, whose formation could also be encouraged with targeted policies. Consequently, these policies towards decent jobs should be carried out while supporting innovation since evidence suggests that African firms that innovate create more jobs but not necessarily better quality jobs (Avenyo et al., 2019).

As innovation matters more than ever in the fourth industrial revolution, the risk of skills mismatch where the curriculum in the education systems does not necessarily match the skill needs could be partly alleviated by promoting short-term migration and the associated circulation of knowledge and ideas. Our results show that the rule of law matters, and that poor governance can be an obstacle both to innovation and to people mobility: this needs to be reviewed.

Given the key contribution of R&D to long-run growth and development, Africa can intensify its efforts to shape a better comparative advantage with respect to the other regions. We provide some evidence that labour mobility could play a role and hence encourage the development of policies that create connectivity, alongside encouraging additional research focussing on the transmission channels that underpin the relationship between short-term migration and innovation.

Acknowledgements

We would like to thank Amadou Boly, Maty Konté, Marco Vivarelli, and Andinet Woldemichael for their comments. Assi Okara provided excellent research assistance. All remaining errors are those of the authors. The views and opinions expressed in this paper are those of the authors and do not necessarily represent the official policy or position of the African Development Bank Group, its Executive Directors, or the countries they represent.

Notes

1 See, for example, http://cf.cdn.unwto.org/sites/all/files/docpdf/glossaryenrev. pdf.
2 Notwithstanding the role of labour and other factor movements, a number of other factors contribute to innovation, as highlighted in research summary

provided by the Oslo Manual (OECD and Eurostat, 2005), like a firm's strategic market position relative to competitors (Tirole, 1995) and uncertainty about product demand (Rosenberg, 1994).

3 Beyond innovation, this could also be linked to the fact that when people migrate they often times need local goods from their origin countries. This increases the exportations of these local goods that are not necessarily new to the market (Vanore, 2020).

4 Data available from 1996.

5 Data from 2010 to 2016.

6 All rankings throughout the text are subject to data availability.

7 Source: http://www.enterprisesurveys.org.

8 In merging these sources with the WBES we matched country and year. As a result, WBES data collected for country X in 2011 and for country Y in 2016, were matched with non-WBES data for 2011 for country X and 2016 data for country Y. The use of lagged dependent variables did not significantly modify the results obtained, and so we match WBES and non-WBES data for a given country using the same year.

9 Table 3.1 presents data for countries for which the information on new product and new process is available.

10 Although the various Enterprise Surveys for African countries have data for some countries since 2002–2003, we focus on the period 2011–2016 because data related to the main interest variables are provided since 2011 (one exception is, however, Madagascar which has a survey in 2013 but which did not include those questions).

11 We find that 53.5% of the firms surveyed in the WBES have introduced an innovation over the past three years (Table 3.1). This proportion rises to 75% in the working sample (Table 3.3), which restricts the observations to countries for which data on informal employment is available. Table 3.2 shows how data are trimmed based on available indicators.

12 Source: McKinsey https://www.mckinsey.com/industries/financial-services/our-insights/mobile-financial-services-in-africa-winning-the-battle-for-the-customer.

13 https://data.worldbank.org/indicator/ST.INT.ARVL?locations=US.

14 The inclusion of a variable capturing trade openness aims to control for innovations occurring through the exchanges of goods (Rapoport, 2018). Similarly, using the stock of FDI as share of GDP accounts for innovation entering the country via foreign direct investments. Finally the share of migrants in the population accounts for innovation arising from long-term or permanent population movements as a distinct channel than short-term labour movements. The two-step approach is itself not without problems, as indicated by Bryan and Jenkins (2015).

15 The second step regression includes lagged GDP growth, the share of informal employment, the share of migrants, openness to trade, the share of foreign FDI, and the number of tourist arrivals per country inhabitant. The coefficients of those variables are typically not statistically different from zero and hence are not reported.

References

Acs, Z. J., Anselin, L., & Varga, A. (2002). Patents and innovation counts as measures of regional production of new knowledge. *Research Policy, 31*(7), 1069–1085.

Adepoju, A. (2008). Migration in Sub-Saharan Africa. Current African Issues, No. 37. Uppsala: The Nordic Africa Institute.

African Development Bank. (2019). African Economic Outlook. https://www. afdb.org/fileadmin/uploads/afdb/Documents/Publications/2019AEO/ AEO_2019-EN.pdf.

African Development Bank (AfDB) and African Union (AU). (2018). Africa Visa Openness Report. https://www.visaopenness.org/fileadmin/uploads/afdb/ Documents/VisaOReport2018_R15jan19.pdf.

Agrawal, A., Cockburn, I., & McHale, J. (2006). Gone but not forgotten: Knowledge flows, labor mobility, and enduring social relationships. *Journal of Economic Geography, 6*(5), 571–591.

Agrawal, A., Kapur, D., McHale, J., & Oettl, A. (2011). Brain drain or brain bank? The impact of skilled emigration on poor-country innovation. *Journal of Urban Economics, 69*, 43–55.

Anderson, E. (2007). Travel and communication and international differences in GDP per capita. *Journal of International Development: The Journal of the Development Studies Association, 19*(3), 315–332.

Andersen, T. B., & Dalgaard, C. J. (2011). Flows of people, flows of ideas, and the inequality of nations. *Journal of Economic Growth, 16*(1), 1–32.

Avenyo, E. K., Konte, M., & Mohnen, P. (2019). The employment impact of product innovations in sub-Saharan Africa: Firm-level evidence. *Research Policy, 48*(9), 103806.

Bahar, D., & Rapoport, H. (2018). Migration, knowledge diffusion and the comparative advantage of nations. *The Economic Journal, 128*(612), F273–F305.

Bathelt, H., & Schuldt, N. (2008). Between luminaires and meat grinders: International trade fairs as temporary clusters. *Regional Studies, 42*(6), 853–868.

Bloom, N., Draca, M., & Van Reenen, J. (2016). Trade induced technical change? The impact of Chinese imports on innovation, IT and productivity. *The Review of Economic Studies, 83*(1), 87–117.

Boly, A., Coniglio, N. D., Prota, F., & Seric, A. (2014). Diaspora investments and firm export performance in selected sub-Saharan African countries. *World Development, 59*, 422–433.

Breschi, S., & Lissoni, F. (2009). Mobility of skilled workers and co-invention networks: An anatomy of localized knowledge flows. *Journal of Economic Geography, 9*(4), 439–468.

Bryan, M. L., & Jenkins, S. P. (2015). Multilevel modelling of country effects: A cautionary tale. *European Sociological Review, 32*(1), 3–22.

Choudhury, P. (2016), Return migration and geography of innovation in MNEs: A natural experiment of on-the-job learning of knowledge production by local workers reporting to return migrants. *Journal of Economic Geography, 16*(3), 585–610.

Dos Santos, M. D., & Postel-Vinay, F. (2003). Migration as a source of growth: The perspective of a developing country. *Journal of Population Economics, 16*(1), 161–175.

Dowrick, S., & Tani, M. (2011). International business visits and the technology frontier. *Economics Letters, 110*(3), 209–212.

Gambardella, A., Mariani, M., & Torrisi, S. (2009). How 'provincial' is your region? Openness and regional performance in Europe. *Regional Studies, 43*(7), 935–947.

Gambetta, D. (1988). *Trust: Making and breaking cooperative relations*. Oxford: Blackwell.

Hamermesh, D. (2006). The value of peripatetic economists: A sesqui-difference evaluation of Bob Gregory. *Economic Record, 82*(257), 138–149.

Hellmanzik, C. (2013). Does travel inspire? Evidence from the superstars of modern art. *Empirical Economics, 45*(1), 281–303.

Hovhannisyan, N., & Keller, W. (2015). International business travel: An engine of innovation? *Journal of Economic Growth, 20*(1), 75–104.

Howells, J. (1996). Tacit knowledge, innovation and technology transfer. *Technology Analysis & Strategic Management, 8*(2), 91–106.

Hunt, J., & Gauthier-Loiselle, M. (2010). How much does immigration boost innovation? *American Economic Journal: Macroeconomics, 2*(2), 31–56.

Jaffe, A. B., Trajtenberg, M., & Henderson, R. (1993). Geographic localization of knowledge spillovers as evidenced by patent citations. *Quarterly Journal of Economics, 108*(3), 577–598.

Keller, W. (2010). International trade, foreign direct investment, and technology spillovers. In B. H. Hall & N. Rosenberg (Eds.), *Handbook of the Economics of Innovation* (Vol. 2, pp. 793–829).Amsterdam: North-Holland, Elsevier.

Kerr, W.R. (2008). Ethnic scientific communities and international technology diffusion. *Review of Economics and Statistics, 90*(3), 518–537.

Miguélez, E. (2018). Inventor diasporas and the internationalization of technology. *World Bank Economic Review, 32*(1), 41–63.

OECD/Eurostat. (2005). Oslo Manual: Guidelines for Collecting and Interpreting Innovation Data, 3rd Edition, The Measurement of Scientific and Technological Activities, OECD Publishing, Paris. DOI: 10.1787/9789264013100-en.

Oucho, J. O. (1990). Migrant linkages in Africa: Retrospect and prospect. In *The Role of Migration in African Development: Issues and Policies for the 1990s Nairobi*. Dakar: UAPS.

Piva, M., Tani, M., & Vivarelli, M. (2018). Business visits, knowledge diffusion and productivity. *Journal of Population Economics, 31*(4), 1321–1338.

Rapoport, H. (2018). *Diaspora externalities: A view from the South* (No. 2018/25). United Nations, World Institute for Development Economic Research (UNU-WIDER), WIDER Working Paper series.

Rogers, M. (1998). *The definition and measurement of innovation*. Parkville, VIC: Melbourne Institute of Applied Economic and Social Research.

Rosenberg, N. (1994). *Exploring the Black Box: Technology, Economics, and History*. Cambridge: Cambridge University Press.

Schumpeter, J. A. (1934). *The Theory of Economic Development*. Cambridge, MA: Harvard University Press.

Schwab, K. (2017). The Global Competitiveness Report 2017/2018, World Economic Forum. https://www.weforum.org/reports/the-global-competitiveness-report-2017-2018.

Storper, M., & Venables, A. J. (2004). Buzz: Face-to-face contact and the urban economy. *Journal of Economic Geography, 4*(4), 351–370.

Tirole, J. (1995). *The Theory of Industrial Organization*. Cambridge, MA: MIT Press.

Vanore, M. (2020). Migration, trade, and development in Africa: Conceptual and empirical links. In M. Konte, L. M. Mbaye & V. Mazzucato (eds.). *Migration, Remittances and Sustainable Development in Africa*. Routledge: Routledge/Taylor & Francis Group.

World Bank. (2019). "Future drivers of growth in Rwanda: Innovation, integration, agglomeration, and competition." Conference Edition. Washington, DC: World Bank. License: Creative Commons Attribution CC BY 3.0 IGO.

4 The impact of internal migration of youth in developing sustainable counties in Kenya

Linda Adhiambo Oucho

Introduction

Internal migration is an old yet relevant form of mobility that provides perspectives explaining international migration drivers. Understanding internal migration within a country reveals development and policy gaps mostly non-operational at a rural level. In Kenya, internal migration began as a result of colonial policies in place that required labour migrants to support the development of upcoming major cities, and taxation policies that were required to be paid by the labour migrants. Back then, internal migration was mostly dominated by men, but women still engaged in migration in search of employment or other income-generating opportunities. The native pass determined who had a right to move from the native reserves to the cities and never on a permanent basis. After independence, these policies were removed which led to increased mobility from underdeveloped provinces from Western and Northern Kenya to developing cities of Nairobi and Mombasa with a promise of economic opportunities. The lack of a policy meant that people were free to move, but the structures in place in cities were ill-prepared to manage large populations of movement. The urban environment we see today is a result of both migration and natural increase with rising fertility rates and relatively moderate mortality rates within the country. Yet governments still do not understand internal migration dynamics or effectively have a plan of action to address the direct and indirect impact of migration in rural and urban areas. The challenges faced today in major cities from pollution, overstretched social services, and competition over employment opportunities are due to the fact that the relevant steps have not been taken to create an enabling environment across the country that makes migration a choice and not a necessity.

This chapter provides an overview of the current state of affairs on internal migration drawing from existing studies. This chapter draws evidence from the study led by the African Migration and Development Policy Centre (AMADPOC) on Youth, Employment and Migration in Eastern and Southern Africa (YEMESA[*]) assessing internal migration patterns of the youth and unpacking the youth-migration-employment nexus within the context of Kenya. The study adopted mixed methods (quantitative and qualitative).

* The project was funded by the International Development Research Centre (IDRC).

A quantitative survey of 1,500 respondents was administered with non-migrant and migrant populations in ten counties[1] in Kenya. The selection of the sub-counties was based on projections of the 2009 population census that outlined in-migrant and lifetime migrant populations across Kenya. The census also pre-dates the devolution of governance which took effect in 2013, thus, the census results were based on eight provinces at the time. In terms of qualitative methods, the study adopted key informant interviews in the ten counties, and focus group discussions with youth groups in three major source and destination counties for migrants provided insight on the realities of migrant and non-migrant youth in search of employment opportunities and the limitations they experience in the process. The focus groups were mixed male and female and broken down into three youth categories – employed, self-employed, and unemployed – with the aim of understanding the realities experienced by different youth groups by employment status.

The results provide a rich database with which to explore the dynamics of the motives for, and policy and operational contexts of, migration, employment, and entrepreneurship. This chapter will provide valuable insights into migration realities in Kenya, with a specific focus on the youth and how the national and county governments can mainstream migration into development activities which will lead to sustainable employment and entrepreneurship that contribute to the realization of national- and county-level growth. With regard to the Sustainable Development Goals (SDGs), it will provide food for thought through a solutions-oriented approach to Target 11 on inclusive cities. The results of this chapter will outline strategies County Governments in Kenya can use to harness the potential of their internal migration by creating an enabling environment through decent jobs and cities that includes the contributions of internal migrants. At the same time, it will paint a realistic picture of the limitations county government face in managing internal migration flows while managing other socio-economic commitments highlighted under the national development plans (Vision 2030) which is currently being implemented through Medium Term Plans III (2018–2022).

Migration in Kenya: a brief overview

Internal migration is well known but not understood or prioritized by state and non-state actors. It is not governed by any policy as all restrictions on internal migration were removed once Kenya received independence in 1963 which allowed free movement across the country. The unequal development that had already taken place in selected parts of the country and the drive to access income-generating opportunities in cities led to many young people to move to cities to access employment to meet their existing needs and those of their household. Those patterns of migration still exist today among young people.

The migration flows in Kenya were outlined in the International Organization for Migration (IOM, 2015) first migration profile of Kenya in 2015. It took stock of different migration patterns in the country revealing gaps of knowledge on internal migration flows within the country from impact to policy. The issues faced by international migrants are also experienced by internal migrants, despite them moving within the country that requires some interest and focus for national and county governments. The report further revealed how national ministries and departments with migration functions had different positions, roles, and activities related to migration, with very few, with the exception of the Ministry of Devolution, focussed on understanding internal migration within the country. The purpose of the profile was to identify gaps of knowledge on internal migration; evidence of available data at a national level reveals the demographic profile along with the impact of migration on development (economic, social, political, and environmental) as well as policies or laws in place aligned with the national development plan (Vision 2030) and how it has mainstreamed migration into the process. After the migration profile was completed, the development of the National Coordination Mechanism for migration was created and hosted by the Department of Immigration which has been tasked with handling all migration-related activities, including the design of the National Migration Policy, the Labour Migration Policy, and the Labour Migration Management Bill currently under review. Hence there is no operational policy or framework, although there is progress.

The governance system is important to consider with regard to migration patterns in Kenya. The devolution of governance in 2013 led to the decentralization of national government activities and empowerment of county governments to implement the national agenda at county level. Devolution gave birth to forty-seven (47) county governments that are currently on their second term (2018–2022). Each county government prior to their term has to provide socio-economic, environmental, and political details concerning their county through the County Integrated Development Plans (CIDPs). Within these CIDPs it is clear that most of the county governments lack evidence and data on migration patterns to, from, and within their County, and often cite internal migration as a threat in terms of loss of labour or bringing in criminal activities. The Kenya National Bureau of Statistics (KNBS) has continued to collect internal migration data through the census identifying some migratory flows giving a sense of different migration patterns taking place within, to, and from Kenya. However, internal migration is not officially recorded in most countries, including Kenya. The dynamics and volume of internal voluntary migration are less understood than forced migration.

Within Kenya, at least five types of internal migration within and between counties are recognized:

a   *Rural to urban*: experienced from the colonial period when migrants moved to cities for employment and better access to social services. This is the most researched form of youth mobility-employment and according to IOM is the dominant form in Kenya. From the early 1990s, return flows to rural areas started to feature, a time when there was a rise in Kenyans emigrating for work and education (Macharia, 2003).

b   *Rural to rural*: migrants travel from rural areas in search of better opportunities or due to landlessness and population pressure to other rural areas. This type of migration is determined by the opportunities available in respective counties in Kenya.

c   *Urban to rural*: this generally involves people moving back to their origin upon retirement or after shock events, such as post-electoral violence in 2007/08, when migrants from Western counties returned from Uasin Gishu and Central Kenya; it is increasingly common as urban economic hardships grow in large informal settlements with poor basic services;

d   *Urban to urban*: migrants re-locate from one town to another to either start or expand a business, or for many public officials as they transfer in education, health, etc. (NCPD, 2013).

e   *"Circular"* migration which is constant with temporary re-location and return cycles (Badoux 2018; Onyango, 2017). The latter was least documented in literature reviewed. Kenyan youth are very mobile, and many are well connected through digital means with their outside world.

Internal migration does not necessarily have or need any formal policies to govern it, as policies related to internal migration can be restrictive and controlling which can be associated with the policies in place during colonialism. Internal migration requires a process or system in place to better understand it through data and research that can be used to develop strategies and programmes that can respond effectively to the drivers and impact (positive and negative) of migration in source, transit, and destination counties. A platform that can achieve that is Kenya Vision 2030, which currently makes minor references to internal migration but does not adequately mainstream migration as a potential contributor to national development. It is guided by the SDGs, which have set up 17 goals to be met by 2060; migration can be viewed as a part of many of the goals.

Understanding these flows within the country, how they impact cities as well as diversify employment in the different sectors is key to resolving international migration associated with negative impact of socio-economic development and environmental shocks which can result in displacement. Specifically, it would be important to understand the realities experienced by youth migrants in search of employment in other counties and whether the receiving counties are ready to receive, integrate and manage these migrant groups. This chapter will focus on Goal 11 of the SDGs on inclusive cities and how understanding internal youth migration flows can benefit those cities that host migrants from other locations.

Youth employment in Kenya to county level

Between 750,000 and one million Kenyan youth enter the labour market annually, but only about 15% of them are successful in securing formal jobs. (African Institute for Development Policy (AFIDEP), 2018a). Three findings from the above report are worth highlighting:

- Youth unemployment is higher than the national unemployment level, with 17.7% of youth unemployed, compared to 7.4% of the national unemployment;
- More female youth are unemployed compared to their male counterparts with 21% and 17% respectively; and
- When young people are employed, they are commonly in the low-paying category, including the informal sector in the *urban* areas, while young people in the *rural* areas tend to be under-employed, e.g. in low-yielding agricultural activities.

Hence, working youth are on salaries which may not meet their needs, and many are not considered eligible under social protection.[2] The YEMESA study results revealed that young people are looking for better employment in comparison to their place of origin. The educational status revealed the reasons why people moved as illustrated in Figure 4.1.

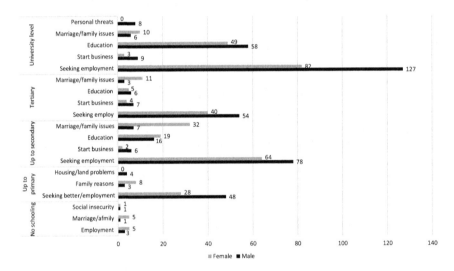

Figure 4.1 Motives for migration by education status.
Source: YEMESA results (AMADPOC, 2019).

Those migrating from rural areas are more likely to search for white-collar jobs under the assumption that they pay more or have better working conditions. Young people are less likely to take up work in rural areas which are often unpaid or under-paid (especially for those working in family farms), and very few young people are interested in agriculture which is associated with the elderly (AMADPOC, 2019).

Unemployment and under-employment estimates vary considerably as some are based on total working-age population, others on youth 15–35 or the 20–24 age-groups. As the formal employment sector is small, labour statistics may not be accurate. The Kenya National Bureau of Statistics unemployment rate[3] for 2017 was 7.4% by late 2016 (Kenya National Bureau of Statistics, 2017). The International Labour Organisation (ILO) estimated 11% among the 20–24 year age-group for the same period. UNDAF (2018) put the level at 14.7% with more women (19%) than men (11%) being out of a job.

The YEMESA study conducted focus group discussions with employed, unemployed, and self-employed youth to understand the dynamics of the three groups. Unemployed youth identified a few issues preventing them from accessing employment and majority of them indicated that they had not been actively searching for work indicating whether some are interested in searching for work. Others did not consider starting their own enterprises. These raise concern as to whether some unemployed youth are actively searching for employment (see Figure 4.2).

A national-level analysis of youth unemployment patterns found that not all youth are equally affected by unemployment with gender, age, education, and social stratification influencing job opportunities. Female youth (1.22 million or so) were the largest unemployed group; then youth 18–25 years old, with primary and secondary education (1.5 million); unemployed rural youth (1.15 million) who migrate to urban areas; youth from poor households (750,000) with little opportunity to engage in self-employment; youth with low or no education (255,000); and youth with tertiary education (18,000 or so) (World Bank Vision 2030, 2014).

Youth under-employment in Kenya is not covered in official data by the KNBS or by ILO. Under-employment[4] is a crucial problem that leaves affected youth behind as dependents, despite their actual economic activity and especially true for rural youth (British Council, 2017). The mix of unemployment, underemployment, inactivity, and poor quality jobs

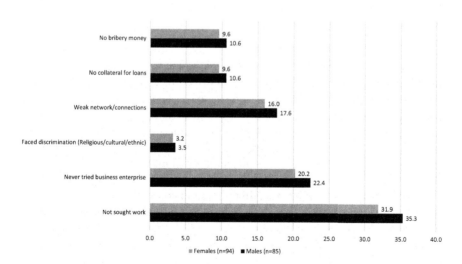

Figure 4.2 Reasons for unemployment (n = 179).
Source: YEMESA results, AMADPOC (2019).

Table 4.1 Estimate of employment 2013–2017 (in 000')

	2013	2014	2015	2016	2017
Modern establishment Wage employees	2,283.1	2,370.21	2,478.0	2,553.5	2,656.6
Self-employment & unpaid family work	83.8	103.0	123.2	132.5	139.4
Sub-total	2,366.9	2,473.2	2,601.2	2,686	2,796
Informal sector (est.)	11,150.11	11,846.0	12,562.4	13,309.7	14,097.5
Totals	13,517	14,319.2	15,163.6	15,995.7	16,893.5

Source: Kenya National Bureau of Statistics (2018).

(informal, unskilled, and low-paid) still *predominantly affects 15- to 24-year-olds compared to the rest of the working age-group* (World Bank and Vision 2030, 2014) (Table 4.1).

Apart from gender, there are spatial and sectoral differences around youth employment patterns in the country (National Council for Population and Development [NCPD] and United Nations Population Fund [UNFPA], 2013), and it is difficult to ascertain the extent to which devolution of governance to 47 counties is impacting at the county level and how this influences in- and out-migration from individual counties. However, a broad spatial picture of youth employment patterns from a gender lens is presented without clarifying whether a person is a migrant or non-migrant.

The youth and internal migration in Kenya

Kenyan youth are mobile, connected, and resourceful, representing human resources that carry skills for development in their areas of re-location and in their original homes. Some households may have both internal and international migrants. Most internal migrants move from poorer to what is perceived as better endowed locations. This is not always the case, however, as many rural youth find themselves living in sprawling informal settlements, often in one-room housing, paying hiked prices for water from vendors, with few people having access to their own toilets (Ezeh *et al.*, 2006) and, for young women in particular, risk of abuse and sexual assault.

Internal migration is, nevertheless, a livelihood option for Kenya's youth. A wide social, environmental, economic, and cultural diversity influences the decision-making in re-location for female and male youth. Labour migration is a very selective process which engages certain sub-groups more than others which include gender, age, disability, and community of origin. Youth mobility for opportunities has far-reaching potential for migrants as well as their communities and counties of origin and destination. A 2016 study on youth migration from Kenya's more densely populated rural areas found that over 90% of reasons given related to employment (63.7% seeking work; received work offer 26%); starting one's own family rated 6.6%, usually among females, while land constraints rated 3.0%, and family conflict was rated at 0.6% (Muyanga *et al.*, 2016).[5]

Previously, Kinyangi's socio-economic study (2014) on rural–urban migrants resident in Kibera and decision making influences around the process found that, in pursuit of employment, unskilled males were most likely to migrate based on a personal decision, while female and male migrants from Nyanza with no social networks in Kibera were more likely to be influenced by family and friends The significance of social circles at place of destination has a long history in Kenya and other countries, especially for securing work, accommodation, and contacts.

Internal labour migration – opportunities and contribution

Tacoli (1998) argued that new forms of migration were emerging at the same time that old ones were intensifying while others were slowing down. A paucity of quality data has hampered informed understanding of internal migration in Kenya. It is assumed that devolution of governance and services to 47 counties with accompanying youth support strategies is changing the face, nature, and scale of out-migration from parts of western Kenya to large cities, especially Nairobi; that increasing jobs opportunities and boosting of training at county and sub-county levels are incentives for youth not to migrate in the same numbers; and that urban–urban and rural-rural migrant flows are evolving within and between counties. But this is not evidence-based as yet. The results of the YEMESA study revealed that youth are driven to migrate mostly by socio-economic factors related to employment opportunities whether they are available or not and further education as illustrated in Figure 4.3.

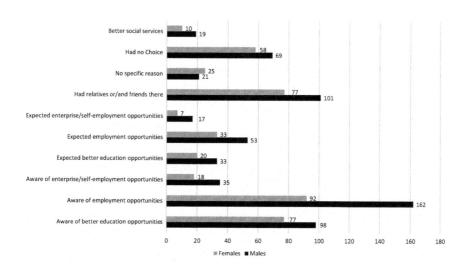

Figure 4.3 Reasons for migration.
Source: YEMESA results, AMADPOC (2019).

Drivers of migration reveal limitations or gaps in counties of origin, which, if included in the development planning, could reduce the need to out-migrate. For instance, lack of social services could be an indication that systems are not working effectively or efficiently, and if the County governments undertake further assessments in their constituencies, they can improve the social services reducing the need for some of their populations to out-migrate, thereby meeting some of the targets in SDG 11. At the same time, the culture of migration cannot be ignored; that is, the historical nature of internal migration that has been taking place before, during, and after colonialism under the impression that cities provide opportunities that are better can be associated with the existing youth migration patterns to date.

Internal migration is a key determinant of sub-national-level population change and population re-distribution in the long-term.[6] The dynamics of geographic mobility of youth in search of employment whether in the form of rural-urban, rural-rural, urban-rural, or urban-urban flows and consequent influence on spatial distribution have social, economic, environmental, and policy response implications at national, county, and sub-county levels (Oucho and Gould, 1993). Rural-urban migration is directly linked to speedy urban growth rates in Kenya (UNFPA and NCPD, 2013). Population characteristics in both regions of origin and regions of destination change with different age structures due to the selectivity of rural-urban migration, meaning that it is predominantly the younger working-age population (female and male) that migrates, with the elderly and young remaining (Nyaoro *et al.*, 2016).

Rather than approaching rural-urban migration as a dynamic and a 'problem' with risks of over-population and consequences of over-stretching resources, including the labour market in cities and towns, Oucho and Gould (2014) brought new and positive analysis and reflection to internal migration, and, to an extent, spatial planning and policymaking – migration is not only a factor in determining population structure (along with birth and mortality) but also a solution in the development process. Coherence and connected urban and rural policymaking are effective when direct urban and rural (and *vice versa*) poverty links are accepted. Ramisch (2014) and Arosio (2016) further reiterated the strong rural-urban connect in the Kenyan internal migration context and, in the case of the latter, the value of improving the quality of life in urban and rural catchment areas in tandem.

The above is pertinent, as many of the current CIDPs (2018–2022), on which spatial and sectoral plans are aligned to, do not reflect joint or unified urban-rural development strategies for effective development delivery. In aligning to the Big 4 Agenda, infrastructure, jobs, value addition, and markets are clearly connected but in a more disparate manner. Furthermore, the Kenya Vision 2030 presents urbanization as one of four key *challenges* (World Bank, 2017). The substantial investments required to sustain large and expanding urban populations, infrastructure are importance of urban and physical planning, including at county levels.

The need for cities to plan for the increase in population with contribution from migrants from other locations is key. The spatial planning (national and county-based) has assumed a high profile since devolution especially when looking at development projects that aim to attract development into the country. Internal migration brings opportunities and challenges to the aspiration and design of resilient and thriving towns and cities as envisaged under Kenya's national and sub-national plans, and the achievement of SDG 11 on sustainable cities and communities.[7] Climate change and environmental issues are very relevant in the Kenyan and East Africa setting and magnify risks and vulnerabilities (UN-Habitat, 2018a, 2018b; Wall *et al.*, 2014). The CIDPs are essential county planning and budgeting documents that could be used to map out migration with the county, the various ways in which it impacts the local community, and existing government responses as well as to identify gaps that need further development. In the next ten years or so, key questions that many counties will face are whether the transformations will take place and whether these emerging towns and cities will be able to absorb excess labour from different parts of the country.

Mainstreaming youth, employment, and migration into Vision 2030

As in most countries there is no consideration, in terms of policy at least, of the synergy between youth, migration, and employment/enterprise for inclusive growth and development. Curbing migration of youth is presented as an important outcome of success in youth employment generation. However, progress is on-going towards a draft Kenya National Migration Policy and a Draft National Labour Migration Policy[8] and the recently revised Youth Policy.

The Kenya Government has come up with various strategies to build and maximize skills among youth. In time, it is expected that this will leverage opportunities at county level to generate decent employment for all youth, from within, and outside the counties. The Big 4 Agenda[9] realization requires a spectrum of skilled and non-skilled workforce. Youth entrepreneurship, employable skills, and innovation are at the heart of the agenda, which relies on strong private sector partnerships and win–win scenarios.[10]

The following are highlights and learning from the implementation Kenya Vision 2030 Medium Term Plan II (MTP II) outcomes of relevance (completed in 2017) and relevant elements of the on-going MTP III (2018–2022).

Kenya Vision 2030 on youth employment/entrepreneurship

Vision 2030 is Kenya's transformative agenda and the country's youthful citizenry are key to its realization. They are part of achievement of the principles of the inclusive 2010 Constitution and sharing in the benefits of devolution to 47 Counties in 2013. Vision 2030 also incorporates the government's approach to mainstreaming the SDGs into planning. The second Medium Term Plan (2013–2017) focussed on '*Transforming Kenya: Pathway to Devolution, Socio-Economic Development, Equity and National Unity*'. Experience during MTP II showed that activities closely linked to the youth-employment-migration theme were:

- **Unemployment and under-employment**, especially for the youth remained high;
- **skills mismatch** between demand and supply;
- **weak linkage between industry and training** institutions
- **skills shortages** in some critical areas within the labour market;
- **poor access to basic services such as electricity** and safe drinking water, which impacts communication, enterprise, and innovation opportunities; and
- **low labour productivity** negatively affects the country's competitiveness. The latter links to Kenya's relatively low ranking of 99 out of 138 counties (World Economic Forum, 2017), with labour productivity stagnating at 2.2 out of 10 over a long time period.

The current MTP III (2018–2022) targets the Economic, Social and Political Pillars that are pegged closely to labour and employment through investments in Infrastructure, ICT, Science, Technology and Innovation, Land Reforms, Public Sector Reforms, Ending Drought Emergencies, and other interventions.[11] The targets in MTP III are currently being guided by the existing Jubilee Government under the Big Four Agenda. Through the Access to Government Procurement Opportunities (AGPO), youth, women, and persons with disabilities, among others, are able to explore potential entrepreneurial goals targeting different sectors, including the informal. AGPO stipulated that 30% of all public tenders target youth, disabled persons, and women; in the *jua kali* sectors, short-term or casual work including transport, domestic or security. There are direct and indirect opportunities to be considered. The MTP III, however, has excluded the role and impact of migration, yet migration has a significant impact on all four pillars.

For instance, in the **Manufacturing Pillar**, the fiscal revenues can be optimized from the emerging oil industry in Kenya. This can be achieved through investments in, and promotion of, technical education, within Technical and Vocational Education Training (TVET) programmes. These programmes should include low-income but work-intense sectors into development strategies will yield benefits for resident and migrant youth. Migrants are a significant segment of the sub-sector where youth dominate in terms of mobility with the country that can be capitalized on. Improved understanding of their mobility and the drivers can assist in improving the policy approach to manufacturing.

In terms of the **food security/nutrition pillar**, strengthened rural-urban linkages have great potential for rural and urban residents and youth. If non-farm activities associated with *inclusive* agronomic and natural resource value chains are fostered, along with investment in connective infrastructure such as warehousing and cold storage, local economic growth will ensue, benefitting communities, including potential out-migrants, migrants returning from larger towns and cities, and downstream to urban entrepreneurs. The CIDPs can develop a strategic approach to meet the next MTPs and benefit from combining migration and youth dividends.

It is not expected that a single sector will address youth unemployment or under-employment in the long term, even at county level. Collaboration and coherent positive disposition towards the development potential of migration are required across sectors with sound integration within particular agenda such as the Big 4, e.g. manufacturing and agriculture and food/nutrition security. Sectors contributing strongly to GDP such as large commercial extractives/mining are not labour intensive.

For successful and inclusive execution of the Big 4 Agenda at county level and employment generation, building on existing progress and lesson-learning is strategic, while recognizing the need for innovation and investment in 'new' infrastructure and other components as required. Innovation, synergy-building, and partnerships are required in policy and practice.

Creating inclusive cities and towns at county level

The devolution of governance in Kenya brought new resources and hope to previously marginalized communities, looking for inclusive economic growth, service delivery, and long-term employment for the youth. The realization of Vision 2030, the Big 4 Agenda, and the ten-point Youth Agenda is taking place at the county, sub-county, ward, location, and household levels.

The 2018 Youth Convention themed 'Create an inclusive society and promote cohesion: a call to action by the Youth' made a call to action to both the youth and the government at national and county levels to accelerate youth development and the country's socio-economic growth. A ten-point agenda was ratified for youth socio-economic development (Mwololo, 2018). This agenda is recent and seen as a useful entry point in exploring the Kenyan youth-internal migration-county governance relationship. They act as reference 'milestones' in this chapter which aims to provide valuable insights for policy formulation and development approaches on internal migration by both national and county governments for sustainable employment and entrepreneurship that contribute to the realization of national- and county-level growth. For the purposes of this report 'youth' refers to female and male 18–35 years old. What government will do is:

Fast track	Speed up the review of the National Youth Policy[*] to reflect on the current status of the youth and their emerging issues, including reviewing the role and impact of migration
Decent Jobs	Ensure that the 'Big Four' delivers decent jobs and opportunities for the youth.
Create	Create a ministry for the youth to effectively handle young people's pressing issues to avoid the progression of challenges into problems like unemployment and lack of access to business grants and start-up capital
Partnerships	Tap into public-private partnerships to accelerate devolution and open up the countries for economic development.
Invest	Invest in youth to bridge the gap between the rich and poor.
Act & Prevent	Act on and prevent corruption as may destroy the future of youth
Prioritize	Keep the interests of youth at the forefront, including their voices in political processes, not as villains or victims of political processes.

While the youth leaders will be expected to

Unite	Unite the youth into a tribe, the Youth, so that they can harness their numbers into a political constituency to deliver the Kenya that carries their aspirations.
Form	Form citizen accountability groups at the county level to enhance their participation in governance, check excesses at county level, and demand financial accountability and better services.
Innovate	Innovate around the 'Big Four' thematic areas and create jobs for themselves.

From the ten-point agenda, the focus is on building relations between youth and government and including youth in policy development and implementation while addressing the bottlenecks that limit some of the existing government initiatives. Migration, interestingly, does not feature in the agenda, raising questions as to whether migrant youth do have an equal standing when it comes to engaging with county government; whether county government understands some of the challenges migrant youth face with regard to access to opportunities in general from services to employment; and whether they have the relevant policies, initiatives, resources, and capacity in place to include the needs of a diverse county population. Yet the results from YEMESA reveal a need for experiences of migration to be considered as young people from another city/town are less likely to have strong connections with their local county government, if they do not belong to a community within the destination country. County governments will

[*] The revised National Youth Policy was passed in November 2019.

also benefit from understanding their internal migration profile as a way of identifying skill sets that they have that can be harnessed for the purposes of building the county economy.

The ten-point agenda presents an opportunity to national/county government and youth representations to assess the realities that represents many counties in Kenya on the role and impact of migration. In the process of delivering decent jobs for the youth, the environment in which employment is offered would need to be enabling and recognize that youth are a dynamic group with different needs. Migrant youth, in particular, have moved for the purposes of securing employment unavailable in their place of origin. Hence, cities would need to develop an efficient strategy of addressing any potential conflict that may arise as a result of competition over jobs but see the value of skills and knowledge transfer of youth. County governments will therefore have to develop a different perspective of migration and not view it as a hinderance to reduce the risk of designing strategies that create more limitations than opportunities.

The Jubilee Government, in their second term, for many Kenyans, it is 'time for action' as the first term was indicated by county leaders as their time for start-ups, plan, recruit, procurement, etc. There is pressure on County Executives, County Assemblies, and those with sectoral mandates to deliver national and county[12] priorities. As Obonyo (2018) pointed out, collaboration between both levels of government is important: youth agenda merits high priority in county investment, while resources made available to the counties need to be realistic based on their function and role in achieving their and contributing to the national agenda.

Counties vary in the economic character and structure. Some counties have infrastructure, roads/transport links, or factories. For instance, Kiambu in 2010, prior to devolution, was second only to Nairobi with 206 factories; Nairobi had 1,090 out of a total of 2,252 (Ndii, 2018). It continues to attract many industries that set up camp within Kiambu in order to have better access to wider markets in Nairobi, while at the same time attracting migrants in search of income-generating opportunities. Other counties are capital intensive, such as Nakuru, a centre for geo-thermal energy, a large floriculture industry, and a tourism/hospitality industry, all related to the Rift Valley and Lake Naivasha. In addition, as outlined above on urban centres and GDP contributions, individual counties, even those with a strong rural sector, have vibrant economies – some generating jobs and some not. The size of a county and its economy according to Ndii (2018) does not reflect on income equality or poverty levels.

Some counties have baseline information, and data on poverty profiles, demographic, employment, some estimate of informal-formal sectors, revenue generation, detailed agro-ecological, maps, etc. are available. This provides a picture of the county needs and identifies entry points where county governments can intervene. However, there is limited evidence of systematic internal migration data being gathered across the 47 counties, either within or between counties. However, in certain cases, the county demographic profiles indicate mobility towards urban/town locations for work, e.g. Kajiado.

Kajiado County is a prominent pastoralist/rangeland county with a diverse population, bordering Nairobi Metropolitan Area and Tanzania. It has a very vibrant and strong economy and according to Ndii (2018) is among the top ten strongest county economies. In 2018, work commenced on an indoor market facility in Ngong for more than 2,000 traders, one of the largest in East Africa. In order to incorporate the youth agenda into their development activities at the county level, the county has focussed on vocational internships targeting the construction and water sectors undertaken by 200 young persons through a partnership between the county government and 20 local companies (Kajiado County Government, 2018). The county government is one of the few counties acknowledging the contributions of labour migration to the development of its local economy, which includes both international and internal migrants.

Incorporating the needs of different types of migrants within a city is essential for growth especially if the strategies are developed to benefit the local residents and the migrants. The county government will also be in a position to effectively respond to relations between migrants and host populations. The extent to which youth and migrant needs are prioritized can be assessed only by the county's approach, especially to recent youth labour migration dynamics in the devolved setting.

There have been criticisms of county governments not prioritizing migration within the development planning as, according to Samba (2018), the CIDPs have yet to consider the needs of young people and associated budgets – not least given their demographic advantage at county levels, with four out of five Kenyans (80%) under 35 years. The National Manpower Survey Basic Report published by the government in 2014 showed that only three out of ten (29%) employees in national and county governments were aged below 35 years (Ministry of Labour and KNBS, 2014). The County government mandates are not fully inclusive of key challenges facing youth – or they are not a priority, and this is a process that needs to be strengthened over time while considering the dynamic profile that youth already exhibit. The National Youth Policy (2006) is under review and it pinpoints two areas which county governments can aim for – inclusive economic opportunities for youth and health-related – the latter commonly refers to drug-abuse among unemployed and poor youth. CIDPs need to reflect both matters. It has, however, not considered the importance of understanding how migration of youth impacts cities and whether the process leads to inclusiveness or increases inequalities among the youth.

A synthesis of youth opinions in Siaya, Turkana, Mombasa, and Nairobi counties (British Council, 2018) revealed the following:

- Migration to cities and towns, inside and outside counties, is a step towards formal employment – large cities are perceived to hold the greatest opportunities, even if more costly.

- Strong education and skills do not guarantee job security or access, even for an interview.
- Entrepreneurship is a more realistic option – and reduces exposure to corruption and bureaucracy around accessing formal employment.
- Employment in farming and agriculture is a 'subsistence', and not a business, option – even in high-potential areas such as Siaya.

Counties are still in the process of understanding devolution as a trial and error period allows them to learn and adapt practices that ensure the development of a county. Migration should be included in those planning activities as a way of capitalizing on the benefits that migration brings especially internally which is assumed to be larger than international. Awareness of the skills that migrants bring and how they contribute to the county economy is critical for county development. County governments will have to ensure that the negative impacts of migration is reduced by putting measures in place the build relations between migrant and host population. This is key to ensuring that cities are inclusive of the needs of all individuals including migrant populations. There is, however, a long road ahead for counties to appreciate migration as an opportunity for development and not a threat, and this can be achieved only by using an evidence-based approach at a decentralized level that showcases the pros and cons of migration to a county.

Conclusion

The results of the YEMESA study revealed that youth continue to move where opportunities exist where they believe they will economically benefit. Their migration is defined by both lack of opportunities in their place of origin and the assumed available opportunities in other localities. The need for county governments to understand the drivers of youth migration today is essential, especially when considering their role and impact on development in general. When considering sustainable cities and communities there is a need to factor in the increasing migratory flows of youth across the county and formulate initiatives and programmes aligned to the national development plans that includes the SDG 11 goals. The youth are educated and are always in search of opportunities, whether in employment or entrepreneurship. They are also in search of an environment that gives them social, economic, political, and environmental security, among others. Kenya is in a strategic position to achieve that through devolution, but it needs to understand the internal migratory flows and include them in their national and county development plans. At the same time, the mainstreaming of migration into the national SDG targets especially with regard to developing inclusive cities would be beneficial to the government.

The chapter revealed that population will continue to increase, partially due to migration, and cities that are ill-prepared to support a growing population will experience difficulties due to lack of planning. The need to value the contributions of migrants but also be aware of the negative impact of migration to cities is key to planning. The answer lies in the migration drivers which identify gaps in policy implementation through existing strategies. These gaps can be used to strengthen government approaches in source, transit, and destination counties. This will also reduce the need for youth to consider international destinations to search for employment opportunities that are otherwise unavailable in their county of origin or the country.

There is, however, an urgent need for county governments to understand their migration profiles to determine the needs of the wider population, including those that are not born there. By including a section in the CIDPs on the migration profile of internal migrant adapted from data from the recent 2019 census, the county government will be able to know the demographic profiles of their population, strengthen their existing development strategies to include them, and explore ways of engaging them in county-level development. To achieve sustainable cities and communities it has to be an inclusive process that requires capturing the perspectives of the local population, including migrants. At present, the government of Kenya is laying the foundation to achieve its national development goals through the Big Four Agenda and would benefit from mainstreaming migration into the activities. This requires the process to be inclusive, by providing the youth a seat at the table of decision-makers and implementers so they are able to influence the process from inception to implementation.

Notes

1 Nairobi, Mombasa, Uasin Gishu, Narok, Nakuru, Laikipia, Naivasha, Kajiado, Nyamira and Nyandarua.
2 The AFIDEP report is part of a larger East Africa Regional Analysis of Youth Demographics.
3 Unemployment rate is the number of people actively seeking employment as a percentage of the labour force https://tradingeconomics.com/kenya/unemployment-rate.
4 Not employing their skills adequately; part-time.
5 The study engaged 500 internal migrants up to 35 years, mostly male with origins in Eastern, Nyanza, Western, Central and Rift Valley.
6 Along with population fertility and mortality.
7 SDG 11 – By 2030, the following targets should be met: access to adequate, safe, affordable housing, sanitation, upgrade slums; sustainable transport and access including for disabled persons; reduce the negative impact of urban environmental pollution; universal access to safe, inclusive and accessible, green and public spaces (all ages) and more.
8 IOM, July 2018. Kenya's Draft National Migration Policy Integrates Global Compact Commitment. Both are informed by the Kenya Vision 2030, the Big 4 Agenda, the Sustainable Development Goals (SDGs), the Global Compact for Migration (GCM), the Migration Governance Framework, the African Union Migration Framework, and the Intergovernmental Authority on Development (IGAD) regional migration policy frameworks.
9 The 'Big Four' agenda aims to further strengthen the economy, progress industrialization, and create jobs, thereby contributing towards the realization of Vision 2030. Its Investment Plan is anchored on Four Key Pillars and pegged

to national development agenda as well as global targets such as the SDGs. The pillars are Manufacturing, Food Security/Nutrition by 2022, Housing and Universal Health Coverage (UHC).
10 Latest News, October 25, 2018. Big Four Agenda's Massive Opportunities For Local And Global Private Sector, Says President Kenyatta. http://www. president.go.ke/2018/03/06/big-four-agendas-massive-opportunities-for-local-and-global-private-sector-says-president-kenyatta/.
11 Enablers for the 2018-'22 phase are Infrastructure, ICT, Science, Technology and Innovation, Land Reforms, Public Sector Reforms, Ending Drought Emergencies, National values and Ethics, Security, Peace Building and Conflict Resolution.
12 These county governments are responsible for county legislation (CoK 2010, Article 185) and executive functions for agriculture, trade development, county health services, county education (pre-school, child care, adult education), county transport (roads), pollution control, culture, public amenities, and coordination (Article 183).

References

African Institute for Development Policy (AFIDEP). (2018a). Boom or burst: New findings on investing in Kenyan youth for a better future. https://www.afidep. org/boom-or-burden-new-findings-on-investing-in-kenyas-youth-for-a-better-tomorrow/.
African Institute for Development Policy (AFIDEP). (2018b). The big four agenda: Just how will Kenya's national and county governments work together for success? www.afidep.org/the-big-four-agenda-just-how-will-kenyas-national-and-county-governments-work-together-for-success/.
Arosio, M. (2016). History, characteristics and consequences of rural-urban migration and urbanization in Kenya. https://www.researchgate.net/publication/301228606_History_Characteristics_and_Consequences_of_Rural-Urban_Migration_and_Urbanization_In_Kenya.
Badoux, M. (2018). Eldoret – A city on the move. Drivers, dynamics and challenges of rural to urban mobility. Research and Evidence Facility. EU Trust Fund and Rift Valley Research.
British Council. (2017). Youth employment in Kenya. *Literature review*. https://www.britishcouncil.co.ke/sites/default/files/ng_kenya_youth_employment_in_kenya.pdf.
British Council. (2018). Next Generation Kenya: Qualitative Research Findings. British Council: Nairobi.
Brooks, K., Amy, G., Goyal, A., and Zorya, S. (2015). Devolved healthcare turns sour as doctors quit service. October 26, 2015. www.businessdailyafrica.com/corporate/.
Brooks, K., Amy, G., Goyal, A., and Zorya, S. (2017). State launches portal for job-seekers. July 12, 2017. https://www.businessdailyafrica.com/economy/.
Brooks, K., Amy, G., Goyal, A., and Zorya, S. (2017). Kenya's youth percentage among the highest globally. August 27, 2017. https://www.businessdailyafrica.com/economy/Kenya-youth-percentage-among-the-highest-globally/3946234-4072946-jvv2x2/index.html.
Ezeh, A.C., Chepngeno, G., Kasiira, A.Z., and Woubalen, Z. (2006). The situation of older people in poor urban settings: The case of Nairobi, Kenya. In: Cohen, B. and Menken, J., editors. *Aging in Sub-Saharan Africa: Recommendation for*

Furthering Research. Washington, DC: National Research Council (US) Committee on Population.

Food and Agriculture Organisation. (2018). Migration – Decent youth employment. http://www.fao.org/rural-employment/work-areas/migration/en/.

Kajiado County Government. (2018). Kajiado report 2018. www.kajiado.co.ke/.

Kenya Institute for Public Policy Research and Analysis. (2018a). Tightening affirmative action on empowerment of people with disability. http://kippra.or.ke/.

Kenya Institute for Public Policy Research and Analysis. (2018b). Realising the 'Big Four' agenda through energy as an enabler. Policy Monitor Issue 9 No. 3. January–March 2018.

Kenya National Bureau of Statistics (KNBS). (2017). *Economic Survey Kenya*. Nairobi: Kenya National Bureau of Statistics.

Kenya National Bureau of Statistics (KNBS). (2018). *Economic Survey Kenya*. Nairobi: Kenya National Bureau of Statistics.

Kinyangi, H. (2014). Migration decision-making: A case study of Kibera, Nairobi. A research project submitted in partial fulfilment of the requirement for the Degree of Master of Arts in Population Studies and Research, University of Nairobi.

Macharia, J. (2003). Migration in Kenya and its impact on the labor market. Conference on African.

Ministry of Labour and Kenya National Bureau of Statistics. (2014). National manpower survey basic report. http://kenyanewsagency.go.ke/.

Ministry of Youth Affairs (2006). *Kenya National Youth Policy*. Nairobi: Ministry of Youth Affairs.

Muyanga, M., Otieno, D., and Jayne T.S. (2016). Land access and outmigration in densely populated areas of Kenya. Transforming small-holder agriculture in Africa: The role of policy and governance. 5th International Conference of AAAE. September 16, 2016. Addis Ababa.

Mwololo, M. (2018). Innovation, counties now the areas to seek jobs. Daily Nation. July 16, 2018. https://nation.africa/kenya/life-and-style/dn2/innovation-counties-now-the-areas-to-seek-jobs-67138.

Ndii, D. (2018). 'The politics of county economies: Why Central Kenya MPs are wrong', The Elephant, November 1, 2018: https://www.theelephant.info/op-eds/2018/11/12/the-politics-of-county-economies-why-central-kenya-mps-are-wrong/.

Nyaoro, D., Schade, J., and Schmidt-Verkerk, K. (2016). Assessing the evidence: Migration, environment and climate change in Kenya. IOM Environmental Migration Portal. https://environmentalmigration.iom.int/assessing-evidence-migration-environment-and-climate-change-kenya.

Obonyo, R. (2018). Change of approach needed to generate more jobs for youth. Daily Nation. February 4, 2018.

Onyango, E. (2017). Institutional entrepreneurship and social innovation at the base of the pyramid: The case of M-Pesa in Kenya. *Industry and Innovation*, 26(4): 369–390.

Oucho, J. and Gould, W.T.S. (1993). Internal migration, urbanization and population distribution. In: Foote, K.A., Hill, K.H., and Martin, L.G., editors. *Demographic Change in Sub-Saharan Africa*, pp. 256–296. Washington, DC: National Research Council.

Ramisch, J.J. (2014). 'We will not farm like our fathers': Multilocational livelihoods, cellphones, and the continuing challenge of rural development in western Kenya. In: Sick, D., editor. *Rural Livelihoods, Regional Economies, and Processes of Change*, pp. 10–35. Routledge: London.

Samba, E. (2018). Factor Youth needs into county plans. March 19, 2018. https://www.the-star.co.ke/news/2018/03/19/factor-youth-needs-in-county-plans_c1727090.

Tacoli, C. (1998). 'Rural-Urban Interactions: A guide to the literature', *Environment and Urbanization, Vol.10:1.* pp. 147–166.

UN-Habitat. (2018b). UN Habitat and the Government of Kenya enter partnership to Empower Urban Youth Economically. March 2018. https://unhabitat.org/un-habitat-and-government-of-kenya-enter-partnership-to-empower-urban-youth-economically/2018/.

United Nations Development Assistance Fund (UNDAF). (2018). Common Country Assessment. *Umoja ni Nguvu.* UN Development Assistance Framework 2018–2022. January 2018. R. Oliver and A. Morara.

United Nations Development Programme (UNDP). (2016). *Human Development Report 2016.* New York: United Nations Development Programme.

United Nations Development Programme (UNDP). (2018). Human Development Indicators and Indices. Kenya 2018 Statistical Update. Briefing. http://hdr.undp.org/sites/all/themes/hdr_theme/country-notes/KEN.pdf.

United Nations Population Fund (UNFPA) and National Council for Population and Development (NCPD). (2013). UN Population Fund and National Council for Population and Development. Kenya Population Situation Analysis, July 2013. www.unfpa.org.

Wall, R.S., Maseland, J., Rochell, K., and Spaliviero, M. (2014). United Nations Human Settlements Programme (UN-Habitat). UN Habitat, 2014. State of African Cities 2014 – Re-imagining urban transitions. https://unhabitat.org/books/state-of-african-cities-2014-re-imagining-sustainable-urban-transitions/.

World Bank. (2017). Appraisal document Kenya urban support programme. July 2017.

World Bank and Vision 2030. (2014). Youth employment initiatives in Kenya. http://vision2030.go.ke/inc/uploads/2018/05/.

World Economic Forum. (2017). *Global competitiveness report 2016'17.* C.K. Schwab (ed.). http://www3.weforum.org/docs/.

5 Remittance prices and welfare

Evidence from Sub-Saharan Africa

Lwanga Elizabeth Nanziri and Paul Gbahabo

Introduction

Remittances by migrant workers to sending countries have increased exponentially over the past decade, making their contribution to GDP surpass foreign direct investments. For instance, in 2016, official remittance flows to developing countries reached over US$400 million, representing over 70% of the global remittance flows (Remittance Prices Worldwide, 2017). At a micro-level, these remittances have improved the welfare of beneficiary households. However, there are concerns that remittance prices as a proportion of the total amount remitted are high. According to the United Nations Sustainable Development Goals (SDG) Report of 2018, the global average cost of sending US$200 was estimated at 7.2% in 2017, more than double the UN's target transaction cost of 3%.[1] This could compromise the aforementioned benefits since a higher cost might reduce the growth in incomes which is the basis of household consumption of goods and services. But the increasing innovations, such as internet-based remittance technologies, should lead to competition among local remittance service providers, thus reducing the cost of sending remittances. It therefore follows that in the absence of alternative channels, an increase in the cross-border cost of remitting should lead to a decline in welfare and vice versa.

This chapter examines if indeed an upward movement in the cross-border cost of remittance transactions has a negative effect on welfare in the Sub-Saharan Africa (SSA) region, which harbours some of the most expensive corridors. The cost of remittances is measured as the average cost of sending US$200 between two countries, which is in line with the UN's definition and policy variable. The Remittances Prices Worldwide data from World Bank is used for the period 2011 to 2018. A sample of 17 countries, for which data is available over the entire period, is extracted. These countries are home to 13 remittance corridors, which yields 351 data points. The biggest remitter in SSA is South Africa which sends to mainly eight countries within the same region.[2] Welfare is then measured by four indicators (household consumption per capita, life expectancy, food availability per capita, and mean years of schooling) whose data is obtained from the World Bank World Development

Indicators. We estimate a panel fixed effects model to overcome the problem of cross-sectional interdependency. In addition, Arellano and Bond's (1991) one-step generalized method of moments (GMM) is employed to mitigate the potential endogeneity problems as a result of reverse causality between the welfare variables and the remittance cost. In this specification, we make use of the remittance volume as an instrument for remittance cost. Remittance volume is captured as total remittance received in a country as a proportion of GDP. Endogeneity may arise if relatively well-off households self-select into migration and subsequently remit back to their relatively wealthy countries of origin.

Our results show that an increase in the remittance fees is associated with a decrease in overall household welfare. Consumption per capita declines by 5 percentage points, food availability per capita by 1%, mean years of schooling by 3 percentage points, and life expectancy by 0.1 percentage points. However, the effect on food availability per capita is more significant when remittance volumes, rather than the actual remittance fees, are considered. Overall, these results are consistent with studies both on the continent and elsewhere. We conclude that if remittance costs remain sticky downwards, SSA region might not realize the full benefits from the increasing trend of remittance flows. These results, therefore, support the pursuit of the SDG target of reducing remittance costs to 3% of every US$200 sent across borders.

The chapter is organized as follows. 'Literature review' provides an overview of the literature. Data and the empirical strategy are discussed in 'Data and empirical strategy', and results are presented and discussed in 'Empirical results'. 'Conclusion' concludes.

Literature review

Remittance cost and remittance funds

Theoretically, a high cost of services has the potential of curtailing demand. This would make the concern about the cost of remitting funds across countries relevant, given its implication on the volume of remittances. However, the causality between cost and volume of remittances is unclear. While the volume of remittances has tripled above what it was in 2000, and it is five times what it was in 1990 (Cecchetti and Schoenholtz, 2018), the cost has declined only very marginally. According to Beck and Soledad Martinez Peria (2009), the cost of remitting is directly related to the number of remitters and inversely related to the degree of competition among remittance service providers (banks, money transfer operators, and fintech companies) especially in the receiving country. Indeed the current surge in financial technology, which provides alternative transfer mechanisms beyond banks, has the potential of reducing the cost of services and subsequently volumes of remittances. For instance, Munyengera and Matumoto (2016) find an increase in the probability of receiving remittances and an associated rise in the total value of the remittances among people using mobile money services in Uganda compared to non-users. These mobile money transfers are associated with low transaction costs. Despite the recent growth in innovations in financial service provision however, some regions are still characterized by high remittance costs such as the SADC region (Truen et al., 2016), albeit with rising volumes. This paradox might be linked to the uses of remittances as we discuss in the next section.

Remittances and welfare

The economic importance of remittances has increased over the past decade. According to the World Bank, remittance were larger than official flows and private non-FDI flows to developing countries by 2004, at about 5% of imports and 8% of domestic investment (Page & Plaza, 2005). In 2018, US$689 billion was remitted, of which US$529 went to low- to middle-income countries, averaging 4.6% as a percentage of GDP in Africa alone (World Bank, 2019).

Empirical evidence suggests that remittances increase income, hence welfare in receiving countries. However, the effect can be in the short-run or in the long-run in that increased household consumption or well-being happens immediately a household receives an income shock (the remittance). If the household instead undertakes investment ventures, then it will be guaranteed of long-run consumption as a result of the current investment. Zhunio, Vishwarao and Chiang (2012) and Adam and Cuecuecha (2010) validate this argument. They find that remittances are a transitory income source used more in human and physical capital investment relative to consumption. Relatedly, Lopez-Cordova (2005) finds that remittances lead to a reduction in child mortality, which is evidence of investment in household health to mitigate future costs associated with bad health. The author also finds an increase in school attendance and a decline in illiteracy, which points to future consumption benefits through increased earnings.

Apart from improving investment, remittances form a safety net for both the receiving households and the remitting household members. Households send away people as migrant labourers to diversify the risk of negative income shocks in originating communities. In the event of adverse welfare shocks of the migrant labourers, members in the sending communities may also send remittances to the migrants (Yang & Choi, 2007). Hence, remittances serve as mutual insurance for the poor through consumption smoothing, thus lessening liquidity traps.

Social safety nets are particularly important for the most vulnerable population in that welfare-improving remittances could also lessen inequalities. Portes (2009) substantiates this evidence with the finding that raising remittances by 1% increases the income of the population in the first decile and that of the seventh decile while decreasing the income of the top 10% (Portes, 2009). However, Cuong and Linh (2018) contrast this evidence arguing that remittances perpetuate inequalities through increased dependency. They find that individuals aged between 23 and 60 in households with a migrant family member are less willing to accept a job when compared to those without a migrant worker. This could be due to increased reservation wages, risking further reduction in household income through voluntary unemployment.

Thus far, literature reveals that remittances are a source of improved household welfare through provision of income for consumption smoothing and investment. However, remittances may also increase inter-household inequality due to selectivity of labour migration.

Remittances in Africa

Africa is one of the continents where important macro- and micro-economic indicators respond to the rising flow of remittances. The prominence of remittances as an alternative or an additional source of financing attracts scholarly work that examines their relationship with welfare on the continent. The African literature finds that remittances lead to improved balance of payments, enhanced fiscal sustainability, accelerated economic growth, increased human capital development, and positive or negative shifts in resource equity. The studies also show that remittances unambiguously reduce poverty. For instance, remittances lead to increased inflow of foreign currency into countries, which arguably improves the balance of payments resulting in increased welfare through enhanced country ability to procure imports. Chami et al. (2008) and Corden and Neary (1982) support this evidence with the finding that remittance flows into a country lead to appreciation of domestic currency. However, Ball, Lopez, and Reyes (2013) and Ojapinwa and Nwokoma (2018) show that these effects are limited to only significantly shifting nominal but not real exchange rates. Therefore, remittances could fall short in enhancing welfare using exchange rate appreciation as the transmission mechanism.

Fiscal sustainability stands as another potential benefit of remittances to receiving countries. Increased remittance flow leads to enhanced revenue through increased tax bases as some countries not only tax the remittances themselves but also collect revenue from the businesses established through investments from remittances, leading to enhanced debt sustainability (Chami et al., 2008). Thus, more government expenditure particularly on social services gets funding from non-debt means that improve fiscal sustainability through reduced debt. As most governments in Africa increase tax rates to repay debts through increased depth of revenue, remittances could stall the increase in tax rates leading to improved disposable income for the population, hence improved well-being.

Economic growth becomes an additional important indicator that benefits from remittance flow into a country. Remittances contribute to this progress through increased availability of resources which loosens liquidity constraints, allowing a larger section of the population to participate in enterprises through investment (Fayissa & Nsiah, 2010; Giuliano & Ruiz-arranz,

2009; World Bank, 2006). The rising private incomes debatably lead to improved well-being. The overall result is increased aggregate income for the remittances receiving countries. However, Barajas et al. (2009) argue that the national income effects of remittances may not be verified due to the absence of empirical evidence. Clemens and Mckenzie (2018) also acknowledge that it is difficult to accurately measure remittance flows on the continent, which might affect the conclusions on the growth and development outcomes.

Development, particularly in human capital, largely benefits from remittance flows. For instance, Lu (2011) shows that households use remittances to educate children. The increased availability of resources due to the remittances not only increases education attainment but also reduces pressure on child labour supply that arguably increases school attendance. Adams and Cuecuecha (2010) substantiate this evidence with the finding that remittances associate with years of schooling, and Zhunio, Vishwarao and Chiang (2012) further show that remittances relate to decreased illiteracy rates. Hence, remittances, through these human capital traits, debatably allow people to obtain better jobs and earn higher incomes in the labour market.

Besides human capital development, remittances lead to shifts in resource equity. For example, Wouterse (2010) found that remittances coming from migrants within Africa reduce inequality through increased income of the less privileged receiving households. This could be the case because most intra-African migrants originate from rural areas where income gradients are flat, leading to less selection into migration. Nevertheless, the author also shows that remittances coming from migrants outside Africa increase inequality. This is likely because intercontinental migration requires high costs of movement such that only rich households send out migrants; hence, remittances come to affluent homes – the problem of endogenous selection into lucrative migration destinations.

Remittances have been associated with reduced poverty in Africa. For instance Anyanwu and Erhijakpor (2010) find that international remittances have a negative and significant effect on poverty headcount across 33 African countries. Akobeng (2016) supports these findings by showing that the size of the coefficient varies depending on the chosen poverty metric. Beyene (2014) also supports these findings, however, with a caution that the poverty-reducing effects of remittances do not associate with reduced inequalities which suggests that remittances lead to perpetual dependence and exacerbate class strata (Beyene, 2014).

Therefore, the increased remittance flows into Africa provide an opportunity for improved welfare. These spill-over effects include appreciation of the currencies that increases access to foreign goods, reduction of debt burden due to improved fiscal position, rising income due to increased private investment, and enhanced human capital development due to increased education financing. Remittances, on the other hand, could either increase or decrease income inequality conditional on selection into migration amongst the remitters, while evidence that they reduce poverty remains unequivocal.

Africa, however, remains one of the regions with the highest cost of remitting in the world. The cost of remitting determines the volume of remitted funds, which, in turn, could negatively impact the welfare of households. This chapter focusses on the relationship between cost of remitting and welfare in some of the most unequal parts of SSA.

Data and empirical strategy

Data description

The data used is Remittance Prices Worldwide (RPW) obtained from the World Bank. RPW monitors the cost incurred by remitters when sending money along major remittance corridors, across all geographic regions of the world. The RPW was launched in 2008. The data is collected on a quarterly basis, covering 48 remittance sending countries and 105 receiving countries, for a total of 365 country corridors worldwide.[3] We extract data for the SSA region. According to the RPW Report for 2017Q1, SSA had the highest above-average cost of remitting USD 200 as shown in Figure 5.1.

A close look at the remittance patterns shows that there are 13 major corridors in 17 SSA countries for which data is complete over the period 2011Q1–2018Q3. The remitting countries in this sample are Ghana, Senegal, South Africa, and Tanzania. As shown in Table 5.1, the busiest remitter is South Africa in SADC, followed by Tanzania in East Africa. Remittances in the SADC sub-region are unidirectional, going from South Africa to the rest – Angola, Botswana, Eswatini (formerly Swaziland), Lesotho, Malawi, Mozambique, Zambia, and Zimbabwe. The only other sending country in this region is Angola which remits to only one country, Namibia. This corridor

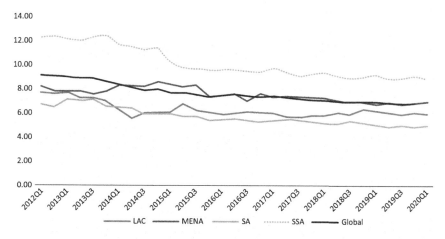

Figure 5.1 Average remittance cost per US$200 sent per region.
Source: RPW report (2017).

Table 5.1 Summary of the data for the period 2011Q1–2018Q3

Sending country	Receiving country	Average cost of sending remittance	Average volume of remittances received as % of GDP	No. of MNOs in receiving country	Welfare indicators in receiving countries			
					Average household consumption per capita	Average food availability per capita	Mean life expectancy	Mean years of schooling
Ghana	Nigeria	10.21	1.19	(6) 4	1,521.29	0	52.91	6
Senegal	Mali	4.58	1.53	(4) 3	538.69	0	57.41	2.25
South Africa	Angola	14.04	0.003	(5) 2	1,596.64	84.02	60.99	4.98
South Africa	Botswana	15.70	0.05	(5) 3	3,686.66	0	65.42	9.19
South Africa	Eswatini	12.40	0.6	(5) 2	3,478.13	87.53	56.61	6.39
South Africa	Lesotho	12.04	4.16	(5) 2	1,257.11	104.76	53.55	6.13
South Africa	Malawi	16.60	0.15	(5) 5	448.08	138.15	62.18	4.43
South Africa	Mozambique	15.85	0.32	(5) 3	377.87	89.88	57.56	3.44
South Africa	Zambia	15.93	0.06	(5) 3	838.27	109.63	60.97	6.9
South Africa	Zimbabwe	12.64	2.38	(5) 3	1,029.89	121.69	59.67	8.07
Tanzania	Kenya	12.34	0.62	(12) 4	861.1	133.47	66.36	6.35
Tanzania	Rwanda	14.00	0.56	(12) 4	578.41	129.83	66.43	3.97
Tanzania	Uganda	13.78	0.99	(12) 6	503.84	70.04	59.41	5.7

Source: Authors' compilation from the World Bank's Remittance Price Worldwide, World Development Indicators. Figures in brackets represent the number of MNOs in the sending countries. The mobile money providers in sending countries are MTN in Ghana, Wari (Tigo) & Orange in Senegal, currently none in South Africa, and Airtel, Vodacom, Tigo plus Zantel in Tanzania.

is excluded from the analysis because remittance price data is available only for the period 2016–2018. A similar unidirectional pattern is observed in the East African region, where the major sending country is Tanzania, servicing Kenya, Rwanda, and Uganda. The West African region is represented by only two major corridors: Ghana to Nigeria and Senegal to Mali.

Table 5.1 shows that with the exception of the Senegal-Mali corridor, the remittance cost in the rest of the countries in our sample exceeds both the global average of 7.2% and the target cost of 3% that was set in UN's SDG 10.7. However, the statistics show a mixed relationship between the number of mobile money service providers, Mobile Network Operators (MNOs), and cost of remitting in the countries in our sample. For instance, Tanzania, which is one of the pioneers of mobile money, with four mobile money providers (and 12 mobile money operators), charges as high as 14% per US$200 compared to Ghana and Senegal, which have up to two mobile money providers. Suffice to add that South Africa, which charges the highest remittance fees in the sample, does not offer mobile money services, although it has five mobile money operators. This inconclusive pattern is in contrast with what Beck and Soldeda Martinez Peria (2009) and Freund and Spatafora (2005) find, that the degree of competition in the financial sector of the sending country (captured by the existence of non-traditional financial services providers such as mobile money providers) can drive remittance cost down. In this paper, however, taking remittance cost as exogenous to the receiving country, we focus more on factors in the recipient countries. The relatively lower cost for sending money from South Africa to Eswatini, Lesotho, and Zimbabwe can be attributed to the large number of migrants from these countries resident in South Africa, a notion that is corroborated by Beck and Soledad Martinez Peria (2009).

The data also shows that there is a mixed relationship between the volume of remittances (the demand for remittances) and the remittance cost. There's also a mixed correlation between the cost of remitting and the receiving countries' welfare indicators. We investigate the significance of this relationship in the next section.

The welfare variables considered include household consumption per capita, food availability per capita, life expectancy, and mean years of schooling. These variables are meant to capture the major uses of remittances by the receiving household as discussed in the preceding section, i.e., for consumption smoothing, investment in education, and health care.

Welfare variables as well as the control variables (trade openness, consumer price indices, population growth, government fixed capital formation, government final expenditure on consumption) are obtained as annual series from the World Development Indicators for the period 2011–2018 to match the RPW series. The food availability data is obtained from the U.S. Department of Agriculture database (www.ers.usda.gov). We convert the annual series into quarterly data using three methods. For stock variables such as household consumption per capita, we use the Denton match-last method, while for flow variables, such as trade openness (imports and exports as a percentage of GDP), the quadratic match–sum method is used. Finally, the quadratic match–average is used to convert the annual consumer price indices into quarterly series. The choice of conversion method for the variables was informed by the extensive literature on temporal disaggregation (see for instance Eurostat 1999; Aziakpono 2005; European Union 2013; Sbia, Shahbaz, & Hamdi, 2014).

The summary of the welfare variables is provided in Table 5.1, and it shows that per capita income in the sample ranges between US$377.87 (Mozambique) and US$3,686.66 (Botswana). Mean years of schooling is lowest in Mali (2.25 years) and highest in Botswana (9.2 years), while life expectancy ranges between 52.9 years (Nigeria) and 66.4 years (Rwanda). For the period under review, the largest volume of remittances as a percentage of GDP was recorded in Lesotho from South Africa (4.19%) while the least was from South Africa to Angola (0.003%). The data does not reveal any meaningful trend between the cost or volume of remittances and the welfare indicators. We investigate this further in the section that follows.

Model specification and estimation

To estimate the effect of remittance prices on the welfare of individuals in recipient countries, we start by estimating a panel fixed effects model with 13 corridors in 17 countries, using quarterly data for the period 2011Q1–2018Q3, which gives us a total of 350 data points. This model allows us to account for the effect of unobservables as well as cross-sectional interdependency. We therefore regress welfare indicators highlighted above (household consumption per capita, food availability per capita, life expectancy, and household expenditure on education) on the average cost of remittances in each corridor, and on a vector of receiving country characteristics. The empirical model is thus specified as follows:

$$\log(W_{it}) = \beta_0 + \beta_1 \log(C_{jt}) + \beta_2 X_{it} + \varepsilon_{it} \tag{1}$$

where W_{it} denotes welfare in receiving country i at time t, C_{jt} is the remittance cost in corridor j, X_{it} denotes a vector of receiving-country-specific control variables (gross domestic product per capita, inflation, gross fixed capital formation, government final expenditure on consumption, population growth, trade openness), and ε_{it} denotes the error term. The choice of regressors follows recent research works such as Ball et al. (2013), Beyene (2014), Bettin, Presbitero and Spatafora (2014), Anyanwu and Erhijakpor (2010), Singh et al. (2010), Akobeng (2016), and Mabrouk and Mekni (2018).

However, the possibility of endogeneity might render our estimates of the fixed effects model biased. For instance, there is a possible reverse causality between welfare in the receiving countries and remittances (Gupta et al., 2009. It is argued that migration, which is the source of remittances, is a costly endeavour that requires substantial amounts of financial resources. Thus, relatively well-off households are likely to send migrants who, in turn, remit back to their countries (Ebeke & Le Geoff, 2011). To deal with this potential problem, we estimate a one-step dynamic GMM model by Arellano-Bond (1991). For this GMM estimation, we make use of the remittance volumes, measured as a proportion of the recipient country's GDP, as an instrument for remittance cost. Indeed, the immediate effect of higher remittance costs, according to consumer theory, would be a potential decline in the overall volume of remittances, which would, in turn, affect the welfare in the recipient country due to reduced incomes. Other instruments used in this model include the lagged dependent variable and the first difference of the control variables. If the GMM estimates are consistent with results from the panel fixed effects model, then endogeneity is not an issue and we can thus accept the fixed effects estimates. Otherwise, we report the GMM estimates.

Empirical results

Table 5.2 presents the estimation results of the effect of remittance transaction costs on the welfare outcomes of major corridors of SSA recipient countries for the period 2011Q1–2018Q3. The *a priori* expectation is that an increase in the cost of remitting could penalize welfare. Columns (1)–(5) present the GMM estimates. With the exception of results in column (2), a rising cost of remittance compromises welfare outcomes. For instance, a 1% increase in remittance costs reduces household consumption per capita by 3 percentage points. This result is in line with Wouterse (2010), who finds a similar effect in relation to within Africa remittances. Life expectancy declines by 0.1 percentage points and mean-years of schooling by 3% as shown in columns (3) and (4) respectively. Although not reported, our fixed effects results show an effect of up to 18.6% decline in education attainment. Relatively larger effect on education have been reported in studies such as Zhunio et al. (2012), Lu (2011), and Adam and Cuecuecha (2010), who argue that remittances provide some form of transitory income that enables investment in human and physical capital. Comparing the two outcomes, life expectancy and mean years of schooling, these results are corroborated by Lopez-Cordova (2005), who finds a decline in mortality of 5% and a decline of 40% in illiteracy. Moreover, the link between welfare indicators has been established by researchers such as Jayachandran and Lleras-Muney (2009), who found that investment in human capital for Sri Lankan girls led to lower mortality, thus increasing the life expectancy of mothers.

Results in column (5) show the effect of remittances on food availability per capita. Remittance volumes are used directly instead of remittance cost as in column (2). The result is a decline in food availability to households by 1%. This result is supported by Mabrouk and Mekni (2018), who find a positive association between total remittances with food security in terms of access, utilization, and stability while negatively associated with food availability

Table 5.2 The effect of remittance cost on welfare in selected SSA countries (2011–2018)

	Arellano-Bond One-Step GMM				
	(1)	(2)	(3)	(4)	(5)
	Household consumption per capita	Food availability per capita	Life expectancy	Mean years of schooling	Food availability per capita
Remittance cost	−0.05	−0.03	−0.001	−0.03	
	(0.01)★★★	(0.27)	(0.00)★	(0.02)★	
Remittance volume (%)					−1.03
					(0.02)★★★
GDP per capita	0.124	−4.14	−0.002	0.66	−0.14
	(0.07)★	(1.14)★★★	(0.00)	(0.02)★★★	(0.05)★★
Inflation	−0.01	−0.08	0.00	0.00	−0.03
	(0.00)★★★	(0.07)	(0.00)★★★	(0.00)	(0.04)
Gross fixed capital formation	−0.015	1.66	−0.003	−0.06	−0.30
	(0.03)	(0.37)★★★	(0.00)★★★	(0.03)★	(0.14)★★★
Gov. consumption expenditure	−0.04	−0.90	0.00	−0.06	−0.04
	(0.04)	(0.52)★	(0.00)	(0.03)★	(0.10)
Pop. growth rate	−0.06	0.21	0.05	0.03	−0.07
	(0.03)★	(0.56)	(0.00)★★★	(0.03)	(0.07)
Lagged dependent variable	0.77	0.21	0.89	0.73	0.78
	(0.03)★★★	(0.07)★★★	(0.00)★★★	(0.03)★★★	(0.09)★★★
Constant	1.06	33.916	0.449	−3.07	5.24
	(0.43)★★	(8.69)★★★	(0.01)★★★	(0.67)★★★	(0.79)★★★
Sargan test	527.57	147.16	712.73	181.76	145
	(0.000)	(0.000)	(0.000)	(0.000)	(0.000)
Wald test	1,574.94	1,482.03	3,579.70	6,457.76	4,371.28
	(0.000)	(0.000)	(0.000)	(0.000)	(0.000)
Obs.	250	250	250	250	250

Notes: Robust standard errors in parentheses. ★, ★★ and ★★★ denote 5%, 10%, and 1% level of significance respectively. All variables are in log form except for the mean years of schooling and personal remittance volume.

dimension. While household expenditure of food would have been a better proxy of welfare, we did not get data for all the countries in our sample over the period under consideration. Indeed Kedir and Ibrahim (2011) find a positive and significant effect of remittances on household expenditure on food in Ethiopia. Overall, our results suggest that an upward movement in remittance costs does have a negative impact on welfare in the receiving countries by compromising affordability and/or investment in basic services. This is consistent with the literature.

Conclusion

We investigate the relationship between remittance cost and recipient countries' welfare in SSA. We focus on remittances within the continent using the

RPW data from the World Bank. We incorporate the volume of remittance as one of the instruments given that volume has the first-order effect. We find evidence of an inverse relationship between remittances cost and several welfare outcomes such as household income per capita, mean years of schooling, life expectancy, and food availability per capita. This implies that if remittance costs remain sticky downwards, welfare in SSA could be compromised, in a continent that is already characterized with high levels of poverty. At a macro-level, the implication of these results is that if cross-border costs of funds transfer within the SSA region remain high, economies therein might not benefit from the associated role of remittances as a source of external resources, in a continent that is heavily reliant on external debt.

These results support the call by the United Nations to keep costs of remitting funds as low as possible. The negative relationship established in our results is a long-run effect, implying that not only do the high costs of remitting affect the volume of funds remitted, but that households focus primarily on immediate consumption and forgo investments that would contribute to better welfare in the future.

Notes

1 See https://unstats.un.org/sdgs/report/2018.
2 South Africa also sends to four countries in the rest of Africa but data for these countries was not complete for the period 2011–2018. Subsequently they were dropped from the analysis.
3 For more on the data see https://remittanceprices.worldbank.org/en.

References

Adams, R. H., & Cuecuecha, A. (2010). Remittances, household expenditure and investment in Guatemala. *World Development*, 38(11), 1626–1641. https://doi.org/10.1016/j.worlddev.2010.03.003.

Akobeng, E. (2016). Out of inequality and poverty : Evidence for the effectiveness of remittances in Sub-Saharan Africa. *Quarterly Review of Economics and Finance*, 60, 207–223. https://doi.org/10.1016/j.qref.2015.10.008.

Anyanwu, J. C., & Erhijakpor, A. E. O. (2010). Do international remittances affect poverty in Africa? *African Development Review*, 22(1), 51–91.

Arellano, M., & Bond, S. (1991). Some tests of specification for panel data: Monte Carlo evidence and an application to employment equations. *Review of Economic Studies*, 58, 277–297.

Aziakpono, M. (2005). Financial development and economic growth in Southern Africa. In *Reducing capital cost in southern Africa*, pp. 137–167. OECD Publishing, Paris.

Ball, C. P., Lopez, C., & Reyes, J. (2013). Remittances, inflation and exchange rate regimes in small open economies. *The World Economy*, 36(4), 487–508. https://doi.org/10.1111/twec.12042.

Barajas, A., Chami, R., Fullenkamp, C., Gapen, M., & Montiel, P. (2009). Do workers' remittances promote economic growth? International Monetary Fund Working Paper WP/09/153, Washington, DC.

Beck, T., & Soledad Martinez Peria, M. (2009). What explains the cost of remittances? An examination across 119 country corridors. World Bank Policy Research Working Paper 5072, World Bank group, Washington, DC.

Bettin, G., Presbitero, A. F., & Spatafora, N. (2014). *Remittances and vulnerability in developing countries*. International Monetary Fund, Washington, DC.

Beyene, B. M. (2014). The effects of international remittances on poverty and inequality in Ethiopia. *The Journal of Development Studies*, 50(10), 1380–1396. https://doi.org/10.1080/00220388.2014.940913.

Cecchetti, S G and K L Schoenholtz (2018), "The stubbonly high cost of remittances" voxeu.org, 27 March https://voxeu.org/article/stubbornly-high-cost-remittances

Chami, R., Barajas, T., Fullenkamp, C., Gapen, M., & Montiel, P. (2008). Macroeconomics consequences of remittances. International Monetary Fund Occasional Paper 259, Washington, DC.

Clemens, M. A., & Mckenzie, D. (2018). Why don't remittances appear to affect growth. *The Economic Journal*, 128, 179–209. https://doi.org/10.1111/ecoj.12463.

Corden, M., & Neary, P. (1982). Booming sector and de-industrialization in a small open economy. *The Economic Journal*, 92(825), 848.

Cuong, N. V., & Linh, V. H. (2018). The impact of migration and remittances on household welfare: Evidence from Vietnam. *Journal of International Migration and Integration*. 19(4), 945–963.

Fayissa, B., & Nsiah, C. (2010). The impact of remittances on economic growth and development in Africa. *The American Economist*, 55(2), 92–103.

Giuliano, P., & Ruiz-arranz, M. (2009). Remittances, financial development, and growth. *Journal of Development Economics*, 90(1), 144–152. https://doi.org/10.1016/j.jdeveco.2008.10.005.

Ebeke, C. H., & Le Goff, M. (2011). Why migrants' remittances reduce income inequality in some countries and not in others? CERDI Working Papers halshs-00554277, HAL.

Eurostat. (1999). *Handbook on quarterly national accounts*. European Commission, Luxembourg.

Gupta, S., Pattillo, C. & Wagh, S. (2009). Effect of Remittances on Poverty and Financial Development in Sub-Saharan Africa. *World Development*, 37(1), 104–115

Jayachandran, S., & Lleras-Muney, A. (2009). Life expectancy and human capital investments: Evidence from maternal mortality declines. *Quarterly Journal of Economics*, 124(1), 349–397.

Kedir, A., & Ibrahim, G. (2011). The role of loans and remittances in consumption and investment decisions in Urban Ethiopia. United Nations Economic Commission for Africa, https://www.uneca.org/sites/default/files/uploaded-documents/AEC/2011/kedir_and_ibrahim-the_role_of_loans_and_remittances_in_consumption_and_investment_decisions_in_urban_ethiopia_0.pdf.

Lopez-Cordova, J. (2005). Globalization, migration, and development: The role of Mexican migrant remittances. *Economia*, 6(1), 217–256.

Lu, Y. (2011). Migration, remittances and educational stratification among blacks in Apartheid and post-Apartheid South Africa. *Social Forces*, 89(4), 1119–1144.

Mabrouk, F. M. & Mekni, M. M. (2018). Remittances and food security in African countries: Remittances and food security. *African Development Review*, 30(3), 252–263.

Munyengera, G. K. & Matumoto, T. (2016). Mobile money, remittances, and household welfare: Panel evidence from rural Uganda. *World Development*, 79, 127–137.

Ojapinwa, T. V., & Nwokoma, N. I. Ã. (2018). Workers' remittances and the Dutch-disease argument : Investigating the relationship in Sub-Saharan Africa. *African Development Review,* 30(3), 316–324.

Page, P., & Plaza, S. (2005). Migration remittances and development: A review of global evidence. A World Bank paper presented at the African Economic Research Consortium Plenary Session Proceedings, August 2005.

Portes, L. S. V. (2009). Remittance, poverty and inequality. *Journal of Economic Development,* 34(1), 127–140.

Remittance Prices Worldwide Report (2017), Issue 12. World Bank Group, Washington, DC.

Sbia, R., Shahbaz, M., & Hamdi, H. (2014). A contribution of foreign direct investment, clean energy, trade openness, carbon emissions and economic growth to energy demand in UAE. *Economic Modelling,* 36, 191–197.

Singh, R.J., Haacker, M., Lee, K.W. & Le Goff, M. (2010). Determinants and macroeconomic impact of remittances in Sub-Saharan Africa. *Journal of African Economies,* 20, 312–340

Truen, S., Kgaphola, K. & Mokoena, M. (2016). Updating the South Africa–SADC remittance channel estimates. FinMark Trust Report.

World Bank. (2006). Global economic prospects 2006: Economic implications of remittances and migration. Washington, DC.

———. (2019). https://blogs.worldbank.org/peoplemove/data-release-remittances-low-and-middle-income-countries-track-reach-551-billion-2019.

Wouterse, F. (2010). Remittances, poverty, inequality and welfare : Evidence from the Central Plateau of Burkina Faso. *The Journal of Development Studies,* 46(4), 1743–9140. https://doi.org/10.1080/00220380903019461.

Yang, D., & Choi, H. (2007). Are remittances insurance? Evidence from rainfall shocks in the Philippines. *World Bank Economic Review,* 21(2), 219–248.

Zhunio, M., Vishwarao, S., & Chiang, E. P. (2012). The influence of remittances on education and health outcomes: A cross-country study. *Journal of Applied Economics,* 44(35), 4605–4616. https://www.tandfonline.com/doi/full/10.1080/00036846.2011.593499.

Part II

Migration, education, and knowledge in Africa

6 Migration, remittances, and child education in Ghana

Evidence from a longitudinal study

Victor Cebotari

Introduction

According to official statistics, there were 417,000 international Ghanaian migrants in 2017 (United Nations. Department of Economic and Social Affairs. Population Division, 2017). Some sources, however, put the number of Ghanaians residing abroad at 1.5 million (Government of Ghana, 2016). Within the country, an estimated eight million Ghanaians have migrated internally, from rural to urban areas in the past two decades (Molini & Paci, 2015). These migrants contribute vital financial resources to their families and the country's economy. In Sub-Saharan Africa, Ghana is second only to Nigeria in the amount of remittances received from nationals working abroad. Specifically, in 2018, the inflow of Ghanaian remittances accounted for US$3.8 billion, up from US$136 million in 2010. The remitting inflow of 2018 represents 7.4% of Ghana's Gross Domestic Product (GDP) (World Bank, 2018). The size and scale of in-kind remittances are unknown, largely due to informality and the undeclared status of these flows.

Many Ghanaian migrants are parents who migrate internally or internationally to provide better opportunities for their children and other family members who often stay behind. Nationwide, about 37% of all Ghanaian children, excluding orphans, have at least one biological parent away, although the parent-child separation is not always due to migration (Ghana Statistical Service-Ghana Health Service and ICF International, 2014). Monetary and in-kind remittances sent back by migrant parents are used to pay for school fees, books, and other educational necessities, thus creating an assumption that children are the net beneficiaries of migration (Bredl, 2010). Under these circumstances, a body of literature on parental migration, remittances, and educational outcomes of children is burgeoning (Acosta, 2011; Antman, 2012; Cebotari, 2018; Cebotari & Mazzucato, 2016; Cortes, 2015; Kroeger & Anderson, 2014).

Through detailed case studies, these studies inform theoretical and empirical evidence on the educational outcomes of children when parents migrate and remit. The evidence shows that parental migration often results in income gains with subsequent benefits for children's education (Antman, 2012;

Cebotari, 2018; Edwards & Ureta, 2003; Kandel & Kao, 2001). Children seem to benefit more when remittances are invested in better schools, educational material, and learning support (Rapoport & Docquier, 2006). These investments, however, may be constrained when parents send no or scarce remittances and when remittances are not invested in children's education (Cebotari, Siegel, & Mazzucato, 2016; Cortes, 2015; Kroeger & Anderson, 2014).

This study builds on existing gaps and intends to make novel contributions in several ways. First, the analysis adds a holistic perspective on migration by simultaneously looking at both internal and international parental migration and the different types of remittances. The literature on parental migration and remittances has predominately looked at international remitting channels, with few studies looking at remittances from internal migration but not necessarily linked to child education (see for instance Ackah & Medvedev, 2012; Molini, Pavelesku, & Ranzani, 2016). We know from recent longitudinal findings in Ghana that parents frequently change their migration status, shifting between being an internal, international, or non-migrant over the years, and it is rather common for children to simultaneously have one parent away internally while the other parent is away internationally (Cebotari, Mazzucato, & Appiah, 2018). There is a gap in the literature on transnational families on how internal and international remittances associate with children's education.

Second, this study includes measurements of both monetary and in-kind remittances. The literature almost exclusively looks at the effects of monetary flows in relation to children's education. Only a handful of studies have used evidence of non-monetary remittances when measuring child education (Cebotari, 2018; Cebotari et al., 2016; Kroeger & Anderson, 2014). This gap in evidence hinders our understanding of whether the effects of remittances on education is entirely due to monetary investments in children.

Third, data used in this study employs child reports for measuring migration, remittances, and education outcomes. Existing studies rely almost exclusively on adult reports to advance empirical and theoretical evidence on child well-being. Recent studies show that children assess and report their educational outcomes differently from adults (Cebotari et al., 2016; Jordan & Graham, 2012).

Finally, this is the first study to employ longitudinal evidence to look at monetary and in-kind remittances and to assess their effects on child education in an African context. Transnational characteristics are dynamic events, and, for the most part, existing studies rely on snapshot data to advance the knowledge on children in transnational care (although see Cebotari et al., 2018; Gatskova, Ivlevs, & Dietz, 2017; Jampaklay, 2006; Nobles, 2011).

This study includes a sample of children aged between 12 and 21 years. The age range reflects the distribution of children in classrooms in the surveyed schools. The term 'children' is therefore used to reflect the relationship pupils have with migrant parents. In the following, I discuss the transnational dynamics and how they associate with child education.

Background

Migration, remittances, and child education

Time and money are two channels through which parents invest resources in their children (Thomson, Hanson, & McLanahan, 1994). Along these lines, there are benefits and risks for children when parents migrate. According to the household strategy theory, parental migration aims to maximize the well-being of children and other family members who stay behind (Stark & Bloom, 1985). Migrant parents enhance the economic welfare of their family by regularly sending remittances. The monetary and in-kind resources improve the socioeconomic status and well-being of children by facilitating investments and their upward social mobility. In Mexico, research shows that children in migrant households are economically better than children in non-migrant households (Morooka & Liang, 2009). Furthermore, evidence from China shows that children in migrant families with a better socioeconomic status have better educational outcomes (Wen & Lin, 2012). In many countries, parental migration was found to boost educational expenditures, with positive effects on children's school attainment, performance, educational aspirations, and school enjoyment (Antman, 2012; Cebotari, 2018; Cebotari & Mazzucato, 2016; Edwards & Ureta, 2003; Kandel & Kao, 2001). It is likely that the effects of remittances on child education depend on the capacity and willingness of families to invest in children's schooling and to mitigate the household constraints that keep children away from school (Brown & Poirine, 2005; Cebotari et al., 2016).

The specific effects of monetary and in-kind remittances on child education are not always straightforward in the literature. Typically, monetary remittances are received by children's caregivers, who use those resources to pay for school expenses but also for a variety of household goods and services (Poeze, 2018). At the same time, in-kind remittances contribute to the commodification of love, in that gifts and material goods attempt to recreate the emotional intimacy and parental care from a distance (Coe, 2011; Parreñas, 2001). The flow of in-kind remittances may be an imperfect replacement of parental care but in practice, intimate connections and child education are deeply intertwined. Empirical studies show that children who have a good quality relationship with their migrant parents have better grades and enjoy school more (Cebotari et al., 2018; Cebotari & Mazzucato, 2016; Jordan & Graham, 2012). Similarly, children whose caregivers are happier are more likely to report an above-average ranking in their class when living transnationally (Cebotari et al., 2016). However, the access to remittances can be a source of conflict between migrant parents and children's caregivers and may affect investments in children, including in education (Poeze, 2018).

Despite the evidence on the effects of remittances on child education, questions remain about whether parental migration and its remitting potential are indeed a successful strategy to improve the well-being of children

(Adams & Page, 2005). A consequence of parental migration is parental absence, which often has emotional costs for the children (Jordan & Graham, 2012; Mazzucato & Cebotari, 2016). According to the attachment theory (Bowlby, 1958), a child's meaningful development relates to the proximity, stability, and long-term attachment with a caregiver. Indeed, parental absence can be injurious to the education of a child due to lessened parental support and guidance during school cycles. These effects are normally independent from the remitting potential of migrant parents. In the Philippines, evidence shows that children in transnational care tend to lag behind in schools when controls for remittances are applied (Cortes, 2015).

For the most part, transnational family studies look at international migration. A large body of research has been conducted in the context of China and looks at internal migration, albeit over large distances (Hu, 2012; Wen & Lin, 2012). To date, the effects of internal *versus* international migration on children's education have not been well examined. One of the few studies that looked at the effects of internal and international parental migration in Mexico and Indonesia found that international migration is more detrimental to children's school attendance than internal migration (Lu, 2014). In Ghana, Cebotari and Mazzucato (2016) found similar patterns in the fact that the school performance of children whose parents migrated internationally was lower compared to that of children whose parents migrated internally. This evidence suggests that internal and international parental migration may have different effects on children. Internal parental migration implies a closer geographical proximity and less administrative and financial difficulties for parents and children to see each other on a regular basis. At the same time, international migration allows for a greater earning potential compared to internal migration, which may directly influence investments in children's education (Cebotari et al., 2016; Lu, 2014). However, international migration brings in higher expectations of reunification and material benefits among children, which may lead to feelings of abandonment and distress when these expectations are not met (Parreñas, 2005; Wu & Cebotari, 2018). The difficult situation that many parents encounter at their destinations may add to these difficulties and may affect children's well-being more negatively (Poeze, 2018).

The evidence from the literature suggests that the relationship between parental migration and child education is also gendered. The dominant narrative is one in which girls are more disadvantaged, compared to boys, when investments are made in domains of well-being such as education. In Ghana, evidence shows that girls are more likely than boys to compensate for shortages in household labor, and they change residences more often when parents migrate (Whitehead, Hashim, & Iversen, 2007). Furthermore, Ghanaian girls are more at risk to have poorer well-being outcomes, including education, when parents migrate internally or internationally (Cebotari et al., 2018). In other contexts, studies found that parental migration does not necessarily affect the education of girls more negatively. For instance, in Mexico and

El Salvador, parental migration associates positively with girls' school attainment (Acosta, 2011; Antman, 2012), while in Tajikistan it associates with girls' normal school progress (Cebotari, 2018).

In this study, the normative context of family functioning is also important to be considered. In Ghana, it is common for many children to live in the care of someone other than their biological parents. When parents migrate, leaving children behind in the care of a trusted family or non-family member is often a preferred choice. When living in foster care, Ghanaian children were found to accommodate well to the new families and they build harmonious relationships with their caregivers (Poeze, 2018). Many schools in Ghana also feature a high-quality boarding service and migrant parents, at times, use these facilities for their children who stay behind (Bledsoe & Sow, 2011).

Drawing on the above-mentioned literature, this study investigates different transnational family configurations that take into account the diversity of internal and international parental migration and their remitting patterns in relation to children education. This evidence and the longitudinal dimension of the analysis provide a more detailed insight into the measures being analyzed and their time-varying effects.

Method

Data

This study uses panel data collected in 2013, 2014, and 2015 among children and youths aged 12–21, in Kumasi and Sunyani, two urban areas with high out-migration rates in Ghana. A national data sampling strategy was not considered due to urban clustering of high out-migration patterns in the country.

Following a stratified sampling procedure, eight low- and high-quality public and private junior high schools (JHS) and senior high schools (SHS) were selected in the two urban locations. The Ministry of Education in Ghana provides annual rankings of public and private schools based on their enrollment rates and final exam performance. A random list generator was employed to select an equal number of JHS and SHS, public and private, and low- and high-quality schools in the two urban locations. Selected schools were approached and asked to participate, all of which agreed to take part in the survey. For the first round of the survey, one class from each of the first two grades was randomly selected in each school. In these classes, all children were asked to fill in the questionnaire. In the remaining classes of the first two grades, a purposive sampling was applied to select a sufficient number of children with internal and international migrant parents. Children of migrants were purposively oversampled to allow for a sufficient number of children in transnational care to fulfill the study's objective of comparing children with a migrant and non-migrant background. All these children were subsequently followed in the next rounds of the survey, ensuring that they have at least two years of participation in the panel.

During data collection, children were informed of the study's purpose and of the voluntary nature of their participation. The questionnaire was administered in English and filled in by students themselves under the guidance of the surveying team. The same team composed of five trained data collection specialists collected the three rounds of data. In JHS, the survival rates of panel children were 83% in the second round and 96% in the third round. Similarly, the survival rates of SHS panel children were 82% and 85% in rounds two and three, respectively. Main reasons for panel attrition were school dropout and children changing schools.

In total, 985 unique respondents were sampled at the start of the survey, of which 405 filled in the questionnaire twice, while 350 completed the full panel. The analysis retained only children who had participated in the survey at least twice.

The data have been collected as part of a study on the Effects of Transnational Child Raising Arrangements on Life-chances of Children, Migrant Parents and Caregivers between Ghana and the Netherlands (TCRA Ghana), financed by the Dutch Research Council (NWO).

Measures

The study employs two self-reported measures of child education: school enjoyment and rank in class. For school enjoyment, children indicated on a scale from 1 to 5 how they generally enjoy school, with higher scores reflecting better outcomes. For rank in class, students were asked to indicate whether they are among the best students in the class, rank in the middle, or most of the classmates rank better than they do. The self-reported measures of child education have previously been used and validated by research on transnational families (Cebotari et al., 2016, 2018; Cebotari & Mazzucato, 2016; Jordan & Graham, 2012). These studies show that self-reported measures of school enjoyment and school performance capture well variations in the education of children in transnational families and are more precise measurements compared to adult-reports of similar outcomes.

The analysis includes two variables of interest that relate to internal and international parental migration and remittances. The first indicator details the type of parental migration and remittances: non-migrant, parent(s) away internationally and sending monetary remittances, parent(s) away internationally and sending in-kind remittances, parent(s) away internationally and sending both monetary and in-kind remittances, parent(s) away internationally and sending no remittances, parent(s) away internally and sending monetary remittances, parent(s) away internally and sending in-kind remittances, parent(s) away internally and sending both monetary and in-kind remittances, parent(s) away internally and sending no remittances. The second indicator measures in a binary form whether monetary remittances are used for child's education.

The control variables include two individual-level characteristics: child's gender and age in full years. In addition, measurements include family characteristics in binary forms such as the education of the child's caregiver (1 = secondary education or more), the marital status of parents (1 = divorced/ separated), and the stability of a child's care arrangement (1 = child changed caregiver one or more times since the parent has migrated). Another measure looks at the duration of child-parent separation: no separation, separation occurred in the past 12 months, and separation occurred over 13 months ago or more.

The study also employs two socioeconomic indicators of wealth. One indicator is an index of household assets that comprises information on assets such as the ownership of durable goods (house, refrigerator, computer, and means of transportation) and the access to private utilities (toilet and bathing facilities). The second indicator is a binary measure of a child's general living conditions related to other children (1 = better living conditions).

Two additional measures account for the total number of children living with the child, and the number of younger children that live in the household. These indicators include both biological and non-biological siblings who currently live with the child.

Finally, a binary family process variable was included to measure the quality of the child-caregiver relationship, where 1 indicates a distant relationship (Cebotari et al., 2018; Jordan & Graham, 2012). The child's main caregiver may be a parent, a family, or a non-family member.

Interaction terms were included to examine the moderating effects between gender and main variables of interest. The interactions were used to observe whether there are gender-specific variations according to specifics of migration in the sample and over years.

Analysis

The analysis employs a fixed effects modeling strategy, which accounts for time-invariant characteristics and time events that may influence both child education and parental migration. The fixed effects approach allows estimating the effects of change in different forms of parental migration and remittances in relation to children's education over time. Considering the time-varying component of fixed effects modeling, the measures employed in this study are those that change over time, except for gender of the child, which is retained in the analysis as part of the interaction terms.

The models included clusters of variables in a step-wise fashion to observe the progressive effects of indicators on child education outcomes. For brevity, only the full models are presented and discussed, but the step-wise regressions are available upon request. Similarly, the full models only display interaction terms with significant coefficients. In the analysis, robust standard errors were estimated and corrected for clustering of observations at individual level. Indicators were tested for collinearity and none was observed.

Results

The descriptive overview of indicators employed in this study is presented in Table 6.1. The average school enjoyment value in the sample and over years is 3.9, on a scale from 1 to 5. It reflects overall positive values of school enjoyment among the sampled population. Similarly, 40% of all children self-ranked themselves as being among the best students in the class. At the same time, 57% of children mentioned that they rank in the middle, with a small proportion of them reporting below-average ranking (3.4%).

Within the sampled population, 53% of children had at least one internal or international migrant parent over the years. A large majority of these parents sent monetary or in-kind remittances. Of those children whose parents

Table 6.1 Means/percentages (standard deviations) of dependent and independent variables

Variables	Full panel sample	
	%/mean (SD)	N
School enjoyment	3.94 (0.95)	1,717
Rank in class	100	1,717
Most of classmates rank better than me	3.44	59
I rank in the middle	56.61	972
I am among the best students in class	39.95	688
Parental migration and remittances	100	1,717
Both parents resident, non-migrant	46.88	805
Parent(s) away internationally: monetary remittances only	2.74	47
Parent(s) away internationally: in-kind remittances only	0.64	11
Parent(s) away internationally: monetary & in-kind remittances	16.25	279
Parent(s) away internationally: no remittances	3.03	52
Parent(s) away internally: monetary remittances only	4.25	73
Parent(s) away internally: in-kind remittances only	1.63	28
Parent(s) away internally: monetary & in-kind remittances	11.24	193
Parent(s) away internally: no remittances	13.34	229
Remittances used for child's education	28.01	481
Child is girl	47.87	822
Child age (years)	15.58 (1.98)	1717
Caregiver's education secondary or more	44.44	763
Duration of separation: none	50.2	862
Duration of separation: ≤ 12 months	25.63	440
Duration of separation: 13 ≥ months	24.17	415
Parents divorced/separated	29.94	514
Child changed caregiver ≥ 1	29.18	501
Living conditions are better when compared to other children	49.56	851
Household asset index	3.69 (1.51)	1,717
Total number of children living with the child	2.97 (2.08)	1,717
Total number of younger children living with the child	1.4 (1.35)	1,717
Distant relationship with the caregiver	18.81	323

Notes: Standard deviations in parentheses.

sent remittances, the greatest proportion were receiving both monetary and in-kind remittances. Children with parents away internally or internationally who received only monetary remittances accounted for 4% and 3%, respectively. A smaller proportion of children whose parents migrated internally or internationally received in-kind remittances only (2% and 1%, respectively). Overall, more children with internal migrant parents did not receive any remittances compared to children whose parents migrated abroad (13% and 3%, respectively). In the sampled population of children, 28% received monetary remittances who were spent on education.

In the data, 48% of all respondents were female. The average age of children in the sample was 15.5 (SD = 1.98). Of all children, 44% had a caregiver who have completed secondary education or more. The proportion of children who have been separated from their migrant parents for less than a year accounted for 26%. At the same time, 24% of children have been separated from their parents for a longer period. The stability of care indicator shows that 29% of children changed their caregiver once or more since parents have migrated. A similar proportion of children (30%) had parents who were divorced or separated. In general, children report having good living conditions: approximately half of all children indicated having better living conditions compared to other children. Furthermore, the average value in the asset index was 3.7 (SD = 1.51), on an asset scale from 1 to 6. Furthermore, children reported living with up to three other children at home and indicated having, on average, 1.4 (SD = 1.35) younger children in the residence. Finally, most children reported a good relationship with their caregiver at home.

To understand how the dynamics of migration and remittances unfold, it is important to observe the change in these dynamics over years. Table 6.2 presents the transition rates of internal and international parental migration as per types of remittances. Data on transition rates revealed changes in parental migration status as well as in the remitting behavior. In the observed period, 87% of children in non-migrant families remained so. Of those children who transitioned from having a non-migrant parent to a migrant parent (23%), more children had parents who migrated internally than internationally. Similarly, when children transitioned from having a parent migrant to living with both parents, more did so who had a parent away internally than internationally.

Of all children with internal and international migrant parents who received only monetary remittances, 26% and 38%, respectively, kept receiving so. When changes in the monetary remittances occurred, most transitions were made toward receiving both in-kind and monetary remittances, and to no remittances. Notably, transition rates from monetary remittances only to in-kind remittances only are insignificant or nonexistent for both internal and international parental migration.

Overall, the least preferred remitting channel over years is for international migrant parents to send only in-kind remittances: all these parents transitioned to sending either both in-kind and monetary remittances (75%)

Table 6.2 Transition rates for parental migration and remittances in the panel years (2013 to 2015)

Parental migration and remittances	Both parents resident, non-migrant	Parent(s) away internationally: monetary remittances only	Parent(s) away internationally: in-kind remittances only	Parent(s) away internationally: monetary & in-kind remittances	Parent(s) away internationally: no remittances	Parent(s) away internally: monetary remittances only	Parent(s) away internally: in-kind remittances only	Parent(s) away internally: monetary & in-kind remittances	Parent(s) away internally: no remittances	Total	N
Both parents resident, non-migrant	86.78	0.21	0	1.71	0.64	1.28	0.21	3.84	5.33	100	805
Parent(s) away internationally: monetary remittances only	8.33	37.50	0	20.73	20.94	8.33	0	0	4.17	100	47
Parent(s) away internationally: in-kind remittances only	0	0	0	75	25	0	0	0	0	100	11
Parent(s) away internationally: monetary & in-kind remittances	7.73	7.18	1.10	68.51	6.08	0	0.55	4.42	4.42	100	279
Parent(s) away internationally: no remittances	12.90	12.90	12.90	22.58	29.03	0	0	3.23	6.45	100	52

Parent(s) away internally: monetary remittances only	12.77	2.13	0	2.13	0	25.53	2.13	31.91	23.40	100	73
Parent(s) away internally: in-kind remittances only	5.88	0	0	0	5.88	0	23.53	23.53	41.18	100	28
Parent(s) away internally: monetary & in-kind remittances	18.02	0	0.90	5.41	0.90	11.71	4.50	42.34	16.22	100	193
Parent(s) away internally: no remittances	15	0.83	0	0	2.50	5.83	2.50	16.67	56.67	100	229

Note: The changes in panel years are reflected in the rows.

or no remittances (25%). The stronger remitting channel over years for both internal and international migrant parents is represented by the ability to send both in-kind and monetary remittances. From one year to another, 42% of internal migrants and 69% of international migrants who were sending both types of remittances kept sending so. At the same time, a relatively high proportion of internal and international migrant parents have not been sending any types of remittances over the years. Children whose internal and international migrant parents did not send any remittances accounted for 57% and 29%, respectively. These data illustrate that remittances and parental migration are dynamic processes. The time-varying patterns of migration and remittances give a greater weight to the need to conduct a longitudinal analysis in the context of this study.

The results of transition rates revealed interesting patterns on how parental migration and the types of remittances unfold over time for children living transnationally. In the next stage of analysis, multivariate models are employed to observe the time-varying effects of migration and remittances on education outcomes. Table 6.3 displays the full fixed effects models for parental migration and the types of remittances in relation to school enjoyment and class ranking.

When parental migration and types of remittances were considered (Table 6.3), children with parents away internationally and receiving both in-kind and monetary remittances were more likely to have higher levels of school enjoyment and class ranking as compared with children in non-migrant families ($\beta = 0.50$ and $\beta = 0.04$, respectively). Furthermore, results show that children were more likely to report a lower rank in class when parents were away internationally and did not send remittances, as compared to children living with both parents ($\beta = -0.04$). In addition, children of internal migrant parents who received in-kind remittances only, or both types of remittances, were more likely to have higher levels of school enjoyment ($\beta = 0.57$ and $\beta = 0.53$, respectively) than children in non-migrant families. Net of other factors, the estimated coefficients for international migration (monetary remittances only, and in-kind remittances only) and internal migration (monetary remittances only, and no remittances) were not statistically significant in relation to both educational outcomes.

When measuring the migration and remittances effects, significant interaction terms were found between these characteristics and child gender. Specifically, interaction effects revealed that girls were less likely to report a higher class ranking when parents were away internally and were not sending remittances (β of the interaction term $= -0.02$). Furthermore, being a girl reduced the overall positive effect on school enjoyment when there was an internal migrant parent who sent only in-kind remittances (β of the interaction term $= -0.21$).

When controlling for the use of remittances, results show that a monetary investment in children's education is a likely predictor for a better class ranking. However, this effect was not replicated for school enjoyment.

Table 6.3 Internal and international parental migration, monetary and in-kind remittances, and educational outcomes – fully adjusted models

	School enjoyment		Rank in class	
	Model 1		Model 2	
	β	SE	B	SE
Parental migration status				
Both parents resident, non-migrant	.	.	.	.
Parent(s) away internationally: monetary remittances only	0.22	(0.24)	0.18	(0.14)
Parent(s) away internationally: in-kind remittances only	−0.09	(0.33)	−0.03	(0.19)
Parent(s) away internationally: monetary & in-kind remittances	0.50★★	(0.22)	0.04★	(0.03)
Parent(s) away internationally: no remittances	−0.02	(0.19)	−0.04★★	(0.10)
Parent(s) away internally: monetary remittances only	0.31	(0.23)	−0.03	(0.12)
Parent(s) away internally: in-kind remittances only	0.57★★	(0.22)	0.08	(0.14)
Parent(s) away internally: monetary & in-kind remittances	0.53★	(0.21)	0.08	(0.11)
Parent(s) away internally: no remittances	0.39	(0.16)	0.12	(0.10)
Remittances used for child's education	0.02	(0.11)	0.09★★	(0.04)
Child is girl	0.43	(0.30)	0.03	(0.09)
Child age (years)	0.11★	(0.05)	0.01	(0.02)
Caregiver's education secondary or more	−0.04	(0.09)	0.04	(0.04)
Duration of separation: none	.	.	.	.
Duration of separation: ≤ 12 months	−0.46★★	(0.16)	−0.05	(0.09)
Duration of separation: 13 ≥ months	−0.44★★	(0.16)	−0.08★	(0.09)
Parents divorced/separated	−0.07	(0.10)	−0.04	(0.06)
Child changed caregiver ≥ 1	−0.02	(0.09)	0.01	(0.04)
Living conditions are better when compared to other children	0.11	(0.07)	0.05	(0.03)
Household asset index	0.01	(0.03)	0.05★★	(0.01)
Total number of children living with the child	0.01	(0.02)	0.02	(0.01)
Total number of younger children living with the child	−0.00	(0.04)	−0.02	(0.02)
Distant relationship with the caregiver	−0.29★★★	(0.08)	−0.01★	(0.04)
Parent(s) away internally: in-kind remittances only x Female	−0.21★	(0.13)	–	
Parent(s) away internally: no remittances x Female	–		−0.02★	(0.01)
Wave-fixed effects	Yes		Yes	
Child-fixed effects	Yes		Yes	
Unique number of children	713		713	
Total number of observations	1717		1717	
R-squared	0.07		0.05	

Notes: Standard errors in parentheses (adjusted to account for clustering within individuals).
★ p <.05, ★★ p <.01, ★★★ p <.001.

Furthermore, age was a significant predictor and shows that older children are more likely to report better levels of school enjoyment. A longer duration of separation, and especially one that lasted for more than a year, corresponded to a lower likelihood that children will report higher levels of school enjoyment and class ranking. The household asset index was a significant predictor for a higher class ranking but not for school enjoyment. Notable, a distant relationship with the caregiver shows a negative association with both educational outcomes.

Taken together, these results suggest that child education benefits when parents migrate internally or internationally and send a steady inflow of both in-kind and monetary remittances. Furthermore, child education additionally benefits when remittances are invested in child education and when children are older and live in wealthier households. At the same time, there are gender differences in children's education that are dependent on settings that include internal migration and volatile remitting channels.

Discussion

This study is the first to employ longitudinal evidence to comparatively assess the effects of internal and international parental migration and remittances in relation to child education in an African context. For the most part, existing studies rely on snapshot data to inform the evidence-base on African transnational families and child well-being. The panel evidence of this study allows for a higher accuracy when modeling the time-varying effects of migration and child education. The findings add two reflections to current knowledge on the effects of migration and child education. First, internal and international parental migration, and monetary and in-kind remittances, are important differentiating factors as to whether child education benefits or suffers. Second, the gender of the child shows patterns of vulnerability when associated with parental migration, remittances, and education. These findings are discussed below.

This study includes measures of internal and international parental migration and different types of remittances to reflect more accurately the multifaceted nature of how children experience with living transnationally. Whether parents migrate internally or internationally and the type of remittances they send are important differentiating factors for child education. Specifically, children whose parents migrate internally or internationally and receive both monetary and in-kind remittances are more likely to have higher levels of school enjoyment and a better class ranking. When remittances are specifically invested in child education, they are likely to predict a better rank in class. At the same time, the absence of monetary and in-kind remittances is likely to negatively affect the education of children, especially of girls. In Ghana and elsewhere, remittances are seen as vital resources to access quality education and to care for children through school (Cebotari, 2018; Kandel & Kao, 2001; Poeze, 2018). Indeed, remittances are used to pay for a variety of school costs and this investment was found to have positive effects on children's educational outcomes (Antman, 2012; Cebotari et al., 2016; Edwards & Ureta, 2003). Furthermore, in Ghana, education is highly prized, and many parents invest in children's schooling as they expect higher returns later in a child's life (Poeze, 2018).

Findings of this study emphasize the preference of Ghanaian parents toward sending both in-kind and monetary remittances when away internally or internationally. Over years, the remitting flow of many migrant parents converge toward sending both types of remittances. Monetary and in-kind remittances represent an exchange that creates a sense of care and connectivity between children and migrant parents (Coe, 2011). Migrant parents are likely to substitute the proximity of care with money and gifts, thus creating what is described by Parreñas (2001) as the 'commodification of love'. In addition to remittances, migrant parents engage with new media and communication technologies to foster intimate ties and help with childcare from afar (Baldassar, Nedelcu, Merla, & Wilding, 2016; Poeze, 2018). Through these channels, migrant parents stay engaged in the family decision-making, including in decisions related to children's schooling (Cebotari & Mazzucato, 2016; Poeze, 2018).

Importantly however, parental access to financial resources defines the way in which parents can meet children's material needs and invest in their education. Findings of this study show that of all children whose parents migrated internally and internationally, 57% and 29%, respectively, did not receive any remittances over years. The absence of remittances may reflect negatively on children's education, especially on girls, as findings of this study show. The high proportion of parents who did not send remittances may reflect the volatile nature of work and the hardship that many Ghanaian parents face at the destination. When parents migrate, there are expectations of material benefits from children and families who stay behind (Poeze, 2018). The difficult situations that many parents encounter at the destination may lead to unmet expectations and unstable remitting flows, which may affect the well-being of children, including their educational outcomes.

The findings of this study also point to gender differences, in that internal migration is more likely to negatively affect girls' school enjoyment and class ranking when parents send no remittances or in-kind remittances only. These findings may echo the weak earning potential of internal migrants in Ghana compared to those away internationally (Ackah & Medvedev, 2012; Mazzucato, Boom, & Nsowah-Nuamah, 2008). Less remittances influence how investments are made in children, with girls more negatively affected (Cebotari et al., 2018; Lu, 2014). When remittances are scarce, Ghanaian girls are more likely to compensate for labor shortages in the household and they change caregivers more often compared to boys (Whitehead et al., 2007). To the extent that parental migration may exacerbate gender inequalities in transnational families, more research is needed on how migration, remittances, and gender differences interlink in Ghana.

There are several limitations to this study. One limitation is the difficulty to model the internal and international migration and remittances as per which parent has migrated. Due to limited sample size, this distinction could not retain enough observations for a viable modeling. The migrant selectivity is an inherent limitation for studies that employ quantitative data. There are no empirical tools to holistically control for migrant selectivity over time, and the reader needs to be alert of this limitation. The data employed in this study comprise three rounds of observations. Therefore, data capture only short- to medium-effects of migration and remittances on child education. Data also include children who attend school and the results may not be generalizable to the entire population of Ghanaian children.

Despite these limitations, this study adds a longitudinal perspective on the effects of parental migration, remittances, and child education in an African context. It does so by employing child reports to measure associations of interest. This is a novel contribution, in that existing evidence on children in transnational care is preponderantly based on assessments made by adults. To the extent that children's voices must feature more prominently in research on child well-being, this study concludes that parental migration is not necessarily a vulnerability for the education of children in Ghana.

References

Ackah, C., & Medvedev, D. (2012). Internal migration in Ghana: determinants and welfare impacts. *International Journal of Social Economics, 39*(10), 764–784. doi:10.1108/03068291211253386.

Acosta, P. (2011). School attendance, child labour, and remittances from international migration in El Salvador. *The Journal of Development Studies, 47*(6), 913–936. doi:10.1080/00220388.2011.563298.

Adams, R. H., & Page, J. (2005). Do international migration and remittances reduce poverty in developing countries? *World Development, 33*(10), 1645–1669. doi:10.1016/j.worlddev.2005.05.004.

Antman, F. M. (2012). Gender, educational attainment and the impact of parental migration on children left behind. *Journal of Population Economics, 25*(4), 1187–1214. doi:10.1007%2Fs00148-012-0423-y.

Baldassar, L., Nedelcu, M., Merla, L., & Wilding, R. (2016). ICT-based co-presence in transnational families and communities: challenging the premise of face-to-face proximity in sustaining relationships. *Global Networks, 16*(2), 133–144. doi:10.1111/glob.12108.

Bledsoe, C., & Sow, P. (2011). Back to Africa: second chances for the children of west African immigrants. *Journal of Marriage and Family, 73*, 747–762. doi:10.1111/j.1741-3737.2011.00843.x.

Bowlby, J. (1958). The nature of the child's tie to the mother. *International Journal of Psycho-Analysis, 39*(5), 350–373.

Bredl, S. (2010). Migration, remittances and educational outcomes: the case of Haiti. *International Journal of Educational Development, 31*(2), 162–168. doi:10.1016/j.ijedudev.2010.02.003.

Brown, R., & Poirine, B. (2005). A model of migrants' remittances with human capital investment and intrafamilial transfers. *International Migration Review, 39*(2), 407–438. doi:10.1111/j.1747-7379.2005.tb00272.x.

Cebotari, V. (2018). Transnational migration, gender and educational development of children in Tajikistan. *Global Networks, 18*(4), 564–588. doi:10.1111/glob.12193.

Cebotari, V., & Mazzucato, V. (2016). Educational performance of children of migrant parents in Ghana, Nigeria and Angola. *Journal of Ethnic and Migration Studies, 42*(5), 834–856. doi:10.1080/1369183X.2015.1125777.

Cebotari, V., Mazzucato, V., & Appiah, E. (2018). A longitudinal analysis of well-being of Ghanaian children in transnational families. *Child Development, 89*(5), 1168–1785. doi:10.1111/cdev.12879.

Cebotari, V., Siegel, M., & Mazzucato, V. (2016). Migration and the education of children who stay behind in Moldova and Georgia. *International Journal of Educational Development, 51*(November), 96–107. doi:10.1016/j.ijedudev.2016.09.002.

Coe, C. (2011). What is love? The materiality of care in Ghanaian transnational families. *International Migration, 49*(6), 7–24. doi:10.1111/j.1468-2435.2011.00704.x.

Cortes, P. (2015). The feminization of international migration and its effects on the children left behind: evidence from the Philippines. *World Development, 65*(January), 62–78. doi:10.1016/j.worlddev.2013.10.021.

Edwards, A., & Ureta, M. (2003). International migration, remittances, and schooling: evidence from El Salvador. *Journal of Development Economics, 72*(2), 429–461. doi:10.1016/S0304-3878(03)00115-9.

Gatskova, K., Ivlevs, A., & Dietz, B. (2017). Does migration affect education of girls and young women in Tajikistan?. *WIDER Working Paper 2017/104*, 47. Retrieved from https://www.wider.unu.edu/sites/default/files/wp2017-104.pdf.

Ghana Statistical Service-Ghana Health Service and ICF International. (2014). *Ghana Demographic and Health Survey 2014*. Retrieved from http://www.dhsprogram.com/.

Government of Ghana. (2016). *National migration policy for Ghana*. Retrieved from Accra: http://migratingoutofpoverty.dfid.gov.uk/files/file.php?name=national-migration-policy-for-ghana.pdf&site=354.

Hu, F. (2012). Migration, remittances, and children's high school attendance: the case of rural China. *International Journal of Educational Development, 32*(2), 401–411. doi:10.1016/j.ijedudev.2011.08.001.

Jampaklay, A. (2006). Parental absence and children's school enrolment. Evidence from a longitudinal study in Kanchanaburi, Thailand. *Asian Population Studies, 2*(1), 93–110. doi:10.1080/17441730600700598.

Jordan, L. P., & Graham, E. (2012). Resilience and well-being among children of migrant parents in South-East Asia. *Child Development, 83*(5), 1672–1688. doi:10.1111/j.1467-8624.2012.01810.x.

Kandel, W., & Kao, G. (2001). The impact of temporary labor migration on Mexican children's educational aspirations and performance. *International Migration Review, 35*(4), 1205–1231. doi: 10.1111/j.1747-7379.2001.tb00058.x.

Kroeger, A., & Anderson, K. H. (2014). Remittances and the human capital of children: new evidence from Kyrgyzstan during revolution and financial crisis, 2005–2009. *Journal of Comparative Economics, 42*(3), 770–785. doi:10.1016/j.jce.2013.06.001.

Lu, Y. (2014). Parental migration and education of left-behind children: a comparison of two settings. *Journal of Marriage and Family, 76*(5), 1082–1098. doi:10.1111/jomf.12139.

Mazzucato, V., Boom, B. v. d., & Nsowah-Nuamah, N. N. N. (2008). Remittances in Ghana: origin, destination and issues of measurement. *International Migration Review, 46*(1), 103–122. doi:10.1111/j.1468-2435.2008.00438.x.

Mazzucato, V., & Cebotari, V. (2016). Psychological well-being of Ghanaian children in transnational families. *Population Space and Place, 23*(3), e2004. doi:10.1002/psp.2004.

Molini, V., & Paci, P. (2015). *Poverty Reduction in Ghana: Progress and Challenges.* Washington, DC. Retrieved from https://openknowledge.worldbank.org/handle/10986/22732.

Molini, V., Pavelesku, D., & Ranzani, M. (2016). Should I Stay or Should I Go? Internal Migration and Household Welfare in Ghana. *Policy Research Working Paper.* Retrieved from http://elibrary.worldbank.org/doi/abs/10.1596/1813-9450-7752. doi:10.1596/1813-9450-7752.

Morooka, H., & Liang, Z. (2009). International migration and the education of left behind children in China. *Asian and Pacific Migration Journal, 18*(3), 345–370.

Nobles, J. (2011). Parenting from abroad: migration, nonresident father involvement, and children's education in Mexico. *Journal of Marriage and Family, 73*(4), 729–746. doi:10.1111/j.1741-3737.2011.00842.x.

Parreñas, R. (2001). Mothering from a distance: emotions, gender, and intergenerational relationships in Filipino transnational families. *Feminist Studies, 27*(2), 361–390. doi:10.2307/3178765.

Parreñas, R. (2005). *Children of global migration: Transnational families and gendered woes.* Stanford, CA: Stanford University Press.

Poeze, M. (2018). *Migration, family separation and caregiving across borders: A multi-sited ethnography of transnational child-raising arrangements between Ghana and The Netherlands.* (PhD), Maastricht University, Maastricht. Retrieved from https://cris.maastrichtuniversity.nl/portal/files/31350116/c6222_embargo_chapter5en7.pdf.

Rapoport, H., & Docquier, F. (2006). The economics of migrants' remittances. In S.-C. Kolm & J. M. Ythier (Eds.), *Handbook of the Economics of Giving, Altruism, and Reciprocity* (Vol. 2, pp. 1135–1198). Amsterdam: Elsevier.

Stark, O., & Bloom, D. E. (1985). The new economics of labour migration. *American Economic Review, 75*(2), 174–178.

Thomson, E., Hanson, T. L., & McLanahan, S. S. (1994). Family structure and child well-being: economic resources vs. parental behaviors. *Social Forces, 1*, 221–242. doi:10.2307/2579924.

United Nations. Department of Economic and Social Affairs. Population Division. (2017). *Trends in International Migrant Stock: The 2017 revision.* Retrieved from https://www.un.org/en/development/desa/population/migration/data/estimates2/estimates17.asp.

Wen, M., & Lin, D. (2012). Child development in rural China: children left behind by their migrant parents and children of nonmigrant families. *Child Development, 83*(1), 120–136. doi:10.1111/j.1467-8624.2011.01698.x.

Whitehead, A., Hashim, I. M., & Iversen, V. (2007). *Child migration, child agency and intergenerational relations in Africa and South Asia.* Development Research Centre on Migration, Globalisation and Poverty. Brighton. Retrieved from http://r4d.dfid.gov.uk/PDF/Outputs/MigrationGlobPov/WP-T24.pdf.

World Bank. (2018). *Migration and remittances. Recent developments and outlook.* Retrieved from https://www.knomad.org/sites/default/files/2018-12/Migration%20and%20Development%20Brief%2030.pdf.

Wu, Q., & Cebotari, V. (2018). Experiences of migration, parent–child interaction, and the life satisfaction of children in Ghana and China. *Population Space and Place, 24*(7), e2160. doi:10.1002/psp.2160.

7 Diaspora knowledge transfer in Sierra Leone and Somaliland

Charlotte Mueller

Introduction

In today's global economy, knowledge is the most important driver of productivity and economic growth, assuring competitiveness and innovation
(Argote & Ingram, 2000; United Nations, 2018). Knowledge is regarded as
an important tool for development (Fagerberg, Srholec, & Verspagen, 2010).
However, a lack of specialized knowledge and skills is a major limitation in
developing country contexts, such as Sierra Leone and Somalia. Sierra Leone's
once striving higher education system was heavily damaged during the country's civil war. While the country has achieved major improvements since,
the higher education sector is unable to meet the great demand for higher
education, with a lack of qualified teaching staff being a serious challenge
(World Bank, 2013; World Bank Group, 2017). Despite major improvements
as well, Somalia remains one of the most fragile states in the world, affected
particularly by attacks by al Shabaab, droughts, and mass displacement. Conflict and fragility have also led to low levels of human capital (The Fund for
Peace, 2019; World Bank Group, 2018).

Diasporas[1] have been increasingly recognized as source of knowledge and
skills that could be used as a tool for development in countries of origin.
Different scholars have demonstrated that migrants and diaspora members
can make important contributions to development in their country of origin through economic, social, and intellectual contributions as well as foster entrepreneurship, innovation, and capacity building (Brinkerhoff, 2016;
Klagge & Klein-Hitpaß, 2010; Levitt, 1998; Levitt & Lamba-Nieves, 2011;
Siar, 2012, 2014; United Nations, 2018). The 2030 Agenda for Sustainable
Development recognizes the positive role migrants can play for sustainable
development in countries of origin, transit, and destination (United Nations
General Assembly, 2015). Despite this recognition, the Agenda sets the main
focus regarding migrants on the need for inclusion, protection, and rights,
portraying migrants as 'beneficiaries of the ends of sustainable development [...] not as [an] agent[s] of the means of sustainable development itself'
(Appave & Sinha, 2017, p. 3). Conversely, existing evidence shows that diasporas can contribute to achieving the Sustainable Development Goals (SDGs)

in their countries of origin through different types of engagement, including knowledge and skills transfer (Appave & Sinha, 2017).

In line with this logic, short-term diaspora return and temporary return programmes emerged in the 1970s as a method to harness this knowledge transfer via the United Nations Development Programme Transfer of Knowledge through Expatriate Nationals. Since this time, several different programmes have emerged for diaspora contributions to development in Africa, most notably the Migration for Development in Africa Programme.[2] Little research, however, has been conducted on the effectiveness of these programmes and the specific modalities that enable diaspora members to achieve successful knowledge transfer that is sustainable over time.

This chapter draws on research conducted within the programme Connecting Diaspora for Development (CD4D), administered by IOM, the Netherlands, from 2016 to 2019. This programme enables Dutch diaspora members to return to their country of origin for approximately three months with the objective of contributing to knowledge transfer and capacity building. The programme has been active in seven countries: Afghanistan, Ethiopia, Ghana, Iraq, Morocco, Sierra Leone, and Somalia. Research has been conducted in all these countries apart from Morocco. In this chapter, I examine how participants in CD4D, who are members of their respective diasporas, transfer both explicit and tacit knowledge to host institutions in their countries of origin. A comparative case analysis is conducted of experiences of CD4D diaspora experts and institutions in the origin countries hosting the diaspora member in Sierra Leone and Somaliland. The cases presented show some of the main forms of knowledge transfer in the CD4D Programme. This study also illustrates that certain factors such as time or type of institution make one knowledge transfer method more suitable than another. It also shows that both explicit and tacit knowledge transfer methods can contribute to individual capacity building and changes at the host institution. While diaspora engagement can contribute to a number of SDGs, depending on the activities diaspora members engage in, two goals and targets are particularly relevant here. First, Goal 4 'Quality Education' and its fourth target regarding the increase in youth and adults who have relevant skills, including technical and vocational skills, for employment, decent jobs, and entrepreneurship. And, second, Goal 9 'Industries, innovation and infrastructure' and its target to support domestic technology development, research, and innovation in developing countries.

The chapter is divided into the following five sections. First, a brief overview of the concepts of diaspora knowledge transfer and capacity building. This is followed by a presentation of the case study and methods. The results are discussed in the third and fourth sections. While the third section focusses on forms of knowledge transfer, the fourth section highlights contributions to the host institutions and to capacity building. In the discussion sections, comparisons are drawn between the cases that elicit understandings of how knowledge can be transferred differently and inferences are drawn regarding the strengths and weaknesses of different forms of knowledge transfer. The final section contains conclusions. The conclusion stresses how diaspora knowledge transfer can be utilized as a mechanism for achieving SDGs.

Diaspora knowledge transfer and capacity building

Diaspora engagement can take a variety of forms, ranging from maintaining contact with family and friends, sending remittances individually or collectively, investments and trade, to volunteerism, skills transfer, and entrepreneurship (Brinkerhoff, 2012; Kuschminder, Sturge, & Ragab, 2014; Newland & Plaza, 2013; Terrazas, 2010). Due to the potential attributed to diaspora members, temporary return programmes have emerged as a means of formalizing diaspora engagement by international organizations. Thereby, temporary return programmes such as CD4D are based on two main assumptions. The first premise is that highly skilled individuals are more likely to leave their country of origin, leading to loss of already scarce human capital for developing countries, also referred to as brain drain (Castles, De Haas, & Miller, 2014; Kuschminder, 2014). By encouraging these emigrants to return temporarily, they may be able to address knowledge gaps and thereby foster individual progress. A second assumption is the ability of diaspora members to make 'diaspora-specific contributions' (Brinkerhoff, 2006, p. 127). Diaspora members are, as they are returning to their country of origin, expected to be familiar with the country's language and culture. Diaspora members are expected to merge values and cultural knowledge from two contexts and easily adapt, interact, and communicate in both. Compared with, for instance, foreign experts, these abilities constitute an operational advantage, also referred to as in-between advantage (Brinkerhoff, 2006, 2016; Kuschminder et al., 2014).

Drawing on existing studies, knowledge transfer will be defined as a multi-stage process of an individual's or group's experiences (here the diaspora expert) affecting another individual or group, in this case staff at the host institutions, also referred to as colleagues (Argote & Ingram, 2000; Bender & Fish, 2000). In contrast to the concept of social remittances, which emphasizes the circularity of knowledge (Levitt, 1998; Levitt & Lamba-Nieves, 2011), knowledge transfer will only be analysed in a unidirectional manner in this chapter as a transfer from the diaspora expert to colleagues as this is the direction defined by the temporary return programme. Yet it should be emphasized that, in practice, knowledge transfer may constitute a multidirectional process, including in this case (Figure 7.1).

Thereby, knowledge refers to 'literally what people know' (UNDP, 2010), including job or sector-specific knowledge, scientific or technical knowledge, communication skills, and cultural and social skills and behaviours. Knowledge is generally divided into explicit and tacit knowledge, a distinction also discussed and applied throughout this chapter. Explicit knowledge

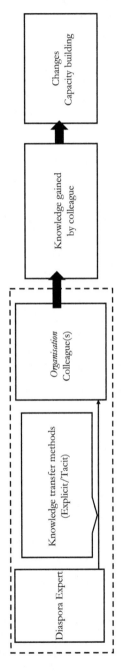

Figure 7.1 Knowledge transfer process. Own elaboration.

is defined as knowledge that may be codified and transmitted through a systematic language. Examples of explicit knowledge include words, sentences, reports, assessments, patents, databases, and computer programmes. Explicit knowledge transfer methods encompass formal trainings, manuals, and up-to-date documentation and memos or guidance notes. Tacit knowledge is defined as knowledge that is difficult to articulate and codify as it is highly personal, context-dependent, and complex. Examples of tacit knowledge may be intuition, leadership, decision making, and language. Best practice meetings, mentoring and coaching, on-the-job training, targeted work assignments, and teamwork encouragement are examples of tacit knowledge transfer methods (Davenport & Prusak, 1998; Fahey & Prusak, 1998; Goh, 2002; Huffman, 2012; Inkpen, 1998; Joia & Lemos, 2010; King, 2009; Kuschminder et al., 2014; Levin & Cross, 2004; Polanyi, 1966). As tacit knowledge transfer is difficult to measure, this study uses an approach previously applied by Kuschminder (2014) which draws on the experiences of CD4D diaspora experts, colleagues, and host institutions to assess knowledge transfer. For the purpose of this study, knowledge transfer is operationalized as 'perceived knowledge transfer', meaning that what is reported as knowledge transfer here are the knowledge senders' and knowledge receivers' perception of what was transferred. Thereby, the diaspora expert's perspective constitutes the knowledge sender perspective, reporting mainly on perceived knowledge transmission, while the colleague's perspective reports perceived knowledge absorption or 'knowledge gained'.

To hold value, transferred knowledge should impact behaviours, policies, processes, and practices within the recipient party, here referred to as 'changes' (Bender & Fish, 2000). Within a temporary return programme knowledge transfer is expected to lead to capacity building which can be defined as:

> Means by which skills, experience, technical and management capacity are developed within an organizational structure (contractors, consultants or contracting agencies) – often through the provision of technical assistance, short/long-term training, and specialist inputs (e.g., computer systems). The process may involve the development of human, material and financial resources).
>
> (OECD, 2002 as cited in Kuschminder, 2014, p. 193)

Case study and methods

As knowledge transfer here is measured in the form of 'perceived knowledge transfer', data used in this chapter was collected through in-depth interviews with staff at CD4D host institutions in Sierra Leone and Somalia in 2017, 2018, and 2019 as well as through interviews with the programme participants, also referred to as CD4D diaspora experts. IOM operates CD4D in Somalia, in Mogadishu and Hargeisa (Somaliland). For logistical reasons, in-country interviews could only be conducted in Somaliland. This chapter therefore focusses only on assignments conducted in Hargeisa. Interviews at host institutions took place at three different points in time to be able to compare between Time 0, 1, and 2 and assess changes that were implemented. The interviews were conducted with staff at higher management level, henceforth referred to as 'managers', and staff who worked with the CD4D diaspora experts at selected host institutions, who will be referred to as 'colleagues' throughout this chapter. Managers were interviewed to gain a broader understanding of the general strengths and challenges of the organization before and during the CD4D Programme, as well as CD4D-specific benefits and challenges as perceived by the respondents. Colleagues were interviewed to understand knowledge transferred from the receiver perspective. Respondents were generally identified and selected by the lead contact (project focal point) at the host institution with guidance from the IOM staff and based on the criteria provided by the researcher.

CD4D diaspora experts were interviewed to understand knowledge transferred from the sender perspective. The participants were generally contacted for an interview after the end of an assignment. Interviews took place via Skype, phone, or in-person in the Netherlands. A few interviews with diaspora experts were also conducted in the assignment countries as participants were still in the country upon the visit of the researcher. Interviews took place on a voluntary basis. The interview guide used in the research evolved through the interview process and focussed on the motivation and pre-assignment experiences with regard to temporary return and knowledge transfer, general assignment information, institutional environment and institution's work culture, knowledge transfer, contributions to change on an organizational level, participant's personal development, and CD4D Programme feedback.

This research, however, is subject to a number of limitations. Two main limitations should be highlighted. First, during the interviews in Somaliland an IOM staff member was present at all times and acted as interpreter whenever necessary. While this served to overcome language barriers to the extent possible, this may have influenced respondents, as IOM is the one operating the programme. In Sierra Leone, an IOM staff member accompanied the researcher to the host institutions; however, the IOM staff member was not present during the interviews. Nonetheless, in both contexts, managers and colleagues at the host institutions overall also voiced critical opinions. Diaspora experts were always interviewed without any IOM staff member present and at a neutral location. Second, this study measures knowledge transfer based on self-reported declarations. Diaspora experts may have an incentive to overreport their achievements as they hope to receive the opportunity to do another assignment. They might also self-select into the interview, as diaspora experts who were less successful with their assignment are probably less eager to be interviewed. However, the researcher interviewed the majority of CD4D diaspora experts in Sierra Leone as well as in Somaliland. Similarly, not all staff members who worked with the diaspora experts were available for an interview.

Using case examples from the CD4D Programme, this chapter aims to illustrate the different forms of knowledge transfer possible within a temporary return programme. For this chapter, two cases were selected. The first case consists of two examples; three examples were chosen for the second case. Each example draws on data from the interviews with diaspora experts, managers, and colleagues. This was complemented with data generated from a questionnaire diaspora experts were asked to complete upon completion of an assignment.

The first case is knowledge transfer at an institute of higher education in Sierra Leone. Higher education has a long tradition in Sierra Leone. Fourah Bay College, now part of the University of Sierra Leone in Freetown, is the oldest higher education institution in West Africa (World Bank, 2013). The progress of Sierra Leone's higher education system since the country's independence in 1961 was affected negatively by one-party politics and structural adjustment programmes in the 1980s. Yet the most significant negative impact was caused by the civil war when higher education institutions became targets of attacks (World Bank, 2013; World Bank Group, 2017). Since the end of the war in 2001, Sierra Leone's higher education sector has been restored and re-organized. With the University of Sierra Leone and Njala University, there are currently two public universities in Sierra Leone. In addition, another 30 higher and tertiary institutions were operating in Sierra Leone in 2011, including one private university, three polytechnics (three public), three teacher training or education colleges (two public, one private), four theological schools or colleges (four private), and eleven technical and professional colleges or institutes (one public, ten private) (World Bank, 2013; World Bank Group, 2017).

The higher education sector in Sierra Leone has seen a sharp increase in enrolments, and there continues to be a high demand for higher education in the country (World Bank, 2013; World Bank Group, 2017). Despite these positive developments, the quality of teaching staff presents a major challenge for higher education institutions in Sierra Leone. Recruitment of sufficiently qualified staff is difficult for institutions. Only 2% of full-time academic staff at the ten core institutions in 2009/2010 were professors or associate professors. Sixty-three per cent held a Master's degree or higher (World Bank, 2013). The lack of qualified staff can be clearly seen in the cases of the CD4D host institutions. Managers described challenges with regard to staff quality and quantity: They reported difficulties to recruit specialized staff with a Master's degree or higher and facing challenges with regard to turnover of staff. Another challenge is a lack of computer skills, for instance, knowledge about how to create a PowerPoint presentation.

The second case is knowledge transfer to human resource (HR) departments at ministries in Somaliland. While Somaliland has managed to gain political stability and establish functioning public institutions since its declaration of independence, Somaliland's population is very young, higher education has only emerged recently, and the self-declared state lacks human capital in several areas (N. M. Ali, 2014; N.-I. Ali, 2016; BBC, 2017). The majority of educational institutions were damaged or destroyed during the war (N. M. Ali, 2014). Somaliland's first university was only established in 1998, making access to university education a relatively recent possibility for many Somalilanders. While the Somaliland higher education sector has grown rapidly within the last decade and demand for university education is high, a lack of human capital remains a major challenge for Somaliland (N.-I. Ali, 2016). As one respondent described, this issue is related to the fact that many Somalilanders have gaps in their primary and secondary level education, even though they might be pursuing graduate education (MAN D, Organisation 3, Somaliland, 2019). Similarly, all CD4D host institutions in Somaliland described a lack of experts, capacity, experience, and training on sector-specific skills such as Monitoring and Evaluation (M&E), plant protection, marketing, logistics, and engineering as the main challenge. In a presentation at the 7th High Level Aid Coordination Forum in 2014, the Chairman of the Somaliland Civil Service Commission stated, 'Somaliland's civil servants [can be] characterized mostly as: overstaff[ed], over aged staff, unskilled, inexperienced, poorly equipped, poorly resourced, and suffer from low morale arising, amongst other, from poor remuneration and terms and conditions of service' (Muse Duale, 2014, p. 2).

The assignments within the HR departments showed that not only do the host institutions lack an HR policy, but ministries do not have clear job descriptions and criteria as a basis for recruitment or clearly defined tasks per position, employee work time and attendance tracking systems, employee records, or forms for sick leave or maternity leave. Additionally, at one of the ministries selected for this case study, the HR department was only established in 2018, and another ministry was only established as a separate institution in the same year. A study conducted in 2004 assessing the training needs of the Somaliland Civil Service already identified the need to introduce job descriptions for all positions, including a definition of minimum qualifications, rightsizing of staff, and the establishment of a performance monitoring system, amongst other measures (Bicker, 2004). A World Bank (WB) assessment for the Somaliland Civil Service Reform Project also highlighted a lack of complete personnel records, with only 30% of civil servants at the WB target ministries having verified and completed personnel records of satisfactory quality in the central HR personnel database (World Bank, 2016).

The two cases were selected for a variety of reasons. First, there are three main types of host institutions in the CD4D Programme: higher education institutions, ministries, and hospitals. Very few hospitals participated in the programme; therefore, I selected a case from ministries and a case from higher education institutions to compare cases from the most common types of organizations. Within CD4D, interventions concentrate on organizations within specific target sectors (IOM, 2018). In Sierra Leone, CD4D targets the education, healthcare, and agriculture sectors, but most host institutions are higher education institutions (IOM, 2019a). CD4D assignments in Somaliland took place in three sectors, namely agriculture, infrastructure, and justice. With the exception of one institution, the Municipality of Hargeisa, all host institutions were ministries (IOM, 2019b). Therefore, the first case was selected from Sierra Leone and the second from Somaliland. Second, the two selected cases show two types of knowledge transfer methods: more informal practices of closely working together in Somaliland versus more formal practices of workshops and trainings in Sierra Leone. Third, in all cases at least some knowledge transfer took place, as reported by the CD4D diaspora experts and colleagues. There are also cases within CD4D where little or no evidence for knowledge transfer could be found.

A total of 28 interviews were included for these case study examples. Table 7.1 shows the number of interviews conducted for each case.

All interviews were transcribed and thematically analysed with an open, emerging coding scheme using the qualitative analysis software NVivo. The codes centred around the respondents' perception of knowledge transfer methods, knowledge transferred or gained, and changes implemented on an organizational and individual level.

Table 7.1 Overview Interviews

		Diaspora expert (DE)	Managers (MAN)		Colleagues (COL)		Total
	Org.		T1 (2018)	T2 (2019)	T1 (2018)	T2 (2019)	
Case 1	*Org. 1*	*DE 1 (2018)* *DE 2 (2018)*	*MAN A*★★ *MAN B* *MAN C* *MAN D* *MAN E* *MAN F* *MAN G*	*MAN H* *MAN I* *MAN J*★ *MAN K* *MAN L*	*(Note: Beneficiaries of trainings in this case were mostly heads of departments, here included as managers.)*		14
Case 2	*Org. 2*	*DE 3 (2019)*	–	*MAN A*★ *MAN B*★★	-★★★	*COL A* 4	14
	Org. 3	*DE 4 (2018; 2019)*	*MAN C*★	*MAN C*★ *MAN D*★★		*COL B* 6	
	Org. 4	*DE 5 (2019)*	*MAN E*★★	–	*COL C*	*COL C* 4	
Total							28

★ = Lead Contact/Project Focal Point; ★★ = Director General/Principal ★★★ = The ministry was established only in 2018.

Forms of knowledge transfer

Knowledge transfer is commonly divided into explicit and tacit knowledge transfer (Polanyi, 1966). Both forms of transfers can be found in the CD4D Programme. As Polanyi (1966), the founder of this distinction, argued, 'all knowledge has a tacit and explicit component'. The cases presented here demonstrate how explicit and tacit components form part of knowledge transfer processes, how both methods are closely interlinked, and how one method complements the other. The two case studies illustrate some of the main forms of knowledge transfer within the CD4D Programme. This includes formal trainings as an explicit knowledge transfer method and close, daily interaction as a tacit knowledge transfer method. As the case studies illustrate, the different methods allow for different types of knowledge to be transferred.

Explicit knowledge transfer through formal trainings

Previous studies on return programmes, such as the Returning Experts component of the CIM 'Migration for Development' programme (Kuschminder et al., 2014) or TRQN to Afghanistan (Kuschminder, 2014), identified tacit knowledge transfer to be more common. However, Kuschminder et al. (2014) found that 'formal training most commonly occurred in academic settings' (p. 24). This study also finds that formal trainings are a more common method of knowledge transfer in academic settings. As the case examples from Sierra Leone illustrate (see Figure 7.2), explicit knowledge transfer may take the form of seminars and trainings. This included one-off full-day trainings of one or two days as well as one-hour seminars that took place more regularly. For instance, as Figure 7.2 shows, Diaspora Expert 1 gave seminars on standards of thesis planning and research project writing that were attended by senior lecturers and students. A staff member who attended the seminars himself explained that staff gained explicit knowledge from the seminar, such as on 'the pattern of writing' as well as on the procedures and tools one needs for a research project.

Diaspora Expert 2 had already launched an entrepreneurship programme for students at Organisation 1 prior to CD4D. During CD4D, the diaspora expert initiated a national workshop on entrepreneurship that was attended by not only staff and students from Organisation 1 but also members of other higher education institutions in Sierra Leone. According to the lead contact, some staff of Organisation 1 were able to gain knowledge from this. The project focal point himself reported to have gained knowledge on the wider concept of entrepreneurship and strategic entrepreneurship, and learnt about start-ups through examples from the Netherlands.

Tacit knowledge transfer through close, daily interaction

In contrast to the first case, the examples selected for the second case show the use of tacit knowledge transfer methods (see Figure 7.3). Here, knowledge transfer took place in the form of close daily interaction between the

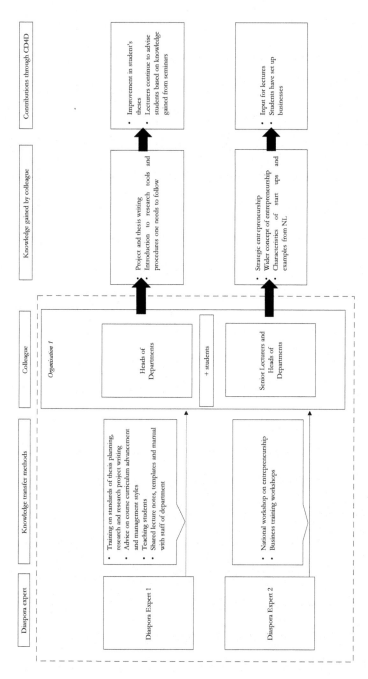

Figure 7.2 Case examples of diaspora knowledge transfer during CD4D in Sierra Leone. Own elaboration; based on interviews with CD4D diaspora experts and staff at the host institutions.

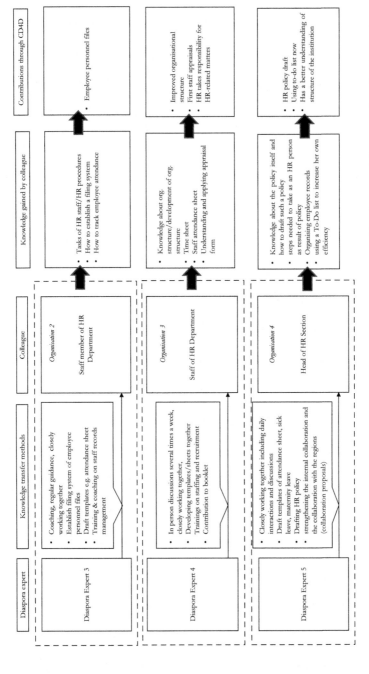

Figure 7.3 Case examples of diaspora knowledge transfer during CD4D in Somaliland. Own elaboration; based on interviews with CD4D diaspora experts and staff at the host institutions.

Note: Some of the diaspora experts also conducted activities with other departments; this was not included here as the focus is on HR departments.

diaspora expert and staff of the host institutions in Somaliland who were working together to build and improve the institutions' HR Management. At Organisation 2, the diaspora expert coached a member of the HR department and transferred knowledge via learning by example and targeted work assignments. During the assignment at Organisation 3, the diaspora expert engaged in almost daily in-person discussions with staff members of the HR department and closely worked together with the HR team for the duration of the assignment. In a similar way, Diaspora Expert 5 and the Head of HR at Organisation 4 closely worked together to draft an attendance sheet, as well as forms and procedures for sick leave and maternity leave and an HR policy for the institution.

Despite the use of a tacit knowledge transfer method, the case examples from Somaliland also show that elements of explicit knowledge were transferred as well. At all three ministries, the diaspora experts generally drafted the templates (in English). Through the templates that the CD4D diaspora experts drafted, staff gained explicit knowledge on the common tasks, procedures, and documents of HR staff in the Netherlands, including a time sheet, staff attendance sheet, and leave sheets. At all three host institutions, one of the main contributions of the diaspora experts was to introduce staff to HR procedures that are standard in most contexts, such as the Netherlands, but were not in place at the ministries in Somaliland. The diaspora experts furthermore played a crucial role in creating the necessary structure, as illustrated by the following quote:

> The [HR] department was not functional to begin with. So when I came in I didn't know much where to start and what to do next. So this is where I benefited from [the diaspora expert], like structuring what we needed to do. Like first and second and the third. And also have those files. I had it in mind but I did not know how to put one first and then which one is second and which one is third. [...] Because of [the diaspora expert] we have something in place right now. [...] Before we did not know how many staff [members] came in in the morning and how many staff [are] in the departments. But now we know because we have an attendance sheet and also the leave request sheet as well is functional. Because before we did not know if someone [...] request[ed] a special leave to go somewhere and do something or they are on maternity leave or on sick leave. But now [we know] because we have a table, a form, that they fill, the staff member will come to the department, fill out [the form] and so I record it and then I know.
>
> (COL A, Organisation 2, Somaliland, 2019)

The diaspora experts were then needed to explain the templates and necessary HR procedures to the staff. The daily and close interaction with the diaspora experts then enabled the transfer of tacit knowledge. The colleagues learnt the steps they needed to take as an HR person, such as how to apply these sheets in practice and how to take responsibility for HR matters. At the same time, staff reviewed the drafts and contributed input to adjust the more general templates to the local and institutional contexts. For instance, the HR staff member working with a diaspora expert at Organisation 4 described working with the diaspora expert in the following way:

> The template has been developed by [the CD4D expert]. Because we did not even have it before. And as a staff member we did not even have any idea [how to develop the templates] – we needed those templates. But when [the diaspora expert] developed the templates, we amended it according to the context of the Ministry so we added in our contribution in that sense.
>
> (Colleague C, Organisation 4, Somaliland, 2019)

As the quotation illustrates, this method of knowledge transfer enabled the transfer of new knowledge while ensuring that the end results were context-appropriate.

Contributions to the host institutions and to capacity building

From a development perspective, it is important to see whether the knowledge transfer contributes to capacity building and changes at the organization. As Kuschminder (2014) described, 'Capacity building occurs once a person has absorbed that knowledge, learned new skills, and developed new capacities. In addition, capacity building can occur at the individual level, institutional level or community level'.

For CD4D, examples of capacity building mostly seem to occur on the individual level. For instance, from the workshops given by Diaspora Expert 1 a manager reported to have observed an improvement in students' theses as a result. According to the respondent, the lecturers are able to continue advising students based on the knowledge gained from the seminars. The institutional focal point, who has closely worked with Diaspora Expert 2 for over ten years, reported to be able to use the knowledge that he has gained on entrepreneurship:

> I benefited a lot on strategic entrepreneurship and for now I became a mentor for the entire campus and I am now the person lecturer in entrepreneurship models right across the entire university. [...] I was able to know [the] wider concept of entrepreneurship and I was able to learn about start-ups.
>
> (MAN J, Organisation 1, Sierra Leone, 2019)

According to the lead contact, some students have also been able to set up businesses as a result of the business training workshops.

For the case examples presented from Somaliland, capacity building seems to have occurred mainly on the individual level as the diaspora experts closely worked with one or a few staff members from the HR department. The diaspora experts did not only introduce their colleagues to HR procedures theoretically, but the assignments allowed for the diaspora experts to put some of the procedures in place together with the colleagues, leading to procedural changes at the departmental or institutional level. This includes the introduction of new HR procedures at Organisation 2, including the filing system. As Diaspora Expert 3 described:

> We bought about 200 files, we ordered them, and we started doing the employee files from job description, ID card, passport photos, personal database.
>
> (Diaspora Expert 3, 2019)

As the following quote illustrates, staff considered this an important first step in the improvement of the HR department:

> [The diaspora expert] totally changed the department. [...] the ministry is new and the HR department is also new. [...] So they are struggling to do many things. So [the diaspora expert] helped and do those things to at least organise all staff of the ministry, even the regional staff, and make this filing system and establishing templates, work templates.
>
> (MAN A, Organisation 2, Somaliland, 2019)

Nonetheless, the manager and the CD4D diaspora expert agreed that an HR manual should be developed to ensure continuity. The diaspora expert considered this particularly important due to the high turnover at the institution, an issue that has been observed at all government institutions in Somaliland. However, a development of the HR manual could not be achieved during the first, three-month assignment which has been analysed here as a case example. Nonetheless, the manager reported that the diaspora expert already started developing the manual while he was still in the country. The diaspora expert conducted two more assignments afterwards. According to the diaspora expert, the manual was developed during the second assignment and the head of the HR department was briefed by the diaspora expert with regard to the manual and coached to finalize the follow-up needed with regard to staff job descriptions and maintaining staff records. Yet no host institution data is available for this assignment.

Similar improvements have been observed as a result of the work of Diaspora Expert 4 at Organisation 3. As a result of the work with the CD4D diaspora expert, the first staff appraisals at Organisation 3 have been conducted. Additionally, the interviews showed that the HR department is now able to take responsibility in HR matters and HR staff has started assuming their roles. As one of the managers described:

> the new HR department [which] was actually developed [...] last year [...]. Now I see that the department actually is very tough now, even

they start actually to make what was recruiting and actually look at the background education of that new staff and see which unit actually can we work with them. And make a connection between the education background and the specific unit he can be working and supporting.
(MAN C, Organisation 3, Somaliland, 2019)

The newly acquired capacity of the institution's HR staff was also illustrated by one example where a department director wanted to undertake an HR-related matter without involving the HR department. Staff of the HR department intervened, clarifying the responsibility of the HR department in this situation, something the colleagues themselves attributed to the work with the diaspora expert.

Finally, diaspora experts through CD4D may also make contributions to capacity building of staff which are not job specific. For instance, the Head of the HR at Organisation 4 started using a to-do list based on the suggestion of the diaspora expert. When asked how they currently apply what they learnt from the diaspora expert, one colleague gave the following example:

[The diaspora expert] advised me strongly when I come to the office I don't just like sit down and open my computer and start work but say 'Okay, what do I have today?' – So list it down and then at the end of the day you tick what you have done and leave the rest for the next day.
(COL C, Organisation 4, Somaliland, 2019)

The case examples from Sierra Leone and Somaliland illustrate ways in which the diaspora experts through CD4D have been able to address the lack of basic skills and knowledge on an individual level by training selected staff members within the selected institutions. Overall, these examples show diaspora experts are able to make contributions to capacity building at the host institutions, and this may involve explicit as well as tacit knowledge transfer methods. Nevertheless, it must be acknowledged that many capacity building contributions through CD4D and changes implemented through the activities of the diaspora experts seem to be rather small scale and ad hoc. Additionally, new or altered procedures that were introduced through the knowledge transfer and are now being implemented by the colleagues will have only longer-term impact through continuous action by the colleagues and support of management staff.

Discussion

Drawing on the case examples, a few similarities and differences can be highlighted. The case examples presented here illustrate some of the main forms of knowledge transfer within the CD4D Programme. This includes explicit knowledge transfer via formal trainings and tacit knowledge transfer through close and regular interaction. As the case studies illustrated, the different methods allow for different types of knowledge to be transferred. Different factors might be taken into consideration to choose a knowledge transfer method. The case examples also illustrated that the transfer of explicit knowledge and the transfer of tacit knowledge are closely intertwined. While the case examples from Somaliland showed that tacit knowledge transfer may be preceded or complimented by the transfer of explicit knowledge, it has also been observed that assignments which focus on formal trainings provide a basis, for instance, for the diaspora expert to challenge the status quo or to mentor or coach staff members on an individual basis.

It is important to understand that within CD4D, different actors are involved in defining how an assignment takes place. The tasks of each diaspora expert were defined by the Terms of References (ToR) of each assignment which were drafted by IOM in coordination with the host institution. In practice, the tasks an expert in the end actually engages in are also framed by additional requests by managers of the host institution as well as by the diaspora expert who, in practice, can decide, to a certain extent, whether to engage in activities that go beyond the initial ToR. Higher education institutions, such as Organisation 1 (similar to other similar host institutions in Sierra Leone), in many cases seem to see more direct benefit from having diaspora experts fill the existing gaps and let them teach students. Yet this 'direct teaching' does not contribute to knowledge transfer and capacity building of staff at the host institution. While such assignments could also contribute to the capacity of staff through the use of co-teaching or sharing the end results of assignments in the form of manuals or the like, this is not always the case within CD4D. Kuschminder (2014) identified that 'the project terms of reference focus on training components' as one of the 'key aspects that appear to contribute to the success' of the TRQN project in Afghanistan. Programme design and implementation should therefore ensure that colleagues are identified for all assignments and make knowledge transfer to those colleagues a task the diaspora expert has to deliver on. Within the context of a temporary return programme, such as CD4D, the role of programme design and implementation is then to ensure that knowledge is transferred, for instance, by making co-teaching a task of the diaspora expert.

Kuschminder (2014) found that for TRQN 'the key drawback of the project indicated by all participants, host institutions, and colleagues, is that the assignment is too short' (p. 204). This aspect has also frequently been mentioned during CD4D. While particularly CD4D diaspora experts who were unemployed prior to CD4D may have an incentive to ask for longer assignments or extensions, this research has also shown that some changes need a longer time to implement. Remaining with the case examples, the manager and participant indicated for Diaspora Expert 3's assignment that the HR manual could not be developed within the timeframe of the first assignment. For the purposes of CD4D, which knowledge transfer method is better suited might also depend on the time frame of the assignment. For diaspora experts to closely work together with colleagues more time is required. Even though attending a training session requires managers and colleagues to set time aside for it, formal trainings may provide an introduction to a topic, and the transfer of explicit knowledge, in less time.

Another factor regarding the knowledge transfer method is that the different approaches also define the setup for the diaspora expert-colleague relationship. In Somaliland, where the focus was on tacit knowledge transfer methods, the diaspora experts worked with one to maximum three or four colleagues. For the examples that were given for Sierra Leone, at least ten staff members attended the formal trainings. While diaspora experts trained a slightly larger number of staff during the formal trainings, these knowledge transfer events only took place every few weeks, restricted mainly by the diaspora expert's time at the institution and availability of staff. Nonetheless, trainings could also be a way of establishing the relationship between diaspora experts and colleagues for consequent tacit knowledge transfer, if time allows.

Conclusion

This study set out to discuss the ways in which diaspora members transfer knowledge in Sierra Leone and Somaliland and assess the methods and tools used by diaspora members to contribute to successful knowledge transfer via case examples. It also discussed managers' and colleagues' perceptions of knowledge transfer and its contributions to changes and capacity building at their institution. Common forms of knowledge transfer within CD4D include, but are not limited to, formal trainings and colleagues closely working together with the diaspora expert. Even for the assignments where the diaspora experts focussed on tacit knowledge transfer methods, explicit knowledge was also transferred as the transfer of tacit knowledge built on the preceding transfer of explicit knowledge.

This chapter illustrated via case examples that diaspora knowledge transfer can contribute to capacity building and changes on an individual and personal level. Therefore, diaspora knowledge transfer, as evidenced in this chapter, should be regarded as contributing to SDGs, particularly to Goal 4 'Quality Education' and its fourth target regarding the increase in youth and adults who have relevant skills, including technical and vocational skills, for employment, decent jobs, and entrepreneurship as well as to Goal 9 'Industries, innovation and infrastructure' and its target to support domestic technology development, research, and innovation in developing countries. The findings observed in this study mirror those of the previous studies on migration and the sustainable development agenda that noted that diaspora members can contribute to achieve SDGs in the country of origin, provided 'skill transfer programmes are well executed' (Appave & Sinha, 2017, p. 15) and given that skills of diaspora members match with the needs of the country of origin.

Acknowledgements

The author expresses gratitude to everyone at the International Organization for Migration (IOM) who supported and assisted in this research. This research was conducted as part of the evaluation of the CD4D Programme for IOM, which has been funded by the Dutch Ministry of Foreign Affairs. I am grateful to Dr Katie Kuschminder for her valuable comments on a previous version of this chapter. I would also like to thank everyone who provided research assistance for this project for their excellent work.

Notes

1 The concept diaspora may be defined as a population 'which has originated in a land other than which it currently resides, and whose social, economic and political networks cross the borders of nation-states or, indeed, span the globe' (Vertovec, 1999, p. 1). The term 'diaspora' is applied in a broad sense here, referring more to migrants in the wider sense. I assume that diaspora characteristics, such as dispersion, homeland orientation, and boundary maintenance, do not necessarily apply here and that whether a diaspora expert identifies as a diaspora members depends on the individual.
2 See: https://www.iom.int/mida.

Bibliography

Ali, N. M. (2014). Building State Capacity in a Post-Conflict Situation: The Case of Somaliland. *American International Journal of Contemporary Research*, *4*(1), 157–170.

Ali, N.-I. (2016). Demand Drivers for University Education in Somaliland. *Afrikan Sarvi. Afrikas Horn of Africa Journal*, *1*. Retrieved from https://afrikansarvi.fi/issue11/117-artikkeli/303-demand-drivers-for-university-education-in-somaliland.

Appave, G., & Sinha, N. (Ed.). (2017). *Migration in the 2030 Agenda*. Retrieved from https://publications.iom.int/system/files/pdf/migration_in_the_2030_agenda.pdf.

Argote, L., & Ingram, P. (2000). Knowledge Transfer: A Basis for Competitive Advantage in Firms. *Organizational Behaviour and Human Decision Processes*, *82*(1), 150–169. https://doi.org/10.1006/obhd.2000.2893.

BBC. (2017). *Somaliland Profile*. Retrieved from https://www.bbc.com/news/world-africa-14115069.

Bender, S., & Fish, A. (2000). Retention of Expertise: The Continuing Need for Global Assignments. *Journal of Knowledge Management*, *4*(2), 125–137.

Bicker, M. (2004). *Report on a Training Needs Assessment of the Somaliland Civil Service*. Retrieved from UNDP website: http://www.oocities.org/mbali/doc43.htm.

Brinkerhoff, J. M. (2006). Diaspora Mobilization Factors and Policy Options. In *Converting Migration Drains into Gains. Harnessing the Resources of Overseas Professionals* (pp. 127–153). Manila, Philippines: Asian Development Bank.

Brinkerhoff, J. M. (2012). Creating an Enabling Environment for Diasporas' Participation in Homeland Development. *International Migration*, *50*(1), 75–95.

Brinkerhoff, J. M. (2016). *Institutional Reform and Diaspora Entrepreneurs. The In-between Advantage*. Oxford: Oxford University Press.

Castles, S., De Haas, H., & Miller, M. J. (2014). *The Age of Migration. International Population Movements in the Modern World* (5th Edition). London: Palgrave Macmillan.

Davenport, T. H., & Prusak, L. (1998). *Working Knowledge: How Organizations Manage What They Know.* Boston, MA: Harvard Business School Press. Retrieved from http://www.kushima.org/is/wp-content/uploads/2013/09/Davenport_know.pdf.

Fagerberg, J., Srholec, M., & Verspagen, B. (2010). The Role of Innovation in Development. *Review of Economics and Institutions, 1*(2), 1–29

Fahey, L., & Prusak, L. (1998). The Eleven Deadliest Sins of Knowledge Management. *California Management Review, 40*(3), 265–276.

Fund for Peace. (2019). *Fragile States Index. Annual Report 2019.* Retrieved from http://fundforpeace.org/wp-content/uploads/2019/04/9511904-fragilestatesindex.pdf.

Goh, S. C. (2002). Managing Effective Knowledge Transfer: An Integrative Framework and Some Practice Implications. *Journal of Knowledge Management, 6*(1), 23–30.

Huffman, K. (2012). *Workplace Knowledge Transfer Methods (Based on Bloom's Taxonomy).* The Knowledge Transfer Guild.

Inkpen, A. (1998). Learning, Knowledge Acquisition, and Strategic Alliances. *European Management Journal, 16*(2), 223–229.

IOM. (2018). About Connecting Diaspora for Development. Retrieved from https://www.connectingdiaspora.org/en/about/.

IOM. (2019a). Host Institutions & Target Sectors Sierra Leone. Retrieved from CD4D IOM UN Migration website: https://www.connectingdiaspora.org/en/countries/sierra-leone/host-institutions-target-sectors-sierra-leone/.

IOM. (2019b). Host Institutions & Target Sectors Somalia. Retrieved from CD4D IOM UN Migration website: https://www.connectingdiaspora.org/en/countries/somalia/host-institutions-target-sectors-somalia/

Joia, L. A., & Lemos, B. (2010). Relevant Factors for Tacit Knowledge Transfer within Organisations. *Journal of Knowledge Management, 14*(3), 410–427.

King W.R. (2009) Knowledge Management and Organizational Learning. In W. King (Ed.), *Knowledge Management and Organizational Learning. Annals of Information Systems,* vol 4 (pp. 3–13). Boston, MA: Springer.

Klagge, B., & Klein-Hitpaß, K. (2010). High-skilled Return Migration and Knowledge-Based Development in Poland. *European Planning Studies, 18*(10), 1631–1651. https://doi.org/10.1080/09654313.2010.504346.

Kuschminder, K. (2014). Knowledge Transfer and Capacity Building through the Temporary Return of Qualified Nationals to Afghanistan. *International Migration, 52*(2), 191–207.

Kuschminder, K., Sturge, G., & Ragab, N. (2014). *Contributions and Barriers to Knowledge Transfer. The Experience of Returning Experts.* Maastricht Graduate School of Governance.

Levin, D. Z., & Cross, R. (2004). The Strength of Weak Ties You Can Trust: The Mediating Role of Trust in Effective Knowledge Transfer. *Management Science, 50*(11), 1477–1490.

Levitt, P. (1998). Social Remittances: Migration Driven Local-Level Forms of Cultural Diffusion. *International Migration Review, 32*(4), 926–948.

Levitt, P., & Lamba-Nieves, D. (2011). Social Remittances Revisited. *Journal of Ethnic and Migration Studies, 37*(1), 1–22.

Muse Duale, N. O. (2014). *PSG 5- Civil Service Reform - CSR 2014 Progress Report Somaliland Special Arrangement.* Presented at the 7th High Level Aid Coordination Forum, Hargeisa. Retrieved from https://www.slministryofplanning.org/images/7HLACF/9_141102%20HLACF%20Presentation%20Civil%20Service%20Reform.pdf.

Newland, K., & Plaza, S. (2013). *What We Know About Diasporas and Economic Development* (Policy Brief No. 5). Retrieved from www.migrationpolicy.org/pubs/Diasporas-EconomicDevelopment.pdf.

Polanyi. (1966). *The Tacit Dimension.* New York: Doubleday.

Siar, S. (2012). *The Diaspora as Knowledge Carrier: Exploring Knowledge Transfer through the Highly Skilled Filipino Migrants in New Zealand and Australia.* University of Auckland.

Siar, S. (2014). Diaspora Knowledge Transfer as a Development Strategy for Capturing the Gains of Skilled Migration. *Asian and Pacific Migration Journal, 23*(3), 299–323.

Terrazas, A. (2010). Connected through Service: Diaspora Volunteers and Global Development. In K. Newland (Ed.), *Diasporas. New Partners in Global Development Policy* (pp. 162–211). Washington, DC: Migration Policy Institute.

UNDP. (2010). *Measuring Capacity.* Retrieved from http://www.undp.org/content/undp/en/home/librarypage/capacity-building/undp-paper-on-measuring-capacity.html.

United Nations. (2018). *Economic Development in Africa Report 2018. Migration for Structural Transformation.* Retrieved from http://unctad.org/en/PublicationsLibrary/aldcafrica2018_en.pdf.

United Nations General Assembly. (2015). *Resolution adopted by the General Assembly on 25 September 2015. 70/1. Transforming our world: the 2030 Agenda for Sustainable Development.* Retrieved from https://sustainabledevelopment.un.org/post2015/transformingourworld.

Vertovec, S. (1999). Three Meanings of "Diaspora," Exemplified among South Asian Religions. *Diaspora, 6,* 277–300.

World Bank. (2013). *Republic of Sierra Leone Higher and Tertiary Education Sector Policy Note.* Retrieved from https://openknowledge.worldbank.org/bitstream/handle/10986/16787/ACS43930PNT0P10x0379833B00PUBLIC00.pdf?sequence=1&isAllowed=y.

World Bank. (2016). *Somalia - Somaliland Civil Service Reform Project : P155123-Implementation Status Results Report : Sequence 01 (English).* Retrieved from http://documents.worldbank.org/curated/en/278251475787548454/pdf/ISR-Disclosable-P155123-10-06-2016-1475787539971.pdf.

World Bank Group. (2017). *SABER Tertiary Education Country Report : Sierra Leone 2017.* Retrieved from http://documents.worldbank.org/curated/en/136221505986774598/SABER-tertiary-education-country-report-Sierra-Leone-2017.

World Bank Group. (2018). *Federal Republic of Somalia. Systematic Country Diagnostic.* Retrieved from http://documents.worldbank.org/curated/en/554051534791806400/pdf/SOMALIA-SCD-08152018.pdf.

8 Harnessing social remittances for Africa's development

The case of skilled returnees and skilled return migrant groups in Ghana

Mary Boatemaa Setrana and Kwaku Arhin-Sam

Introduction

The impact of migration in the broader context of development has over the years been studied in relation to the gaps (e.g. brain drain) that migration creates in the home country. Gradually over the years, the debates have begun to incorporate changes in attitudes and behaviours of the people in both host and home countries with whom migrants have direct contacts. Despite its popularity, the concept of migration and development faces contestations without clear positions (Castles, de Haas, & Miller, 2009). The mere underlining assumption in development that some societies are lower and have less differentiated status and as a result, need to be moved to a higher differentiated and better status, is questioned (Hammar & Tamas, 1997: 18). Also, the relationship between the key concepts of the nexus has come under scrutiny. As de Haas (2010) pointed out, often the major criticism of migration and development is the widespread treatment of migration as an external factor that affects development, rather than one that is an inherent element of change (de Haas, 2010 cf. Borchgrevink & Erdal, 2016).

Nevertheless, the role of migration in development continues to yield evidence to support the understanding that migration plays a key role in development and subsequently the entire role of remittances in this union. That is, the migration and development nexus acknowledges the key role of remittances. Even so, the idea to 'bring culture back into migration debates' (Levitt & Lamba-Nieves, 2011: 2), thus, frames the role of social remittances in migration and development. Indeed, while the economic impact of financial remittances is important, and have received much attention in research and policy circles, extending the view onto non-monetary transfers is equally needed and important in the conceptualization of the nexus. Interestingly, the achievement of sustainable development goals (SDG) does not give prominent attention to the concept of social remittances. What is underlined in the SDGs is the need to leverage financial remittances (Target 10.c *reduce to less than 3% the transaction costs of migrant remittances and eliminate remittance corridors with costs higher than 5%).* An examination of the nexus between social remittances and SDGs exposes the invisible and unrecognized achievement of many of these goals through social remittances. For instance, social remittances of returnees have impact on the following SDGs: Goal 3, 'Good health and well-being for people'; Goal 7, Target 10.7 to facilitate orderly, safe, regular, and responsible migration and mobility of people; and Goal 9, 'Build resilient infrastructure, promote inclusive and sustainable industrialization, and foster innovation'. These are explored in the discussion of the findings.

Even though the non-financial aspects of remittances hardly have footprints in the SDGs, scholars of transnational migration have recognized the enormous contribution of social remittances.

The coining of the term 'social remittances' by Levitt (1996) delineates economic and non-monetary remittances (Nowicka & Šerbedžija, 2016). Among such non-monetary transfers include information, values, and ideas (Levitt, 1998; Levitt & Lamba-Nieves, 2011; Grabowska & Garapich, 2016). Despite these growing interests, there is still more to be achieved with regard to evidence-based research on the nuances and impact of social remittances. This chapter contributes to the on-going scholarship on social remittances by exploring how return migrants utilize their knowledge, values, and networks acquired in the home country. Using Ghana as a case, the chapter examines the reasons, knowledge, and values of skilled return migrants to Ghana and how they mobilize themselves for development of the home country as well as sustain their return.

First, the paper provides an understanding of the social dimension of remittances. This is followed by a conceptual framing of social remittances in the context of return migration. Then there is a presentation on the elements of social remittances in the Ghanaian context and how they impact on the achievement of the SDGs. The paper ends with conclusions.

Understanding the social dimension of remittances

According to Cliggett (2003), money continues to have symbolic value for all people involved in remittances. However, in recent times, scholars of transnational migration are gradually shifting their attention to recognize the fact that remittances from migrants are more than money. Social remittances are the constant iterative circulation of ideas, values, and practices, and are also about demonstrating power and success (Levitt, 2016). It is an iterative circulation because what is remitted in social remittances is, in fact, influenced by the different places that the person who is transmitting the remittances has moved through and what she or he has been exposed to. These accumulated 'social wealth' gathered between the different times and spaces is thus circulated. It is also important to acknowledge the power constellations that are inherent within these transfers. Within this understanding, migrants' pre-migration experiences and exposure in the country of origin, in addition to exposures abroad, are important (Arhin-Sam, 2019). These exposures can influence the kind of non-monetary transfers as well. A migrant or returnee's knowledge of the country of origin is important because for social remittances to be successfully exchanged, there is the need for what Levitt (2016) calls a 'cultural and discursive backdrop'. That is, while people may be considered to have acquired new ideas and behaviours as a result of moving around, it is the cultural and discursive background (shared in common with the origin society) that makes them more open to new ideas and behaviours, and vice versa. In other words, a stranger cannot exchange new ideas and behaviours as easily as a native can.

As with financial remittance, social remittances also demonstrate the power of success between the remitter and the receiver of social transfers (Levitt, 2016). That is, in whichever form social remittances take one should be aware of the power relations between the sender and the receiver. Often, the person transmitting social remittance comes up as the successful one (for having acquired new ideas and behaviour), and, with such projection and power, they are able to transmit social remittance to the less successful person. The fact that people can choose to whom to remit what social remittance further underscores the purposeful nature of social remittances and the power of the remitter (Levitt, 2016).

The idea of social transfers is not new to the migration literature. Yet by coining and revisiting social remittances Levitt (1998, 2001) and Levitt and Lamba-Nieves (2011, 2013) categorized social remittances into three domains: (1) normative structures; (2) systems of practices; (3) social capital. Normative structures are ideas, values, and beliefs. The application and the practising of ideas, values, and believes through actions make up the systems of practices, while harnessed values and norms, including social and political networks, form the social capital of social remittances (Levitt, 1998, 2001). For social remittances to occur, one or all of the following must take place: migrants have to return to live in or visit their communities of origin; non-migrants must visit those in the receiving country; or letters, videos, cassettes, e-mails, messaging, or telephone calls must be exchanged between migrants and the home communities (Levitt, 1998; Levitt & Lamba-Nieves, 2011, 2013). At the same time, in the case of return migrants, social remittances can be exchanged face to face in addition to the above transfer channels. Social remittances can also be collective in nature when individual exchanges are gathered as part of their role in an organization or group and are used in organizational and group settings (Levitt & Lamba-Nieves, 2013). Examples of such collective social remittances are old schoolmate associations and hometown associations, among others.

As with many social science concepts, social remittance faces distinct challenges aside from the critiques for Levitt's definition and categories of the concept. First, it is imperative to acknowledge that the impact of social remittances is not always positive (Levitt & Lamba-Nieves, 2013). The existence of power relations means that there is the likelihood that such influences are used negatively or abused for personal gains of the one remitting, for either the short term or the long term. Also, the ideas, values, and behaviours that are remitted may be negative to the receiving society and its norms. Second, social remittance as a term is still underdeveloped theoretically (Grabowska & Garapich, 2016). Third, with all the attention it is getting, the discourses on non-monetary transfer which forms social remittances are still intertwined in the literature with the dominant economic views on remittances (Nowicka & Šerbedžija, 2016). For instance, within the broader migration system theories, de Haas (2010) sees social remittances as contextual and as a second-order effect of migration by calling it 'migration-driven forms of cultural change' (p. 1592). Indeed, every economic activity may have a social function (Levitt, 2016) and social remittances are seen as a derivative of 'economic remittances' (Paasche, 2016). Nevertheless, while scholars are busy devising ways to keep social remittances within economic remittances, the fact is that remittances come in different forms, transferred via different channels, and affect different people in the migration cycle. The imperative is to find ways to fully understand social remittances and their transformative roles.

Conceptual framing of social remittance in the context of return migration

Remittances are divers and context-dependent but not a unitary package (Durand, 1994; cited in Goldring, 2003). The social, political, and economic status of migrants who transfer social remittances is also different, and likewise are the non-migrants who are involved in these transfers. The differences in status of both migrants and non-migrants also determine the influence of social remittances in terms of impact (Levitt, 2001), for example, between men and women, married couples, and single men and women. In this chapter, therefore, we refer to social remittances as diffusion and circulation of knowledge, technology skills, political identities, ideas, values, and different social practices into both sending and receiving countries (Levitt, 1998; Fitzgerald, 2000; Nicholas, 2002). Specifically, we look at social remittances from the perspective of return migrants in the home country.

First, social remittances are constrained in societies where the remittance is expected to impact when the said society is relatively different from the source society of the remittance (Levitt, 1996; Levitt & Lamba-Nieves, 2013). Even so, the relative difference in West African (Ghanaian) and Western societies (many of the return migrants in this study came from Western Europe and North America) is the starting point where the social remittance assessment is conceptualized. That is, we see certain socio-cultural values, ideas, and practices in Ghana to be relatively different from Western countries.

Second, social remittances are not only exchanges but more than the mere fact that people have acquired new values, ideas, or practices and are ready to share. There is the need for a broader cultural background that makes social remittances exchanges possible by making people open to the new idea, practice, and behaviour (Levitt, 2016). Here we see returnees and non-migrants sharing to some degree similarities in terms of knowledge of the country of origin. Considering that we look at returnees who started their migration journey from the home country, their pre-migration experiences on certain ideas, values, and practices are not entirely different from non-migrants (Arhin-Sam, 2019). Social remittances are therefore chiefly enabled if the one remitting the new ideas and values understands and is knowledgeable of the old ideas of the values of the receiver. The power dynamic, however, is derived from the influence that the person remitting the new ideas and values has, which in many instances comes from the show of social, political, and economic superiority (Levitt, 2016). Therefore, we are aware of the inequalities that could be created by this idea of differences. On the one hand, returnees are likely to assume that the country of destination in this context is a better environment where they had acquired some knowledge and values that need to be imposed on the Ghanaian non-migrant. They may neglect the values of the home country and replace them with the acquired values with the assumption that everything 'Western' is the best. On the other hand, the expectations of the non-migrant or families left behind towards these destinations contribute to the perceived inequalities embedded in social remittances that are not rightfully defined. In cases where return migrants have come with certain luxurious and elegant lifestyles, the youth are tempted to assume that 'streets of destination countries (especially advanced Western countries) are made of gold'.

Third, we see social remittance transfers from returnees as potentially constrainable in the context of the home country's norms, ideas, knowledge, and values. In the definition of social remittances, Levitt (1998) mentions social capital in addition to norms and practices. As part of social remittances, social capital in this paper explores the collective social norms, networks, and trust (Putnam, 2000) either among returnees or between returnees and non-migrants or among non-migrants that can improve the efficiency of society. For example, returnee groups, old school associations, and others serve as social networks. Also, we align social capital to 'individual's obligations and expectations that take the form of a "capital" invested in one person for future use' (Coleman, 1988: 2 cited in Markley, 2011).

Fourth, in both individual and collective sense, the conceptualization of social remittances in this chapter follows the three distinctions of social remittances proposed by Levitt (1998) and Levitt and Lamba-Nieves (2013). Even so, returnees come back to the home countries with ideas that are often based on expectations, and values and beliefs that are informed by their interactions in the home society. These normative structures include how, after return, the individual returnee approaches household responsibilities, including participation in religious, political, and other social activities and groups. For example, the attitude of returnees towards social institutions like marriage, funerals, and festivals and the intrinsic gender and social roles are capped within the normative structure of social remittances.

Furthermore, the ideas, values, and approaches towards social, political, and religious activities are put into actual practice when returnees participate in these systems or reject them and/or set up entirely new systems of practice. In whichever way, the returnees put into practice certain systems of norms, values which define how they interact in groups, generate networks, and establish management and leading roles. These systems of practices may confirm, contradict, or complement existing systems of practices in the return society.

Fifth, skilled returnees constitute powerful people who both have the financial resources and possess certain information, ideas, values, and behaviours which can enable them to benefit from the social and political networks that they interact within. These social capitals provide the platform for harnessing different social, cultural, economic, and political values and norms (Levitt, 1998, 2001, 2016). These power relations, often in favour of returnees, can be further exploited by returnees as a group or as individual returnees to the disadvantage of non-migrants.

Lastly, the period of impact of social remittances can be both short- and long-term. In the short term, we conceptualize the impact of social remittances by returnees as part of the negotiation strategies with non-migrants as they resettle. For example, the display of differences in ideas and values and the show of acquired new behaviour and ideas in the short term can impact the society if these ideas are accepted. The returnee, in this case, gets the benefits of the short-term impact of what he or she is remitting. In the long term, social remittances can impact both the society and the returnee after the potential clash of these new ideas and behaviour with old ideas and behaviours. The resulting impact begins to manifest when the negotiations of these exchanges have taken place and the cultural and discursive backdrops are ripe for long-term impact. We analyse the timeframe for the impact of social remittances in the discussion part of the paper.

Methods

The data used to write the chapter was gathered from secondary sources, such as books, and administrative reports from state and private agencies. Primary data were collected through oral communication with 15 return migrants. Phone interviews were conducted with a leading international return association in Ghana. The chapter also benefitted from research works and publications of the authors. The returnees interviewed were between the ages of 24 and 45 and above, with a majority of them within the ages of 25–34 and 35–44. The returnees were within their productive ages. Male respondents were nine, while females were six. Their educational levels were high, with seven of them having a graduate certificate; four had post-graduate certificate, and five had undergraduate certificate. All of them said they had either furthered their education or acquired some kind of training or skills abroad. The returnees were found in all sectors of the

Ghanaian labour market with the majority in the education sector as lecturers or researchers, four medical doctors, three bankers, two consultants, and two administrators. This is attributed to the fact that recent recruitment of skilled personnel appears limited to the teaching sector as well as some non-governmental organizations (compare Anarfi & Jagare, 2005). Six of the returnees were married, while the rest were single, divorced, or separated and widowed. Many of the return migrants had lived in the UK, Germany, the United States, the Netherlands, and Italy (Refer to Table 8.1). The average time spent abroad was about nine years. The majority of return migrants who came to Ghana had completed their training or ended their contract abroad or wanted to start their own businesses or projects. Further to these reasons, the returnees had much more expectations towards home because they felt with their higher level of education, they could easily find jobs in Ghana and also be fulfilled in Ghana in terms of career aspirations than elsewhere. Several socio-economic factors attracted the return of these migrants (Setrana & Tonah, 2016) (Table 8.1):

> the stellar performance of the national economy during the period of the researches; the achievement of a middle-income country status in 2008; the per capita income reached US $1500 in 2009 as well as the income earned from the production of gold, cocoa, tourism, exports of non-traditional goods and remittances from Ghanaians abroad, Ghana started the commercial production of oil in December 2010. These developments resulted in considerable confidence in the economy by foreign and local investors. Furthermore, macro-economic conditions relevant to the performance of any business venture were quite favourable. Economic growth reached a peak of 14.4 per cent in 2011. The rate of inflation and interest rates were falling and the exchange rate was relatively stable. Thus, the general economic conditions for doing business in Ghana were quite favourable during the period of research (in Setrana & Tonah, 2016:553).

The context: elements of social remittances

Return migrants are able to recoup the benefits of their networks at both ends of migration based on the kind of investment they made to sustain and build the trust of the networks. Social remittances are presented as any simplistic measure of societal values, norms, and ideas. However, unlike financial remittances which can be measured quantitatively, it is difficult to do the same with social remittances. To better understand social remittances is to rather talk about the nuances and details of what make up social remittances and how they impact left behind families as well as the migrants themselves. For this section, we focus on the networks, values, norms, and knowledge transfer of return migrants.

Table 8.1 Background characteristics of the returnees

Variable	N (15)	Percentage (%)
Sex		
Male	9	60
Female	6	40
Education		
Post-Graduate	5	33.3
Graduate	7	46.7
Under-Graduate	3	20
Married status		
Married	6	40
Single	4	26.7
Divorced/separated	3	20
Widowed	2	13.3
Age		
25–34	7	46.7
35–44	5	33.3
45+	3	20
Employment		
Lecturer/Researcher	6	40
Medical Doctor	4	26.7
Banker	3	20
Consultant	2	13.3
Country of Destination		
Canada	2	13.3
United Kingdom	6	40.1
Germany	2	13.3
United States of America	3	20
Netherlands	1	6.7
Italy	2	13.3

Transnational networks as forms of social remittances

The transnational network of the return migrants can be categorized into two based on the nature of contacts (Setrana & Tonah, 2016: 556–558). These categories are very relevant to our discussion on social remittances of return migrants. The first is a group of professionals, such as doctors and university lecturers who have ties with former colleagues and institutions abroad. Through these transnational networks, the return migrants learn new skills and technology and earn some additional income. These transnational networks allow the returnees to spend their sabbaticals in some hospitals and universities abroad. The visits are, among others, a means by which returnees learn new and modern techniques that are relevant in their fields of work. Such transnational professional networks have a positive benefit for both the home and the host countries. One of the key elements that enabled the return migrants to continue with this kind of network was either they had permanent residence, citizenship of the destination or could easily acquire visitors' visas from the home country. The story of Kweku tells the story of such returnees.

> Kweku the forty years health professional migrated from his home region in Ghana after his vocation training and some years of practising as a nurse to pursue his dream of becoming a doctor. He migrated to the United States where he started his training as a medical doctor. After his studies in the United States, he moved on to the United Kingdom where he had the opportunity to specialise and also work with one of the renowned hospitals. In the early 2000s, Kweku returned to Ghana permanently and has since then been working as a medical health professional in the country. His former employers abroad sometimes call him to help out in the hospital, especially during the summer breaks. He confirmed that the intermittent call for support gives him the opportunity to earn more income as well as learn new skills in his area of specialisation. He is a member of the Medical Association in both Ghana and the UK. With his kind of profession and his previous travelling experience, he has never been refused a visa.
>
> (Kweku, interview in Accra)

The second group of transnational networks consists of returnees who have business collaboration with foreign partners abroad (Setrana & Tonah, 2016: 557). These partners provide financial and/or technical support to the business here in Ghana. The partners sustain their relationship on a reciprocal basis; both the returnee who serves as the business associate in Ghana and the foreign partner enjoy benefits from the collaboration. For example, Ama has a business partner who supplies her with electrical accessories. She explained their relationship thus:

> Ama, the 30 years old lady migrated to the Netherlands in search of a better life. In 2009, she decided to return to Ghana permanently because she had managed to earn some income and also pursued her diploma education in Information systems. She felt satisfied and thought she could find a better job in Ghana and also help her to be with her family, and settle down for marriage since she was growing in age. Prior to her decision to return permanently to Ghana, she discussed with some of her colleagues to trade in electrical accessories, especially the unused electrical gadgets. With this agreement, she returned to Ghana in 2009 and since then, her friends have supplied her shop with these accessories. The deal is that her colleagues in the Netherlands and even sometimes those living

in other countries ship her the goods so that she pays for them after-sales. The business has expanded and employs other Ghanaians as well.

(Ama, interview in Accra)

In the case of Ama, she had acquired further knowledge from the country of destination which she didn't have prior to migration. She returns with knowledge in information systems which helps her set up her own business and employs others to reduce the unemployment rate in the country. She also finds herself in a network she is benefitting from to support and sustain her business in Ghana. The knowledge has had a triple positive effect on her as a migrant, the community, and the nation as a whole. The amount earned from the business is used to improve the livelihoods of the migrant, her family and friends, as well as other non-migrants.

Home-grown return networks as forms of social remittances

Apart from transnational ties, current trends in returnee networks also show an increasing number of home-grown networks. In Ghana, returnees are heterogeneous, spread across different parts of the country and involved in many activities and professions (Arhin-Sam, 2019). Nevertheless, returnees still organize themselves into many networks such as forming returnee groups. Here, the social, professional, and cultural groupings of returnees are the focus.

According to Arhin-Sam (2019), home-grown return networks in Ghana can be grouped into external networks and internal networks. External networks are those that come about as a result of institutions or organizations whose efforts create platforms that bring together return migrants in the home country. These platforms can be governmental or non-governmental. Examples of government network platforms are the Diaspora Affairs Bureau, and Ghana National Investment Promotion Council. These governmental institutions specifically organize events and outreach programs that create avenues for returnees to mingle and interact. Non-governmental local institutions that provide networking platforms for returnees include professional associations such as the Ghana Medical Association (GMA), the Ghana Bar Association (GBA), and the Ghana Chamber of Commerce (GCoC). Similarly, returnees' other institutions and setups such as universities provide networking opportunities for returnee professors and lecturers.

International organizations and embassies of other countries are among the external platforms for return migrants' mobilization. These institutions mobilize their alumni to take part in voluntary activities using their acquired experience and knowledge during their stay in the host country. Mostly, embassies organize exchange programmes or give scholarship to Ghanaian citizens to take part in various activities with the aim of knowledge exchanges and capacity building. Once they return, the embassies organize them to give back to their communities through either policy or voluntary services.

Examples are the US Department of State, British Council, the Dutch embassy as well as the German embassy, German Development Cooperation, and the Canadian International Development Agency (CIDA), among others. For example, the Centre for International Migration's (CIM) programme under the German development cooperation (GIZ) organizes programmes to bring together returnees from Germany. Aside these international organizations, some Western country universities have alumni networks (German Academic Exchange Service [DAAD] alumni network,[1] Harvard University Alumni network, etc.) and foreign language/cultural centres such as Alliance Française and Goethe-Institut. These networks are organized to share information with returnees but also to mobilize the transfers of social remittances from returnees.

Internal networks are homegrown returnee networks that are set up by returnees themselves usually informed by sharing of information and social events. An example is *Ahaspora*.[2] These returnees-initiated networks become trans-local spaces. For example, Gene, a human resource professional who returned from the UK, shared insights on some of the returnee associations:

> 'Ahaspora' is one of these return groups. It is a group of networks of young Ghanaian professionals who have lived or been educated outside Ghana and have returned home. We want to use our knowledge, skills and resources to make Ghana a better place to live. For those of us in Ghana, we tend to meet. I also belong to a group called the Inter-nations. They are also another returnee group from all over the world as well. I belong to these groups because they provide the platform for young professionals like us to impact positively on our nation Ghana.
>
> (Gene, interview in Accra)

In addition, many returnees mobilize themselves on lines of alumni, cities where they lived abroad and even from countries where they have returned from and according to city or village in Ghana where some of these returnees originate. Returnee networks/groups are continuations of diaspora communities back home. Thus, due to many ethnic diaspora associations abroad (Manuh, 1998; Byfield, 2000; Mohamoud, 2003), when members of these communities return, they tend to continue to organize themselves along these lines.

Returnee networks are also used as ways to mobilize resources that are remitted into the home community. For example, Nii shared one of the activities of the *Ahaspora* network:

> When I realized that I really wanted to stay, I started looking for new networks, new friends and came across 'Ahaspora'. They know how the snow-ball thing goes. Now people know that I'm here, students are coming and I'm mentoring and coaching and supervising them. Ahaspora has this mentoring program where they pair returnees professionals with

high school students and youth so that we can mentor these young people. It is a way for us to impact the new generation.

(Nii, Interview in Accra)

The complexities of gendered norms as a form of social remittances

Here in Ghana if you are above 30 and are not married people look at you as if something is wrong with you. For me, I am changing that by working on my business and showing success. My girls who work with are all learning from how I work with professionalism and therefore I am not afraid if am not around. Some men see returnee women as easy to "sleep" around with only because we returnees show that we are independent women and therefore can decide who we want and do not want to be with regardless.

(Abena, Interview in Accra)

Showing a sense of independence and non-reliance on men is thus seen as being contradictory to the social structure. Nevertheless, a reflection on these social values and the desire to affect social structures are among the ways in which returnees' shape gender perspectives and expectations as ways of social remittance. The gendered norms usually acquired from Western countries by returnees may not align with existing traditional norms. For instance, the Ghanaian environment is mainly patriarchy; women are expected to lead a certain kind of life in order to attract the necessary respect from their male counterparts. While men are accorded much respect back home, women returnees rather face difficulties because they are compelled to return to the traditional norms of men as breadwinners and women as housewives. In that sense, what happens is that the acquired empowerment and values the women return with are shelved by families and communities. The few women who plan to overlook such comments are nicknamed as in the story of Abena.

Some return couples admitted the challenging nature of sharing household responsibilities with their partners upon coming back to live in Ghana. Adwoa and Kojo have such experience:

Adwoa and Kojo are both professionals in different fields. Adwoa is a nutritionist who runs her own consultancy as well as work full time in a hospital. She acquired her master's degree in the UK. Kojo her husband is a civil engineer who works with a construction company. They both have returned to live in Ghana with their three kids. Adwoa has a bitter experience upon return. She thinks that Kojo is not helpful as he used to be. To Adwoa, she is not sure if he is the same man she lived with the UK. She feels she is overburdened with the house duties as well as the caring for the children. She does all these in addition to her job as a career woman. Unfortunately, Kojo has the same feeling towards Adwoa. Kojo complains about the attitude of not contributing to the running of the house financially. Kojo thinks his wife has enough money because of her job, just as he does. So, he has decided that so long as the wife refuses to contribute financially as they did in the UK, he has also resolved not to involve himself in any house chores because he is the breadwinner. Kojo said he was sad because sometimes he had to eat from restaurants just because his wife refused to cook.

Nonetheless, women like Adwoa also now desire for duties to be shared, which was the practice abroad. However, they found it more challenging to retain such arrangements, although they perceived them as good values. This finding supports the literature that says that women enjoyed a more independent lifestyle abroad, partly because of their experience of paid work in a more open society (Kosack, 1976; Phizacklea, 1983; Anarfi, Kwankye, & Ahiadeke, 2005). As a result of these restraining roles imposed by local traditions and cultural norms, some marriages could not be sustained upon return, and among the returnees of this study, some women divorced their partners and left the country while the men stayed to marry new wives. Some male returnees interviewed had re-married, while one was in the process of making a new marriage proposal because their intended wives decided not to live with them in Ghana. In the case of a returnee couple – Isaiah and his wife – the continuous contention over these housekeeping duties and financial obligations, and the wife's inability to cope with the challenges on return led to a break-up of their marriage. Isaiah is now re-married and lives in Ghana with his new family, while the ex-wife has relocated back overseas.

Harnessing social remittances for sustainable development

The nexus between social remittances and the SDGs is important but complex. Leveraging social remittances is key to the sustainable development of many African countries, of which Ghana is one. Unlike financial remittances, social remittances have not received attention in the SDGs. Yet, the voluntary return of skilled migrants with the intentions of finding better opportunities at home constitutes social remittances and an achievement of the SDG Goal 10, Target 10.7, which seeks to *facilitate orderly, safe, regular, and responsible migration and mobility of people.* Encouraging the return of skilled migrants promotes humane and dignified homecoming. The stories of Kojo, Adwoa, Ama, and Kwaku who returned voluntarily show that they prepared their return by furthering their education abroad and expanding their transnational networks. Ghana and other countries receiving such skilled returnees have less burden promoting the economic inclusion of such skilled returnees. Governments per SDG Goal 10, Target 10.2 are compelled to provide support to all persons, including the economic reintegration of returnees; it is worth noting that the greatest burden taken off African governments is when the returnees come home with skills, knowledge, and capital to start their own businesses or fill in the vacancy needs of a country. The government is left with fewer mechanisms of reintegrating them into their social environments, even though studies have shown that, in Ghana, families provide the most support to their return migrants (Setrana & Okyerefo, 2018; Arhin-Sam, 2019). Related to the SDG Target 10.2, which focusses on empowering/promoting the social, economic, and political inclusion of all, is the creation of external and internal networks known as the homegrown return networks. The networks support the social and psychological inclusion of their members into the Ghanaian structures. Aside economic benefits, the formation of returnee networks along the lines of socio-cultural and professional groups provide returnees with mechanisms for social, political, and psychological reintegration. These networks support their members to overcome the challenges of return and reintegration and aid their sustainable return.

One of the latent functions of such networks is the creation of a category of class with their own sets of lifestyles and regulations which widens the income and inequality gap. Non-migrants feel pressurised to migrate and acquire certain qualifications in order to 'belong' to this growing upper class. Added to these challenges is the negative feedback this growing upper class has on the non-migrant youth or unsuccessful potential migrants. While the return of skilled migrants promotes safe, regular, and orderly migration, the feedback loop from these returnees can exacerbate the desire of the youth to migrate by any means, whether 'regular or unregular', 'safe or unsafe', 'orderly or unorderly', in order to acquire such resources to belong to the increasing upper class. It was usual for returnees to be immersed in visits and telephone calls from friends and relatives, many of whom expect to be given gifts and support in one form or the other. Some of the presents given away by the returnees in the first few weeks of returning home include clothing, perfumes, mobile phones, cameras, toiletries, footballs, as well as cash donations to relatives and friends. Although these may be described as burdensome by the return migrants, it must also be acknowledged that they are a means by which returnees gain social acceptance into the family and communities in Ghana. To some extent, the returnees themselves contribute to the kind of behaviour that is expected of them in their communities. Having 'seen the world', they exhibit an arrogant and superior attitude (King, 2000). In some parts of Ghana, the behaviour of returnees reflected the irritation of modern imagery of social status and therefore previously known as 'Burgers' (Nieswand, 2011). In terms of behavioural changes, people from the supposedly more developed countries exhibited certain traits in terms of language and the level of confidence espoused make them stand out differently from others. According to Dahya (1973), these kinds of attitudes become more symbolic since returnees are trying to present themselves as part of the new middle class. In many instances these attitudes reinforce non-migrants' perception on returnees (Arhin-Sam, 2019) as well as motivate non-migrant youth to migrate mostly using irregular channels.

Kwaku, the return medical practitioner, through his transnational network, enhances his skills continually. Although he earns money, his skills and knowledge contribute to Goal 3 of the SDG, 'good health and well-being for people'. As part of this SDG, countries are encouraged to ensure healthy lives and promote well-being for all at all ages. Among the various measures is to reduce the gap between doctor-patient ratio and improve maternal and child mortality in some African countries such as Ghana. Hence, among the various means of leveraging social remittances is for the government of Ghana to motivate short- and long-term return of medical doctors like Kwaku. Such initiatives, as hinted earlier, have been carried out by IOM under the Migration for Development in Africa (MIDA) project and GIZ under the return experts' program (Setrana, 2019).

One of the ways of promoting SDG Goal 9, 'Build resilient infrastructure, promote inclusive and sustainable industrialization, and foster innovation', is through the skills and knowledge return migrants bring to Ghana. Ama, the entrepreneur, and the members of the *Ahaspora* create small-, medium-, and large-scale businesses. These businesses add value to the Ghanaian goods, create jobs, and pay taxes to government, among others. The return migrants interviewed foster innovation and resilience for their own enterprises. Employment creation has a ripple effect on the well-being of the returnee as well as generating income through taxes for the country's economy. However, most of these enterprises struggle to survive due to the absence of government support. The government has the responsibility to leverage such social remittances in order to achieve the full potential benefits of these enterprises by creating an enabling business environment for these businesses to thrive in. Financial and business strategic fora should be organized frequently to support the initiatives of the existing platforms of the return networks. Concessions to support return migrant businesses should be enhanced to sustain return migrants' enterprises for the economic growth of Ghana. Additionally, the home-grown networks assist returnees to sustain their return and reintegration into the home society (Arhin-Sam, 2019). They provide information on useful and important events and needs. They also engage in the development of the communities.

Migration empowers both the Ghanaian man and woman. Once couples or individuals migrate, they tend to acquire some flexible gender roles contrary to rigid patriarchal norms in many traditional contexts. The stories of Adwoa and Ama are examples of such skilled female return migrants who have been empowered through their migration experiences abroad. However, the challenge is how to ensure that these acquired values and norms are perpetuated and enjoyed in a male-dominated environment. The home country context, in this case, prevents the women from exercising their obtained values. Although the females have all it takes to promote SDG 5 (Achieve gender equality and empower all women and girls), its transfer into such a male-dominated environment makes the women vulnerable. Ama and Adwoa have overcome these hurdles by forgoing what many women cherish in the traditional custom, such as having a husband. They are labelled by society as women of deviant attitudes just because they want to assert their rights and apply the learned values from migration. They can make an impact on other young girls only through such means.

Some return migrants were concerned with what they considered to be the excessive religiosity of Ghanaian residents (Setrana & Tonah, 2014; Setrana & Okyerefo, 2018). They were alarmed by the number of churches in Ghana. Returnees were amazed about the ease with which religious explanations were provided as a cure for all sorts of challenges in life and the impact of such attitudes on residents. Though they considered themselves to be religious, their experiences abroad, in largely secular environments, had shown them the importance and limits of religious explanations. It was difficult for some returnees to 'comprehend the ridiculousness associated with the number of hours Ghanaians spend in churches instead of engaging in productive activities, only for them thereafter to beg for alms'. The return migrants describe the excessive religiosity of Ghanaians as unproductive, having a negative impact on the amount of time spent on making economic progress in their workplaces. One of the skilled returnees said, 'I am so upset with my own staff. Time for work is spent in religious gathering ... I wonder how they can improve their economic statuses when they engage in such' (Eselali, interview in Dormaa, March 2015).

As we have shown, the impact of social remittances in the Ghanaian context is both short term and long term in nature. In the short term, returnees are challenged by their own new ideas, values, and behaviours which are sometimes in contrast with the society of origin. On the one hand, such an impact may be negative as it discourages, demotivates, and leads to lack of sense of belonging and less productivity (Arhin-Sam, 2019). On the other hand, social remittances can have short-term positive impact for returnees through the knowledge transfers within their networks that can be harnessed for reintegration purposes. The long-term impact of social remittances in the Ghanaian context is visible from the increasing change in taste, ideas, values, and practices that continue to challenge existing cultural and discursive backgrounds. The long-term impacts result in changing attitudes towards work habits, entrepreneurial behaviours, shifts in gender roles and norms, social tastes, and the overall increase in returnee networks and groups.

Conclusion

The invisible nature of social remittances presents its complexities and challenges with regard to measuring its impact on sustainable development. It is a hard to define and conceptualize concept that can further be disaggregated. Social remittances have the potential to affect many of the SDGs if only it is made less complex in its definition and conceptualization. A more friendly approach to the concept can attract more governments, policymakers, and governments to tap into such aspects of development. The point is that many of such stakeholders do not envisage the direct impact because it cannot be quantified in economic terms. It has mostly been studied in qualitative terms. Other critics have also complained about the expensive cost associated with governments' attempt to harness social remittances for development.

Although much of the discussions on remittances are on the financial aspect, this study among return migrants also shows the social dimensions of the remittances which include the transfer of knowledge, skills, values, and networks, among others. Harnessing social remittances for the achievement of sustainable development is possible under many circumstances. The return of skilled migrants is a source of brain gain to Ghana. Qualitatively, they contribute enormously to the achievement of the following SDGs: Goal 3, 'Good health and well-being for people'; SDG Goal 5, 'Achieve gender equality and empower all women and girls'. Goal 7, Target 10.7, to facilitate orderly, safe, regular, and responsible migration and mobility of people; Goal 9, 'Build resilient infrastructure, promote inclusive and sustainable industrialization, and foster innovation'. Despite the positive impacts, it is worth noting that they also have a negative impact on the country through the creation of an upper-middle-class through the kind of wealth they exhibit. The increasing migration of youth through all kinds of channels and the taste for foreign goods by local people eventually have a negative impact on the promotion of Ghanaian goods.

The study recommends a more comparative and large-scale data collection on social remittances and its impact for countries of origin. There is also the need for governments, through diaspora and migration policies, to create an enabling environment for return migrants to contribute to the home country economy through the knowledge, values, and norms gained.

Notes

1 http://ic.daad.de/accra/alumni.htm.
2 'Aha' is a Twi (Akan) word for 'Here' and 'spora' is a stem of Diaspora. This name befits our status of being home as global citizens. The group aims to bridge the gap between those who are 'Ahas', Ahasporans, and Diasporans, by sharing ideas and experiences to build a true 'Gateway to Africa'. http://www.ahaspora.com/.

References

Anarfi, J.K., & Jagare, S. (2005). *Towards the Sustainable Return of West African Transnational Migrants: What are the Options?* Conference paper, World Bank Conference: New Frontiers of Social Policy Development in a Globalizing World. Arusha.

Anarfi, J.K., Kwankye, S., & Ahiadeke, C. (2005). Migration, Return and Impact in Ghana: A Comparative Study of Skilled and Unskilled Transnational Migrants. In Manuh, T. (ed.), *At Home in the World? International Migration and Development in Contemporary Ghana and West Africa* (pp. 204–226). Accra: Sub-Saharan Publishers.

Arhin-Sam, K. (2019). *Return Migration, Reintegration and Sense of Belonging: The Case of Skilled Ghanaian Returnees.* Baden-Baden: Nomos Verlag. https://doi.org/10.5771/9783845294223.

Boccagni, P., & Decimo, F. (2013). Mapping Social Remittances. *Migration Letters, 10*(1), 1–10.

Borchgrevink, K., & Erdal, M.B. (2016). *The Circulation of Transnational Islamic Charity In Migration and Social Remittances in a Global Europe* (pp. 259–280). Basingstoke: Palgrave Macmillan.

Byfield, J. (2000). Introduction: Rethinking the African Diaspora. *African Studies Review, 43*(1), 1–9.

Carling, J. (2008). The Determinants of Migrant Remittances. *Oxford Review of Economic Policy, 24*(3), 582–599.

Castles, S., de Haas, H., & Miller, M.J. (2009). *The Age of Migration: International Population Movements in the Modern World.* 4th edition. New York: Guilford Press.

Cliggett, L. (2003). Gift Remitting and Alliance Building in Zambian Modernity: Old Answers to Modern Problems. *American Anthropologist, 105*(3), 543–552.

Dahya, B. (1973). Pakistanis in Britain: Transients or settlers? *Race, 14*(3), 241–277.

De Haas, H. (2010). Migration and Development: A Theoretical Perspective. *International Migration Review, 44(1),* 227–264.

Durand, J. (1994). Mas alla de la linea: Patrones migratoroi entre Mexico y Estados Unidos. In Goldring, L. (ed.) (2003), *Re-thinking Remittances: Social and Political Dimensions of Individual and Collective Remittances.* Toronto: York University Press.

Fitzgerald, D. (2000). *Negotiating Extra-Territorial Citizenship: Mexican Migration and the Transnational Politics of Community.* La Jolla, CA: Center for Comparative Immigration Studies.

Grabowska, I., & Garapich, M.P. (2016). Social Remittances and Intra-EU Mobility: Non-Financial Transfers Between U.K. and Poland. *Journal of Ethnic and Migration Studies, 42*(13), 2146–2162.

Hammar, T., & Tamas, K. (1997). Why Do People Go or Stay? In Hammar, T., Brochmann, G., Tamas, K., & Faist, T. (eds.), *International Migration, Immobility and Development* (pp. 1–19). Oxford: Berg.

King, R. (2000). Generalizations from the History of Return Migration. In Ghosh, B. (ed.), *Return Migration, Journey of Hope or Despair?* Geneva: IOM/UN.

Kosack, G. (1976). Migrant Women: The Move to Western Europe - A Step towards Emancipation? *Sage Journals, 17*(4), 369–380.

Levitt, P. (2016). Social Remittances and More: Reflections on 25 Years of Migration Studies. *Central and Eastern European Migration Review, 5*(2), 15–19. https://doi.org/10.17467/ceemr.2017.02.

Levitt, P. (2001). Transnational Migration: Taking Stock and Future Directions. *Global Networks, 1*(3), 195–216.

Levitt, P. (1998). Social Remittances: Migration Driven Local-Level Forms of Cultural Diffusion. *The International Migration Review, 32*(4), 926–948.

Levitt, P. (1996). Social Remittances: A Conceptual Tool for Understanding Migration and Development. *Working Paper Series, 96*(4), 1–24. Retrieved from http://citeseerx.ist.psu.edu/viewdoc/download;jsessionid=BA74A366998C0B36D81BDFF333AFF023?doi=10.1.1.196.2278&rep=rep1&type=pdf.

Levitt, P., & Lamba-Nieves, D. (2013). Rethinking Social Remittances and the Migration-Development Nexus from the Perspective of Time. *Migration Letters, 10*(1), 11–22.

Levitt, P., & Lamba-Nieves, D. (2011). Social Remittances Reconsidered. *Journal of Ethnic and Migration Studies, 37*(1), 1–22. https://doi.org/10.1080/1369183X.2011.521361.

Manuh, T. (1998). Ghanaians, Ghanaian Canadians, and Asantes: Citizenship and Identity Among Migrants in Toronto. *Africa Today, 45*(3), 481–493. Retrieved from http://www.jstor.org/stable/4187240.

Markley, E. (2011). Social Remittances and Social Capital: Values and Practices of Transnational Social Space. *Quality of Life, 22*(4), 365–378.

Mohamoud, A. (2003). African Diaspora and African Development. *Background Paper for AfroNeth, Presented December, 5.* Retrieved from http://www.diaspora-centre.org/DOCS/Diaspora_Developme.pdf.

Nicholas, G. (2002). Dynamic Effects of Migrant Remittances on Growth: An Econometric Model with an Application to Mediterranean Countries. *Discussion Paper,* 74, KEPE.

Nieswand, B. (2011). *Theorising Transnational Migration. The Status Paradox of Migration.* New York and London: Routledge.

Nowicka, M., & Šerbedžija, V. (eds.). (2016). *Migration and Social Remittances in a Global Europe.* Basingstoke: Palgrave Macmillan. https://doi.org/10.1057/978-1-137-60126-1.

Paasche, E. (2016). The Role of Corruption in Workplaces Experiences of Iraqi Kurds upon Return from Europe. *Journal of Ethnic and Migration Studies, 42*(7), 1076–1093.

Phizacklea, A. (ed.). (1983). *One Way Ticket. Migration and Female Labour.* London: Routledge and Kegan Paul.

Putnam, R. (2000). *Bowling Alone: The Collapse and Revival of American Community.* New York: Simon and Schuster.

Setrana, M.B. (2019) *A continental policy forum and workshop on the role of academic Diaspora in revitalization of Africa's Higher Education: The Case of Ghana, Nigeria, Zambia.* Report published by CIDO–AU/Carlton University, funded by The Carnegie Corporation New York (CCNY). Retrieved from http://diasporaforum2019.com/download/a-continental-policy-forum-and-workshop-on-the-role-of-academic-diaspora-in-revitalization-of-africas-higher-education-the-case-of-ghana-nigeria-zambia/.

Setrana, M.B., & Okyerefo, P.K.M. (2018). Internal and International Migration Dynamics in Africa. In Triandafyllidou, A. (ed.), *Handbook of Migration and Globalisation* (pp. 281–196). Cheltenham and Northampton, MA: Edward Elgar Publishing.

Setrana, M.B., & Tonah, S. (2016). Do Transnational Links Matter after Return? Labour Market Participation among Ghanaian Return Migrants. *Journal of Development Studies, 52*(4), 549–560.

Setrana, M.B., & Tonah, S. (2014). Return Migrants and the Challenge of Reintegration: The Case of Returnees to Kumasi, Ghana. *A Journal of African Migration,* 7, 116–142.

9 The impact of mobile money on remittance recipients' household welfare and education

Evidence from Kenya

Romain Fourmy

Introduction

Although they represent a smaller total value compared to international transfers, internal remittances have represented a stable and large source of income for recipient households in Kenya[1] (Jena, 2017). As advanced by the literature, remittances are recognized as an important factor to enhancing welfare in developing countries as a result of their risk-diversification and capital accumulation features (Ratha et al., 2011). Nonetheless, the welfare impact generated by remittances may depend on their count, regularity, and value, which are all strongly influenced by the efficiency of the remitting channel (Ackah & Medvedev, 2010). Prior to 2007, these channels were characterized as being either costly or risky and hence impeding the potential impact of remittances on recipient households (Mohapatra & Ratha, 2011).

In 2007, mobile money was introduced for the first time in Kenya, permitting people to deposit, withdraw, and transfer money using their mobile phones. This new service facilitated the way to process internal remittances, not only because it was cheaper, but also because it became faster and safer to transfer money (Jack & Suri, 2011). Subsequently, this increase in efficiency to remit could lead to consequences on the welfare of recipient households. First, recipient households using mobile money could magnify the count, regularity, and value of remittance receipts, directly improving their welfare. Second, Suri (2017) suggests that this maximization of receipts could lead recipients to allocate more of their household expenditures towards education to finance future migration, as returns to migration increase. Consequently, mobile money could also have a rather indirect, but long-term, positive impact on the welfare of remittance recipient households through this relationship. However, the literature has never empirically investigated this relationship.

Thus, the aim of this chapter is to empirically investigate the impact of mobile money on the household welfare of remittance recipients. This chapter uses a household panel survey data collected between 2008 and 2014 in Kenya, which allows to quantify the actual use of mobile money in internal remittance receipts (Suri & Jack, 2017). In order to assess the effect of mobile money, the empirical approach is structured in two different steps. First, it examines how mobile money has expanded remittance receipts for recipient households. Second, it investigates the changes in expenditure allocation of recipient households caused by the use of mobile money. The findings reveal that mobile money directly improves the welfare through the maximization of receipts, caused by an increase in the count and regularity of remittances. Besides, this maximization of receipts indirectly affects the welfare of recipient households through a higher allocation of expenditures towards education in the long run. Even though this later finding is not statistically significant at the conventional statistical levels, the effect on education expenditures remains the strongest compared to any other expenditure category. Thus, this later finding relates to SDG 4 on education. If this investment is turned into quality education, the use of mobile money in remittance transfers would thus contribute to Target 4.1, which aims to ensure quality primary and secondary education leading to relevant and effective learning outcomes.

The remainder of this chapter proceeds as follows. 'Literature review' reviews the literature on remittances and mobile money. 'Hypotheses' motivates and introduces the working hypotheses of this chapter. 'Data and descriptive statistics' presents the dataset used for the analysis and provides some descriptive statistics. 'Methodology' describes the methodology applied to test the hypotheses. 'Results' reports and interprets the results obtained. 'Conclusion' concludes and discusses the policy implications based on the findings, as well as the limitations of this study.

Literature review

Remittances

As advanced by the new economics of labour migration, remittance transfers rely on a household strategy aiming to overcome imperfect insurance and credit markets in developing countries (Taylor, 1999). First, remittances allow to diversify the risks experienced by households. For instance, negative shocks may reduce their consumption levels. In this case, remittances act as an insurance, which helps households to recover from the consumption loss (Gubert, 2002; Lucas & Stark, 1985; Yang, 2011). Second, remittance receipts are also found to be pro-cyclical, and used for physical capital accumulation once a certain consumption level has been reached (Freund & Spatafora, 2008). As remittance income relies principally on the ability of the migrant to send money, this stream may remain uncertain. For instance, the migrant may also experience negative shocks, such as losing his or her job. Due to this uncertainty, Adams (1998) advances that remittance income is seen as transitory rather than permanent, hence, stimulating the interest in investing in physical capital to maximize long-term welfare. Whereas these investments also support the risk-diversification of households, they equally enable the migrant to secure a base of physical capital at return (Hoddinott, 1994).

As this strategy helps to circumvent market failures in developing countries, households may seek to expand their chances of having a migrant in order to benefit from remittances. To understand the factors determining migration, numerous studies have investigated the characteristics of migrants, for which education has been identified to be among the most deterministic ones (Hagen-Zanker & Siegel, 2007). Using household-level data from Ghana, Ackah and Medvedev (2010) find a higher probability to migrate for younger and more educated individuals, as they tend to have more chances to encounter a job in urban areas. Thus, remittance income may be invested in human capital to finance future migration and enhance the likelihood of benefiting from remittances in the long run (Brown & Poirine, 2005). Although this study is limited to international remittances, Hines and Simpson (2019) provide evidence of a positive effect of remittance receipts on education expenditures for Kenyan households.

Through the improved risk-diversification and accumulation in both physical and human capital, remittances have been recognized as being an important factor contributing to development in developing countries (Ratha et al., 2011). However, the welfare impact of remittances depends on the count, regularity, and value of receipts (Ackah & Medvedev, 2010). The literature advances that these three elements are primarily influenced by the efficiency of the remitting channel (Carling, 2009; Russel, 1986). In Kenya, internal remittances were often processed through informal channels due to the limited access and high costs of the formal ones in the last decades (Ratha, 2005). Prior to 2007, it has been shown that migrants in Kenyan urban areas primarily remitted through bus and taxi companies, friends, and relatives, or carried themselves when returning home (Mohapatra & Ratha, 2011). Even though these informal channels were cheaper than formal ones, remittances could potentially not reach their final destination due to theft or loss, reducing the efficiency of these channels (Mas & Radcliffe, 2011).

Mobile money and remittances

While remittances were principally sent through informal channels during decades, the recent introduction of mobile money has considerably facilitated the way to transfer remittances. This new service was introduced for the first time in Kenya in 2007 under the name of M-PESA, allowing people to deposit, withdraw, and transfer money using their mobile phones (Suri, 2017). One of the main contributions of M-PESA was to supply financial services to the unbanked population in Kenya (Mas & Radcliffe, 2011). This contribution is noteworthy, because financial exclusion has remained a solid barrier to poverty alleviation in developing countries (World Bank, 2012).

As it was conceived at first, another contribution of M-PESA was to optimize the internal remittance market (Jack & Suri, 2011). Indeed, this new formal channel is not only significantly cheaper but also a more secure and faster way to send and receive money compared to former channels. To send money, the sender simply needs to send an SMS including the recipient's M-PESA identifier and the amount desired; then, the recipient receives the amount instantly on his or her mobile phone. As advanced by the literature, the efficiency gain provided by M-PESA could bring many benefits. First, the reduction in transfer costs would increase the likelihood of receiving remittances (Siegel & Fransen, 2013). Using household-level data from two regions in Kenya, Kibera and Bukura, Morawczynski and Pickens (2009) demonstrate that the decrease in fees offered by M-PESA allowed senders to remit more regularly, often with a smaller value per transfer, but still resulting in an increased total value received. This effect is thus consistent with the findings of Aycinena et al. (2010), who detect that the improvement in total value received is mainly driven by the intensification of regularity of receipts rather than the value per transfer. Second, the speed of transaction would facilitate the responsiveness of remittance receipts in case of negative shocks. Jack and Suri (2014) investigate this relationship and find that M-PESA users are more likely to receive remittances when experiencing a negative shock. Moreover, they report evidence that consumption levels were unaffected for M-PESA users during these shocks, while non-users suffered from a loss in consumption by 7%. Third, the security feature of M-PESA would also affect positively the remittance market. When looking at the reasons behind the intensification of remittances in times of negative shocks, Jack et al. (2013) observe that M-PESA has allowed households to receive greater transfers over larger distances.

Based on these findings, it can be advanced that the use of mobile money could maximize remittance receipts, impacting directly and positively the welfare of recipients. Additionally, Suri (2017) suggests that this maximization of receipts could lead remittance recipients to allocate more of their household expenditures towards education to finance future migration, as returns to migration increase thanks to this new channel. Consequently, mobile money could also have a rather indirect but long-term positive impact on the welfare of remittance recipient households through this relationship. Nonetheless, there exists little evidence identifying this effect. The only study touching upon this relationship has been conducted by Munyegera and Matsumoto (2016). Using household surveys from Uganda, their study shows a rise in household expenditures in terms of food, health, education, and social contribution, and that this growth is highly correlated to the enhancement of remittance receipts caused by mobile money. Yet there remain many limitations to their findings. First, both remittance recipient and non-remittance recipient households are included in their sample. As argued in the literature, remittance recipient households are a non-random sample of the population and tend to behave differently compared to non-recipient households (Hoddinott, 1994; Russel, 1986). Second, their identification strategy induces some noise and bias; hence, their results can be interpreted as correlation and not causation.

Hypotheses

The aim of this chapter is thus to provide empirical evidence on this relationship, for which two hypotheses are derived.

First, the effect of mobile money usage on remittance receipts needs to be evaluated, which investigates the direct impact of mobile money on the welfare of remittance recipients. Although it has already been advanced that mobile money enhances the count and regularity of remittances, it is not known whether this is caused by an increase in the intensive or extensive margin (Jack & Suri, 2014; Morawczynski & Pickens, 2009). Therefore, there is a need to eradicate this noise to attain a proper identification of the effects. Accordingly, the first hypothesis proposed is as follows:

H1. Mobile money directly enhances the welfare of remittance recipient households, by increasing the count, regularity, and/or average value of remittance receipts.

To complement this first hypothesis, the reasons for using mobile money in remittance transfers will be examined. These reasons are important, as current directives, such as the SDGs, are shaped towards a reduction in transfer costs in the remittance market (UNSD, 2017). Nevertheless, other reasons may even be more relevant, such as the easiness, speed, and security of remittance channels (Van Doorn & Date, 2002).

Second, the first hypothesis may provide evidence that the remitting channel has gained in efficiency due to mobile money, which may facilitate trade on both the intensive and extensive margin. As suggested by Suri (2017), this facilitation to remit could lead to an improvement in the allocation of human capital, such as in education, as the returns to migration improve. Through this relationship, mobile money could indirectly improve the welfare of remittance recipients through. Accordingly, the second hypothesis proposed is as follows:

H2. Mobile money indirectly enhances the welfare of remittance recipient households, by influencing them to allocate more of their budget towards education.

This second hypothesis thus contributes to providing empirical evidence of an impact of mobile money on investment in education, which is a dimension that has not been properly investigated by the literature.

Data and descriptive statistics

The analysis is based on a household panel survey data collected between 2008 and 2014 in Kenya (Suri & Jack, 2017). These surveys randomly selected households across the country, covering 92% of the national population.

Out of the total number of respondents in the first round, 1,729 are identified as households receiving remittances from household members, relatives, or friends. As this study focusses exclusively on remittance recipients, only these households are considered in the sample for the empirical analysis. Even though the surveys were run through five rounds, the first round in 2008 and second round in 2009 are primarily used to capture the short run. Moreover, the latest round in 2014 complements these two first rounds for the investigation of the second hypothesis, which may require a longer-term view in order to observe the effects. The third and fourth rounds are excluded due to the unavailability of some or all variables of interest.

The main advantage of using this dataset is that it provides detailed remittance records for each recipient household. For instance, these records offer detailed information about remittances received over the last six months, such as the value, the channel, as well as the reason for using the latter. Hence, this information is extremely valuable in the scope of this chapter as it helps to correctly identify the actual use of mobile money in transferring remittances. In addition, extensive information related to weekly, monthly, and yearly expenditures of each household, as well as asset ownership, is available.

However, some limitations present in this dataset need to be addressed. First, the sample attrition across rounds is relatively high. While the sample size is constituted of 1,729 households in the first round, the size decreases to 1,252 and 911 in the second and latest round, respectively. In order to resolve this issue, most of the analysis is conducted using a balanced panel of the two first rounds, as it has been applied by previous research (Jack et al., 2013; Jack & Suri, 2014). Subsequently, 802 households remain in the sample for this balanced panel. Concerning the analysis involving the longer run, an unbalanced panel is used including strictly the latest round and either the first and/or second round, which includes 706 households. Second, none of the variables containing personally identifiable information, such as the district or city of respondents, are available. Therefore, this analysis is constrained to knowing the province where respondents live and whether they reside in a rural or urban area. Lastly, a devastating drought occurred in Kenya in late 2008, leading to a decrease in annual per capita consumption between the first and second rounds. All these later limitations have implications for the empirical strategy to be considered, which are discussed further in 'Methodology'.

Table 9.1 presents descriptive statistics of household characteristics depending on their use of M-PESA for remittance transfers across the two first rounds. In the first round, 408 households reported not receiving remittances through M-PESA, while 394 reported receiving part or all of remittances through M-PESA using their own account. In the second round, 141 households started adopting mobile money to receive remittances. In total, 535 remittance recipient households report using M-PESA to receive part or all of their remittances, whereas 267 households still rely on other channels. In respect of household characteristics, the share of households having a migrant becomes significantly higher for households using M-PESA. As suggested by Medhi et al. (2009), having a migrant would increase the likelihood of receiving remittances, hence

Table 9.1 Descriptive statistics: household characteristics

	Round 1		Round 2	
Variables	*Household* **not** *receiving remittances through M-PESA*	*Household receiving remittances through M-PESA*	*Household* **not** *receiving remittances through M-PESA*	*Household receiving remittances through M-PESA*
Gender of household head	0.784	0.797	0.769	0.796
(male=1)	(0.412)	(0.403)	(0.422)	(0.403)
Age of household head	41.855	39.414	42.758	41.168
(in years)	(14.264)	(13.118)	(14.476)	(13.431)
Education of household head	10.402	12.086	10.424	11.869
(in years)	(4.839)	(4.153)	(3.885)	(3.567)
Household size	4.015	3.794	4.227	4.058
(in absolute numbers)	(2.087)	(1.945)	(2.281)	(1.999)
Share of children in household	0.314	0.294	0.293	0.288
(as a percentage)	(0.243)	(0.250)	(0.246)	(0.246)
Migrant in household	0.907	0.939	0.848	0.940
(migrant=1)	(0.291)	(0.239)	(0.359)	(0.237)
Household wealth index	10.862	11.245	10.690	11.222
(in logarithms)	(1.389)	(1.566)	(1.255)	(1.354)
Negative shocks experienced	1.194	1.231	0.667	0.798
(in numbers)	(0.989)	(0.981)	(0.782)	(0.850)
Household holds bank account	0.547	0.662	0.553	0.613
(holds a bank account=1)	(0.498)	(0.473)	(0.498)	(0.487)
Household owns a cell phone	0.821	0.957	0.833	0.964
(owns a cell phone=1)	(0.384)	(0.203)	(0.373)	(0.185)
Observations	408	394	267	535

Notes: Standard errors are reported in parentheses. The values displayed in the table are proportions of the sample for dummy variables and averages of the sample for continuous variables. The *share of children in household* is computed using the number of children in the household, divided by the household size. The *household wealth index* is computed been computed based on the asset ownership reported by households, which has been transformed as logarithms. Summary statistics for the latest round are not displayed, because most of respondents (88%) use M-PESA to receive remittances and no clear comparison between groups can be performed.

stimulating the adoption of mobile money to facilitate these transfers. Table 9.2 displays the allocation of annual household budget into six expenditure categories, which are based on the classification used by Adams and Cuecuecha (2010). Consistent with the descriptive statistics provided by the same authors, both groups spend a significant share of their budget on strictly consumption items, such as food and consumer goods in the two rounds.

Table 9.2 Descriptive statistics: average household budget shares

Expenditure category	Round 1		Round 2	
	Households **not** receiving remittances through M-PESA	Households receiving remittances through M-PESA	Households **not** receiving remittances through M-PESA	Households receiving remittances through M-PESA
Food	0.560 (0.174)	0.487 (0.175)	0.576 (0.170)	0.502 (0.168)
Consumer goods	0.109 (0.095)	0.126 (0.114)	0.105 (0.098)	0.113 (0.102)
Housing	0.049 (0.082)	0.067 (0.101)	0.061 (0.096)	0.074 (0.094)
Health	0.038 (0.099)	0.034 (0.077)	0.034 (0.077)	0.031 (0.070)
Education	0.061 (0.102)	0.068 (0.117)	0.049 (0.084)	0.064 (0.093)
Other goods	0.182 (0.098)	0.218 (0.116)	0.176 (0.097)	0.215 (0.113)
Observations	408	394	267	535

Notes: Standard errors are reported in parentheses. Summary statistics for the latest round are not displayed, because most of respondents (88%) use M-PESA to receive remittances and no clear comparison between groups can be performed.

Methodology

Following the hypotheses presented in 'Hypotheses', the empirical strategy is divided in two stages. In the first sub-section, the strategy to investigate the effect of mobile money on remittance receipts is described. Then, the strategy to evaluate the impact of mobile money on the allocation of expenditures of recipient households is presented.

Mobile money and remittance receipts

In order to evaluate the impact of mobile money on remittance receipts, a balanced two-period panel is adopted, including the first and second rounds. On top of avoiding potential biases induced by an unbalanced panel, this strategy is consistent with the potential effect that mobile money can already have in the short run, as has been demonstrated by other studies (Jack & Suri, 2014). As mentioned earlier, the use of mobile money could have an impact on the count, regularity, and value of remittances, which are thus used as dependent variables to test the first working hypothesis. The count of remittances is computed by enumerating all the remittances received by the household over the last six months. As the count of remittances might be associated with the experience of negative shocks, the regularity variable needs to be measured in a way that eradicates this potential correlation. Therefore, the regularity variable is calculated as the sum of months in which remittances were received at least once, divided by the period covered by the survey. In terms of interpretation, this variable measures the probability of receiving remittances at least once per month. Then, the average value is computed by summing the value of all remittances received, divided by the total count of receipts.

Concerning the variable of interest, many studies measured mobile money use as whether the household was registered to the service or not. In contrast, this chapter uses the share of remittances that were received through their M-PESA account. This share thus allows us to estimate the actual use of this service in remittance transfers, avoiding either overestimating or underestimating the effect. Furthermore, it enables to eradicate some potential noise generated by the financial inclusion feature of mobile money.

A household fixed effects model is considered to evaluate the effect of mobile money on remittance receipts:

$$receipts_{it} = \beta_0 + \beta_1^{IV} ShareMPESA_{it} + \beta_k X_{it} + \alpha_i + t_{it} + n_{jt} + \mu_{rt} + \varepsilon_{it} \tag{1}$$

where $receipts_{it}$ represents the count, regularity, and average value of remittances for each household i at time t. $ShareMPESA_{it}$ is the share of remittances received through M-PESA for each household. X_{it} is a vector of control variables, including household demographics, financial and asset ownership, and the number of negative shocks experienced over the last six months. Furthermore, t_{it} is a time dummy that is complemented with n_{jt} and μ_{rt}, which are respectively the interactions between time and provinces, and time and the urban dummy in order to control for differential trends across these locations. Lastly, α_i is the household fixed effects term.

As raised in the literature review, the whole population was eligible and free to register to M-PESA, suggesting the presence of self-selection-based endogeneity bias. If not properly addressed, this issue would introduce a bias in the causal interpretation of the effect of mobile money. To minimize this endogeneity concern, the adoption of M-PESA, $ShareMPESA_{it}$, is instrumented. The distance to the closest M-PESA agent is used as the instrumental variable, which is captured by a dummy variable, taking a value of 1 if the household lives within 5 kilometres from the nearest agent, as done by Jack and Suri (2014).

While the self-selection issue is addressed by instrumenting the use of mobile money, endogeneity may still persist. Subsequently, previous studies often complement their strategy by providing a robustness test, which they refer to as a reduced form analysis[2] (Jack & Suri, 2014; Munyegera & Matsumoto, 2016). This test regresses the outcome variable on the distance to agent rather than the use of mobile money, because agent rollout is advanced to be strongly exogenous. Therefore, this allows to see whether the sign and significance levels are consistent across the core strategy and this robustness check. Even though the aim of this test is not to compare coefficient sizes, these are expected to be lower. As argued by Jack and Suri (2014), access to agents greatly facilitates, but does not fully capture, mobile money adoption, explaining the inferior size of coefficients. This robustness test is conducted using a household fixed effects model:

$$receipts_{it} = \beta_0 + \beta_1 Agent_{it} + \beta_k X_{it} + \alpha_i + t_{it} + n_{jt} + \mu_{rt} + \varepsilon_{it} \tag{2}$$

where *Agent* is a dummy variable which takes a value of 1 if the household *i* lives within 5 kilometres from the nearest agent at time *t*. The remaining variables follow the same specification and typology as in Equation 1.

Mobile money, remittances, and household expenditures

From the findings obtained from Equation 1, the impact of mobile money on remittance receipts will be assessed. If mobile money proves to influence one of the mechanism variables, this could imply some indirect effects on the household, as motivated by the second hypothesis. In order to evaluate the effect that mobile money has on recipients' household expenditures, a balanced two-period panel including the first and second rounds is considered as before. However, the effect on recipient households' spending behaviour may not be perceived in the very short run. Therefore, an unbalanced panel including strictly the latest round is used to capture this long-term effect to avoid a significant loss of observations. To estimate the changes in expenditure allocation of households, the strategy employed by Adams and Cuecuecha (2010) is closely mirrored. In their study, the authors use a Working-Leser model, relating budget shares linearly to the logarithm of total annual expenditures, hence appropriately assessing the expenditure patterns of households. As the sum of all budget shares respects the additivity axiom, this functional form allows for rising, falling, or constant change in budget shares, which avoids observing the same slope for all expenditure categories. Moreover, this strategy helps to resolve the issue concerning the decrease in consumption levels faced by Kenyan households between 2008 and 2009. The Working-Leser model used to verify the second hypothesis is as follows:

$$C_{itc} / EXP_{it} = \beta_0 + \beta_1^{IV} ShareMPESA_{it} + \beta_2 \, 1 / EXP_{it} + \beta_3 \left(log \, EXP_{it} \right) \\ + \beta_k X_{it} + \beta_h X_{it} / EXP_{it} + \alpha_i + t_{it} + n_{jt} + \mu_{rt} + \varepsilon_{it} \tag{3}$$

where C_{itc} / EXP is the share of expenditure of category *c* in total expenditure *EXP* for the household *i* at time *t*. The rest of the equation follows the same typology as in Equation 1. As in the previous sub-section, a robustness test is provided using the distance of agent instead of mobile money use. This robustness test is conducted using a household fixed effects model:

$$C_{itc} / EXP_{it} = \beta_0 + \beta_1 Agent_{it} + \beta_2 1 / EXP_{it} + \beta_3 \left(log \, EXP_{it} \right) \\ + \beta_k X_{it} + \beta_h X_{it} / EXP_{it} + \alpha_i + t_{it} + n_{jt} + \mu_{rt} + \varepsilon_{it} \tag{4}$$

again, where *Agent* is a dummy variable which takes a value of 1 if the household i lives within 5 kilometres from the nearest agent at time t.

Results

Mobile money and remittance receipts

The results regarding the effect of mobile money on remittance receipts are presented in Table 9.3. Concerning the instrument variable used in the estimations, the first-stage regression confirms the relevance condition of the distance to the closest mobile money agent. First, the share of M-PESA use has a positive and significant effect on the count of remittance received. In the case of households using exclusively their own M-PESA account to receive remittances, they tend to receive 1.59 remittances more compared to non-users, holding everything else constant. Second, user households tend to receive remittances on a more regular basis. Specifically, households using exclusively their own M-PESA account have a higher probability by 18 percentage points to receive remittances at least once per month compared to non-users. Third, the average value of remittances is not significantly affected by the use of mobile money; nonetheless, the sign of the coefficient reveals to be negative, which relates to the findings of Morawczynski and Pickens (2009), who report a higher regularity and a lower average value of remittance receipts, but still resulting in an increased total value received.

All these results are confirmed by the robustness check analysis. The sign, as well as the significance of coefficients, is consistent with the findings. Therefore, the results illustrate a consistent story that the use of M-PESA expands the count and regularity of remittances for recipient households. The increase in regularity of remittance receipts has often been associated by the literature with a reduction in transfer costs (Aycinena et al., 2010). However, it is important to note that the effects generated by mobile money may not exclusively be attributed to this reduction. As can be seen in Table A.1, the main reasons for using M-PESA are primarily related to the speed and easiness in processing remittances rather than a reduction in transfer costs.

Mobile money, remittances, and household expenditures

Tables 9.4 and 9.5 present the results concerning the impact of the use of M-PESA on household expenditures in the short and long run, respectively. In the short run, households receiving remittances exclusively through M-PESA tend to allocate significantly more of their budget towards the category of other goods by 6.71 percentage points. These results are supported using the robustness check analysis, which reports the same level of significance and direction of the sign. As this category includes various items, thus difficult to interpret, Equation 3 has been estimated relatively to this category. From this estimation, households using M-PESA tend to allocate more

Table 9.3 Regression results Hypothesis 1: mobile money and remittance receipts

Variables	Count of remittances received	Regularity of remittances received	Average value of remittances received
ShareMPESA	1.595★★	0.180★★	−175.2
	(0.792)	(0.0860)	(1,511)
Gender of household head	0.521	0.103★★	1,523
	(0.443)	(0.0459)	(1,041)
Age of household head	0.00550	0.00149	36.07
	(0.0130)	(0.00149)	(62.88)
Education of household head	−0.0744★★	−0.0113★★★	4.593
	(0.0309)	(0.00354)	(60.95)
Household size	0.132	0.00180	−551.5
	(0.0932)	(0.0104)	(396.2)
Share of children in household	0.851	0.145★	1,867
	(0.788)	(0.0851)	(2,364)
Migrant in household	1.426★★★	0.153★★★	−1,256★
	(0.301)	(0.0366)	(654.6)
Bank account	−0.215	−0.0143	138.0
	(0.202)	(0.0222)	(284.2)
Mobile phone	−0.329	−0.0482	1,135
	(0.496)	(0.0556)	(892.5)
Log wealth index	0.0723	0.00297	810.1
	(0.0903)	(0.0101)	(575.7)
Number of negative shocks	0.0519	0.00453	857.2
	(0.103)	(0.0115)	(713.9)
Time	0.637★	0.0957★★★	−1,506★★
	(0.335)	(0.0365)	(610.2)
Time★Province	−0.241★★★	−0.0291★★★	275.8★
	(0.0667)	(0.00706)	(150.6)
Time★Urban	0.00195	−0.000804	−429.9
	(0.343)	(0.0350)	(1,137)
Constant	0.270	0.152	−6,892
	(1.142)	(0.132)	(6,585)
Observations	1,604	1,604	1,594
Robustness check:			
Distance to agent dummy	0.371★★	0.0419★★	−41.22
	(0.185)	(0.0201)	(716.3)
First stage results:			
Instrument: Distance to agent dummy	0.233★★★		
	(0.0320)		
Kleibergen–Paap LM test	45.087		
LM test p-value	0.0000		
Kleibergen–Paap F statistic	53.30		

Notes: Heteroskedasticity-robust standard errors are reported in parentheses. Asterisks ★, ★★, and ★★★ represent significance at the 10%, 5%, and 1% levels, respectively. The count of remittances received variable is expressed as the absolute value. The regularity of remittances received variable is expressed as the probability of receiving remittances at least once per month. The average value of remittances received is expressed in KShs, for which is exchange rate during the period covered was KShs 75 = US$1. The same independent variables have been used for the robustness check analysis, however, these are not reported in the table.

Table 9.4 Regression results Hypothesis 2: mobile money, remittance receipts, and household expenditures: short run analysis

Variables	Food	Consumer goods	Housing	Health	Education	Other goods
ShareMPESA	−0.0269	−0.0497★	0.0250	−0.0253	0.00983	0.0671★★
	(0.0400)	(0.0292)	(0.0251)	(0.0267)	(0.0293)	(0.0313)
log(EXP)	−0.162★★★	0.0447★★★	0.0484★★★	0.0630★★★	0.0525★★★	−0.0467★★★
	(0.0182)	(0.0168)	(0.0186)	(0.0195)	(0.0191)	(0.0175)
Gender of	0.0427	0.0117	−0.0312	0.00417	−0.0318★	0.00442
household head	(0.0283)	(0.0235)	(0.0278)	(0.0256)	(0.0188)	(0.0231)
Age of	−0.00146	−0.00232★★	0.000250	0.00222★★★	0.00247★★★	−0.00117
household head	(0.00106)	(0.000967)	(0.000780)	(0.000844)	(0.000821)	(0.000962)
Education of	0.00221	0.00162	0.00157	−0.00145	−0.00184	−0.00212
household head	(0.00199)	(0.00178)	(0.00168)	(0.00211)	(0.00182)	(0.00195)
Share of	−0.153★★★	0.0798★★	0.0199	0.0948★★★	0.0540	−0.0952★★
children in household	(0.0502)	(0.0394)	(0.0373)	(0.0355)	(0.0378)	(0.0446)
Migrant in	−0.0108	0.00277	−0.00490	0.0277★★	0.00814	−0.0229
household	(0.0223)	(0.0194)	(0.0174)	(0.0124)	(0.0150)	(0.0214)
Log wealth	−0.0153★★	0.00926★	0.00697	−0.00913★	−0.00137	0.00959★★
index	(232.1)	(157.1)	(167.3)	(162.6)	(178.0)	(178.6)
Mobile	−0.0159	0.00179	−0.0295	0.00191	0.0140	0.0277
phone	(0.0418)	(0.0299)	(0.0233)	(0.0272)	(0.0279)	(0.0354)
Bank account	−0.0403★★★	0.0111	0.000870	−0.00173	0.0110	0.0191
	(0.0153)	(0.0135)	(0.0136)	(0.0108)	(0.0113)	(0.0147)
Number of	−0.00754	0.00279	−0.00362	0.0125★★★	0.00230	−0.00639
negative shocks	(0.00494)	(0.00398)	(0.00359)	(0.00295)	(0.00365)	(0.00442)
Time	−0.0113	−0.00238	0.0199	0.0113	−0.00412	−0.0134
	(0.0155)	(0.0124)	(0.0124)	(0.0109)	(0.0113)	(0.0128)
Time★Urban	−0.00640	0.0120	−0.0117	0.0110	−0.0119	0.00696
	(0.0156)	(0.0128)	(0.0119)	(0.0109)	(0.0126)	(0.0130)
Time★ Province	0.00141	0.00201	−0.00235	−0.00169	0.000874	−0.000250
	(0.00302)	(0.00245)	(0.00236)	(0.00193)	(0.00216)	(0.00260)
Constant	2.621★★★	−0.428★★	−0.559★★	−0.715★★★	−0.625★★★	0.707★★★
	(0.220)	(0.201)	(0.228)	(0.224)	(0.235)	(0.210)
Observations	1,604	1,604	1,604	1,604	1,604	1,604
Robustness check:						
Distance	−0.00621	−0.0115★	0.00577	−0.00586	0.00228	0.0155★★
to agent dummy	(0.00931)	(0.00669)	(0.00618)	(0.00561)	(0.00667)	(0.00746)

Notes: Heteroskedasticity-robust standard errors are reported in parentheses. Asterisks ★, ★★, and ★★★ represent significance at the 10%, 5%, and 1% levels, respectively. The model also includes interactions of each variable with the inverse of total expenditure, the inverse of total expenditure, but coefficients for these variables are not reported. The same independent variables have been used for the robustness check analysis, however, these are not reported in the table.

Table 9.5 Regression results Hypothesis 2: mobile money, remittance receipts, and household expenditures: long run analysis

Variables	Food	Consumer goods	Housing	Health	Education	Other goods
ShareMPESA	−0.00897	−0.0220	0.0344	−0.0344	0.0643★	−0.0333
	(0.0407)	(0.0309)	(0.0269)	(0.0329)	(0.0350)	(0.0303)
log(EXP)	−0.127★★★	0.0603★★★	0.0853★★★	0.0283★★	0.000257	−0.0473★★★
	(0.0136)	(0.0137)	(0.0207)	(0.0135)	(0.0114)	(0.0102)
Gender of household head	−0.0336★	0.0228	0.0238	−0.00782	−0.00380	−0.00142
	(0.0199)	(0.0174)	(0.0153)	(0.0162)	(0.0161)	(0.0146)
Age of household head	−0.00122	−0.00154★★	0.00150★★	0.00185★★	0.000296	−0.000874
	(0.000949)	(0.000646)	(0.000623)	(0.000758)	(0.000632)	(0.000720)
Education of household head	−0.00185	0.00138	−0.00264★	0.000820	0.00122	0.00108
	(0.00189)	(0.00168)	(0.00144)	(0.00133)	(0.00177)	(0.00153)
Share of children in household	−0.155★★★	0.0674★★	0.105★★★	0.0472★★	0.0176	−0.0814★★★
	(0.0355)	(0.0303)	(0.0267)	(0.0232)	(0.0281)	(0.0257)
Migrant in household	−0.00624	−0.0185	0.0114	0.0134	0.00470	−0.00476
	(0.0196)	(0.0174)	(0.0140)	(0.0109)	(0.0138)	(0.0141)
Wealth index	−0.00838	0.0180★★★	−0.00802★	−0.0122★★★	−0.00264	0.0132★★★
	(0.00602)	(0.00511)	(0.00424)	(0.00406)	(0.00490)	(0.00436)
Mobile phone	0.0105	−0.0620★★	0.0104	−0.00256	−0.0208	0.0645★★
	(0.0428)	(0.0298)	(0.0245)	(0.0324)	(0.0299)	(0.0282)
Bank account	−0.0225	0.0193	−0.0139	0.0155	−0.00578	0.00739
	(0.0148)	(0.0124)	(0.0114)	(0.0103)	(0.0114)	(0.0111)
Number of negative shocks	−0.00681	−0.00136	−0.00192	0.0150★★★	−0.000988	−0.00392
	(0.00509)	(0.00385)	(0.00281)	(0.00403)	(0.00390)	(0.00387)
Time	−0.00846	0.000261	0.0128	0.00462	−0.00213	−0.00712
	(0.0147)	(0.0120)	(0.0101)	(0.0118)	(0.0127)	(0.0114)
Time★Urban	−0.0146★★	0.00391	0.00116	0.00359	0.0101★★	−0.00419
	(0.00624)	(0.00436)	(0.00382)	(0.00339)	(0.00440)	(0.00488)
Time★Province	0.00272	0.00103	−0.00399★★	−0.000571	0.000626	0.000187
	(0.00220)	(0.00177)	(0.00156)	(0.00154)	(0.00179)	(0.00164)
Constant	2.180★★★	−0.665★★★	−0.965★★★	−0.240	0.0607	0.628★★★
	(0.160)	(0.169)	(0.234)	(0.157)	(0.137)	(0.121)
Observations	1,732	1,732	1,732	1,732	1,732	1,732
Robustness check:						
Distance to agent dummy	−0.00244	−0.00600	0.00937	−0.00937	0.0175★	−0.00908
	(0.0111)	(0.00836)	(0.00719)	(0.00885)	(0.00906)	(0.00804)

Notes: Heteroskedasticity-robust standard errors are reported in parentheses. Asterisks ★, ★★, and ★★★ represent significance at the 10%, 5%, and 1% levels, respectively. The model also includes interactions of each variable with the inverse of total expenditure, the inverse of total expenditure, but coefficients for these variables are not reported. The same independent variables have been used for the robustness check analysis, however, these are not reported in the table.

their budget towards the purchase of cell airtime in the short run. Although this effect might not be intuitive at first, there exists a consistent story behind this effect, which has been motivated by Batista and Vicente (2016) and Mbiti and Weil (2015). Prior to the introduction of mobile money, cell airtime was widely accepted as a proxy for money in developing countries (Maurer, 2012). Thus, early M-PESA adopters tended to buy airtime in order to make payments, because this service was not yet adopted by everyone in the very short run. However, this effect has been advanced to vanish over time as the adoption of mobile money increases (Batista & Vicente, 2016).

Looking at the long run, the allocation of expenditures has diverged compared to the short run. Indeed, the allocation towards the other goods category, and more especially cell airtime, has disappeared as predicted by the literature. Instead, the budget allocation towards education is relatively stronger. Households receiving remittances exclusively through M-PESA tend to allocate more of their budget towards education by 6.43 percentage points in the long run, holding everything else constant. Even though the coefficient is only significant at 90% confidence level, the allocation towards education due to mobile money use remains stronger compared to any other expenditure category. Moreover, the results are supported by the robustness check analysis, for which the sign and significance level regarding education remain consistent.

Conclusion

In developing countries, former channels for internal remittances were often characterized as being costly and risky over the last decades. This inefficiency hindered not only remittance receipts but also the potential benefits they could generate on the welfare of recipient households. Consequently, the introduction of mobile money represented a real opportunity to make the remittance market more efficient. By being a cheaper, safer, and faster way to remit, mobile money could enhance remittance receipts, directly improving the welfare of recipient households. As suggested by Suri (2017), this facilitation to remit could even lead to an improvement in the allocation of human capital, such as in education, as the returns to migration improve. Thus, this second implication could have a rather indirect positive impact on the welfare of recipient households in the longer term. Nonetheless, no empirical studies have examined these potential effects.

This chapter investigated empirically this channel of causation using household panel surveys from Kenya. This dataset provided transfer records for each recipient household, enabling to precisely identify the actual use of mobile money in remittance transfers. Therefore, this strategy discarded any potential noise generated by the financial inclusion feature of mobile money, which has often been disregarded in previous studies. In order to address endogeneity concerns of mobile money adoption and unobserved time-invariant household characteristics, an instrumented household fixed effects model was used throughout this chapter.

The results confirm that the use of mobile money in transferring remittances has a positive impact on the welfare of recipient households. First, mobile money directly improves welfare through the maximization of remittance receipts, generated by both an increase in the count and regularity of remittances received. Second, the maximization of receipts through mobile money affects positively the welfare of recipient households through a better allocation of expenditures in the long run. Even though the coefficient is significant at 90% confidence level, this effect remains the strongest among all expenditure categories. All these results were confirmed through robustness test analyses. Linking these two findings gives some empirical support to what has been suggested by Suri (2017), that the increased returns to migration enabled by mobile money may influence households to invest in future migration, by allocating more of their budget towards human capital accumulation.

Based on these findings, many implications can be derived. First, these findings may provide implications concerning international remittances. On the contrary to internal remittance markets, international remittance channels have not significantly developed over the last decades, remaining costly and slow in processing transfers[3] (Mohapatra & Ratha, 2011). In order to improve and maximize the benefits for the recipient households, the United Nations have set the following target for SDG 10.C: 'By 2030, reduce to less than 3 per cent the transaction costs of migrant remittances and eliminate remittance corridors with costs higher than 5 per cent' (United Nations Statistical Commission, 2017). However, the reduction of costs may not be the sole component making remittance channels more efficient. As has been showed in this study, recipient households claimed to use mobile money because it was primarily faster and easier to send and receive remittances.

Second, this chapter has provided some evidence regarding the effect of mobile money on another dimension that has never been explored empirically, which is one of investment in education. Inspired by the suggestion provided by Suri (2017), this chapter provided some evidence of a higher allocation of expenditures towards education in the long run for households using mobile money to transfer remittances. On the one hand, this growth in demand for education should be grasped by policy makers in developing countries, by converting this demand into quality education, which would contribute to Target 4.1 that aims to ensure quality primary and secondary education leading to relevant and effective learning outcomes. On the other hand, this increase might drive even more human mobility in developing countries when investment in education can increase the chances to migrate. Although migration can bring several benefits, the loss of educated migrants in communities of origin may lead to a potential brain drain (Schiff & Özden, 2005). Therefore, policies should be aimed at handling this brain drain issue, as migration is a phenomenon that is even more likely to expand in the future.

While many limitations imposed by the dataset were addressed through a specific methodology, the study was not able to consider the spatial dimension due to data constraints on the localization of respondents. As advanced by Adams and Cuecuecha (2010), there tends to exist a high correlation among respondents within a municipality. In this study, the spatial dimension was restricted to the province level, hence its not being accurate enough to control for this correlation. Furthermore, the total number of provinces is relatively low, driving the clustering of the standard errors at this level to be inappropriate (Cameron & Miller, 2015).

Notes

1 As internal remittances were mainly processed through informal channels in the last decades, data on the actual amount of these flows are scarce. Based on older survey-based research, Johnson and Whitelaw (1974) document that 88.9% of male respondents in Nairobi reported sending money to rural areas on a regular basis.
2 The name used by the authors for this robustness test might be misleading, because a reduced form analysis commonly refers to a first-stage regression in a 2SLS. Nevertheless, it should be noted that in this case, the dependent variable remains the outcome variables hypothesised in H1 and H2, rather than the use of mobile money.
3 As of now, only 12 countries authorize sending or receiving international remittances through mobile money. These countries are: Benin, Burkina Faso, Cote d'Ivoire, Kenya, Malawi, Mali, Niger, Rwanda, Senegal, Tanzania, Togo, and Zambia (Naghavi & Scharwatt, 2018).

References

Ackah, C., & Medvedev, D. (2010). *Internal migration in Ghana: Determinants and welfare impacts.* The World Bank, Washington, DC.

Adams, R. H. (1998). Remittances, investment, and rural asset accumulation in Pakistan. *Economic Development and Cultural Change, 47*(1), 155–173.

Adams, R. H., & Cuecuecha, A. (2010). Remittances, household expenditure and investment in Guatemala. *World Development, 38*(11), 1626–1641.

Aycinena, D., Martinez, C., & Yang, D. (2010). The impact of remittance fees on remittance flows: Evidence from a field experiment among Salvadoran migrants. *Report.* University of Michigan. [1672].

Batista, C., & Vicente, P. C. (2016). Introducing mobile money in rural Mozambique: Evidence from a randomized field experiment. NOVAFRICA Working Paper, 2016.

Brown, R. P. C., & Poirine, B. (2005). A model of migrants' remittances with human capital investment and intrafamilial transfers. *The International Migration Review, 39*(2), 407–438.

Cameron, A. C., & Miller, D. L. (2015). A practitioner's guide to cluster-robust inference. *Journal of Human Resources, 50*(2), 317–372.

Carling, J. (2009). The determinants of migrant remittances. *Oxford Review of Economic Policy, 24*(3), 581–598.

Freund, C., & Spatafora, N. (2008). Remittances, transaction costs, and informality. *Journal of Development Economics, 86*(2), 356–366.

Gubert, F. (2002). Do migrants insure those who stay behind? Evidence from the Kayes area (Western Mali). *Oxford Development Studies, 30*(3), 267–287.

Hagen-Zanker, J., & Siegel, M. (2007). The determinants of remittances: A review of the literature. *Maastricht Graduate School of Governance Working Paper*, Maastricht, Netherlands.

Hines, A. L., & Simpson, N. B. (2019). "Migration, remittances and human capital investment in Kenya." *Economic Notes: Review of Banking, Finance and Monetary Economics 48*(3), e12142.

Hoddinott, J. (1994). A model of migration and remittances applied to western Kenya. *Oxford Economic Papers, 46*(3), 459–476.

Jack, W., Ray, A., & Suri, T. (2013). Transaction networks: Evidence from mobile money in Kenya. *American Economic Review, 103*(3), 356–361.

Jack, W., & Suri, T. (2011). Mobile money: The economics of M-PESA. *National Bureau of Economic Research (No. w16721)*. Cambridge, MA.

Jack, W., & Suri, T. (2014). Risk sharing and transactions costs: Evidence from Kenya's mobile money revolution. *American Economic Review, 104*(1), 183–223.

Jena, F. (2017). Migrant remittances and physical investment purchases: Evidence from Kenyan households. *The Journal of Development Studies, 54*(2), 312–326.

Johnson, G. E., & Whitelaw, W. E. (1974). Urban-rural income transfers in Kenya: An estimated-remittances function. *Economic Development and Cultural Change, 22*(3), 473–479.

Lucas, R. E. B., & Stark, O. (1985). Motivations to remit: Evidence from Botswana. *Journal of Political Economy, 93*(5), 901–918.

Mas, I., & Radcliffe, D. (2011). Scaling mobile money. *Journal of Payments Strategy & Systems, 5*(3), 298–315.

Maurer, B. (2012). Mobile money: Communication, consumption and change in the payments space. *Journal of Development Studies, 48*(5), 589–604.

Mbiti, I., & Weil, D. N. (2015). Mobile banking: The impact of M-Pesa in Kenya. In Edwards, Johnson, S., and Weil, D. N (Eds.), *African Successes, Volume III: Modernization and Development* (pp. 247–293). Chicago, IL: University of Chicago Press.

Medhi, I., Ratan, A., & Toyama, K. (2009). "Mobile-banking adoption and usage by low-literate, low-income users in the developing world." In *International conference on internationalization, design and global development*. Berlin, Heidelberg: Springer.

Mohapatra, S., & Ratha, D. (2011). *Remittance markets in Africa*. The World Bank, Washington, DC.

Morawczynski, O., & Pickens, M. (2009). Poor people using mobile financial services: Observations on customer usage and impact from M-PESA. *CGAP Brief*. Retrieved from https://www.cgap.org/sites/default/files/CGAP-Brief-Poor-People-Using-Mobile-Financial-Services-Observations-on-Customer-Usage-and-Impact-from-M-PESA-Aug-2009.pdf

Munyegera, G. K., & Matsumoto, T. (2016). Mobile money, remittances, and household welfare: Panel evidence from rural Uganda. *World Development, 79*, 127–137.

Naghavi, N., & Scharwatt, C. (2018). *Mobile money: Competing with informal channels to accelerate the digitisation of remittances*. Retrieved from. https://www.gsma.com/mobilefordevelopment/resources/competing-with-informal-channels-to-accelerate-the-digitisation-of-remittances/

Ratha, D. (2005). Workers' remittances: An important and stable source of external development finance. *Remittances: development impact and future prospects*, 19–51.

Ratha, D., Mohapatra, S., Özden, C., Plaza, S., & Shaw, W. (2011). *Leveraging Migration for Africa: Remittances, Skills, and Investments.* The International Bank for Reconstruction and Development/The World Bank, Washington, DC.

Russel, S. S. (1986). Remittances from international migration: A review in perspective. *World Development, 14*(6), 677–696.

Schiff, M., & Özden, Ç. (2005). *International migration, remittances, and the brain drain.* The World Bank, Washington, DC.

Siegel, M., & Fransen, S. (2013). New technologies in remittance sending: Opportunities for mobile remittances in Africa. *African Journal of Science, Technology, Innovation and Development, 5*(5), 423–438.

Suri, T. (2017). Mobile money. *Annual Review of Economics, 9*(1), 497–520.

Suri, T., & Jack, W. (2017). M-PESA Kenya, Harvard Dataverse, V1, Harvard United-States.

Taylor, E. J. (1999). The new economics of labour migration and the role of remittances in the migration process. *International Migration, 37*(1), 63–88.

United Nations Statistical Commission. (2017). Global indicator framework for the sustainable development goals and targets of the 2030 agenda for sustainable development. *UN Resolution A/RES/71/313.*

Van Doorn, J., & Date, N. (2002). Migration, remittances and development. *Labour Education, 4*(129), 48–53.

World Bank. (2012). *Information and communications for development 2012: Maximizing mobile.* World Bank Publications, Washington, DC.

Yang, D. (2011). Migrant remittances. *Journal of Economic Perspectives, 25*(3), 129–152.

Appendix

Table A.1 Reasons for using M-PESA to receive and send remittances

Reasons for using M-PESA in remittance transfers	Round 1		Round 2	
	Frequency	*Percent*	*Frequency*	*Percent*
Fast	1,542	50.89	2,012	62.84
Easy	679	22.41	611	19.08
Cheap	364	12.01	251	7.84
Safe	210	6.93	248	7.75
Other reasons	235	7.76	80	2.50
Total	3,030	100	3,202	100

Notes: The frequency is computed by summing all the remittance records processed through M-PESA according to the specific reason.

Part III

Migration, remittances, corruption and conflicts

10 Remittances and bribery in Africa

Maty Konte and Gideon Ndubuisi

Introduction

According to the World Bank (2019) report on migration and development, recorded remittances to low- and middle-income countries reached $466 billion in 2017 from their previous value of $429 billion in 2016. Measured as a share of GDP, Africa has continuously topped the chart on the volume of remittances inflow. Amid this rise, quantitative analysis on the impact of remittances on socioeconomic outcomes, including poverty and inequality, labour productivity, consumption stability, and education and financial development (Acosta et al., 2008; Azizi, 2019; Combes & Ebeke, 2011; Edwards & Ureta, 2003; Giuliano & Ruiz-Arranz, 2009; Mamun et al., 2015) have also proliferated. While most of these studies show that remittances improve socioeconomic outcomes, its net effect on economic growth remains elusive (Barajas et al., 2009).

More recently, a growing body of literature has examined the impact of remittances on the institutional quality and political outcomes of the remittance recipient countries. Studies in this literature evaluated the effects of remittances on the political regime types and transitions (Deonanan & Williams, 2017; Escriba-Folch et al., 2015; Williams, 2018), political participation (Goodman & Hiskey, 2008; O'Mahony, 2013; Tyburski, 2012), political patronage or clientelism (Baudase et al., 2018; Combes et al., 2015; Pfutze, 2014), and the level of corruption in the government or government effectiveness in providing public goods (Abidh et al., 2012; Ahmed, 2013; Beriev et al., 2013).

However, only few studies have focussed on African countries (Escribà-Folch et al., 2018; Konte, 2016 and Williams, 2017, among others[1]), despite the region hosting a significant portion of global remittances. Moreover, discussions in these studies show a mixed effect of remittances on institutional quality and political outcomes in Africa. For instance, Williams (2017) found that increasing migrant remittances had a positive effect on democracy in sub-Saharan Africa, whereas Escribà-Folch et al. (2018), using data for eight nondemocracies in Africa, discovered that remittance receipt increased protest in opposition areas but not in progovernment regions. In addition,

Konte (2016) empirically showed that receiving remittances can undermine the endorsement of and support for democracy, depending on whether the recipients prioritize freedom and rights over the economic conditions in their countries.

While these studies have helped us gain important insights on the relationship between remittances and governance or political outcomes in Africa, the question of how migrant remittances affect corruption in Africa has received little attention in the literature. This is surprising because in the last few years more than 130 million citizens interviewed across 35 African countries have paid bribes to access public services and that more than half of the people think that corruption is worsening and that governments are not doing enough to tackle it (see Pring and Vrushi, 2019).

Against this backdrop, in this chapter we examine whether receiving remittances from abroad increases or decreases the likelihood of bribing public officials to access public goods and services, such as official documents and household services, or avoiding run-ins with the police. We identify and empirically test two potential pathways by which this situation may occur: the income and norm channels. First, because remittances increase the receiver's income, s/he is better placed to pay bribes in exchange for public services or goods. Alternatively, depending on the nature of the services or goods, the receiver may prefer to use private services/goods to avoid interactions with public officials. Second, remittances represent a direct link between senders and receivers, making it possible for the former to influence the values of the latter. The sender, for instance, can inveigle the receiver to comply with certain norms and beliefs by withholding transfer. This argument is consistent with Levitt's (1998) social remittance thesis, which suggests that in addition to financial remittances, migrants transfer new knowledge, practices, and norms to their home countries.

For our empirical analysis we used the Afrobarometer surveys administered in 36 African countries between 2008 and 2016 to evaluate the impact of remittances on the corrupt practices of remittance recipients such as bribe payments for public goods and services. The results corroborate our conjectures on the income and norm channels as potential pathways by which remittances affect corruption, such as bribe payments, among remittance recipients. Specifically, while we find that remittance receivers are more likely to pay bribes than non-receivers to access public goods or services, we obtain additional evidence that individuals who live in countries with higher levels of remittances as a share of GDP are more likely to pay bribes to access public goods and services than individuals who live in countries with lower levels of remittances as a share of GDP which is in line with the income channel. However, the positive association between remittance inflows and bribe payments diminishes in countries with a high level of control over corruption, suggesting that strong institutional quality can attenuate the potential negative effects of remittance.

When considering the stock of migrants living in OECD countries, we further find that citizens of African countries with a high stock of migrants living in those OECD countries are less likely to pay bribe to government officials than citizens of countries with lower levels of stock of migrants in those OECD countries which is in line with the norm channel. As we argue further in the main test, however, more data and empirical analyses are needed to provide stronger evidence on remittances, norms, and bribe payments in Africa. Overall, as policy recommendation, the findings in this chapter suggest that policies for the success of SDG 17.3 that, in one of its indicators, calls for an increase in remittances should be coupled with anti-corruption policies advocated in SDG 16.5. If not, the positive effects of remittances on the economic conditions of the recipients may result in increased corruption in remittance-receiving countries.

The remainder of this chapter is structured as follows: 'Remittances, institutions and politics' presents a review of related literature. 'Data and empirical strategy' describes the research methodology including data sources and model specification; 'Results and discussions' discusses the results, whereas 'Concluding remarks' provides some concluding remarks.

Remittances, institutions, and politics

The continuous rise in the volume of workers' remittances, together with its potential as an alternative source of development finance, has proliferated academic researches on its socioeconomic effects. One such area of research related to the current study is the literature on 'remittances and institutional quality'. The major issue analysed in this literature is whether remittances act as a curse or a blessing to the remittance recipient country. Along this line, Abdih et al. (2012) developed a model wherein remittances lead to moral hazard by reducing households' incentive to hold the government accountable for lack of public goods provision. This occurs because remittances enable the recipient households to purchase public goods themselves rather than rely on the government. The government can then free ride and engage in rent-seeking behaviours.[2] Using national indices on control of corruption, government effectiveness, rule of law, and the ratio of remittances to gross domestic product (GDP) in a cross-sectional sample of 111 countries, the authors found empirical evidence for their model's prediction. A similar conclusion has been reached by Ahmed (2013), among others. However, other studies, such as Tyburski (2014), Baudassé et al. (2018), and Tusalem (2018), have found contradictory evidence. Tyburski (2014), for instance, showed that remittances lead to a higher income for people, which makes it easier for them to express their concerns and demand greater control of corruption. Similarly, Baudassé et al. (2018) argued that remittances lower clientelism, thereby allowing people to voice their concerns against the government and to demand higher accountability.

Some other studies argue that remittances' lower clientelism leads to a less corrupt government and fairer elections where citizens can express their actual opinions (Deonanan & Williams, 2017; Escriba-Folch et al., 2015, 2018). It also facilitates political opposition to develop, thereby decreasing the autocratic regime types (Combes et al., 2015). Williams (2017), for example, showed that higher remittances increase the level of democratization in sub-Saharan countries. On the other hand, it could also lead to political disengagement. Escriba-Folch et al. (2018) argue that remittances increase government revenues through higher consumption taxes and/or a reduction in the provision of public goods, as previously explained, which means that the government has more resources available for clientelism. In addition, because of the substitution effects induced by remittances, people could become less interested in politics, thereby making it easier to politically manipulate them before an election (Combes et al., 2015). Along this line, Goodman and Hiskey (2008) found empirical evidence that cities in Mexico with higher levels of emigration and remittances have a population 'that is far less inclined to participate in politics and more likely to view formal politics more ineffective in meeting their daily needs than those citizens living in low migration town' (p. 171). A similar result has also been reached by Ebeke and Yogo (2013) in a sample comprising Sub-Saharan African countries.

Overall, the existing literature on the impact of remittances on institution remains inconclusive, which is largely explained by the research context and idiosyncrasies of the remittance recipient household. The current study contributes to the above literature by evaluating the potential impacts of remittance on the preponderance of corruption among remittance recipient households. We argue that remittances represent a direct link between migrants and those left behind. According to Levitt (1998), this link is a pathway for financial flows and social values transfers through direct communication, which may alter the beliefs of the recipient. Accordingly, the current study is also related to the erstwhile literature on the impact of (e)migration on the migrant's home country institutional quality which takes the social remittances thesis suggested by Levitt (1998) as a starting point.

As a retrospection, social remittances are values, practices and principles, normative structures, systems of practice, and social capital which are transmitted by migrants to their home country (Levitt, 1998). Depending on the differences between the institutional qualities at home and abroad, the literature then argues that migrants could transfer either good or bad values to the home country through direct communication with those left behind, voting and lobbying from abroad, and/or as returned migrants. Spilimbergo (2009) provides a first cross-country empirical evidence in this literature by examining the impact of foreign-trained students on the democratization of their home country. More detailed micro studies have found supportive evidence that migration to countries with good quality governances increases the demand for greater political accountability (Batista & Vicente, 2011), democratization (Pfutze, 2012), and higher electoral competitiveness (Chauvet & Mercier, 2014) at home, respectively.

Data and empirical strategy

Data description

To study the effects of migrant remittances on bribe payment to public officials, we use Afrobarometer data, which contain a collection of nationally representative surveys collected from 36 African countries. The surveys inform us about the attitudes of citizens towards democracy, markets, civil society, and other aspects of development. To our knowledge, only the fourth (collected between 2008 and 2009) and sixth rounds (collected between 2014 and 2016) have a question about whether respondents receive migrant remittances at the time this project started.[3] We combine these two rounds and provide a cross-sectional analysis controlling for country, region, and time-fixed effects.

Both rounds include the following question: 'How often, if at all, do you or anyone in your household receive money remittances from friends or relatives living outside of the country?' The possible answers range from at least once a month to never. We create a dummy variable, *remit_receiver*, that equals 1 if the respondent receives remittances and zero otherwise. We code missing values for the responses 'I don't know' or 'refused to respond'. For a robustness check, we will also use a categorical variable that will group those who receive remittances into different categories defined by the frequencies at which they receive remittances.

We also consider remittance inflows as share of GDP to explore if individuals living in different countries with different levels of remittance inflows behave differently in terms of bribe payment. The data of remittances as share of GDP is taken from the World Development Indicators. This variable enters in our estimation in logs and is denoted by Remit / GDP.

Table 10.1 shows the share of the respondents who received remittances in each of the countries. We observe some heterogeneity across the countries. Cape Verde records the highest proportion of people who receive migrant remittances, with 42%, followed by Algeria, which has a proportion of 39%. The country with the lowest proportion is Burundi, where only 4.6% of respondents report having received migrant remittances, followed by Tanzania, with a proportion of around 6%.

To measure the incidence of corruption, we rely on the questions in the surveys that ask respondents how often (if ever) they have had to pay a bribe by giving a gift to or doing a favour for a public official to get a document, a permit, a household service such as water or sanitation, or to avoid any problems with the police. The possible replies to this question are the following: 'never', 'once or twice', 'a few times', or 'no experience with this in the past year'. We construct a dummy variable, *bribe_payment*, that equals 1 if the respondent ever paid a bribe to a public official and zero otherwise.

Table 10.2 presents the proportion of people who paid bribes in each country. We first report the proportion for the aggregated measure that records a

Table 10.1 Remittance receivers in Africa (%)

Country	Percentage of remittance receivers
Burundi	4.59
Tanzania	5.82
Tunisia	6.68
Madagascar	6.7
Mauritius	7.43
Zambia	9.69
Botswana	10.65
Kenya	11.18
Malawi	11.92
South Africa	11.97
Uganda	12.28
Namibia	13.46
Benin	13.56
Sierra Leone	15.26
Gabon	15.28
Togo	15.98
Cote d'Ivoire	19.43
Swaziland	20.4
Burkina Faso	20.47
Ghana	20.52
Mozambique	21.15
Guinea	21.99
Lesotho	26.85
Tome and Principe	26.87
Mali	26.91
Niger	27.45
Nigeria	27.78
Zimbabwe	27.83
Egypt	28.58
Senegal	28.7
Liberia	30
Morocco	30.08
Cameroon	35.04
Sudan	36.55
Algeria	38.87
Cape Verde	42.06

Notes: This table reports the percentage of people who received migrant remittances from friends or relative living abroad.

bribe payment to get a permit or an official document, receive a household service, or avoid a problem with the police. Countries are sorted by level of bribe payment, and those that have the highest proportion of people who paid a bribe are placed at the top of the first column. Liberia has the highest proportion, with roughly 38% of the population paying a bribe during the year before the survey interviews. Morocco and Kenya have the second- and third-highest proportions of people who made a bribe payment. Mauritius

Table 10.2 Percentage of people who paid bribe in Africa (2008–2015)

Country	Bribe payment (overall)	Bribe payment (official document)	Bribe payment (police)	Bribe payment (household services)
Liberia	38.26	27.16	27.27	19.64
Morocco	33.78	25.65	15.86	8.85
Kenya	32.24	22.62	18.12	6.45
Egypt	31.60	24.49	15.81	18.01
Nigeria	31.43	20.73	21.46	18.75
Uganda	30.15	16.43	18.60	13.15
Sudan	30.13	23.91	11.99	9.18
Cameroon	26.35	18.62	10.29	11.24
Mozambique	24.72	17.17	12.27	13.19
Zimbabwe	19.70	15.01	9.99	3.45
Sierra Leone	19.70	10.13	13.41	6.21
Gabon	18.20	10.53	2.34	9.35
Ghana	16.18	8.28	7.97	6.66
Benin	16.02	12.85	3.92	4.93
Mali	14.56	10.79	5.85	3.74
Cote d'Ivoire	14.01	11.26	2.25	2.17
Zambia	13.80	8.42	8.94	3.35
Burkina Faso	12.98	9.53	5.53	4.35
Senegal	12.90	11.58	2.01	2.51
Togo	11.33	8.50	2.08	3.01
Guinea	11.08	8.10	2.17	2.92
Tome and Principe	10.97	8.06	2.86	3.80
Tanzania	10.47	4.78	6.97	3.32
Madagascar	8.86	7.28	2.68	0.47
South Africa	8.36	5.19	4.27	4.09
Malawi	8.35	4.06	4.50	2.38
Algeria	8.18	5.79	2.84	2.80
Namibia	8.01	4.97	2.56	3.52
Lesotho	7.51	5.60	2.51	1.58
Cape Verde	7.09	4.89	1.57	4.21
Burundi	6.75	3.67	3.09	0.42
Swaziland	6.00	5.13	0.75	0.50
Niger	4.17	3.35	1.75	0.33
Tunisia	3.25	1.83	0.92	0.92
Botswana	1.96	0.75	1.42	0.21
Mauritius	1.08	0.25	0.67	0.17

Notes: The percentages reported are the averages over the Afrobarometer survey years. Countries are ranked on a descending order of the level of bribery.

and Botswana are the two countries with the lowest proportion of people who made a bribe payment for a permit or document or a household service or to avoid a problem with the police.

In addition to our key variable, *remit_receiver*, we control for various individual socio-economic characteristics, such as the gender of the respondents, their age categories, geographical locations, and levels of education. We also add information about access to information using the survey questions asking whether the respondents have access to information through TV, radio, or newspapers. One limitation of the data is that it does not include income information. Therefore, we propose to create the dummy variable *poverty*, which equals 1 if a respondent has gone without food, water, medicine, or cash during the last 12 years and zero otherwise. We also add another dummy indicating whether the respondent is interested in public affairs.

Furthermore, we control for country-level variables to account for time-varying information that may affect the environment in which people live. One variable that we consider is country level of control for corruption, available from the Worldwide Governance Indicators. Control of corruption measures perceptions on the extent to which public power is exercised for private gain, including both petty and grand forms of corruption. This variable varies between −2.5 and 2.5, where a higher value indicates a higher control of corruption in a given country.

Another country-level variable that we include in our analysis is the stock of migrants in OECD countries measured as the difference between the number of migrants from a given country of our sample who migrate to OECD countries and the number of migrants from the same country who exit the OECD country in the same year. Table 10.3 shows the stock of migrants in OECD countries averaged over the Afrobarometer survey years. These data are available from the OECD data portal and include the countries in our dataset and the survey years. This table combined with the previous Table 10.2 shows a mixed picture because some countries such as Morocco, Egypt, and Nigeria record among the highest levels of stock of migrants living in OECD countries but are also among countries with the highest levels of bribe payments. In contrast other countries like Algeria and South Africa have high stocks of migrants in OECD countries but lows level of incidence of bribe payments. To control for the difference in the level of development between the countries, we include the GDP per capita in the empirical analysis.

Empirical strategy

We have data for J = 1, 2, . . . 36 countries, and n_j defines the number of observations for a given country j. In the data, the respondents are nested within regions, and, in turn, regions are nested within countries. To cluster at the region and country levels simultaneously, we estimate a three-level varying-intercept multilevel (or hierarchical) logit model. We are interested in estimating the probability that an individual i, living in region r from country j and interviewed at time t, paid a bribe over the last 12 months to get a permit or document or a household service or to avoid a problem with the police.

Let us denote this probability by π_{irj}. The equation of estimation can be written as follows:

$$\pi_{irjt} = Prob\left(bribe\_payment_{irjt} = 1, \omega_{irjt}\right) \tag{1}$$

Table 10.3 Stock of African migrants in OECD by country

Country	Average (inflow-outflow)
Morocco	48,523
Algeria	35,934
Nigeria	34,636.5
Egypt	31,938
Tunisia	20,861
South Africa	18,951.5
Senegal	15,561.5
Ghana	15,180
Cameroon	14,425
Sudan	11,373
Kenya	9,352
Cote d'Ivoire	9,046
Guinea	7,456
Mali	7,258
Cape Verde	6,656.5
Liberia	6,143
Togo	3,518
Madagascar	2,785
Zimbabwe	2,781
Mauritius	2,769
Sierra Leone	2,598
Uganda	2,447
Burkina Faso	2,276
Benin	1,779.5
Tanzania	1,420.5
Burundi	1,146
Zambia	883
Gabon	872
Niger	629
Sao Tome and Principe	541
Mozambique	540.5
Malawi	213
Botswana	200.5
Namibia	195.5
Swaziland	96
Lesotho	30.5

Notes: This table reports the stock of migrants from African countries living in OECD countries average over the Afrobarometer survey years. Countries are ranked in a descending order of the level of stock of migrants living in OECD countries.

Where,

$$Level\ 1: \omega_{irjt} = \beta_{0rc} + \beta_1 remit\_receiver_{irjt} + \beta_2 \left(Remit\ /\ GDP \right)_{jt} + \beta_3 Z_{jt} + \beta_4 X_{irjt} + t + \varepsilon_{irjt} \tag{2}$$

By allowing the intercept to vary among the countries we have then:

$$Level\ 2: \beta_{0rj} = \beta_{0j} + u_{rj},\ u_{rc} \sim N\left(0,\ \sigma^2\right)$$
$$Level\ 3: \beta_{0j} = \beta_{00} + v_j,\ v_c \sim N\left(0,\delta^2\right) \tag{3}$$

Thus, the general model can be written as follows:

$$\omega_{ijt} = \beta_{00} + \beta_1 remit\_receiver_{irjt} + \beta_2 \left(Remit / GDP \right)_{jt} + \beta_3 Z_{jt} \\ + \beta_4 X_{irj} + time + u_{rj} + v_j + \varepsilon_{irjt}$$ (4)

Z is the vector that contains the additional country-level variables such as GDP, control of corruption, stock of migrants in OECD countries, and GDP per capita. X is the vector that includes all the variables at the individual level. The term $u_{rj} + v_j + \varepsilon_{ij}$ in Equation 4 represents the random part of the model where u_{rc} is the region-specific effect, v_c the country-specific effect, and ε_{ij} is the individual-level error term.[4]

Results and discussions

Aggregate measure of bribe payment

Table 10.4 presents the estimation results of the probability of paying a bribe to a government official in order to receive public goods or services such as official documents, permits, household services, or to avoid problems with the police. In column (1), we only control for our key explanatory variable, the dummy *remit_receiver*, which equals 1 if the respondent receives remittances from relatives or friends abroad and zero otherwise. The coefficient on *remit_receiver* is positive and statistically significant at the 1% significance level. This indicates that an individual who receives remittances from friends or relatives abroad is more likely to pay a bribe to receive public goods or services than a non-remittance receiver. In the next column (2), we add the four country-level variables: the log of remittances received in a country as a percentage of GDP (RemitGDP), control of corruption at the country level (CCE), the log of stock of migrants in OECD countries (inflows–outflows), and the log of the GDP per capita to control for the countries' level of development (GDP). We find that the coefficient on remit_receiver is still positive and highly significant, confirming the conclusion of column (1).

Interestingly, the coefficient on the country level of remittances as a share of GDP is also positive and significant. This means that people who live in countries with a higher level of remittances are more likely to pay a bribe than are people who live in countries with a lower level of remittances. As expected, the coefficient on the country level of corruption is negative and statistically significant at the 1% significance level. In fact, individuals in countries with greater control of corruption are less likely to pay a bribe than are individuals living in countries with lesser control of corruption. These findings support the income channel where more income from migrant remittances increases the incentives of people to pay more bribe to public officials for easier access to public goods and services.

Turning now to the variable, inflows–outflows, which captures the number of migrants living in OECD countries, we find a negative and statistically

Table 10.4 Remittances and bribe payment in Africa

	(1)	*(2)*	*(3)*	*(4)*
remit_receiver	0.460★★★	0.455★★★	0.395★★★	0.389★★★
(1=receiver)	(0.025)	(0.025)	(0.025)	(0.025)
Country-level variables				
Remittances/GDP		0.223★★★	0.218★★★	0.208★★★
		(0.030)	(0.030)	(0.030)
CCE		−1.048★★★	−1.084★★★	−1.060★★★
		(0.125)	(0.123)	(0.122)
Inflow-outflows		−0.254★★★	−0.181★★	−0.159★★
		(0.090)	(0.080)	(0.079)
GDP		0.183	0.159	0.189★
		(0.122)	(0.116)	(0.114)
Individual-level variables				
gender(1=female)			−0.437★★★	−0.412★★★
			(0.021)	(0.021)
educ_someprimary (1=some primary education)			0.129★★★	0.102★★
			(0.041)	(0.041)
educ_primarycompleted (1=primary education completed)			0.388★★★	0.332★★★
			(0.036)	(0.037)
educ_secondary (1=secondary education completed)			0.543★★★	0.488★★★
			(0.042)	(0.042)
educ_postsecondary (1=post-secondary education)			0.652★★★	0.622★★★
			(0.042)	(0.043)
age26to35 (1=aged between 26 and 35)			0.156★★★	0.141★★★
			(0.027)	(0.027)
age35(1= above 35)			−0.075★★★	−0.084★★★
			(0.027)	(0.027)
Urban(1= Yes)			0.153★★★	0.165★★★
			(0.026)	(0.026)
access_information(1=Yes)				0.393★★★
				(0.043)
Poverty(1= experienced poverty)				0.477★★★
				(0.033)
public_affairs(1=interested in public affairs)				0.192★★★
				(0.028)
Constant	−2.365★★★	−2.507★★	−3.089★★★	−4.388★★★
	(0.157)	(1.190)	(1.056)	(1.042)
Observations	80,534	80,270	79,497	78,796
Nb regions	457	457	457	457
Number of countries	36	36	36	36

Notes: This table reports the estimation results of the multilevel logit model. The dependent variable is the probability to pay bribe to access official document or permit, household services, or to avoid a problem with police. Clustered standard errors are in parenthesis. ★★★ p<0.01, ★★ p<0.05, ★ p<0.

significant result. This indicates that countries with more emigrants living in OECD countries are also countries where people have a lower probability of paying a bribe for public goods or services. There may be different plausible interpretations of this result, and one may think that because bribe payment is less common in OECD countries than in the countries considered in our sample, emigrants living in OECD countries may share this norm to their family and friends in their home country, who, in turn, may be less willing to pay a bribe in exchange for public goods and services.

This result is therefore in line with the norm channel discussed in the preceding sections and the findings in the broader literature on the impact of international migration on the institutional development of migrants' home country (Batista & Vicente, 2011; Chauvet & Mercier, 2014; Pfutze, 2012). More specifically, our result suggests that receiving remittances, which indicates a direct communication between migrants and their loved ones that are left behind, induces a positive effect on home country institutional development. For the GDP per capita variable, the coefficient is not statistically significant. Thus, we cannot conclude whether respondents from richer countries are more or less likely to pay a bribe than respondents living in poor countries.

In the last two columns of Table 10.4, we control for numerous individual socio-economic characteristics such as gender, education, age, and geographical location. Furthermore, in column (4), we add the dummies access_information, poverty, and public_affairs. The positive effect of receiving remittances on bribe payment still holds in columns (3) and (4). Turning to the individual socio-economic characteristics that are controlled for, the results in column (3) show that the respondent's gender matters: being a woman reduces the probability of paying a bribe. This finding is in line with previous studies that have provided evidence that women are less corrupt than men (e.g. Dollar et al., 2001; Swamy et al., 2001).

Interestingly, we find that respondents who experienced poverty in the past record a higher probability to pay a bribe in exchange for a public good or service. This result confirms previous evidence in the literature that has shown that the poorest in Africa are more likely to pay bribe to access public services (see Emram et al., 2013; Peiffer & Rose, 2018). Lack of strong network with public officials and/or influential people is one of the key factors explaining the higher incidence of bribe payment to access basic services among poor people (Osei, 2019). Among the remittance receivers in our data many experienced poverty in the past, but we do not know if receiving remittances has improved their network and social capital over time. The results also highlighted that educated people are more likely to pay a bribe than people with no formal education. This finding holds regardless of the level of education. In addition, people located in urban areas have a higher probability of paying a bribe than those living in rural areas. Finally, the results in column (4) show that the respondents accessing information through radio, TV, or newspapers and the respondents interested in public affairs are more likely to pay a bribe. More research is needed to analyse the type of information accessed by the respondents and the frequency at which they access them.

Disaggregate measures of bribe payment

To deepen our analysis, Table 10.5 displays the results when we run separate regressions for the different types of bribe payments such as bribe payment for official documents, household services, and police issues.

The results displayed in Table 10.5 show that the effects of receiving remittances on bribe payment are positive and statistically significant across the different columns. This confirms that remittance receivers are more likely to pay a bribe regardless of the type of public good or service they would like to access. However, the coefficient on remittances as a share of GDP at the country level becomes insignificant in the last two columns when we estimate the probability to pay a bribe to access public school services and the probability to pay a bribe for public health services. The country control of corruption still has a negative effect on the probability of paying a bribe regardless of which measure we use.

The variable stock of migrants in OECD countries affects the probability to pay bribes to access official documents or household services. However, it is insignificant when we consider bribe payment to avoid problems with the police, suggesting that remittance receivers are as likely as non-receivers to face issues with the police. The respondent's gender remains a key determinant of bribe payment; we still find that women are less corrupt than men are. Individual level of education still plays an important role except in a few cases where it has no statistically significant effect on some categories of bribe payments. Overall, the results indicate that across the different columns, educated people are more likely to pay a bribe than uneducated ones are.

In Table 10.6, we separate remittance receivers into different groups depending on how often they receive remittances from friends or relatives abroad. We then have three groups of remittance receivers: those who receive remittances at least once a year, those who receive them three or six times a year, and those who receive them every month. In the estimations we then control simultaneously for the following three dummies: remit_receiver_once, remit_receiver_sixthree, and remit_receiver_month. The control group is people who never receive migrant remittances.

In the first column of Table 10.6, we use our aggregate measure of bribe payment, which takes a value 1 for respondents who paid a bribe to get official documents or permits, to receive household services, or to avoid problems with the police. We can see that the coefficients on all the different categories of remittances are positive and statistically significant at the 1% significance level. These findings highlight the fact that remittance receivers are more likely to pay a bribe than non-receivers, regardless of the frequencies at which they receive the money.

Table 10.5 Remittances and bribe payment by public services

	(1)	(2)	(3)
	Bribery for official document	Bribery for household services	Bribery to avoid a run-in with the police
remit_receiver	0.454***	0.517***	0.472***
(1=receiver)	(0.029)	(0.036)	(0.033)
Country-level variables			
Remittances/GDP	0.216***	0.264***	0.300***
	(0.042)	(0.049)	(0.038)
CCE	−1.275***	−2.715***	−0.660***
	(0.152)	(0.284)	(0.174)
Inflow-Outflows	−0.461***	−1.188***	−0.104
	(0.147)	(0.172)	(0.085)
GDP	0.375**	0.239	−0.075
	(0.159)	(0.283)	(0.152)
Individual-level variables			
gender (1=female)	−0.402***	−0.198***	−0.475***
	(0.025)	(0.032)	(0.029)
educ_someprimary (1=some primary education)	0.125***	0.031	0.051
	(0.049)	(0.066)	(0.056)
educ_ primarycompleted (1=primary education completed)	0.353***	0.295***	0.240***
	(0.043)	(0.058)	(0.050)
educ_secondary (1=secondary education completed)	0.511***	0.387***	0.353***
	(0.050)	(0.065)	(0.056)
educ_postsecondary	0.681***	0.517***	0.460***
	(0.049)	(0.065)	(0.057)
age26to35 (1=age between 26 and 35)	0.094***	0.101**	0.190***
	(0.031)	(0.040)	(0.036)
age35 (age above 35)	−0.125***	−0.053	0.027
	(0.031)	(0.041)	(0.036)
Urban (1=yes)	0.101***	0.258***	0.199***
	(0.030)	(0.039)	(0.034)
access_information (1=yes)	0.321***	0.419***	0.430***
	(0.051)	(0.074)	(0.060)
Poverty (1=yes)	0.458***	0.634***	0.415***
	(0.039)	(0.051)	(0.044)
public_affairs (1=interested in public affairs)	0.189***	0.242***	0.189***
	(0.033)	(0.044)	(0.039)
Constant	−4.041***	0.528	−3.531***
	(1.537)	(2.677)	(1.346)
Observations	78,278	78,463	78,462
Nb regions	457	457	457
Number of countries	36	36	36

Notes: This table reports the estimation results of the multilevel logit model. The dependent variable is the probability to pay bribe to access official document (1), household services (2) and avoid problem with the police (3). Clustered standard errors are in parenthesis. *** $p<0.01$, ** $p<0.05$, * $p<0.1$.

Table 10.6 Remittances and bribe payment by frequency of receipt

Variables	(1) Bribery(Overall)	(2) Bribery for Official document	(3) Bribery household services	(4) Bribery to avoid a run-in with the police
remit_receiver_once	0.413★★★	0.489★★★	0.488★★★	0.497★★★
	(0.035)	(0.039)	(0.049)	(0.044)
remit_receiver_six-three	0.415★★★	0.481★★★	0.577★★★	0.533★★★
	(0.039)	(0.043)	(0.054)	(0.050)
remit_receiver_month	0.300★★★	0.338★★★	0.479★★★	0.304★★★
	(0.048)	(0.054)	(0.069)	(0.066)
Remittances/GDP	0.208★★★	0.216★★★	0.263★★★	0.299★★★
	(0.030)	(0.042)	(0.049)	(0.038)
Inflow-outflows	−0.157★★	−0.451★★★	−1.187★★★	−0.100
	(0.079)	(0.146)	(0.172)	(0.085)
GDP	0.188	0.373★★	0.237	−0.076
	(0.114)	(0.159)	(0.283)	(0.151)
Individual-level variables				
gender (1=female)	−0.411★★★	−0.401★★★	−0.198★★★	−0.475★★★
	(0.021)	(0.025)	(0.032)	(0.029)
educ_someprimary (1=some primary education)	0.102★★	0.125★★	0.031	0.050
	(0.041)	(0.049)	(0.066)	(0.056)
educ_ primarycompleted (1=primary education completed)	0.332★★★	0.353★★★	0.296★★★	0.239★★★
	(0.037)	(0.043)	(0.058)	(0.050)
educ_secondary (1=secondary education completed)	0.488★★★	0.510★★★	0.388★★★	0.352★★★
	(0.042)	(0.050)	(0.065)	(0.056)
educ_postsecondary	0.622★★★	0.681★★★	0.518★★★	0.459★★★
	(0.043)	(0.049)	(0.065)	(0.057)
age26to35 (1=age between 26 and 35)	0.139★★★	0.092★★★	0.101★★	0.187★★★
	(0.027)	(0.031)	(0.040)	(0.036)
age35 (age above 35)	−0.086★★★	−0.128★★★	−0.053	0.024
	(0.027)	(0.031)	(0.041)	(0.036)
Urban (1=yes)	0.165★★★	0.102★★★	0.258★★★	0.201★★★
	(0.026)	(0.030)	(0.039)	(0.034)
access_information (1=yes)	0.393★★★	0.321★★★	0.419★★★	0.431★★★
	(0.043)	(0.051)	(0.074)	(0.060)
Poverty (1=yes)	0.475★★★	0.455★★★	0.634★★★	0.412★★★
	(0.033)	(0.039)	(0.051)	(0.044)
public_affairs (1=interested in public affairs)	0.192★★★	0.188★★★	0.241★★★	0.188★★★
	(0.028)	(0.033)	(0.044)	(0.039)
Constant	−4.394★★★	−4.087★★★	0.539	−3.545★★★
	(1.039)	(1.524)	(2.678)	(1.341)
Nb Obs	78,796	78,278	78,463	78,462
Nb regions	457	457	457	457
Nb countries	36	36	36	36

Notes: This table reports the estimation results of the multilevel logit model. The dependent variable is the probability to pay bribe to access official document (1), household services (2) and avoid problem with the police (3). Clustered standard errors are in parenthesis. ★★★ p<0.01, ★★ p<0.05, ★ p<0.

In columns (2)–(6), we separate the different categories of bribe payments as we did in Table 10.4. We find that regardless of the frequency at which an individual receives remittances, a receiver is more likely to pay a bribe to get official documents. Similarly, s/he is less likely to pay a bribe to receive household services or to avoid problems with the police compared to a non-receiver. The effects of all other country- and individual-level variables are similar to those presented in the previous tables.

Interactions between remittances and control of corruption

We argue that the effect of remittance receipt on corruption may depend on the institutional environment of the countries. For instance, in societies where corruption is high and poorly controlled, people may be more exposed to pay bribe when they receive more income. We add a term of interaction between the country level of remittances (Remit/GDP) and the country level of control of corruption (CC) as shown in Table 10.7. In the first column of the table, we use our main variable of bribe payment, and in the following columns, we use disaggregate measures of bribe payment. The coefficients on the interaction term are negative and statistically significant in almost all columns. This means that the effect of remittances as a share of GDP becomes negative when the level of control of corruption increases. In fact, if we have two countries with similar levels of remittances as a share of GDP, people living in the country with a higher level of control of corruption are less likely to pay a bribe to public officials than the people in countries with a lower level of control for corruption.

Because we have added the interaction term, the coefficient on the variable Remit_GDP is the effect of remittances on bribe payment incidence when the control of corruption is equal to zero. As one can see, this coefficient is not statistically significant. Besides, in our dataset there are no countries for which the control of corruption, which varies between −2.5 and 2.5, is equal to zero.

Concluding remarks

The 2019 report of the Transparency International has highlighted that bribe payments in exchange for public goods and services are prevalent in Africa and, according to a large number of African citizens, corruption is poorly handled by governments. Both internal and external factors may affect incidence of corruption. In this chapter we examined how international inflows such as migrant remittances, i.e. external factor, affect the level of corruption in African countries. This chapter complements the growing literature that shed light on the effects of remittances on institutions, political involvement, and preferences but did not pay enough attention to the potential effect of remittances on corruption in Africa. For our empirical

Table 10.7 Remittances and bribe payment with interaction between control over corruption and remittance inflows

Variables	(1) Bribery	(2) Document	(3) Household services	(4) Police
remit_receiver	0.377***	0.443***	0.499***	0.460***
	(0.025)	(0.029)	(0.037)	(0.033)
Remit/GDP	−0.062	−0.079	−0.085	0.004
	(0.039)	(0.050)	(0.061)	(0.051)
CCE	−0.497***	−0.582***	−2.235***	−0.416**
	(0.144)	(0.167)	(0.288)	(0.188)
CCE*Remit/GDP	−0.916***	−0.918***	−1.370***	−1.012***
	(0.078)	(0.089)	(0.133)	(0.118)
Inflow-Outflows	−0.068	−0.292***	−0.650***	0.040
	(0.080)	(0.106)	(0.148)	(0.091)
GDP	0.323**	0.461***	0.711***	0.098
	(0.138)	(0.170)	(0.273)	(0.170)
Individual-level variables				
gender (1=female)	−0.412***	−0.402***	−0.197***	−0.476***
	(0.021)	(0.025)	(0.032)	(0.029)
educ_someprimary (1=some primary education)	0.100**	0.124**	0.024	0.048
	(0.041)	(0.049)	(0.066)	(0.056)
educ_ primarycompleted (1=primary education completed)	0.329***	0.351***	0.292***	0.235***
	(0.037)	(0.043)	(0.058)	(0.050)
educ_secondary (1=secondary education completed)	0.483***	0.507***	0.380***	0.344***
	(0.042)	(0.050)	(0.065)	(0.056)
educ_postsecondary	0.623***	0.683***	0.521***	0.456***
	(0.043)	(0.049)	(0.065)	(0.057)
age26to35 (1=age between 26 and 35)	0.139***	0.093***	0.098**	0.188***
	(0.027)	(0.031)	(0.040)	(0.036)
age35 (age above 35)	−0.083***	−0.124***	−0.053	0.029
	(0.027)	(0.031)	(0.041)	(0.036)
Urban (1=yes)	0.165***	0.101***	0.262***	0.203***
	(0.026)	(0.030)	(0.039)	(0.034)
access_information (1=yes)	0.381***	0.310***	0.409***	0.418***
	(0.043)	(0.051)	(0.074)	(0.060)
Poverty (1=yes)	0.474***	0.456***	0.629***	0.414***
	(0.033)	(0.039)	(0.051)	(0.044)
public_affairs	0.194***	0.190***	0.239***	0.186***
	(0.028)	(0.033)	(0.044)	(0.039)
Constant	−6.073***	−5.869***	−7.605***	−6.144***
	(1.267)	(1.534)	(2.457)	(1.526)
Nb obs	78,796	78,278	78,463	78,462
Nb regions	457	457	457	457
Nb countries	36	36	36	36

Notes: This table reports the estimation results of the multilevel logit model. The dependent variable is the probability to pay bribe to access official document (1), household services (2), avoid problem with the police (3). Clustered standard errors are in parenthesis. *** $p<0.01$, ** $p<0.05$, * p<0.

analysis, we used the Afrobarometer surveys conducted in 36 African countries between 2004 and 2016. We considered bribe payments for different public goods and services such as access to official documents or permits; household, public school and health care services; or payments to avoid problems with police.

The results showed that remittance receivers are more likely to pay bribes than non-receivers, regardless of the public goods or services under consideration. Furthermore, they suggested that individuals living in countries with higher levels of remittances as a share of GDP are more likely to pay bribes to access public goods and services than individuals living in countries with lower levels of remittances as a share of GDP. This positive relationship between remittances and bribe payments is in line with the income channel hypothesis, whereby remittances increase individual and household income, and, in turn, recipients are more likely to pay bribes for ease of access to public goods and services. In addition, we found that in countries wherein the control of corruption is high, the positive effect of remittances on corruption diminishes. The estimation results on the stock of migrants in OECD countries highlighted that people who live in African countries with a high level of migrants living in OECD countries are less likely to pay bribes than the respondents living in African countries with fewer people who migrate to OECD This result is in line with the norm effect, suggesting that migrants in OECD countries may share anti-corruption attitudes with the compatriots they left behind. However, more data and empirical analyses are needed to provide stronger evidence on remittances, norms, and bribe payments in Africa. It is also worth noting that the findings in this chapter can only be interpreted as correlation and not as causality because of a number of technical issues such as measurement errors and omitted variable biases that need to be solved in future research.

The findings in this chapter have implications for SDGs 17.3 and 16.5 and highlight the importance of effective policies of SDG 16.5 in terms of countries successfully achieving SDG 17.3 without increasing the level of corruption. In fact, the SDG 17.3 target calls for more mobilization of resources in developing countries, including African nations. One of the target indicators is to increase the volume of migrant remittances as a proportion of total GDP. Such an increase may have positive effects on poverty and hunger, among other variables. However, if no anti-corruption actions are effectively implemented in the receiving countries, remittances may increase the incidence of bribery as shown in this chapter The SDG 16.5 target seeks to substantially reduce corruption and bribery in all their forms. One of the indicators of this target is the significant reduction in the proportion of people who pay bribes to – or are asked to pay bribes by – public officials. The findings in this chapter indicate that higher control of corruption at the national level tends to reduce the effect of remittances on bribery. Therefore, the evidence in this chapter claims that policies for the success of SDG 17.3 should be coupled with the anti-corruption policies advocated in SDG 16.5.

Notes

1 See also Ebeke & Yogo (2013) and Dionne et al. (2014) for earlier research on the effects of remittances on political participation in Africa.
2 Two other channels through which remittances can affect the corruption level in the government or the quality of governance, in general, include the following. First, remittances although untaxed, can increase the base for other taxes (e.g. VAT) which makes it less costly for the government to appropriate resources for its own gain (Abdih et al., (2012, p. 658). Second, by affecting the internal political discontent (see Ahmed, 2013, p. 1181).
3 Round 7 of the Afrobarometer was not released when this project started.
4 We use the command melogit of Stata 15 to run the estimations.

References

Abdih, Y., Chami, R., Dagher, J., & Montiel, P. (2012). Remittances and institutions: Are remittances a curse? *World Development,* 40(4), 657–666.

Acosta, P., Calderón, C., Fajnzylber, P., & Lopez, H. (2008). What is the impact of international remittances on poverty and inequality in Latin America? *World Development,* 36, 89–114.

Ahmed, F. (2013). Remittances deteriorate governance. *Review of Economics and Statistics,* 95(4), 1166–1182.

Azizi, S. (2019). The impacts of workers' remittances on poverty and inequality in developing countries. *Empirical Economics,* doi: 10.1007/s00181-019-01764-8.

Barajas, A., Chami, R., Fullenkamp, C., Gapen, M., & Montiel, P. (2009). *Do workers' remittances promote economic growth?* IMF Working Paper 153, Washington, DC.

Batista, C., & Vicente, P. (2011). Do migrants improve governance at home? Evidence from a voting experiment. *World Bank Economic Review,* 25(1), 77–104.

Baudassé, T., Bazillier, R., & Issifou, I. (2018). Migrations and institutions: Exit and voice (from abroad)? *Journal of Economic Surveys,* 32(3), 727–766.

Chauvet, L., & Mercier, M. (2014). Do return migrants transfer political norms to their origin country? Evidence from Mali. *Journal of Comparative Economics,* 42(3), 630–651.

Combes, J-L., & Ebeke, C. (2011). Remittances and household consumption instability in developing countries. *World Development,* 39(7), 1076–1089.

Combes, J-L., Ebeke, C., & Maurel, M. (2015). The effect of remittances prior to an election. *Applied Economics,* 47(38), 4074–4089.

Deonanan, R., & Williams, K. (2016). The effect of remittances on democratic institutions. *Applied Economics,* 49(5), 403–416.

Dionne, K., Inman, K., & Montinola, G. (2014). *Another resources curse? The impact of remittances on political participation.* Afrobarometer Working Paper No. 145.

Dollar, D., Fisman, R., & Gatti, R. (2001). Are women really the "fairer" sex? Corruption and women in government. *Journal of Economic Behavior and Organization,* 46(4), 423–429.

Ebeke, C., & Yogo, T. (2013). Remittances and the voter turnout in sub-Saharan Africa: Evidence from macro and micro level data. *African Development Bank Group Working Paper,* (185), 1–43.

Edwards, A., & Ureta, M. (2003). International migration, remittances, and schooling: Evidence from El Salvador. *Journal of Development Economics,* 72(2), 429–461.

Escriba-Folch, A., Meseguer, C., & Wright, J. (2015). Remittances and democratization. *International Studies Quarterly*, 59(3), 571–586.

Escriba-Folch, A., Meseguer, C., & Wright, J. (2018). Remittances and protest in dictatorships. *American Journal of Political Science*, 62(4), 889–904.

Giuliano, P., & Ruiz-Arranz, M. (2009). Remittances, financial development, and growth. *Journal of Development Economics*, 90 (1), 144–152.

Goodman, G., & Hiskey, J. (2008). Exit without leaving: Political disengagement in high migration municipalities in Mexico. *Comparative Politics*, 40(2), 169–188.

Konte, M. (2016). The effects of remittances on support for democracy in Africa: Are remittances a curse or a blessing? *Journal of Comparative Economics*, 44(4), 1002–1022.

Levitt, P. (1998). Social remittances: Migration driven local-level forms of cultural diffusion. *International Migration Review*, 32(4), 926–948.

O'Mahony, A. (2013). Political investment: Remittances and elections. *British Journal of Political Science*, 43(4), 799–820.

Osei, D. (2019). *Corruption and the poor: Is social capital an exit option?* New York: Mimeo.

Peiffer, C., & Rose, R. (2018). Why are the poor more vulnerable to bribery in Africa? The institutional effects of services. *The Journal of Development Studies*, 54.1(2018), 18–29.

Pfutze, T. (2012). Does migration promote democratization? Evidence from the Mexican transition. *Journal of Comparative Economics*, 40(2), 159–175.

Pfutze, T. (2014). Clientelism versus social learning: The electoral effects of international migration. *International Studies Quarterly*, 2(1), 295–307.

Pring, C., & Vrushi, J. (2019). Global corruption barometer Africa 2019 citizens' views and experiences of corruption, 2019 Transparency International. Retrieved from https://images.transparencycdn.org/images/Full-Report-Global-Corruption-Barometer-Africa-2019.pdf

Mamun, M., Sohag, K., Uddin, G., & Shahbaz, M. (2015). Remittance and domestic labor productivity: Evidence from remittance recipient countries. *Economic Modelling*, 47, 207–218.

Spilimbergo, A. (2009). Democracy and foreign education. *American Economic Review*, 99(1), 528–543.

Swamy, A., Knack, S., Lee, Y., & Azfar, O. (2001). Gender and corruption. *Journal of Development Economics*, 64(1), 25–55.

Tusalem, R. (2018). Do migrant remittances improve the quality of government? Evidence from the Philippines. *Asian Journal of Comparative Politics*, 3(4), 336–366.

Tyburski, M. (2012). The resource curse reversed? Remittances and corruption in Mexico. *International Studies Quarterly*, 56(2), 339–350.

Tyburski, M. (2014). *Curse or Cure. Remittances and Corruption in the Developing World* (Doctoral dissertation). Retrieved from https://dc.uwm.edu/cgi/viewcontent.cgi?referer=https://www.google.be/&httpsredir=1&article=1551&context=etd

Williams, K. (2017). Do remittances improve political institutions? Evidence from sub-Saharan Africa. *Economic Modelling*, 61, 65–75.

Williams, K. (2018). Is the relationship between remittances and political institutions monotonic? Evidence from developing countries. *South African of Economies*, 86(4), 449–467.

World Bank. (2019). *Migration and remittances recent developments and outlook*. Migration and Development Brief 31. Retrieved from https://www.knomad.org/sites/default/files/2019-04/Migrationanddevelopmentbrief31.pdf

11 Shaping the migration journey – the role of corruption and gender

Ortrun Merkle, Julia Reinold, and Melissa Siegel

Introduction

The migration journey is a complex phenomenon with a multitude of actors and locations involved, and, while large parts of the relationship have been investigated, several gaps still remain. For one, the complex relationship between migration and corruption has only recently started to receive increased attention, with many gaps still existing. While initial research focussed mostly on corruption as a facilitator of migration (e.g. Bales, 2007; Richards, 2004; UNODC, 2013), an increasing body of literature also explores the role of corruption as a push factor for migration (Ariu & Squicciarini, 2013; Dimant, Krieger, & Redlin, 2015; Merkle, Reinold, & Siegel, 2017b) and the impact of migration on corruption in the country of origin (Batista & Vicente, 2010; Beine & Sekkat, 2014; Ivlevs & King, 2017).Yet the emerging discussion on this multifaceted relationship is still lacking nuance. Research considering the role of corruption is especially interesting in the African context. The Global Corruption Barometer 2019 suggests that 55% of citizens in Africa think that corruption has increased in the last 12 months and shows that poor and young citizens are much more vulnerable to corruption (Pring & Vrushi, 2019). However, national levels of corruption as well as the institutions that are considered the most affected by bribery vary widely. Hence, the research presented in this chapter can shed further light on some areas that are especially at risk for corruption and a population that is especially vulnerable to experiencing it.

Second, with increasing numbers of female migrants and changing migration patterns for both men and women, more research is needed on the gendered aspect of migration. This chapter will address these three gaps in the research by analysing how corruption shapes migration journeys and how these experiences are gendered. Even though research that has been conducted on corruption and migration separately suggests that experiences of men and women are fundamentally different, there has been no research (until now) on how the link between corruption and migration is gendered and potentially impacted by gender norms. The study presented in this chapter will add to this ongoing debate by taking a closer look at the migration journeys themselves.

An estimated 47.2% of international migrants in Africa are female (UN DESA, 2017), and the gendered experiences of migration have received increasing attention (Donato & Gabaccia, 2015; Fleury, 2016). While initially female migration was mainly considered in the context of the migration of husbands or households, as increasing numbers of women are migrating independently (Oishi, 2002; Pedraza, 1991) the focus of migration research has also evolved. These studies show that women and men can be affected very differently by migration and that the effects vary widely.

Women might experience social stigma when migrating without a partner or husband (Malkin, 2004), while this is often not the case for men. At the same time, migration can also serve as a chance to become economically independent and has been linked to women's empowerment and changing gender roles (Lodigiani & Salomone, 2015; Lopez-Ekra, Aghazarm, Kötter, & Mollard, 2011). While increased economic independence through migration has been shown to help women to escape abusive relationships (Taylor, Moran-Taylor, & Ruiz, 2006), women often end up in abuse and precarious work environments in host communities, such as bars and domestic work. Importantly, how easy it is to migrate is also highly gendered. For women, the question if migration is acceptable without a husband or family member is highly dependent on the societal norms in the home country. A more patriarchal society makes female individual migration more difficult or impossible as decision making power rests solely with the male household members (Boyd, 2006; Massey, Fischer, & Capoferro, 2006). However, research shows that while gender discrimination can make migration more difficult it can also be a reason for women to choose to migrate (e.g. Baudassé & Bazillier, 2014; Black, Hilker, & Pooley, 2004; Ruyssen & Salomone, 2018; Zachariah, Mathew, & Rajan, 2001).

Third, there is still a limited amount of literature discussing the journey itself (Mainwaring & Brigden, 2016; as an exception Kuschminder, 2018) and, especially how it is gendered. Hence, this chapter will contribute to the literature by addressing these three gaps by looking at the question of how corruption experiences shape the migration journey and how these journeys are gendered.

For this chapter, two important things should be kept in mind regarding corruption. To understand the effects of corruption, it must be understood that corruption can directly and indirectly affect individuals. An example of a direct effect is when individuals participate in corrupt acts, for example paying a bribe to get travel documents. In contrast, indirect effects refer to cases where individuals are affected by the corrupt acts of others (Boehm & Sierra, 2015). An example could be that of the embezzlement of development aid, which was supposed to benefit a certain population is rather flowing into the pockets of corrupt officials. Here corruption does not only affect those that were directly involved in the corrupt transaction but also those who were supposed to benefit from the development project. As will be shown in

'Shaping the migration path – corruption in the home country' and 'Facilitator and hindrance – corruption throughout the migration journey' both of these play a role in the migration journey. Additionally, corruption experienced throughout the journey, of course, is highly dependent on the overall level of corruption in the home and transit countries. It is likely that migrants are exposed much more to corruption in countries that have structurally high levels of corruption. However, as will be discussed in the later sections, especially migrants without proper documents are often an easy target for corruption and therefore the sectors involved with migrants, e.g. immigration, police, or humanitarian aid, might have disproportionally high corruption levels.

Researching this topic in more detail is also essential for the achievement of the Sustainable Development Goals (SDG). Understanding the role of corruption in the migration process will help to create better anti-corruption initiatives which can help to 'facilitate orderly, safe, regular and responsible migration and mobility of people, including through the implementation of planned and well managed migration policies' (Target 10.7). The reduction of corruption (Target 16.5) is also an essential element of achieving SDGs. The research presented here sheds light on corrupt practices and can strengthen anti-corruption reforms, by linking them with migration policies. This chapter also contributes to a better understanding of gender inequality in migration and the findings can be used to create a safer environment for women on the move (SDG 5).

This chapter presents the findings from exploratory research. Conducting semi-structured interviews with experts, service providers, and migrants, the chapter explores how migrants from African countries travelling on the Central and Western Mediterranean route experience corruption and how these experiences are gendered.

The next section gives an overview of the methodological approach. 'Shaping the migration path – corruption in the home country' will discuss the experiences of corruption in the country of origin and 'Facilitator and hindrance – corruption throughout the migration journey' dives deeper into the role corruption can play throughout transit. Next, there is a short discussion on the role of gender norms and the final section concludes the discussion.

Methodology

Previous studies have shown that literature on the migration-corruption nexus is scarce (see for instance Merkle et al., 2017b) and usually does not apply a gender perspective. This chapter is therefore largely exploratory in nature and follows a qualitative research approach. It is based on desk research and 67 semi-structured interviews, conducted between November 2016 and May 2017. Interview guides were developed based on a review of key academic literature on migration, corruption, and gender, and aimed at addressing the three key gaps identified in the literature presented in the introduction.

Two rounds of interviews with experts were conducted by the authors and three research assistants. The first round (n=24) focussed on the role of corruption as a push factor for migration, with a particular focus on Mali and Ukraine. The interviewed experts include policy makers, representatives of local, national, and supranational government organizations, international organizations, non-governmental organizations, practitioners and scholars in the field of migration, corruption, and/or gender. The second round (n=43) focussed on gendered experiences of corruption during the migration process. The interviews focussed on service providers working with (female) migrants, who had arrived in Europe, as well as activists and experts from international organizations and non-governmental organizations working on gender, corruption, and migration. The interviews for the second round were conducted in the Netherlands, Germany, Italy, Spain, and Greece. Between March and May 2017, eight migrants were also interviewed. Six migrants were from Nigeria and two from non-African countries. Due to the sensitivity of the topic, all interviews were anonymized and the references to interviews throughout the chapter have been randomly assigned.

Shaping the migration path – corruption in the home country

This section examines corruption experiences of (potential) migrants in the country of origin and how these affect their migration journey. When looking at the role corruption can play in the origin country, it is important to distinguish between three different kinds effects of corruption: first, as a reason for migration aspirations; second, as a facilitator of the migration process; and, third, as an impediment to migration.

Already the decision to migrate can directly or indirectly be shaped by corruption. Merkle, Reinold, and Siegel (2017a), in a first comprehensive study of migration as a potential driver of migration, find that there is less evidence for corruption as a direct driver of migration aspirations; instead, the role seems to be mainly indirect. This was also confirmed by the interviews.

> Corruption is an enabling factor for people to leave. Corruption is an enabling factor for economic decline, it is an enabling factor for conflict and you can even say it is an enabling factor for climate change - but very few people say 'I have had it with this corruption stuff I will pack my bags and leave'.
>
> (Expert Interview 17)

Interviewees agree that high levels of corruption within a country can affect (democratic) institutions and social protection systems leading to unequal opportunities for citizens and resulting imbalances in terms of access to power and resources can encourage individuals, especially from disadvantaged populations, to seek opportunities abroad (Barbieri & Carr, 2005 and Expert Interviews 29,4).

The second effect focusses on corruption as a facilitator of (ir)regular migration within and from the country of origin. In the context of regular migration, corruption can be a way to speed up administrative processes: for instance, when issuing travel documents. Where options for regular migration are limited, corruption is crucial in facilitating irregular migration, such as obtaining fake travel documents and bribing border officials when leaving/entering the country (OECD, 2015 and Expert Interviews 11,35,21,26,41). In addition, migrants oftentimes need the help of smugglers who know the route out of/into the country, and smuggling is facilitated through corruption (Expert Interviews 11; 35). The more rigorous regular migration channels become, the higher the dependency of migrants on corrupt exchanges to be able to migrate. As one expert stated:

> As countries of destination are tightening a little bit their migration laws and trying to be more protective of their borders et cetera, they need to understand that this creates more vulnerabilities to smuggling and more vulnerabilities to trafficking. If you restrict the number of people that can get a visa, you will naturally have people that still want to enter the country and these people will be exposed to more corruption, to more abuse, to more risks of trafficking.
>
> (Expert interview 10)

Corruption can enable female migration in and from countries where it is prohibited and thereby help to overcome involuntary immobility (Ferrant & Tuccio, 2015; Fleury, 2016). In many prominent countries of origin, women seem to be more dependent on intermediaries such as smuggling networks due to their disadvantaged position in societies limiting their access to information, financial, and social capital. This dependency increases their risk of exploitation and vulnerability to becoming victims of human trafficking (Fleury, 2016; Gosh, 2009; Kawar, 2016). Hence, women's vulnerability to corruption and associated risks like becoming victims of trafficking can be attributed to patriarchal structures in their home countries, which assign different roles to men and women.

Finally, corruption can impede (regular) migration in and from the country of origin. High levels of corruption in countries of origin can increase the costs of migration and consequently make (regular) migration less affordable, for instance when high bribes are required to obtain regular travel documents. This can ultimately lead to involuntary immobility. This concept refers to a situation in which an individual wants to migrate but is not able to do so (Carling, 2002). In some countries, women can be disproportionately affected by involuntary immobility due to patriarchal structures. Where the access of women and girls to economic and social capital is restricted, or women are not allowed to travel or leave the country without the consent of a male relative or household member, their options for migration are limited.

Facilitator and hindrance – corruption throughout the migration journey

Once migrants leave their countries of origin with or without corruption, transit for most of them is filled with corrupt encounters. It is important to remember that the separation between origin and transit countries is not always clear-cut as 'all countries can be categorized as either. In the case of Nigeria, it's an origin country for trafficking to Europe but a destination country for many West Africans' (Expert Interview 16). For the purpose of this chapter, transit migration is defined as a situation between emigration and settlement. It is assumed that migrants do not have the intention to re-main living in transit countries. Interviewees agree that migrants experience the most intense forms of corruption during this time.

> [Transit often is] a period where opportunist use corruption, where you have corrupt officials, corrupt systems. They see opportunities in mi-grating populations, and they're quick to jump and exploit those op-portunities whereas perhaps in the source countries it's more deliberate, more planned, more structured.
>
> (Expert Interview 36)

Vulnerability to corruption during transit

The question of why migrants are more vulnerable to corruption during transit is often simply a case of lack of connections and the necessity to use corrupt exchanges for things that would usually be achieved by a social net-work or a more open policy environment. Hence, the idea of vulnerability is a difficult concept which covers many different areas and combines many factors:

> It can be about a lack of networks and a lack of social capital and of course the more you move from your country of origin, along that transit route to your destination country, the further and further you move away from your social network, from family, from things you're familiar from, by virtue of being a stranger, you become vulnerable.
>
> (Expert Interview 36)

Much of the vulnerability and the power imbalances migrants face through-out the journey are due to the lack of legal channels for migration. 'Legal status' has to be considered as an integral intersectional category, not only in the destination country but also throughout the journey. In migration research this has been well documented. Research on the United States has shown that race is a major determinant of legal status of immigrants (e.g. Ngai, 2004) and that individuals experience their lack of legal status as a similar distinction to distinctions based on race, class, or gender (Dreby, 2015; Menjívar, 2006).

The research for this chapter shows that in many instances, where legal channels are not available, corruption is a necessity to enable the migration process. As migrants are moving further from their social networks, they rely on corruption to create connections to navigate their journey and to allow them to cross borders. Corruption in these cases is often considered a means to overcome the limitations of the lack of legal status and is, therefore, seen as not necessarily negative. As one expert stated:

> If you made a conscious decision to migrate and a conscious decision to use an illegal route then the degree of agency, cooperation, acceptance, indeed the degree of welcoming corruption can be vastly different. There will be people who say I want to migrate from A to B, legal systems don't allow me to do it. So, I will use illegal systems and I am very grateful that there are corrupt officials that can help me.
>
> (Expert Interview 36)

Yet the irregular status during transit makes people more vulnerable to corruption and exploitation.

> In Lebanon for example, we have some reports of people forced to have sex in order to have their legal status recognized or in order to cross the borders. This is really a key issue. In a legal situation, most of these risks are gone because corruption arises from contacts with smugglers and so on. This is kind of a repeated pattern, not context specific, that we see everywhere.
>
> (Expert Interview 31)

Corruption as an enabler

Just as in the home country, corruption can enable migration during transit. Interviews revealed that bribes are expected, for instance, for sharing information with migrants, for letting migrants continue their journey, for officials to ignore fake travel documents, and to prevent denunciation (OECD, 2015). This applies to transit countries in various parts of the world, including West African countries, Turkey, Bulgaria, and Mexico to name a few examples from the interviews. Migrants are especially vulnerable to corruption and abuse during transit since they depend on intermediaries like smugglers.

Crossing the Sahara Desert without smugglers, for example, is a task that the interviewees determined impossible. The harsh environmental conditions and the presence of bandits in the region would almost certainly lead to death (Expert Interviews 11; 6). One Nigerian migrant described her encounter with these bandits: 'They [the armed groups say] come, if you don't have sex with me I will kill you, with a gun or a knife, all those things. So many girls were afraid. They had no choice' (Female Migrant).

In particular, when crossing borders migrants experience corruption in various forms. Border officials have been reported to let migrants pass only in return for bribes whether they are travelling through regular means or not (Female Migrant). In addition to monetary forms of corruption, it has been reported that middlemen, including smugglers and traffickers, pay border officials with female migrants (Expert Interviews 26; 31; 7; 4; 6; 13), implying that each vehicle transporting migrants always has to carry female migrants for payment (Expert Interview 6). The same is true for checkpoints guarded by soldiers along the route (Expert Interview 13, Migrants). This showed an important nuance regarding experiences of sextortion. Women's bodies are frequently used as a means of exchange not only for herself but for an entire group. A male migrant recounts:

> The border guards see that there are women in your convoy, they stop the pick-up and take the women. You can wait three or four days, sometimes one week, you never know how long, until the time they can satisfy all their desires [pause] and they come back.
>
> (Expert Interview 18)

Besides experiencing corruption as a means to organize the journey, it is also sometimes experienced as the only way for (irregular) migrants and refugees to get access to basic services like (reproductive) health care (Expert Interview 16) or humanitarian aid (OCCRP, 2014). Displaced women also can experience different forms of corruption in the context of humanitarian assistance or when living in refugee camps. Countries affected by emergencies such as natural disasters and conflict are often poor and face high levels of corruption (Chêne, 2009). In this context inflows of aid resources can actually increase corrupt practices, which then negatively impacts the quality and quantity of humanitarian assistance. Women are assumed to be most affected by such emergencies – not least because they often lack information regarding their rights. Hence, they are also most affected by corruption in the context of humanitarian aid. It has been reported that Syrian refugees in Lebanon had to pay bribes for humanitarian aid (OCCRP, 2014). Furthermore, limited financial resources make them vulnerable to sexual exploitation, in particular because of patriarchal attitudes, gender discrimination, and the fact that it is oftentimes men who deliver basic services (e.g. shelter, food distribution, health services, and education) (Amnesty International, 2016;

Chêne, 2009; Gosh, 2009; UNHCR & Save the Children, 2002). Single and widowed women are most vulnerable to sexual exploitation for aid because they are not protected by male household members (Chêne, 2009). Having male household members, however, does not necessarily protect women from exploitation. UNHCR and Save the Children (2002) report cases of men having to offer their female (underage) family members to humanitarian aid workers in exchange for access to aid.

Corruption and sexual exploitation curtail women's and girl's access to basic services and can lead to severe physiological, psychological, and social consequences for them (Chêne, 2009). In a study on the Calais refugee camp, researchers found that the presence of smugglers within the camp leads to fears of sexual exploitation, with roughly 73% of women saying they felt unsafe in the camp (Hangul, Paton, Stanton, & Welander, 2016).

Corruption as an impediment to migration

Just like in the home country, corruption can also make migration impossible once the migrant is on the way. One female migrant interviewed reported that she was stranded in Libya, one of the main transit countries for migration from Africa to Europe, for almost one year until she had enough money to pay corrupt border officials to migrate onwards. This concept of involuntary immobility in Libya is also receiving more attention as a consequence of the European Union's and Italy's deal with the Libyan government (Dalhuisen, 2017; Times of Malta, 2017). In the 2017 Malta Declaration, the European Council, in accordance with a prior European Commission Communication (European Commission, 2017), decided to expand collaboration with Libya as the 'main country of departure' beyond Operation SOPHIA in order to 'significantly reduce migratory flows along the Central Mediterranean route and break the business model of smugglers' (European Council, 2017). Consequently, thousands of migrants are stranded in Libyan detention centres under inhumane conditions, which was confirmed by our interviews with migrants and experts. This is underlined especially by migrants being reluctant to talk about their experiences in Libya. As one interviewee puts it:

> It is pure violence and women hardly talk about it. It must be appalling experiences that they cannot talk about. They can talk about their forced prostitution in Italy, Spain and Greece but about their experiences in Libya [...] they say 'it was no good'.
>
> (Expert Interview 10)

Female migrants in Libyan prisons have also been reported to be forced into transactional sex for basic goods and services (Expert Interview 23). Corruption has been reported to facilitate exploitation of women and girls during transit. As one expert explained, corruption enables a form of temporary marriages in Syria's neighbouring countries.

> You have religious figures and official authorities facilitating these kinds of marriages even though they are illegal. So, if you take Lebanon or Jordan, there were Syrian girls subject to these kinds of marriages. So, that Jordanian or Lebanese or also sex tourists could come, have the marriage for a few days or weeks, sexually abuse them and then leave.
>
> (Expert Interview 31)

The amounts of bribes migrants report can vary extensively: It has been reported, for instance, that Turkish officials let migrants continue their journey towards Europe for very small fees. In contrast, migrants in the ECOWAS region often arrive at their destination without having any money left due to the high amounts and high frequency of corruption throughout the journey (Expert Interviews 11;1). As already pointed out, where enormous bribes are expected this can lead to involuntary immobility until the migrant receives or earns the required sums. Migrants also reported severe punishments for the inability to pay for corruption.

> There was a lot of police. When you get to the border they say stop. You bring money for them and then if you didn't give them money they would beat you, they will tell you to sit down in the sun. You will be there until you find something on you or beg someone to just give me some money. […] They will make sure that they will beat you as nastily as possible. Oh God I hated it. (Female Migrant)

Here another gendered difference became noticeable. While men who could not comply with demands for bribes were severely beaten, women faced sexual violence and abuse (Bruni & Merkle, 2018).

The role of gender norms

Even though men and women migrate for similar reasons, gender norms, power relations, expectations, and unequal rights fundamentally shape the migration choices and experiences (O'Neil, Fleury, & Foresti, 2016) as well as the experiences of corruption. This section gives a short overview of the role of patriarchal structures in the way migrants experience corruption throughout their journey.

The first is the form of corruption; while men have described facing extreme violence throughout their journey and our interviewees reported severe beatings for men by corrupt officials, in the context of corruption their experience is significantly different. While men pay with money, 'women's experiences [of corruption] are shaped by the fact that, if they have nothing, they still have female bodies' (Expert Interview 2). This form of corruption, sextortion, in itself, is fundamentally a manifestation of patriarchal power structures.

This does not remain the only role that patriarchy plays in determining the lived experiences of corruption throughout the journey. As many of our expert interviews recounted, the availability of funds for corruption in both the home country and throughout the journey is often determined by gender norms in the home country. While families in patriarchal societies often collect money to send a male relative on the migration journey, women travelling alone frequently leave against the will of their family and hence without the family's financial and emotional support. This is especially the case when migration is seen as a risk to 'corrupt' women (Shaw, 2005) or when women and girls migrate to escape family control (Temin, Montgomery, Engebretsen, & Barker, 2013). This leaves them not only more vulnerable to sextortion, as the only available means of payment is their body, but also increases their risk to be caught up in trafficking networks.

With changing dynamics in female migration, more and more families also support their female members' journey; however, patriarchal structures remain and shape the journey from the start. In some cases, families actually take the decision to migrate for the women (Yeoh, Graham, & Boyle, 2002), for example, because women are believed to send remittances more regularly (Kanaiaupuni, 2000). Families might also deceive women in order to get them to migrate:

> Very often corruption impacts on the reasons to migrate in a first place because women are often convinced by trusted people with the deception of a better future. Instead, men are more aware of the difficulties of the journey. Women are often convinced to migrate by relatives or friends in the country of origin, so since the first connection with the smuggler or trafficker corruption is crucial, because a trusted person mediates the process.
>
> (Expert Interview 12)

Patriarchal structures in the countries of origin and transit also determine who is considered an easy and viable target for corruption and violence:

> With a lot of cultures, the abuse of a woman is less likely to bring retribution than the abuse of a man. An example, if you're [...] mistreating a man, there's always the chance, as a corrupt official, that you might upset someone, that might be related to someone important, they might be related to this and so on. Women are, in a lot of places, seen much more as a commodity or a good, or something that's fair game. You know, and once women have left their country of origin, they're in that transit

space, there are less powerful factors about the honor of the women or the family will protect them – these things are gone and have fallen away during the transit journey.

(Expert Interview 21)

Interviewees agree that women travelling alone are especially vulnerable to abuse and exploitation during transit. They are more likely to be pressured into corruption, especially sextortion, and as previously discussed usually have less resources available. It has been reported several times that women might have to engage in transactional sex for protection with men (Interviews 27; 11; 23). They pretend to be couples during transit and/or upon arrival in order to be less vulnerable to violence from other migrants or groups they meet along the way and to increase their chances of being accepted or granted asylum in the destination country (Interview 8). Another example of this is female migrants in Libyan prisons having to engage in sexual acts for food, water, and health services (Interview 23). This also applies to housing needs, especially in Algeria and Morocco, where abusive landlords often claim sexual services as a form of complementing a low rent (Interview 6). It is also reported that sextortion, or, as one interviewee preferred to call it, 'survival sex', is common in refugee camps such as the former so-called 'Calais Jungle', where one respondent highlighted that single mothers in the camp were particularly vulnerable to transactional sexual relationships built around protection (Interview 12). Yet travelling with male family members does not automatically guarantee protection. Where women do not have a say over what will happen to them, male family members frequently use females as a pawn to get ahead in the migration journey (Expert Interview 29) and evidence suggests that migrant women are forced to 'pay down [their] husband's debt to smugglers by making [themselves] available for sex along the way' (Bennhold, 2017).

Interviews with former sex workers who were trafficked from Nigeria to Italy highlighted that women were especially and overwhelmingly sexually abused by corrupt officials whilst in transit in Libya (Interview female migrant). Whilst most of the migrants interviewed for this report were reluctant to talk about Libya and their journey, the few words that they used to describe it are enough to understand the situation. In fact, they described their life in Libya as 'terrible', 'hell', 'lots of suffering', and 'no freedom'. Respondents explained that women would be told that they would have to go with the men, and if they refused they would be beaten or whipped (Female Migrant). It was also clear that the impact of being in a transit country where the women had no command of the language contributed to feelings of insecurity and a loss of autonomy (migrant woman, Europe). One girl pointed out that she was stuck in Libya for more than ten months because they were waiting for the money needed to pay corrupt border police in order to gain safe passage (Female Migrant).

Conclusion

Migrants can experience corruption during all points in the migration journey. Corruption can lead to migration aspirations, enable migration, or impede it (i.e. involuntary immobility). This chapter finds that corruption comes into play whenever legal options for migration are limited and is a constant throughout all stages of the migration process for many migrants. Despite being exploratory in nature, this research provides some crucial insights into the gendered experiences and forms of corruption during migration. While both men and women routinely encounter corruption during different stages of the migration process, this chapter finds that women are especially vulnerable to atypical forms of corruption such as sextortion in addition to more typical forms of corruption that are also experienced by men. Women travelling alone are especially exposed to corruption and sexual exploitation along the way. Furthermore, we find that underlying gender norms play a crucial role in shaping the experiences of corruption both in the home country and during the journey. For example, we find that women from highly patriarchal societies frequently travel with little financial resources and are, therefore, often more vulnerable to sextortion and abuse. The research also discovered another layer in the relationship between gender and corruption. Frequently, women are not only participants in the corrupt exchanges but are also commodified as the means of exchange for groups of migrants when crossing borders. Lastly, experiences with corruption and consequences of non-payment have serious consequences for male and female migrants' short-, medium-, and long-term physical and mental health.

The findings presented in this chapter show the importance of interlinking efforts to achieve SDGs 5, 10, and 16. Pooling efforts to include anti-corruption efforts into migration policy can not only help make migration safer for both men and women but can also help fight corruption on a national level. However, policy makers have to take care to gender mainstream both anti-corruption and migration policies and make sure that anti-corruption policies are not used as another layer to make migration more dangerous. Hence, more nuanced research is needed to further inform policy decisions.

The research presented in this chapter is only a starting point in analysing migrants' experiences with corruption and due to its explorative nature, and does not claim to be able to include all aspects that play a role in the analysis. There are several limitations to this exploratory study that should be overcome in future research. These experiences do not happen in isolation and are not shaped by gender alone but, as hinted at in the analysis for this research, intersect with many other factors of oppression, such as race, class, and ability. Future research on experiences of corruption, especially in the context of migration, should therefore take an intersectional approach to better understand the nuances of the phenomenon. The research presented in this chapter also heavily focusses on interviews with service providers and experts, and includes only a small number of migrants' voices. Additionally, the results presented in this chapter and research on sextortion as a whole focus solely on the experiences of women; while one can assume that sextortion does predominantly affect women, one should also investigate in more detail how men, and especially boys, are affected. Last but not least, the study has a wider geographical focus, and it is probably useful to take a closer look at specific countries of origin and transit in more detail.

References

Amnesty International. (2016, January 18). Female refugees face physical assault, exploitation and sexual harassment on their journey through Europe. Retrieved February 15, 2018, from https://www.amnesty.org/en/latest/news/2016/01/female-refugees-face-physical-assault-exploitation-and-sexual-harassment-on-their-journey-through-europe/.

Ariu, A., & Squicciarini, P. (2013). *The Balance of Brains: Corruption and High Skilled Migration* (Discussion Papers (IRES - Institut de Recherches Economiques et Sociales) No. 2013010). Retrieved from Université catholique de Louvain, Institut de Recherches Economiques et Sociales (IRES) website: https://ideas.repec.org/p/ctl/louvir/2013010.html.

Bales, K. (2007). What Predicts Human Trafficking? *International Journal of Comparative and Applied Criminal Justice, 31*(2), 269–279. https://doi.org/10.1080/0192403 6.2007.9678771.

Barbieri, A. F., & Carr, D. L. (2005). Gender-Specific Out-Migration, Deforestation and Urbanization in the Ecuadorian Amazon. *Global and Planetary Change, 47*(2), 99–110.

Batista, C., & Vicente, P. C. (2010). Do Migrants Improve Governance at Home? Evidence from a Voting Experiment. *IZA Discussion Paper*, (4688) Bonn, Germany: Institute for the Study of Labor.

Baudassé, T., & Bazillier, R. (2014). Gender Inequality and Emigration: Push Factor or Selection Process? *International Economics, 139*, 19–47. https://doi.org/10.1016/j.inteco.2014.03.004.

Beine, M., & Sekkat, K. (2014). Emigration and Origin Country's Institutions: Does the Destination Country Matter? *Middle East Development Journal, 6*(1), 20–44. https://doi.org/10.1080/17938120.2014.898411.

Bennhold, K. (2017, December 21). On Perilous Migrant Trail, Women Often Become Prey to Sexual Abuse. *The New York Times*. Retrieved from https://www.nytimes.com/2016/01/03/world/europe/on-perilous-migrant-trail-women-often-become-prey-to-sexual-abuse.html.

Black, R., Hilker, L. M., & Pooley, C. (2004). *Migration and Pro-Poor Policy in East Africa* (Working Paper No. C7; p. 53). Sussex: Sussex Centre for Migration Research.

Boehm, F., & Sierra, E. (2015). *The Gendered Impact of Corruption: Who Suffers More—Men or Women?* (U4 Brief 2015 No. 9). Retrieved from Chr. Michelsen Institute website: http://www.u4.no/publications/the-gendered-impact-of-corruption-who-suffers-more-men-or-women/downloadasset/3882.

Boyd, M. (2006). Push Factors Resulting in the Decision for Women to Migrate. In UNFPA-IOM (Ed.), *Female Migrants: Bridging the Gaps throughout the Life Cycle* (pp. 29–38). Retrieved from https://www.unfpa.org/sites/default/files/resource-pdf/bridging_gap.pdf.

Bruni, V., & Merkle, O. (2018). Gendered Effects of Corruption on the Central Mediterranean Route. *ECDPM Great Insights*, 7(1 (Winter 2018)). Retrieved from http://ecdpm.org/great-insights/migration-moving-backward-moving-forward/gendered-corruption-central-mediterranean/.

Carling, J. (2002). Migration in the Age of Involuntary Immobility: Theoretical Reflections and Cape Verdean Experiences. *Journal of Ethnic and Migration Studies*, 28(1), 5–42. https://doi.org/10.1080/13691830120103912.

Chêne, M. (2009). *Gender and Corruption in Humanitarian Assistance* (U4 Expert Answer No. 223). Retrieved from Chr. Michelsen Institute (CMI) website: https://www.u4.no/publications/gender-and-corruption-in-humanitarian-assistance/.

Dalhuisen, J. (2017, December 12). Libya's Wretched Web of Collusion [Online News]. Retrieved February 15, 2018, from Al Jazeera website: http://www.aljazeera.com/indepth/opinion/eu-complicity-refugee-abuse-libya-171212072937704.html.

Dimant, E., Krieger, T., & Redlin, M. (2015). A Crook is a Crook ... But is He Still a Crook Abroad? On the Effect of Immigration on Destination-Country Corruption. *German Economic Review*, 16(4), 464–489. https://doi.org/10.1111/geer.12064.

Donato, K. M., & Gabaccia, D. (2015). *Gender and International Migration*. New York, NY: Russell Sage Foundation.

Dreby, J. (2015). *Everyday Illegal: When Policies Undermine Immigrant Families*. Oakland, CA: University of California Press.

European Commission. (2017). *Managing Migration along the Central Mediterranean Route – Commission Contributes to Malta Discussion* (European Commission-Press Release No. IP/17/134). Retrieved from http://europa.eu/rapid/press-release_IP-17-134_en.htm.

European Council. (2017). *Malta Declaration by the Members of the European Council on the External Aspects of Migration: Addressing the Central Mediterranean Route—Consilium* (Press Release No. 43/17). Retrieved from European Council website: http://www.consilium.europa.eu/en/press/press-releases/2017/02/03/malta-declaration/.

Ferrant, G., & Tuccio, M. (2015). South–South Migration and Discrimination against Women in Social Institutions: A Two-way Relationship. *World Development*, 72, 240–254. https://doi.org/10.1016/j.worlddev.2015.03.002.

Fleury, A. (2016). Understanding women and migration: A literature review. *Global Knowledge Partnership on Migration and Development Working Paper, 8*. Washington, WC: World Bank.

Ghosh, J. (2009). *Migration and gender empowerment: Recent trends and emerging issues* (Human Development Research Paper (HDRP) Series No. 2009/4). UNDP.

Hangul, Ö., Paton, E., Stanton, N., & Welander, M. (2016). *Unsafe Borderlands Filling Data Gaps Relating to Women in the Calais Camp*. Retrieved from Refugee Rights Data Project website: http://refugeerights.org.uk/wp-content/uploads/2016/06/RRDP_UnsafeBorderlands.pdf.

Ivlevs, A., & King, R. M. (2017). Does Emigration Reduce Corruption? *Public Choice*, 171(3–4), 389–408. https://doi.org/10.1007/s11127-017-0442-z.

Kanaiaupuni, S. M. (2000). Reframing the Migration Question: An Analysis of Men, Women, and Gender in Mexico. *Social Forces, 78*(4), 1311–1347. https://doi.org/10.2307/3006176.

Kawar, M. (2016). Gender and Migration: Why are Women more Vulnerable? In F. Reysoo & C. Verschuur (Eds.), *Femmes en mouvement: Genre, migrations et nouvelle division internationale du travail* (pp. 71–87). Retrieved from http://books.openedition.org/iheid/6256.

Kuschminder, K. (2018). Afghan Refugee Journeys: Onwards Migration Decision-Making in Greece and Turkey. *Journal of Refugee Studies, 31*(4), 566–587. https://doi.org/10.1093/jrs/fex043.

Lodigiani, E., & Salomone, S. (2015). *Migration-Induced Transfers of Norms. The Case of Female Political Empowerment* (SSRN Scholarly Paper No. ID 2622394). Retrieved from Social Science Research Network website: https://papers.ssrn.com/abstract=2622394.

Lopez-Ekra, S., Aghazarm, C., Kötter, H., & Mollard, B. (2011). The Impact of Remittances on Gender Roles and Opportunities for Children in Recipient Families: Research from the International Organization for Migration. *Gender & Development, 19*(1), 69–80. https://doi.org/10.1080/13552074.2011.554025.

Mainwaring, Ċ., & Brigden, N. (2016). Beyond the Border: Clandestine Migration Journeys. *Geopolitics, 21*(2), 243–262. https://doi.org/10.1080/14650045.2016.1165575.

Malkin, V. (2004). "We go to Get Ahead": Gender and Status in Two Mexican Migrant Communities. *Latin American Perspectives, 31*(5), 75–99. https://doi.org/10.1177/0094582X04268402.

Massey, D. S., Fischer, M. J., & Capoferro, C. (2006). International Migration and Gender in Latin America: A Comparative Analysis. *International Migration, 44*(5), 63–91. https://doi.org/10.1111/j.1468-2435.2006.00387.x.

Menjívar, C. (2006). Liminal Legality: Salvadoran and Guatemalan Immigrants' Lives in the United States. *American Journal of Sociology, 111*(4), 999–1037. https://doi.org/10.1086/499509.

Merkle, O., Reinold, J., & Siegel, M. (2017a). *A Gender Perspective on Corruption Encountered During Forced and Irregular Migration.* Retrieved from GIZ Anti-Corruption and Integrity Programme website: https://i.unu.edu/media/migration.unu.edu/attachment/4665/A-Gender-Perspective-on-Corruption-Encountered-during-Forced-and-Irregular-Migration.pdf.

Merkle, O., Reinold, J., & Siegel, M. (2017b). *A Study on the Link between Corruption and the Causes of Migration and Forced Displacement.* Retrieved from GIZ Anti-Corruption and Integrity Programme website: https://i.unu.edu/media/migration.unu.edu/publication/4597/A-Study-on-the-Link-between-Corruption-and-the-Causes-of-Migration-and-Forced-Displacement.pdf.

Merkle, O., Reinold, J., & Siegel, M. (2018). Corruption, gender and migration. *Planet Integrity: Building a Fairer Society.* Presented at the OECD Global Anti-Corruption & Integrity Forum 2018, Paris.

Ngai, M. M. (2004). *Impossible Subjects: Illegal Aliens and the Making of Modern America.* Retrieved from ACLS Humanities E-Book http://hdl.handle.net/2027/heb.06691.

OCCRP. (2014, May 19). Syria: Aid Corruption Worsens Plight of Syrian Refugees. Retrieved February 15, 2018, from Organized Crime and Corruption Reporting

Project website: https://www.occrp.org/en/daily/2452-syria-aid-corruption-worsens-plight-of-syrian-refugees.

OECD. (2015). *Responses to the refugee crisis: Corruption and the smuggling of refugees* Paris, France: OECD.

Oishi, N. (2002). *Gender and Migration: An Integrative Approach* (Working Paper No. 49). Retrieved from The Center of Comparative Immigration Studies website: https://ccis.ucsd.edu/_files/wp49.pdf.

O'Neil, T., Fleury, A., & Foresti, M. (2016). *Migration, Gender Equality and the 2030 Agenda for Sustainable Development* (No. Briefing Report; p. 16). Retrieved from ODI website: https://www.odi.org/sites/odi.org.uk/files/resource-documents/10731.pdf.

Pedraza, S. (1991). Women and Migration: The Social Consequences of Gender. *Annual Review of Sociology, 17*(1), 303–325. https://doi.org/10.1146/annurev.so.17.080191.001511.

Pring, C., & Vrushi, J. (2019). *Global Corruption Barometer Africa 2019: Citizen's Views and Experiences of Corruption.* Retrieved from Transparency International website: https://www.transparency.org/files/content/pages/2019_GCB_Africa.pdf.

Richards, K. (2004). The Trafficking of Migrant Workers: What are the Links between Labour Trafficking and Corruption? *International Migration, 42*(5), 147–168. https://doi.org/10.1111/j.0020-7985.2004.00305.x.

Ruyssen, I., & Salomone, S. (2018). Female Migration: A Way Out of Discrimination? *Journal of Development Economics, 130*(Supplement C), 224–241. https://doi.org/10.1016/j.jdeveco.2017.10.010.

Shaw, J. (2005). Overseas Migration in the Household Economies of Microfinance Clients: Evidence from Sri Lanka. In J. Shaw (Ed.), *Remittances, Microfinance and Development: Building the Links. Vol. 1: A Global View* (pp. 84–91). Retrieved from http://www.geoffbertram.com/fileadmin/publications/Remittances%20bibliograhy.pdf.

Taylor, M. J., Moran-Taylor, M. J., & Ruiz, D. R. (2006). Land, Ethnic, and Gender Change: Transnational Migration and Its Effects on Guatemalan Lives and Landscapes. *Geoforum, 37*(1), 41–61.

Temin, M., Montgomery, M. R., Engebretsen, S., & Barker, K. M. (2013). *Girls on the Move: Adolescent Girls & Migration in the Developing World* (p. 136). Retrieved from Population Council website: https://www.popcouncil.org/uploads/pdfs/2013PGY_GirlsOnTheMove.pdf.

Times of Malta. (2017, November 22). EU-Libya Deal on Migration may be Breaching Geneva Convention—Kofi Annan. Retrieved February 15, 2018, from Times of Malta website: https://www.timesofmalta.com/articles/view/20171122/world/eu-libya-deal-on-migration-may-be-breaching-geneva-convention-kofi.663768.

UN DESA. (2017). International Migrant Stock: The 2017 Revisions. Retrieved September 13, 2019, from https://www.un.org/en/development/desa/population/migration/data/estimates2/estimates17.asp.

UNHCR, & Save the Children. (2002). *Sexual Violence and Exploitation- The Experience of Refugee Children in Guinea, Liberia and Sierra Leone* [Programme/project review]. Retrieved from Save the Children website: https://www.alnap.org/system/files/content/resource/files/main/825.pdf.

UNODC. (2013). *Corruption and the Smuggling of Migrants* [Issue Paper]. Vienna: United Nations Office on Drugs and Crime.

Yeoh, B. S. A., Graham, E., & Boyle, P. J. (2002). Migrations and Family Relations in the Asia Pacific Region. *Asian and Pacific Migration Journal, 11*(1), 1–11. https://doi.org/10.1177/011719680201100101.

Zachariah, K. C., Mathew, E. T., & Rajan, S. I. (2001). Social, Economic and Demographic Consequences of Migration on Kerala. *International Migration, 39*(2), 43–71. https://doi.org/10.1111/1468-2435.00149.

12 Do remittances fuel electoral violence?

Empirical evidence from Africa?

Rasmane Ouedraogo and Windemanegda Sandrine Sourouema

Introduction

Remittances are an important source of external financing in sub-Saharan African countries. According to the World Bank's World Development Indicators database, inflows of remittances to the region increased from 0.76% of GDP in 1980–1984 to 2.42% over the last five years (2013–2017). Countries including Cabo Verde, Comoros, the Gambia, Lesotho, Liberia, Senegal, and Zimbabwe are the largest recipients, with remittances representing more than 10% of their GDP during the period 2013–2017. It is in this context that the international community recognized that remittances are a key financing source for the sustainable development goals (SDGs) and called for policies to reduce the cost to remit money and boost remittances.

Yet the literature on the effects of remittances is vast and not clear-cut. There are some optimisms about the positive impact of remittances. Several studies show that remittances boost economic growth and investment (Akinlo and Egbetunde, 2010; Batu, 2017; Combes et al., 2019), improve education and health outcomes (Adams and Cuecuecha, 2010; Ambrosius and Cuecuecha, 2013; Azizi, 2018; Bouoiyour and Miftah, 2016; Yang, 2008), reduce income inequality and poverty (Bang et al., 2016; Li and Zhou, 2013; Rapoport and Docquier, 2006), and relax financial constraints and contribute to the development of the financial sector (Aggarwal et al., 2011; Anzoategui et al., 2014; Demirguc-Kunt et al., 2011; Giuliano and Ruiz-Arranz, 2009). However, there are some studies that underline the negative side of remittances. Ahmed (2013), Abdih et al. (2012), and Chami et al. (2008) showed that remittances worsen governance and increase corruption. Other empirical studies also highlighted that remittances lead to 'hazard moral' (Ebeke, 2012; Yol, 2017) and brain drain (Bredtmann et al., 2019; De Haas, 2010; Faini, 2007) and that the infusion of money from migrants may have an inflationary influence on the local economy (Ball et al., 2013; Ulyses-Balderas and Nath, 2008). Vadean et al. (2019) and Chami et al. (2018) showed that remittances could reduce the recipients' likelihood of working.

To date, there is no empirical study on the impact of remittances on electoral violence. Electoral violence is widespread in Africa and according to

Buchard (2015) around 50% of elections in the African region are subject to violence. There are several allegations that remittances could be diverted to finance and fuel conflicts, but no empirical evidence has been provided so far. For instance, Van Hear (2003) argued that contributions by the diaspora financed much of the conflict between Eritrea and Ethiopia as the Eritrean government attempted to direct individual remittances into government channels and the country's diaspora has been asked to pay 2% of their income to the state as a 'healing tax'. Also, Kapur (2003) noted that in Somalia, a large portion of the remittances went to supply arms to the rural guerrillas who toppled the government in January 1991. Similarly, Agunias (2006) revealed that migrants from the Dominican Republic have had an especially long history of political involvement with their country via large campaign donations, while the diaspora from the Philippines provided crucial support to pro-democracy forces that ultimately ended the regime of dictator Ferdinand Marcos. Seddon (2004) claimed that remittances from the Sri Lankan Tamil diaspora contributed to the Tamil secessionist struggle, and that the Indian Hindu diaspora in the UK contributed money to extremist groups in India. Unfortunately, neither side has strong empirical evidence to back up or substantiate its claims.

Remittances could be used to support social movements and political groups that may encourage and/or engage in conflicts and electoral violence. A review of the literature suggests two prominent mechanisms – direct and indirect – linking remittances to the dynamics of conflicts. Direct mechanisms include money, arms, and other material assistance provided by the diaspora (Anderson, 1999; Duffield, 2001; Kaldor, 2001). Remittances enable migrants to serve active and important roles in national politics. Migrants could support existing political and/or economic regimes and contribute to internal political transformation and fuel conflicts. Collier (2000) argued that a large diaspora is a powerful risk factor predisposing a country to civil war, or to its resumption. Indirect mechanisms include the appropriation by warring parties of remittances sent to individual families, converting a part of such remittances to military resources. The indirect support could be achieved through various forms of taxation or extortion, including checkpoints and blockades controlled by government forces, insurgents, warlords, or freelancers (Kaldor, 2001). The money captured could be used to finance for military operations, or material support in the form of food, weapons, or other supplies. Beyond this indirect channel, Duffield (2001) stated that some diaspora members can also be conduits for the laundering of the proceeds of illicit trade and businesses controlled by warring parties.

However, remittances can dampen conflicts and electoral violence through their impact on social development and democratic institutions. In fact, remittances improve household earnings, giving people better food, health, housing, and educational standards, which, in turn, can reduce the occurrence of conflicts/violence (Goodhand, 2001; Humphreys and Weinstein 2008). Furthermore, remittances can contribute to promote democracy in the migrants' countries of origin (Deonanan and Williams, 2017; Escriba-Folch, Meseguer and Wright, 2015; Ivlevs and King, 2017; Shain, 1991), which can reduce the use of violence to resolve electoral disputes. Escriba-Folch, Meseguer, and Wright (2015) argued that worker remittances undermine the capacity of autocratic regimes to mobilize electoral support through the delivery of goods and services to voters. Diasporas can transfer funds to civil society organizations and become critical factors in running democratic political campaigns inside their homelands (Shain, 1991).

This chapter improves the literature by estimating the causal effect of remittances on electoral violence in Africa. We do this by exploiting some micro-level data from the sixth round of Afrobarometer surveys, which conducted detailed individual-level surveys in several African countries. Afrobarometer represents a strong, reliable source of public opinion data within African states. Our sample covers nearly 40,000 individuals from 30 African countries. The Afrobarometer database contains the respondents' geographic areas (districts), their experience and perception of electoral violence, and whether or not they are remittances receivers. We supplemented this database with some data on precipitations and temperature from Ben Yishay et al. (2017). To deal with the problem of endogeneity, we use an instrumental variable approach. Attempts to estimate the effect of remittances on electoral violence obviously suffer from the reserve causality issue, the measurement errors, and omitted variables problem, which can lead to biased estimates. To overcome this endogeneity concern, we use exogeneous variations in rainfalls and temperature to instrument remittances, and to identify the causal link between remittances and electoral violence. This is consistent with the literature as several previous studies pointed out that migrants remit money to support their families back home when they face extreme economic difficulties (OECD, 2013; Ratha, 2007). We use an instrumental variable probit method to perform our estimates.

The results from our empirical estimations provide strong evidence that remittances reduce electoral violence in Africa. Specifically, while controlling for a battery of covariates including the respondents' sociodemographic and economic conditions, their political affiliations and elections-related characteristics, and the trust of respondents in the electoral commission, we find that remittances have a statistically significant negative effect on electoral violence. These results are robust to a range of sensibility checks. In addition, we find that the key transmission channels are the promotion of democratic institutions and the improvement in human capital. The findings of the chapter have several implications for SDGs, and most particularly Targets 16 and 17. Indeed, the SDG Target 16 is intended to promote peaceful societies by significantly reducing all forms of violence and related death rates (16.1) and reducing illicit financial and arm flows (16.4). As for the SDG Target 17, it aims at strengthening the means of implementation and revitalizing the global partnership by mobilizing additional financial resources for developing countries (17.3). As such, this chapter implies that achieving the SDG Target 17 through an increase in remittances could help to attain Target 16 related to the reduction in violence. As several African countries are in conflict and regularly experience electoral violence, attaining Target 16 under SDGs is crucial. This chapter shows that an increase in remittances can contribute to make peace in Africa and, therefore, achieve one of important SDG targets.

This chapter, to our best knowledge, is the first to empirically explore the effect of remittances on electoral violence. It contributes to the literature in three ways. First, we fill the gap in the literature on the effects of remittances by focusing on the specific case of electoral violence. The chapter provides an empirical evidence of the impact of remittances on electoral violence on a large sample of countries and rejects the country-based claims that remittances fuel violence. Second, we rely on exogeneous variations in rainfalls and temperature to identify the causal effect of remittances on electoral violence. Previous studies used imperfect instruments such as the lagged values of remittances (Catrinescu et al., 2006) and internal instruments-lagged explanatory variables (Giuliano and Ruiz-Arranz, 2009). The use of lagged values can violate the condition of exogeneity as they could be subject to serial autocorrelation.

Third, we use micro-level data which have several advantages compared to country-level data used in many studies. As violence is typically localized, occurring largely within specific regions of a country, the use of country-level data for both remittances and electoral violence could be problematic. Furthermore, previous papers have shown that the measurement of remittances at the country-level is imperfect in developing countries (Alvarez et al., 2015). Regarding the election-related violence, country-level data rely exclusively on physical and observable signs of occurrence of events such as killings and demonstrations. However, electoral violence is not only about observable events and physical acts of violence that take place in the public sphere. Electoral violence also includes political intimidation, blackmail, co-ercion, threat, psychological manipulation, and verbal abuse (UNDP, 2009). Using micro-level data allows us to cover all these forms of electoral violence. Another drawback of macro-level data is that electoral violence that happens in remote areas, with limited media coverage, is often not reported.

The rest of the chapter is organized as follows. 'Data sources and descriptive statistics' presents the data and some descriptive statistics. 'Empirical strategy' outlines the empirical strategy employed in the chapter and discusses relevant estimation issues. 'Results' presents the empirical results, while 'Robustness checks' describes in detail all the robustness tests. 'Conclusion' concludes.

Data sources and descriptive statistics

Data sources

Our main source of data is the sixth wave of the Afrobarometer surveys which cover 36 African countries. The surveys were conducted in 2014/2015. As an independent, nonpartisan research project that measures the social, political, and economic conditions in Africa, Afrobarometer represents a strong, reliable source of public opinion data within African states. There is an increasing use of Afrobarometer data in the literature (Isaksson and Kotsadam 2018; Khemani 2015; Konte, 2016), which reflects a certain confidence on the reliability and quality of the data. Nationally representative samples of individuals who are more than 18 years old are selected in both rural and urban areas of the different countries. Multilevel random selection methods are used to generate the samples, which are presentative cross-section of the population. In the sixth round of Afrobarometer, more than 53,000 people have been surveyed, with sample sizes ranging between 1,200 and 2,400 people in function of each country population size.

Measurement of electoral violence

We rely our measure of electoral violence on one question about respondents' own perception and experience of electoral violence (see question 49 of the questionnaire). Regarding the question Q49, the respondents were asked 'During election campaigns in this country, how much do you personally fear becoming a victim of political intimidation or violence?' Responses include 'A lot', 'Somewhat', 'A little bit', and 'Not at all'. We merge the three first answers and code them as 1, which indicates that the respondent has experienced political intimidation or violence, and 0 for the last answer 'Note at all'. The question Q49 refers to electoral violence according to the definition by the United Nations Development Program (UNDP) (2009). UNDP (2009) defines electoral violence as 'Acts or threats of coercion, intimidation, or physical harm perpetrated to affect an electoral process or that arise in the context of electoral competition. When perpetrated to affect an electoral process, violence may be employed to influence the process of elections—such as efforts to delay, disrupt, or derail a poll—and to influence the outcomes: the determining of winners in competitive races for political office or to secure approval or disapproval of referendum questions'. In the same vein, Fischer (2002) describes electoral violence as any random or organized act or threat to intimidate, physically harm, blackmail, or abuse a political stakeholder in seeking to determine, delay, or to otherwise influence an electoral process. Question (Q49) provides an assessment about the respondent perception and personal experience regarding political intimidation and violence.

Remittances

We refer to the question Q9 of the sixth round of the Afrobarometer surveys to measure remittances. On this question, respondents were asked, 'how often, if at all, do you or anyone in your household receive money remittances from friends or relatives living outside of the country?' Possible responses include 'At least once a month', 'at least every three month', 'at least every six months', 'at least once a year', 'less than once a year', and 'never'. We merge the five first answers and code them as 1, which indicates that the respondent receives remittances of money from friends or relatives living outside of the country, and 0 for the last answer 'never'.

Control variables

We control for the several covariates to alleviate problems of confounding caused by omitted variables. Table A.2 in appendices provides the list of control variables.

Descriptive statistics

The sample covers 30 countries and consists of around 40,000 respondents. The number of individuals in the sample range from 630 people in Liberia to 2,395 in Malawi. Table 12.1 presents some descriptive statistics. On average, 46% of total respondents reported being a victim of electoral violence. Furthermore, around 19% of respondents are recipients of remittances. There are some disparities between the countries. Table 12.1 presents the average values of the share of respondents who receive remittances and electoral violence by country. We observe that electoral violence is widespread in Nigeria, Cote d'Ivoire, Liberia, and Kenya where more than two-thirds of respondents reported being victim of political intimidation and violence. On the contrary, the share of respondents who have been targeted by electoral violence is low in Niger, Madagascar, Mauritius, and Burkina Faso. In these countries, less than one-fourth of respondents reported being subjects of electoral violence. The share of respondents receiving money of remittances is high in Algeria, Sudan, Cameroon, and Liberia, with more than one-third of respondents being recipients, and low in Burundi, Tanzania, Tunisia, and Mauritius where less than 10% of respondents benefit from remittances (Table 12.2).

Empirical strategy

To examine the impact of remittances on electoral violence in Africa, we estimate the following equation:

$$Electoral\ Violence_{ij} = \alpha + \beta Remittances_{ij} + \gamma X'_{ij} + \mu_{ij} \tag{1}$$

Where for individual i from country j, *Electoral Violence*$_{ij}$ is a binary variable equal to 1 if the individual reports being victim of electoral violence and 0 otherwise, *Remittances*$_{ij}$ represents a binary variable equal to 1 if the respondent receives remittances and 0 otherwise. Vector X'_{ij} includes socioeconomic and demographic, political, and election-related variables. μ_{ij} is the error term.

Table 12.1 Descriptive statistics

Variable	Obs.	Mean	Std. Dev.	Min	Max
Electoral violence	39,853	0.46	0.50	0	1
Remittances	39,853	0.19	0.39	0	1
GDP growth	39,853	-0.01	0.03	-0.16	0.04
Employment	39,717	0.39	0.49	0	1
Illiterate	39,752	0.15	0.18	0	1
Age, Log	39,651	3.55	0.37	2.89	4.65
Urban	39,853	0.39	0.49	0	1
Male	39,853	0.50	0.50	0	1
Political party member	36,570	0.63	0.48	0	1
Fair election	36,487	0.44	0.50	0	1
Voters' views reflected	32,762	0.37	0.48	0	1
Votes counted fairly	37,242	0.35	0.48	0	1
Non-participation of opposition parties	36,135	0.07	0.26	0	1
Trust electoral commission	36,774	0.27	0.44	0	1
Non-social media	39,853	0.89	0.31	0	1
Social media	39,279	0.25	0.43	0	1
Access to food	39,801	0.54	0.50	0	1
Access to water	39,799	0.54	0.50	0	1
Access to medical care	39,743	0.50	0.50	0	1
Access to cash income	39,729	0.25	0.43	0	1
Democracy	37,591	4.00	4.36	0	10
Human development	39,853	0.54	0.10	0	1
Rainfall shock	39,853	0.14	0.70	-0.81	8.17
Rainfall shock square	39,853	0.51	4.97	0.00	66.80
Temperature shock	39,853	1.01	0.03	-0.19	2.20

Generally, there are three main problems related to the estimation of Equation 1, which can lead to endogeneity issue and biased estimates. The first issue is the reverse causality between remittances and electoral violence. Although the objective of this study is to estimate the impact of remittances on electoral violence, one could argue that electoral violence can also reversely affect the inflows of remittances. Indeed, there is no doubt that immigrants will support their family back home when electoral violence occurs. The studies by OECD (2013), Ratha (2007), and Maimbo and Ratha (2005) show that remittances increase when crises occur in the immigrants' origin countries. The second issue is the measurement error, which may result from an under- or over-reporting related to right-hand-side variables including

Table 12.2 Electoral violence (%) and remittances (%) by country (average values)

Country	Electoral violence (%)	Remittances (%)
Algeria	40.4	38.0
Benin	36.0	13.6
Burkina Faso	23.7	17.8
Burundi	25.9	4.6
Cameroon	40.3	35.0
Cote d'Ivoire	71.7	19.3
Gabon	63.2	12.5
Ghana	34.6	18.1
Guinea	45.4	21.7
Kenya	67.4	11.3
Liberia	65.3	31.7
Madagascar	13.8	8.3
Malawi	43.3	12.6
Mali	35.4	29.6
Mauritius	23.3	7.5
Morocco	37.0	30.0
Mozambique	61.6	26.7
Namibia	34.8	10.5
Niger	10.4	27.6
Nigeria	81.9	29.7
Senegal	33.2	26.1
Sierra Leone	49.6	12.0
South Africa	38.2	8.3
Sudan	51.0	35.7
Swaziland	37.3	20.4
Tanzania	51.8	6.0
Togo	51.3	15.1
Tunisia	32.9	6.8
Zambia	54.3	10.0
Zimbabwe	60.7	26.7

remittances. Some individuals may choose to underreport or misreport the fact that they receive transfers from abroad. Several studies have noted that remittances tend to be underreported in household survey data (Acosta et al., 2006; Freund and Spatafora, 2008). The third issue that can lead to endogeneity is the omitted variables. As in any econometric estimate, controlling for all possible determinants of electoral violence in one regression is unconceivable. Consequently, simple probit regressions are likely to be biased.

To address this endogeneity issue, we employ an instrumental variable probit model to estimate Equation 1. We rely on the exogenous variations in rainfalls and temperature and instrument remittances with the shocks in rainfalls and temperature between 2013 and 2014. We include the square of rainfall shock to take into account the cases of flooding. The intuition is that an economic shock emerging from extreme rainfalls and temperature in the immigrants' origin countries may incite them to send money back home in order to support their families. Ratha (2007) argued that the main reason immigrants send money is to support their families during tough economic times. Remittances function as a shock absorber in low-income countries by providing critical income support after economic shocks or natural disasters (Kapur, 2004; World Bank, 2006). African countries are subject to extreme temperature and floods which destroy agricultural crops and lead to food insecurity. We acknowledge that shocks in rainfall and temperature can impact electoral violence through other channels such as economic growth and unemployment. Thus, we control for these variables in the regressions.

The data on rainfalls and temperature are extracted from Ben Yishay et al. (2017), who provide geocoded data at various geographic levels, including municipalities/districts. The data are originally from the Combined Precipitation Dataset of NASA's Global Precipitation Climatology Project (Willmott and Matsuura, 2001). Station values of annual total rain gauge–measured precipitation were interpolated to a 0.5 degree by 0.5 degree latitude/longitude grid, where the grid nodes are centered on the 0.25 degree. The geocoded data of Ben Yishay et al. (2017) are then used to match with the respondent's district as coded by Afrobarometer. Therefore, all respondents within the district would be matched with the temperature and rainfalls level recorded by Ben Yishay et al. (2017). We were able to match the administrative district names for 30 countries out of the 36 countries in the sixth round of Afrobarometer surveys (see in Appendix Table A.1 the list of countries). Only the administrative districts of Egypt and Uganda did not match with the district names in Ben Yishay et al. (2017). Thus, we exclude these countries from the study. Furthermore, there is a lack of rainfalls and temperature data at the district level for Botswana, Cabo Verde, Lesotho, and Sao Tome and Principe. These countries are not included in the study. We extracted the data for the period 1990–2014, and then calculated the shocks in temperature and rainfall as the deviations from the long-term trend.

Results

We report in Tables 12.3 and 12.4 the results of the regressions obtained through the simple probit model and the instrumental variable probit method, respectively. As can be observed, the coefficient associated with remittances is negative and highly significant at the 1% level in both Tables 12.3 and 12.4, suggesting that remittances are negatively associated with electoral violence. However, the coefficient associated with remittances is lower in Table 12.3 than in Table 12.4.

We will focus our analysis on the results using the instrumental variable probit model as the issue of endogeneity is addressed. The Wald test scores about the exogeneity of the instrumented variable are reported at the bottom of Table 12.4. This statistical test shows that we can reject the null hypothesis of no endogeneity, and therefore our empirical strategy is appropriate. Furthermore, the coefficients associated with rainfall shock, rainfall shock

Table 12.3 Results using simple probit model

Variables	(1)	(2)	(3)	(4)	(5)	(6)	(7)	(8)
Remittances	−0.121*** (0.014)	−0.109*** (0.014)	−0.078*** (0.017)	−0.071*** (0.018)	−0.071*** (0.018)	−0.075*** (0.018)	−0.065*** (0.019)	−0.070*** (0.019)
Remittances*democracy							−0.008** (0.003)	
Remittances*human development								−0.002** (0.001)
GDP growth	−2.146*** (0.200)	−2.456*** (0.205)	−1.616*** (0.292)	−1.707*** (0.296)	−1.715*** (0.297)	−1.533*** (0.302)	−1.495*** (0.303)	−1.535*** (0.305)
Employment		−0.004 (0.012)	−0.003 (0.015)	−0.001 (0.015)	−0.004 (0.016)	−0.022 (0.016)	−0.034** (0.017)	−0.020 (0.016)
Illiterate		0.213*** (0.018)	0.167*** (0.024)	0.169*** (0.024)	0.170*** (0.025)	0.181*** (0.025)	0.188*** (0.026)	0.181*** (0.025)
Age, Log		−0.215*** (0.016)	−0.197*** (0.021)	−0.200*** (0.021)	−0.205*** (0.022)	−0.196*** (0.022)	−0.204*** (0.023)	−0.194*** (0.023)
Urban		0.009 (0.012)	0.045*** (0.015)	0.046*** (0.015)	0.046*** (0.016)	0.036** (0.017)	0.049*** (0.017)	0.033** (0.017)
Male		−0.104*** (0.012)	−0.099*** (0.015)	−0.090*** (0.015)	−0.089*** (0.015)	−0.096*** (0.015)	−0.098*** (0.016)	−0.097*** (0.015)
Political party member			0.061*** (0.015)	0.061*** (0.016)	0.058*** (0.016)	0.048*** (0.016)	0.049*** (0.017)	0.048*** (0.016)
Fair election			−0.367*** (0.016)	−0.356*** (0.017)	−0.362*** (0.017)	−0.355*** (0.017)	−0.356*** (0.018)	−0.356*** (0.017)
Voters' views reflected			−0.094*** (0.015)	−0.098*** (0.016)	−0.097*** (0.016)	−0.080*** (0.016)	−0.095*** (0.017)	−0.080*** (0.016)
Votes counted fairly			−0.371*** (0.017)	−0.343*** (0.018)	−0.344*** (0.018)	−0.332*** (0.018)	−0.321*** (0.019)	−0.329*** (0.018)

	(1)	(2)	(3)	(4)	(5)	(6)	(7)	(8)
Non-participation of opposition parties			0.329***	0.320***	0.318***	0.305***	0.311***	0.303***
			(0.030)	(0.030)	(0.030)	(0.030)	(0.031)	(0.031)
Trust electoral commission				-0.150***	-0.148***	-0.140***	-0.149***	-0.141***
				(0.019)	(0.020)	(0.020)	(0.021)	(0.020)
Non-social media					0.033	0.063**	0.062**	0.060**
					(0.027)	(0.028)	(0.029)	(0.028)
Social media					0.024	-0.014	-0.018	-0.014
					(0.018)	(0.019)	(0.019)	(0.019)
Access to food						-0.119***	-0.116***	-0.118***
						(0.018)	(0.019)	(0.018)
Access to water						-0.055***	-0.055***	-0.055***
						(0.017)	(0.018)	(0.018)
Access to medical care						-0.045**	-0.054***	-0.045**
						(0.019)	(0.020)	(0.019)
Access to cash income						-0.060***	-0.054**	-0.061***
						(0.021)	(0.022)	(0.021)
Democracy							-1.279***	
							(0.295)	
Human development								-0.045
								(0.031)
Observations	39,853	39,432	25,634	24,487	24,221	24,058	22,448	23,972
Number of countries	30	30	29	28	28	28	27	28
Log likelihood	-47118.2	-46307.4	-29662.1	-28312.1	-27983.0	-27685.4	-25703.3	-27585.4
Wald chi²	187.5***	657.2***	2001.2***	2043.7***	2037.1***	2230.1***	2209.7***	2227.3***

Note: Robust standard errors in parentheses. *** p<0.01, ** p<0.05, * p<0.1.

square, and temperature shock are significant. Thus, our instruments, which capture extreme economic shocks, are a good predictor of remittances in Africa. The Wald test and the Anderson-Rubin test regarding the strength of the instrument are strongly significant; thus, we reject the hypothesis that our instruments are weak.

Table 12.4 presents the estimates with a set of control variables included subsequently in each column. In column 1, we control for only GDP growth. We find that the marginal coefficient associated with remittances, our key variable of interest, is negative and significant at the 1% level. Quantitatively, being a receiver of remittances from abroad reduces the likelihood of reporting electoral violence in Africa by nearly 14 percentage points.[1] This finding contradicts some previous claims which underlined that remittances are used to finance and fuel conflicts (Anderson, 1999; Duffield, 2001; Kaldor, 2001). Our results suggest that remittances do not fuel electoral violence in Africa. Previous literature has shown that remittance-receiving households make higher investments in health care and education than those households that do not receive this type of income (Yang 2008; Adams and Cuecuecha, 2010), which can, in turn, increase human capital and reduce the use of violence to resolve electoral disputes. Moreover, remittances can play an important role in supporting the development of local infrastructure, which fosters growth and productivity. As such, remittances could improve social development and the prospects and thereby dampen the risks of electoral violence.

In column (2) we control for some basic socio-demographic variables, including respondents' level of education, gender, age, living area, and employment status. We see that the coefficient associated with remittances remains negative and significant at the 1% level.

In column (3) we control for the political affiliation of the respondents as well as some elections-related variables. These variables include whether the respondent is a member of a political party, and judgment about the election: fairness of votes and participation of opposition parties and the counting of votes. In Africa, the outbreak of electoral violence is often related to the misjudgment of people about the electoral process and the exclusion of opposition parties from the electoral violence. Even after controlling for these important covariates, we still find that the coefficient associated with remittances is negative and significant at the 1% level. Furthermore, we find that the respondents who believe that opposition parties have been prevented from participating in the elections are more likely to report electoral violence. This suggests that more political inclusion could contribute to lower electoral violence in Africa. Not surprisingly, we also observe that respondents who reported that the election was fair and free, and that the votes were counted fairly, are less likely to be involved in electoral violence. Thus, ensuring a free and fair election is key to reduce suspicions among voters and electoral violence.

In column (4) we control for the trust of the respondents in the national electoral commission. There is no doubt that a lower level of trust in the national electoral commission could lead to protest and electoral violence. We still find that the baseline finding holds. The marginal coefficient associated with remittances remains negative and highly significant at the 1% level. Moreover, the coefficients associated with the trust in the national electoral commission are negative and significant, suggesting that a more accountable, transparent, and effective electoral commission could help prevent electoral violence in Africa.

In column (5), we control for the role of media during the election period by including the respondent's media channel. The media can act as a watchdog to ensure plurality of views, opinions, and transparent political processes, and offer a platform for candidates and voters to discuss important issues. However, the media can also amplify or even incite national prejudices or tensions during contentious elections. As can be seen in column (5), the coefficient associated with remittances remains negative and strongly significant at the 1% level. Thus, controlling for the respondents' media channel does not change our results. Furthermore, we also find that the coefficients associated with the two types of media channels are positive and significant, suggesting that the media contributes to increase electoral violence in Africa. In fact, the media could spread widespread rumors and trigger violence among the populations. Abdi and Deane (2008) argued that the media had undermined democracy during the Kenya's post-election violence of 2008.

In column (6) we control for the access of the respondents to basic needs, including food, water, medical care, and cash income. Goodhand (2001) argued that some politicians can exploit the impoverished conditions of populations to mobilize and lead them to rebellion. Poverty compounds vulnerability to insurgency at the individual and community levels by lowering the opportunity cost of mobilizing for violence (Humphreys and Weinstein 2008). Thus, the lack of human basic needs could cause public protest and lead to electoral violence. Even after controlling for these variables, the coefficient associated with remittances in column (6) remains negative and strongly significant at the 1% level. Furthermore, we also find that respondents who have never been without food, water, and medical care are less likely to experience electoral violence.

Finally, in columns (7) and (8), we include the interactive variables between remittances and democracy and human development to test whether remittances reduce electoral violence by promoting democratic institutions and improving human development. The data on the degree of democracy come from the Polity IV database with higher values representing a high degree of democracy. The human development index, which is produced by the United Nations Development Programme, is a composite index covering longevity, education, and income per capita. The results show that the coefficients associated with the two interactive variables in columns (7) and (8) are all negative and strongly significant at the 1% level. This finding implies that the dampening effect of remittances on electoral is higher in countries with democratic institutions and better human development outcomes.

Table 12.4 Baseline results

Variables	(1)	(2)	(3)	(4)	(5)	(6)	(7)	(8)
Remittances	-2.9538***	-2.9834***	-3.5397***	-3.7285***	-4.2351***	-3.8804***	-2.6486***	-1.6495***
	(0.526)	(0.367)	(0.535)	(0.535)	(0.682)	(0.702)	(0.640)	(0.436)
Remittances* democracy							-0.0605***	
							(0.014)	
Remittances*human development								-0.0170***
								(0.003)
GDP growth	-1.3285***	-2.0409***	-1.3186***	-1.0354**	-0.9423	-0.7713	-1.4379***	-1.4588***
	(0.385)	(0.317)	(0.499)	(0.526)	(0.574)	(0.559)	(0.451)	(0.396)
Employment		0.0089	-0.0406	-0.0503*	-0.1251***	-0.0973**	0.0006	-0.0187
		(0.019)	(0.028)	(0.029)	(0.038)	(0.038)	(0.027)	(0.026)
Illiterate		0.3189***	0.1799***	0.1625***	0.0832*	0.0975**	0.1312***	0.1297***
		(0.028)	(0.038)	(0.040)	(0.044)	(0.043)	(0.036)	(0.031)
Age, Log		-0.2895***	-0.2702***	-0.2804***	-0.1204***	-0.1219***	-0.1674***	-0.1690***
		(0.024)	(0.035)	(0.037)	(0.045)	(0.043)	(0.038)	(0.031)
Urban		0.1033***	0.0844***	0.0754**	-0.0375	-0.0213	0.0482*	-0.0232
		(0.022)	(0.031)	(0.031)	(0.030)	(0.030)	(0.025)	(0.022)
Male		-0.1020***	-0.0941***	-0.0774***	-0.1224***	-0.1277***	-0.1291***	-0.1140***
		(0.018)	(0.025)	(0.026)	(0.028)	(0.027)	(0.024)	(0.020)
Political party member			0.1916***	0.2030***	0.2323***	0.2195***	0.2190***	0.1534***
			(0.028)	(0.029)	(0.034)	(0.034)	(0.038)	(0.023)
Fair election			-0.6560***	-0.6332***	-0.6199***	-0.5873***	-0.5116***	-0.4841***
			(0.041)	(0.040)	(0.043)	(0.041)	(0.033)	(0.027)
Voters' views reflected			0.0105	0.0010	0.0034	0.0160	-0.0033	-0.0046
			(0.027)	(0.028)	(0.030)	(0.029)	(0.027)	(0.021)
Votes counted fairly			-0.4675***	-0.4124***	-0.4319***	-0.4165***	-0.3584***	-0.3741***
			(0.029)	(0.030)	(0.033)	(0.032)	(0.027)	(0.023)
Non-participation of opposition parties			0.2465***	0.2529***	0.2686***	0.2615***	0.2438***	0.2381***
			(0.049)	(0.051)	(0.055)	(0.052)	(0.044)	(0.038)
Trust electoral commission				-0.2842***	-0.2735***	-0.2518***	-0.2421***	-0.2041***
				(0.034)	(0.037)	(0.035)	(0.031)	(0.024)
Non-social media					0.2000***	0.2171***	0.2006***	0.1454***
					(0.052)	(0.051)	(0.046)	(0.036)

	(1)	(2)	(3)	(4)	(5)	(6)	(7)	(8)
Social media	0.5379**				0.5352***	0.5229***	0.3797***	0.2621***
	(0.085)				(0.085)	(0.083)	(0.071)	(0.050)
Access to food						−0.0461	−0.0768**	−0.0909***
						(0.035)	(0.030)	(0.024)
Access to water						−0.1556***	−0.0961***	−0.0916***
						(0.035)	(0.028)	(0.024)
Access to medical care						−0.1073***	−0.1146***	−0.0924***
						(0.033)	(0.029)	(0.024)
Access to cash income						0.0365	0.0284	−0.0229
						(0.040)	(0.035)	(0.028)
Democracy							−1.1183***	
							(0.430)	
Human development								−0.3432***
								(0.071)
Constant	1.3085***		1.8242***	1.9388***	1.3228***	1.2837***	1.4522***	1.0035***
	(0.156)		(0.184)	(0.191)	(0.172)	(0.169)	(0.172)	(0.116)
First stage								
Rainfall shock	−0.0109**	−0.0189**	−0.0261**	−0.0589***	−0.0571***	−0.0565***	−0.0680***	−0.0506***
	(0.004)	(0.008)	(0.011)	(0.012)	(0.012)	(0.012)	(0.013)	(0.012)
Rainfall shock square	0.0286***	0.0297***	0.0294***	0.0745***	0.0589***	0.0548***	0.0390***	0.0067
	(0.008)	(0.008)	(0.008)	(0.013)	(0.013)	(0.013)	(0.013)	(0.0132)
Temperature shock	0.8154***	0.8642***	0.9623***	0.8288***	0.6747***	0.6118***	0.4420***	0.7078***
	(0.108)	(0.109)	(0.117)	(0.119)	(0.120)	(0.122)	(0.137)	(0.121)
Observations	39,853	39,432	25,634	24,487	24,221	24,058	22,448	23,972
Number of countries	30	30	29	28	28	28	27	28
Wald chi²	121.9***	418.9***	1021.8***	1010.3***	881.1***	1042.7***	1419.5***	1895.7***
Wald chi-squared test of exogeneity	138.4***	130.3***	106.4***	123.9***	111.4***	79.8***	31.9***	20.7***
Anderson-Rubin test of weak instrument	137.4***	119.9***	101.1***	123.2***	126.3***	99.9***	102.0***	118.6***
Wald test of weak instrument	63.3***	60.9***	43.7***	48.6***	38.5***	30.5***	17.1***	14.3***

Moreover, we observe that the coefficients associated with remittances are lower in columns (7) and (8) than in column (6), suggesting that the effect of remittances on electoral violence is partially through democracy and human development.

Robustness checks

Additional variables

In this section, we control for several covariates to check the robustness of our findings to the inclusion of more variables in the baseline specification.

First, we include some variables capturing the respondents' perception of freedom in their country (see column 1, Table 12.5). The respondents are asked whether or not they are free to speak and free to join any political organizations or choose who to vote for. Electoral violence is more likely to occur when voters feel that there is a lack of freedom in the country. The inclusion of the respondents' perception of freedom does not change our findings. The coefficient associated with remittances is still negative.

In column (2), we control for the respondents' religious group member-ship. Some previous studies have found that religious fractionalization can spur on conflict (Montalvo and Reynal-Querol, 2005a, 2005b) and that election-related violence in Africa is fueled by religious divisions (Colombo et al., 2019; Eifert et al., 2010). Our findings remain consistent even after controlling for these important predictors of electoral violence in Africa. The coefficient associated with remittances remains negative and significant.

Third, we control for the respondents' perception of corruption in the country (see column 3, Table 12.5). In the survey, the respondents were asked whether they think that there is corruption in the office of the Pres-ident, members of parliament, government, police, and judges. Corruption is an issue in Africa, while high perception of corruption can be a motive of demonstrations and rejection of election poll results, thereby leading to more electoral violence. To capture the effect of corruption, we first create a binary variable taking the value of 1 if the respondent thinks that there is corrup-tion in the offices of President, members of parliament, government, police, or judges, and 0 otherwise. We then generate an aggregate index which is a simple average of the perception of corruption in the five institutions. The control of corruption in the key five institutions highlighted above does not alter our findings. In addition, the coefficient associated with corruption is positive and statistically significant, suggesting that a high perception of cor-ruption can lead to more electoral violence.

Fourth, we include some variables related to the safeness in general in the respondents' surrounding living places (see column 4, Table 12.6). As Wallsworth (2015) argued, it is important to account for the experience that led the respondent to report a given perceived level of violence. We suspect that the areas with high insecurity risks may be more likely to experience

Table 12.5 Robustness: inclusion of more covariates

Variables	(1)	(2)	(3)	(4)	(5)	(6)	(7)
Remittances	-4.0270***	-3.1995***	-3.5894***	-3.5591***	-3.6584***	-3.6157***	-3.8182***
	(0.757)	(0.611)	(0.698)	(0.646)	(0.672)	(0.637)	(0.728)
Freedom of speech	-0.1200***						
	(0.034)						
Freedom of association	-0.1021**						
	(0.040)						
Freedom to choose who to vote for	-0.2482***						
	(0.049)						
Member of a religious group		0.2346***					
		(0.026)					
Corruption			0.1602***				
			(0.060)				
Safe walking in neighborhood				-0.0706**			
				(0.034)			
Never feared crime in home				-0.1254***			
				(0.036)			
Never had something stolen from house				-0.1979***			
				(0.042)			
Never been physically attacked				-0.5207***			
				(0.073)			
Area size					0.0341		
					(0.021)		
Density of the population					0.0016		
					(0.008)		
Inflation						0.0144**	
						(0.006)	

(Continued)

Variables	(1)	(2)	(3)	(4)	(5)	(6)	(7)
Fiscal deficit						-0.0792 (0.114)	
Share of women in parliament						0.0006 (0.008)	
Gini index						-0.0419 (0.060)	
Oil deposits							0.1439*** (0.050)
Constant	1.4684*** (0.180)	1.2250*** (0.151)	1.1382*** (0.186)	1.9653*** (0.196)	1.3102*** (0.168)	2.9325 (2.897)	1.3431*** (0.169)
First stage							
Rainfall shock	-0.0622*** (0.012)	-0.0550*** (0.012)	-0.0573*** (0.013)	-0.0527*** (0.012)	-0.0623*** (0.013)	-0.0054 (0.014)	-0.0547*** (0.012)
Rainfall shock square	0.0589*** (0.013)	0.0566*** (0.013)	0.0555*** (0.013)	0.0511*** (0.013)	0.0581*** (0.013)	0.0068 (0.014)	0.0482*** (0.013)
Temperature shock	0.4914*** (0.123)	0.6690*** (0.123)	0.6076*** (0.128)	0.6796*** (0.121)	0.5761*** (0.122)	-0.1231 (0.139)	0.5801*** (0.122)
Observations	23,822	24,088	21,972	24,054	24,133	22,522	24,133
Number of countries	28	28	28	28	28	28	28
Wald chi^2	1059.5***	1311.5***	1028.8***	1246.8***	1105.4***	259.9***	1056.7***
Wald chi-squared test of exogeneity	75.9***	58.8***	63.6***	70.6***	72.7***	10.9***	70.4***
Anderson–Rubin test of weak instrument	119.8***	70.1***	83.7***	87.4***	97.8***	73.4***	102.9***
Wald test of weak instrument	28.3***	27.4***	26.4***	30.4***	29.6***	0.9	27.5***

Note: Standard errors in parentheses. *** $p<0.01$, ** $p<0.05$, * $p<0.1$.

electoral violence. Fortunately, in the sixth round of Afrobarometer surveys, there are some questions related to the security environment where the respondents live. The respondents were asked whether they feel unsafe walking in neighborhood, and whether they fear crime in home or if they have ever been physically attacked. In column 4, Table 12.5, we report the results of the estimates including these security-related variables. We see that the coefficients associated with remittances remain negative and significant at the 1% level. Thus, our findings do not change after incorporating the respondents' perception of security risks in their living areas.

Fifth, we control for the density and the size of respondents' districts (see column 5, Table 12.5). We extracted the population and density data at the district level from the Center for International Earth Science Information Network. Our baseline results remain strongly robust as the coefficient associated with remittances is still negative and strongly significant.

Sixth, to account for other macroeconomic conditions in the country, we include the inflation rate, and fiscal deficit over GDP in column 7. The data are from the IMF's World Economic Outlook. We also control for the share of women in the parliament and the level of income inequality, which are from the World Bank's World Development Indicators. We computed the average of these variables for the last five years (2010–2014) to avoid the simultaneity issue. In fact, violence can originate from difficult macroeconomic conditions or a high level of inequality. As reported in column 6 (Table 12.5), we observe that our findings are robust to the inclusion of these macroeconomic variables.

Finally, we control for the presence of a petroleum sites in the administrative region of the respondents. Some studies have found that naturally rich countries are prone to conflicts and violence (Collier and Hoeffler, 2004; Lei and Michaels, 2014). We use onshore petroleum and gas site data from the US Geological Society (United States Geological Survey [USGS], 2014), and match with the administrative region names in Afrobarometer surveys. Our findings remain unchanged.

Excluding countries of the sample

In this section, we undertake a series of robustness checks by dropping the countries of the sample one by one. The impact of remittances on electoral violence may be driven by some countries that have some specific characteristics that are not controlled for. To account for this potential misspecification, we drop the countries of the sample, one by one, and report the coefficients associated with our variables of interest. It is worth noting that all control variables of column 6 in Table 12.4 are included in the regressions. Tables 12.6 and 12.7 report the results. We mention in each column the name of the country that is dropped. The coefficients associated with remittances remain negative and strongly significant at the 1% level. Thus, our findings are consistent regardless of the country excluded from the sample.

Table 12.6 Robustness: excluding countries from the sample

Variables	(1)	(2)	(3)	(4)	(5)	(6)	(7)
	Burundi	Benin	Burkina Faso	Cote d'Ivoire	Cameroon	Algeria	Gabon
Remittances	−3.8221***	−4.2942***	−3.6631***	−3.1857***	−4.2475***	−4.1040***	−4.1179***
	(0.707)	(0.753)	(0.705)	(0.620)	(0.840)	(1.501)	(0.782)
Constant	1.3508***	1.5228***	1.4303***	1.2923***	1.3407***	1.5327***	1.3440***
	(0.172)	(0.187)	(0.169)	(0.158)	(0.179)	(0.255)	(0.177)
First stage							
Rainfall shock	−0.0550***	−0.0582***	−0.0549***	−0.0586***	−0.0437***	−0.0456***	−0.0417***
	(0.012)	(0.012)	(0.012)	(0.012)	(0.012)	(0.012)	(0.012)
Rainfall shock square	0.0519***	0.0561***	0.0525***	0.0571***	0.0492***	0.0361**	0.0469***
	(0.013)	(0.013)	(0.013)	(0.013)	(0.013)	(0.015)	(0.013)
Temperature shock	0.6114***	0.5931***	0.5873***	0.6175***	0.5801***	0.0082***	0.6522***
	(0.123)	(0.122)	(0.121)	(0.122)	(0.120)	(0.133)	(0.122)
Observations	23,353	23,381	23,263	23,259	23,482	23,483	23,577
Number of countries	27	27	27	27	27	27	27
Wald chi^2	999.3***	937.9***	1087.7***	1205.9***	947.4***	954.5***	938.7***
Wald chi-squared test of exogeneity	75.3***	95.5***	66.6***	57.2***	74.3***	19.9***	78.1***
Anderson-Rubin test of weak instrument	101.0***	111.6***	97***	94.9***	93.3***	115.2***	96.9***
Wald test of weak instrument	29.2***	32.5***	27.0***	26.3***	25.6***	7.5***	27.7***

Note: Standard errors in parentheses. *** p<0.01, ** p<0.05, * p<0.1

Table 12.7 Robustness: excluding countries from the sample

Variables	(1)	(2)	(3)	(4)	(5)	(6)	(7)
	Mauritius	Malawi	Namibia	Niger	Nigeria	Senegal	Sudan
Remittances	−2.9449***	−3.6603***	−5.9473***	−3.0508***	−4.2910***	−4.3906***	−2.6241***
	(0.554)	(0.733)	(1.150)	(0.641)	(0.786)	(0.848)	(0.493)
Constant	1.1288***	1.3395***	1.5393***	1.3169***	1.3754***	1.4555***	1.1774***
	(0.142)	(0.175)	(0.236)	(0.155)	(0.186)	(0.191)	(0.137)
First stage							
Rainfall shock	−0.0656***	−0.0696***	−0.0532***	−0.0626***	−0.0529***	−0.0317**	−0.0680***
	(0.012)	(0.012)	(0.013)	(0.012)	(0.012)	(0.013)	(0.012)
Rainfall shock square	0.0548***	0.0620***	0.0565***	0.0573***	0.0610***	0.0370***	0.0268**
	(0.013)	(0.013)	(0.013)	(0.013)	(0.013)	(0.013)	(0.016)
Temperature shock	0.6489***	0.3849***	0.4800***	0.5254***	0.5611***	0.6786***	0.6583***
	(0.122)	(0.139)	(0.127)	(0.121)	(0.122)	(0.121)	(0.12)
Observations	23,434	22,672	23,415	23,370	22,628	23,391	23,488
Number of countries	27	27	27	27	27	27	27
Wald chi^2	1261.6***	1067.8***	594.6***	1139.5***	859.2***	878.9***	1454.1***
Wald chi-squared test of exogeneity	56.7***	62.5***	120.9***	47.9***	87.2***	79.5***	52.0***
Anderson-Rubin test of weak instrument	95.4***	116.9***	133.6***	75.8***	100.9***	95.9***	69.5***
Wald test of weak instrument	28.2***	24.9***	26.7***	22.6***	29.8***	26.8***	28.3***

Note: Standard errors in parentheses. *** p<0.01, ** p<0.05, * p<0.1

(8)	(9)	(10)	(11)	(12)	(13)	(14)	(15)
Ghana	*Guinea*	*Kenya*	*Liberia*	*Morocco*	*Madagascar*	*Mali*	*Mozambique*
-3.4688★★★	-3.5484★★★	-4.0352★★★	-3.8886★★★	-3.7913★★★	-2.9420★★★	-4.0083★★★	-3.8433★★★
(0.652)	(0.649)	(0.668)	(0.712)	(0.699)	(0.590)	(0.756)	(0.707)
1.3477★★★	1.3967★★★	1.4355★★★	1.3107★★★	1.3380★★★	1.3071★★★	1.3391★★★	1.1193★★★
(0.163)	(0.166)	(0.178)	(0.167)	(0.167)	(0.149)	(0.173)	(0.161)
-0.0610★★★	-0.0583★★★	-0.0777★★★	-0.0597★★★	-0.0566★★★	-0.0495★★★	-0.0452★★★	-0.0611★★★
(0.012)	(0.012)	(0.012)	(0.012)	(0.012)	(0.012)	(0.012)	(0.012)
0.0582★★★	0.0580★★★	0.0654★★★	0.0618★★★	0.0548★★★	0.0475★★★	0.0470★★★	0.0610★★★
(0.013)	(0.013)	(0.013)	(0.013)	(0.013)	(0.013)	(0.013)	(0.013)
0.5884★★★	0.6217★★★	0.5249★★★	0.5457★★★	0.5955★★★	0.7222★★★	0.6395★★★	0.5351★★★
(0.121)	(0.121)	(0.125)	(0.12)	(0.121)	(0.124)	(0.121)	(0.121)
23,308	23,500	22,568	23,738	24,133	23,275	23,272	23,283
27	27	27	27	27	27	27	27
1173.1★★★	1099.6★★★	917.2★★★	1019.3★★★	1064.6★★★	1318.2★★★	1015.8★★★	1028.5★★★
66.3★★★	70.8★★★	100.8★★★	77.5★★★	74.9★★★	49.6★★★	74.9★★★	74.6★★★
95.1★★★	89.5★★★	112.7★★★	96.6★★★	97.1★★★	67.4★★★	94.6★★★	96.4★★★
28.3★★★	29.8★★★	36.5★★★	29.8★★★	29.4★★★	24.8★★★	28.1★★★	29.5★★★

(8)	(9)	(10)	(11)	(12)	(13)	(14)	(15)
Sierra Leone	*Swaziland*	*Togo*	*Tunisia*	*Tanzania*	*South Africa*	*Zambia*	*Zimbabwe*
-3.8629★★★	-3.7913★★★	-3.6875★★★	-2.8014★★★	-4.5026★★★	-3.7778★★★	-3.5362★★★	-3.9496★★★
(0.707)	(0.699)	(0.673)	(0.503)	(0.850)	(0.675)	(0.676)	(0.680)
1.3703★★★	1.3380★★★	1.3329★★★	1.2164★★★	1.5212★★★	1.1992★★★	1.2989★★★	1.3363★★★
(0.172)	(0.167)	(0.166)	(0.139)	(0.198)	(0.161)	(0.162)	(0.174)
-0.0551★★★	-0.0566★★★	-0.0591★★★	-0.0672★★★	-0.0481★★★	-0.0360★★★	-0.0536★★★	-0.0536★★★
(0.012)	(0.012)	(0.012)	(0.012)	(0.013)	(0.013)	(0.012)	(0.012)
0.0557★★★	0.0548★★★	0.0571★★★	0.0608★★★	0.0573★★★	0.0418★★★	0.0531★★★	0.0585★★★
(0.013)	(0.013)	(0.013)	(0.013)	(0.013)	(0.013)	(0.013)	(0.013)
0.6099★★★	0.5955★★★	0.6025★★★	0.7502★★★	0.5770★★★	0.8729★★★	0.6840★★★	0.6795★★★
(0.121)	(0.121)	(0.121)	(0.123)	(0.124)	(0.134)	(0.134)	(0.121)
23,803	24,133	23,674	23,459	22,522	22,618	23,545	22,937
27	27	27	27	27	27	27	27
1037.8★★★	1064.6★★★	1081.9★★★	1396.0★★★	842.1★★★	975.8★★★	1142.2★★★	938.8★★★
77.9★★★	74.9★★★	74.4★★★	60.0★★★	89.4★★★	79.9★★★	65.0★★★	90.0★★★
97.5★★★	97.1★★★	95.9★★★	86.9★★★	102.9★★★	98.9★★★	87.8★★★	98.0★★★
29.9★★★	29.4★★★	30.0★★★	30.9★★★	28.0★★★	31.3★★★	27.3★★★	33.8★★★

Table 12.8 Robustness: using remittances in percentage of GDP

Variables	(1)	(2)	(3)	(4)	(5)	(6)	(7)	(8)
Remittances	−0.0813*** (0.015)	−0.0679*** (0.015)	−0.0791*** (0.013)	−0.0724*** (0.013)	0.0627*** (0.013)	−0.0682*** (0.013)	−0.0379*** (0.013)	−0.0229** (0.012)
Remittances*democracy							−1.4524*** (0.355)	
Remittances*human development								−0.1843*** (0.040)
GDP growth	−4.4418*** (0.453)	−4.3671*** (0.443)	−2.7632*** (0.588)	−2.0745*** (0.551)	−2.0692*** (0.550)	−2.0139*** (0.536)	−0.6345 (0.544)	−1.5761*** (0.512)
Employment		−0.0152 (0.015)	−0.0359** (0.018)	−0.0410** (0.018)	−0.0356* (0.019)	−0.0532*** (0.018)	−0.0556*** (0.019)	−0.0556*** (0.018)
Illiterate		0.2298*** (0.020)	0.1420*** (0.026)	0.1470*** (0.027)	0.1357*** (0.027)	0.1511*** (0.027)	0.1612*** (0.028)	0.1522*** (0.027)
Age, Log		−0.2620*** (0.019)	−0.2493*** (0.023)	−0.2537*** (0.024)	−0.2348*** (0.025)	−0.2254*** (0.025)	−0.2478*** (0.026)	−0.2209*** (0.025)
Urban		0.0029 (0.014)	0.0433** (0.017)	0.0495*** (0.018)	0.0689*** (0.018)	0.0523*** (0.019)	0.0719*** (0.020)	0.0480** (0.019)
Male		−0.0946*** (0.013)	−0.0995*** (0.017)	−0.0877*** (0.017)	−0.0949*** (0.017)	−0.1016*** (0.017)	−0.1014*** (0.018)	−0.1033*** (0.017)
Political party member			0.1261*** (0.017)	0.1265*** (0.018)	0.1248*** (0.018)	0.1132*** (0.018)	0.0926*** (0.019)	0.1126*** (0.018)
Fair election			−0.4470*** (0.018)	−0.4275*** (0.018)	−0.4254*** (0.018)	−0.4187*** (0.018)	−0.4263*** (0.019)	−0.4166*** (0.018)
Voters' views reflected			−0.0428** (0.017)	−0.0435** (0.018)	−0.0441** (0.018)	−0.0256 (0.018)	−0.0461** (0.019)	−0.0225 (0.018)
Votes counted fairly			−0.4133*** (0.019)	−0.3732*** (0.020)	−0.3758*** (0.020)	−0.3658*** (0.020)	−0.3397*** (0.021)	−0.3554*** (0.020)
Non-participation of opposition parties			0.2361*** (0.033)	0.2240*** (0.033)	0.2254*** (0.034)	0.2154*** (0.034)	0.2295*** (0.035)	0.2098*** (0.034)
Trust electoral commission				−0.1876*** (0.021)	−0.1818*** (0.021)	−0.1752*** (0.021)	−0.1718*** (0.022)	−0.1686*** (0.021)

	(1)	(2)	(3)	(4)	(5)	(6)	(7)	(8)
Non-social media					0.0768***	0.1090***	0.1151***	0.1031***
					(0.029)	(0.030)	(0.031)	(0.030)
Social media					0.0531**	0.0980***	0.1163***	0.0920***
					(0.022)	(0.022)	(0.023)	(0.022)
Access to food						-0.1180***	-0.1376***	-0.1206***
						(0.021)	(0.022)	(0.021)
Access to water						-0.0625***	-0.0514**	-0.0530***
						(0.020)	(0.021)	(0.020)
Access to medical care						-0.0909***	-0.0914***	-0.0861***
						(0.021)	(0.022)	(0.021)
Access to cash income						-0.0442	0.0166	-0.0307
						(0.027)	(0.028)	(0.026)
Democracy							0.0012	
							(0.004)	
Human development								-0.0064***
								(0.001)
Constant	0.2385***	0.9612***	1.0545***	1.0144***	0.8863***	0.9059***	0.8398***	0.8235***
	(0.062)	(0.092)	(0.107)	(0.108)	(0.114)	(0.112)	(0.118)	(0.110)
First stage								
Rainfall shock	-1.8073***	-1.8160***	-2.5969***	-2.6478***	-2.6714***	-2.6805***	-2.9710***	-2.9192***
	(0.091)	(0.091)	(0.114)	(0.128)	(0.128)	(0.127)	(0.137)	(0.129)
Rainfall shock square	0.5962***	0.6018***	0.8812***	0.4832***	0.5121***	0.5651***	0.4339***	0.5955***
	(0.061)	(0.061)	(0.080)	(0.133)	(0.134)	(0.132)	(0.136)	(0.135)
Temperature shock	2.8444***	2.5945***	3.0783**	-0.0196	-0.047	2.5475**	6.8786***	3.5291***
	(0.937)	(0.945)	(1.193)	(1.215)	(1.229)	(1.230)	(1.386)	(1.233)
Observations	39,545	39,099	25,240	24,089	23,817	23,652	22,031	23,568
Number of countries	30	30	29	28	28	28	27	28
Wald chi^2	137.8***	638.0***	2063.4***	2123.5***	2124.6***	2268.2***	2223.2***	2298.8***
Wald chi-squared test of exogeneity	44.4***	33.4***	6.5***	1.2	1.0	1.7	3.3*	0.0
Anderson–Rubin test of weak instrument	127.6***	113.2***	103.6***	121.2***	124.7***	101.1***	104.5***	120.0***
Wald test of weak instrument	28.3***	19.8***	1.8	0.0	0.1	0.1	9.1***	0.8

Note: Standard errors in parentheses. *** $p<0.01$, ** $p<0.05$, * $p<0.1$.

Using remittances in percentage of GDP

Finally, we use remittances as a share of GDP instead of the binary variable used so far. This allows us to take into account the size of remittances in our sample of countries. The results are reported in Table 12.8. We find that the coefficient associated with remittances remains negative and strongly significant in all columns. Therefore, the use of remittances in percentage of GDP does not alter our findings.

Conclusion

Two of the SDGs are to increase financial resources such as remittances in developing countries and reduce conflicts and violence. However, there is an increasing concern about the use of remittances to finance ongoing conflicts and fuel violence. In this regard, several claims have been done on the specific cases of some countries, including the conflict between Eritrea and Ethiopia, the Philippines, Dominican Republic, and Sri Lanka. Yet all these country-based claims lack substantial empirical evidence. In this chapter, we provide an empirical analysis of the impact of remittances on electoral violence in Africa using some micro-level data from the sixth round of Afrobarometer surveys. The sample covers nearly 40,000 individuals from 30 African countries. To address the problem of endogeneity and identify the causal effects of remittances on electoral violence, we rely on some very exogeneous instruments including rainfall and temperature shock and employ an instrumental variable probit model.

We find a strongly significant and negative impact of remittances on electoral violence in Africa. The findings are robust to a variety of alternative specifications, such as the inclusion of several covariates in the estimates and the exclusion of countries of the sample. This empirical study – the first of its kind on remittances and electoral violence – makes a significant contribution to the literature and provides some implications for SDGs. Alongside other financing means, remittances have been considered one of the potential external sources of funding for SDGs during the United Nations' Third International Conference on Financing for Development in Addis Ababa in July 2015. The importance of remittances in supporting families back home in developing countries was recognized, and some policies are being implemented to promote and reduce the transaction costs of money transfers and create greater options and opportunities to leverage the potential benefits of remittances for development. While there are some claims that remittances can be used to fuel conflicts, our findings suggest that remittances are not to blame for the widespread electoral violence in the African continent. They have instead contributed to lessening electoral violence. In this regard, pursuing the goal of increasing remittances in developing countries, including Africa, under the SDGs initiative can contribute to reduce electoral violence and promote peace in Africa. Furthermore, our results show that remittances reduce electoral violence by contributing to the building of strong democratic institutions and improving human development. Therefore, remittances contribute to several of the goals set in the 2030 SDGs Agenda, such as education, good health, and well-being. Governments, regulators, and the private sector have an important role to play in leveraging the effects of remittances and contributing to reach SDGs by 2030.

Note

1 Marginal effects calculated when the respondent is a receiver (the binary variable remittances are equal to 1).

References

Abdi, J., and Deane, J., 2008. *The Kenyan 2007 elections and their aftermath: the role of media and communication.* Policy Briefing No. 1. London: BBC World Service Trust.

Abdih, Y., Chami, R., Dagher, J., and Montiel, P., 2012. Remittances and Institutions: Are Remittances a Curse? *World Development* 40(4): 657–666.

Acosta, P., Calderon, C., Fajnzylber, P., and Lopez, H., 2006. Remittances and Development in Latin America. *World Economy* 29(7): 957–987.

Adams, R. J., and Cuecuecha, A., 2010. Remittances, Household Expenditure and Investment in Guatemala. *World Development* 11(38): 1626–1641.

Aggarwal, R., Demirguc-Kunt, A., and Pería, M. S. M., 2011. Do Remittances Promote Financial Development? *Journal of Development Economics* 96(2): 255–264.

Agunias, D. R., 2006. *Remittances and Development: Trends, Impacts, and Policy Options – A Review of the Literature.* Washington, DC: Migration Policy Institute.

Ahmed, F. Z., 2013. Remittances Deteriorate Governance. *The Review of Economics and Statistics* 95(4): 1166–1182.

Akinlo, A. E., and Egbetunde, T., 2010. Financial Development and Economic Growth: The Experience of 10 Sub-Saharan African Countries Revisited. *The Review of Finance and Banking* 2(1): 17–28.

Alvarez, S. P., Briod, P., Ferrari, O., and Rieder, U., 2015. Remittances: how reliable are the data? *Migration Policy Practice* V(2), United Nations, New York.

Ambrosius, C., and Cuecuecha, A., 2013. Are Remittances a Substitute for Credit? Carrying the Financial Burden of Health Shocks in National and Transnational Households. *World Development* 46: 143–152.

Anderson, M. B., 1999. *Do No Harm: How Aid Can Support Peace – Or War.* London: Lynne Rienner.

Anzoategui, D., Demirgüç-Kunt, A., and Pería, M. S. M., 2014. Remittances and Financial Inclusion: Evidence from El Salvador. *World Development* 54: 338–349.

Azizi, S., 2018. The Impact of Workers' Remittances on Human Capital and Labor Supply in Developing Countries. *Economic Modelling* 75: 377–396.

Bang, J. T., Mitra, A., and Wunnava, P. V., 2016. Do Remittances Improve Income Inequality? An Instrumental Variable Quantile Analysis of the Kenyan Case. *Economic Modelling* 58: 394–402.

Ball, C., Lopez, C., and Reyes, J., 2013. Remittances, Inflation and Exchange Rate Regimes in Small Open Economies. *The World Economy* 36(4): 487–507.

Batu, M., 2017. International Worker Remittances and Economic Growth in a Real Business Cycle Framework. *Structural Change and Economic Dynamics* 40: 81–91.

Ben Yishay, A., Rotberg, R., Wells, J., Lv, Z., Goodman, S., Kovacevic, L., and Runfola, D., 2017. Geocoding Afrobarometer Rounds 1–6: Methodology & Data Quality. AidData. Retrieved from http://geo.aiddata.org.

Bouoiyour, J., and Miftah, A., 2016. Education, Male Gender Preference and Migrants' Remittances: Interactions in Rural Morocco. *Economic Modelling*, 57: 324–331.

Bredtmann, J., Flores, F. M., and Otten, S., 2019. Remittances and the Brain Drain: Evidence from Microdata for Sub-Saharan Africa. *The Journal of Development Studies* 55(7): 1455–1476.

Buchard, S. M., 2015. *Electoral Violence in Sub-Saharan Africa: Causes and Consequences.* Boulder, CO: Lynne Rienner Publishers.

Catrinescu, N., León-Ledesma, M., Piracha, M., and Quillin, B., 2006. *Remittances, Institutions, and Economic Growth.* IZA Discussion Paper No. 2139. Bonn: IZA.

Chami, R., Barajas, A., Cosimano, T., Fullenkamp, C., Gapen, M., and Montiel, P., 2008. *Macroeconomic Consequences of Remittances.* Washington, DC: International Monetary Fund.

Chami, R., Ernst, E., Fullenkamp, C., and Oeking, A., 2018. Are Remittances Good for Labor Markets in LICs, MICs and Fragile States? Evidence from Cross-Country Data. IMF Working Paper WP/18/102, Washington, DC.

Collier, P., 2000. *Economic Causes of Civil Conflict and Their Implications for Policy.* Washington, DC: World Bank.

Collier, P., and Hoeffler, A., 2004. Greed and Grievance in Civil War. *Oxford Economic Papers* 56(4): 663–595.

Colombo, A., D'Aoust, O., and Sterck, O., 2019. "From rebellion to electoral violence: Evidence from Burundi." *Economic Development and Cultural Change* 67(2): 333–368.

Combes, J-L., Kinda, T., Ouedraogo, R., and Plane, P., 2019. Financial Flows and Economic Growth in Developing Countries. *Economic Modelling* 83: 195–209.

De Haas, H., 2010. Migration and Development: A Theoretical Perspective. *International Migration Review* 44(1): 227–264.

Demirguc-Kunt, A., Cordova, E. L., Peria, M. S. M., and Woodruff, C., 2011. Remittances and Banking Sector Breadth and Depth: Evidence from Mexico. *Journal of Development Economics* 95(2): 229–241.

Deonanan, R., and Williams, K., 2017. The Effect of Remittances on Democratic Institutions. *Applied Economics* 49(5): 403–416.

Docquier, F., and Rapoport, H., 2003. *Remittances and Inequality: A Dynamic Migration Model.* IZA Discussion Paper No. 808. Bonn: Institute for the Study of Labor.

Duffield, M., 2001. *Global Governance and the New Wars: The Merging of Development and Security.* London: Zed Books.

Ebeke, C. H., 2012. Do Remittances Lead to a Public Moral Hazard in Developing Countries? An Empirical Investigation. *The Journal of Development Studies* 48(8): 1009–1025.

Eifert, B., Miguel, E., and Posner, D., 2010. Political Competition and Ethnic Identification in Africa. *American Journal of Political Science* 54(2): 494–510.

Escriba-Folch, A., Meseguer, C., and Wright, J., 2015. Remittances and Democratization. *International Studies Quarterly*, 59(3): 571–586.

Faini, R., 2007. Remittances and the Brain Drain: Do More Skilled Migrants Remit More? *World Bank Economic Review* 21(2): 177–191.

Fischer, J., 2002. Electoral Conflict and Violence: A Strategy for Study and Prevention. IFES White Paper, 1. Retrived from https://www.ifes.org/sites/default/files/econflictpaper.pdf

Freund, C., and Spatafora, N., 2008. Remittances, Transaction Costs and Informality. *Journal of Development Economics* 86(2): 356–366.

Giuliano, P., and Ruiz-Arranz, M., 2009. Remittances, Financial Development, and Growth. *Journal of Development Economics* 90(1): 144–152.

Goodhand, J., 2001. *Violent Conflict, Poverty, and Chronic Poverty.* CPRC Working Paper 6. London: Chronic Poverty Research Centre, ODI.

Humphreys, M., and Weinstein, J. M., 2008. Who Fights? The Determinants of Participation in Civil War. *American Journal of Political Science* 52(2): 436–455.

Isaksson, A., and Kotsadam, A., 2018. Racing to the Bottom? Chinese Development Projects and Trade Union Involvement in Africa. *World Development* 106: 284–298.

Ivlevs, A., and King, R. M., 2017. Does Emigration Reduce Corruption? *Public Choice* 171(3–4): 389–408.

Kaldor, M., 2001. *New and Old Wars: Organised Violence in a Global Era.* Oxford: Polity, and Cambridge: Blackwell.

Kapur, D., 2004. *Remittances: The New Development Mantra?* G-24 Discussion Paper No. 29, Retrieved from https://unctad.org/en/Docs/gdsmdpbg2420045_en.pdf.

Khemani, S., 2015. Buying Votes versus Supplying Public Services: Political Incentives to Under-invest in Pro-poor Policies. *Journal of Development Economics* 117: 84–93.

Konte, M., 2016. The Effects of Remittances on Support for Democracy in Africa: Are Remittances a Curse or a Blessing? *Journal of Comparative Economics* 44(4): 1002–1022.

Lei, Y.-H., and Michaels, G., 2014. Do Giant Oil Field Discoveries Fuel Internal Armed Conflicts? *Journal of Development Economics* 110: 139–157.

Li, X., and Zhou, Y., 2013. An Economic Analysis of Remittance of Unskilled Migration on Skilled–Unskilled Wage Inequality in Labor Host Region. *Economic Modelling,* 33: 428–432.

Maimbo, S. M., and Ratha, D., 2005. *Remittances: Development Impact and Future Prospects.* Washington, DC: World Bank.

Montalvo, J. G., and Reynal-Querol, M., 2005a. Ethnic Polarization, Potential Conflict and Civil War. *The American Economic Review* 95(3): 796–816.

Montalvo, J. G., and Reynal-Querol, M. 2005b. "Ethnic diversity and economic development." *Journal of Development Economics* 76(2): 293–323.

Organization for Economic Cooperation and Development (OECD), 2013. *Fragile States: Resource Flows and Trends,* Conflict and Fragility. Paris: OECD Publishing. https://doi.org/10.1787/9789264190399-en.

Rapoport, H., and Docquier, F., 2006. The Economics of Migrants' Remittances: 1135–1199. In S. C. Kolm and J. M. Ythier (eds.) *Handbook of the Economics of Giving, Altruism and Reciprocity: Volume 2,* North-Holland: Amsterdam.

Ratha, D., 2007. *Leveraging Remittances for Development.* Washington, DC: Migration Policy Institute Policy Brief.

Seddon, D., 2004. South Asian Remittances: Implications for Development. *Contemporary South Asia* 13(4): 405–406.

Shain, Y., 1991. *The Frontiers of Loyalty.* Middletown, CT: Wesleyan University Press.

Ulyses-Balderas, J., and Nath, H. K., 2008. Inflation and Relative Price Variability in Mexico: The Role of Remittances. *Applied Economics Letters* 15(3): 181–185.

UNDP, 2009. *Elections and Conflict Prevention: A Guide to Analysis, Planning and Programming.* New York: UNDP.

United States Geological Survey (USGS), 2014. Mineral Facilities of Africa and the Middle East. National Minerals Information Center.

Vadean, F., Randazzo, T., and Piracha, M., 2019. Remittances, Labour Supply and Activity of Household Members Left-Behind. *The Journal of Development Studies* 55(2): 278–293.

Wallsworth, G., 2015. Electoral Violence: Comparing Theory and Reality. http://econ.msu.edu/seminars/docs/WallsworthElectionViolenceSept2014Draft.pdf.

Willmott, C. J., and Matsuura, K., 2001. Terrestrial Air Temperature and Precipitation: Monthly and Annual Time Series (1950–1999). http://climate.geog.udel.edu/~climate/html_pages/README.ghcn_ts2.html.

World Bank, 2006. Trends, Determinants, and Macroeconomic Effects of Remittances. Chapter 4 *Global Economic Prospects.* Washington, DC.

Yang, D., 2008. International Migration, Remittances and Household Investment: Evidence from Philippine Migrants' Exchange Rate Shocks. *Economic Journal* 118(528): 591–630.

Yol, N., 2017. The Ambiguous Effects of Remittances on Health Expenditure: A Panel Data Analysis. *Economics Bulletin* 37(4): 2561–2573.

Appendices

Table A.1 List of countries

Algeria	Morocco
Benin	Mozambique
Burkina Faso	Namibia
Burundi	Niger
Cameroon	Nigeria
Cote d'Ivoire	Senegal
Gabon	Sierra Leone
Ghana	South Africa
Guinea	Sudan
Kenya	Swaziland
Liberia	Tanzania
Madagascar	Togo
Malawi	Tunisia
Mali	Zambia
Mauritius	Zimbabwe

Table A.2 List of control variables

Sociodemographic variables

Age	Continuous variable (years, in Logarithm)
Education	Dichotomous variable taking the value of 1 if the respondent is not formally educated, and 0 otherwise
Male	Dichotomous variable taking the value of 1 if the respondent is a male, and 0 otherwise
Urban	Dichotomous variable taking the value of 1 if the respondent resides in urban area, and 0 otherwise
Employment	Dichotomous variable taking the value of 1 if the respondent is employed, and 0 otherwise

Political affiliation and election-related variables

Political party member	Dichotomous variable taking the value of 1 if the respondent is affiliated to a political party, and 0 otherwise
Fair election	Dichotomous variable taking the value of 1 if the respondent thinks that the last election was completely free and fair, and 0 otherwise.
Voters' views reflected	Dichotomous variable taking the value of 1 if the respondent thinks that elections ensure that voters' views are reflected, and 0 otherwise
Votes counted fairly	Dichotomous variable taking the value of 1 if the respondent thinks that votes are always counted fairly, and 0 otherwise
Non-participation of opposition parties	Dichotomous variable taking the value of 1 if the respondent thinks that opposition has been prevented from running, and 0 otherwise
Trust electoral commission	Dichotomous variable taking the value of 1 if the respondent trusts the national electoral commission, and 0 otherwise

Media-related variables

Non–social media	Dichotomous variable taking the value of 1 if the respondent gets news from the radio, TV, and newspapers, and 0 otherwise
Social media	Dichotomous variable taking the value of 1 if the respondent gets news from the social media, and 0 otherwise

Socioeconomic variables

Access to food	Dichotomous variable taking the value of 1 if the respondent has never been without food, and 0 otherwise
Access to water	Dichotomous variable taking the value of 1 if the respondent has never been without water, and 0 otherwise
Access to medical care	Dichotomous variable taking the value of 1 if the respondent has never been without medical care, and 0 otherwise
Access to cash income	Dichotomous variable taking the value of 1 if the respondent has never been without cash income, and 0 otherwise

Part IV

Challenges in the management of migration flows

13 Mainstreaming the global compact on migration on irregular migration in Africa

Linda Adhiambo Oucho

Background

In recent years, migration has become a topical subject due to the impact it has on sending, receiving and transit countries. Although the benefits and challenges of migration have been well known, it was not recognized as a key Sustainable Development Goal (SDG) until 2015. This was after a lengthy process through the Global Forum for Migration and Development (GFMD) that made a case for including migration as one of the SDGs due to the positive impact it has on development of a country, but also recognized the need to protect the rights of migrants. In 2015, during the United Nations General Assembly, the 2030 Agenda for Sustainable Development Goals recognized the important contribution migration has to sustainable development as a crosscutting issue in 11 out of 17 goals. In addition, the New York Declaration for Refugees and Migrants committed to addressing irregular border crossings through state engagements with commitment 27 aiming to *address*

> unsafe movement of refugees and migrants with particular reference to irregular movement of refugees and migrants. We will do so without prejudice to the right to seek asylum. We will combat the exploitation, abuse and discrimination suffered by many refugees and migrants.
> (United Nations General Assembly, 2016, p. 5/24)

Alongside protecting the rights of migrants, SDGs aimed to create safer pathways of regular migration, a process that has contributed to the development of the Global Compact for Safe, Orderly and Regular Migration (GCM) which was agreed upon in December 2018 during the GFMD process.

Flahaux and De Haas (2016: 2) argued that 'African migration is "exceptional" and essentially different from migration elsewhere', highlighting mixed migratory patterns occurring across the continent. Irregular migration has become one of the key discussion points among countries experiencing irregular flows to and through their countries as receiving and transit countries in Africa. More and more people are seeking irregular routes to access countries that have better opportunities than their own no matter how high the risk as irregular patterns have been identified among asylum seekers and refugees seeking alternative locations to settle, migrants who are trafficked and smuggled to different destinations. Although Flahaux and De Haas (2016) argued that migration aspirations depend on an individual's life aspirations, they are also influenced by social, cultural, economic, and political factors. Those that migrate greater distances may have the resources to facilitate their migration which includes selling their assets such as land, while individuals who come from a poor household are less likely to migrate greater distances and are more likely to migrate within their country.

Reports of Eritreans and Somali migrants travelling through the Northern corridor bound for Europe via Libya as well as the Eastern migration corridor bound for the Middle East countries via war-torn Yemen. Figure 13.1 illustrates the estimated stock of irregular migrants in selected countries in Africa between 1996 and 2008.

A recent study by the United Nations Development Programme (2019: 21), focused on a sample of 3,098 respondents from Africa, described the profile of the respondents stating that the average age of departure for most irregular migrants was 24 years, majority were single (71%), with no children (60%), and majority were male (77%). This is not surprising as the youth have increasingly dominated migratory flows which may represent the lack of opportunities, especially employment, in their country of origin.

There have been different interpretations of how and why irregular migration continues to persist. Karagueuzian and Verdier-Chouchane (2014) argue that irregular migration occurs when the socio-economic conditions in countries of origin are not conducive for its citizens. People are driven out due to human rights abuses, limited access to basic service as well as violation of labour rights in their country. They are attracted to destinations that offer these values and those unable to meet the legal requirements to migrate regularly choose irregular pathways knowing the risks of such movements but bearing in mind the benefits of migrating to their chosen destinations. While Ogu (2017) argues that irregular migration continues to be motivated by economic, political, and socio-cultural conditions in the source country, the present irregular migration patterns are a re-enactment of the transatlantic slave trade, what he terms as the *backward syndrome*. That is the perception that taking perilous routes to a destination that will offer them the solutions that they presently do not have access to in their place of origin. A common factor most authors agree on is that people are motivated to migrate due to conditions in their country of origin. The reality in many African countries is the lack of employment opportunities in their countries of origin which drives youth to seek opportunities elsewhere, sometimes seeking irregular paths to destinations on the continent such as South Africa and off the continent such as European countries. The thin line between migrant smuggling and human trafficking is evident with the experiences of migrants bound for Europe who were kidnapped along the migration corridors via North Africa and ransomed by the smugglers along the Sinai corridor where families left behind and those in destination countries are expected to pay exorbitant fees for the release of their loved ones (SAHAN & Inter-Governmental Authority

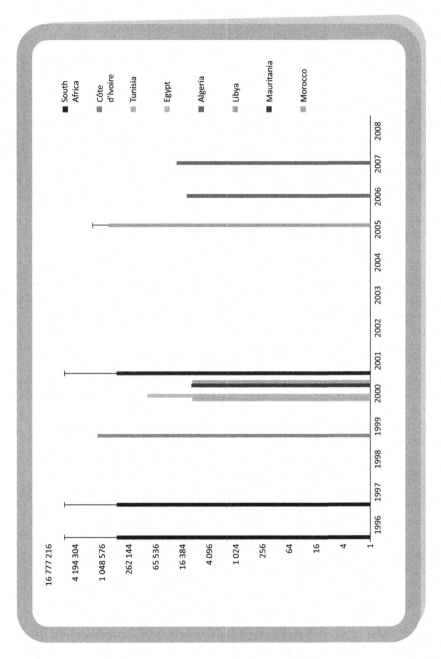

Figure 13.1 Estimated irregular migrant stock in selected countries, 1996–2008.
Source: Karagueuzian & Verdier-Chouchane (2014: 11).

for Development, 2016). The recent Arab Spring[1] from 2010 also heightened insecurity along the borders in North Africa putting many smuggled migrants at risk of being trafficked or enslaved.

Recent international media reports on irregular migration showcase stories on migration patterns from Western African countries such as Niger where cases of enslavement have been identified in Libya, a country torn by political instability, increasing the risks of human rights violation. The media representation also creates the impression that a large population of African migrants using irregular routes are leaving the continent influencing public opinions about migration. Yet recent research has found that there are more intra-African migratory movements which were 12.5 million in 2000 and increased to 19.4 million in 2017, with the largest stock of migrants found in Western and Eastern Africa. Top destinations within the continent include South Africa, Cote d'Ivoire, Uganda, Nigeria, Ethiopia, and Kenya respectively (United Nations Conference on Trade and Development, 2018). According to the African Development Bank (2019: 14), East African countries[2] face severe inequalities as out of 48% of income earners, 20% is for the richest of income earners in the region and only 6% goes to the poorest population in the region. This inequality exists despite the number of programmes in place to address poverty in the different countries. Poverty is a major driver of migration as people are constantly seeking income-generating opportunities to rise out of poverty. Employment also is a challenge in Eastern Africa and other parts of the continent as although between 2000 and 2009 African economies have experienced growth, it has not resulted in sufficient decent jobs to absorb the growing population of youth and it is highly dependent on selected commodity exports (African Development Bank, 2019) which is not sustainable. The risks of people migrating irregularly increases where opportunities are lacking within their place of origin. Eastern African countries are taking significant steps through their national development or transformational programmes to address some of the structural challenges that exist within their countries which may reduce the need for people to consider irregular pathways of migration to access employment or income-generating opportunities.

Nevertheless, irregular migration has led to serious complications for the migrants and governance structures of countries that are receiving or transit countries within the continent and beyond. Furthermore, it has led to questions as to what continues to be some of the driving factors that has led to the increased irregular flows across the continent. The challenge set by the member states that signed the non-binding GCM agreement in December 2018 is how to reduce the risks faced by migrants and create more regular pathways for migration that do not violate the laws and regulations of member states that receive them.

The premise of this chapter is to unpack the reality of implementing the GCM within Africa, a continent with diverse migration governance systems, mixed migration patterns, and differing perspectives on migration. The chapter takes stock on some of the efforts being led by the African Union to reduce irregular migration through the development of the Free Movement

Protocol and the Africa Free Continental Trade Areas, which allow migrants to consider the option of temporary or permanent migration depending on their needs. Furthermore, it will take stock of regional efforts led by or in partnership with the Regional Economic Communities (RECs), looking to best practices and lessons learned. In addition, examples will be drawn from member states that are implementing policies and laws that are akin to creating an enabling environment where safe, orderly, and regular migration can take place aligned to SDG 10 on reducing inequalities, specifically Target 10.7 of facilitating orderly, safe, regular migration.

Irregular migration systems

There are different types of irregular migrants, including overstayers, migrants taking advantage of the asylum system, irregular workers, migrants illegally crossing the borders using fraudulent documents and other means, migrants violating the rules of sojourn of non-nationals, trafficked victims, and smuggled migrants. Irregular migration systems outline ways and means in which people become irregular within a destination country. It is usually associated with a person accessing a country without the proper documentation, thereby going against the law of accessing the country illegally. Or it can be a case where people access legally through a temporary process, that is, a visitor's visa, and overstaying and becoming irregular or undocumented (Cvajner & Sciortino, 2010b).

According to Cvajner & Sciortino (2010a), the differentiation theory argued that the

> structural origins of irregular migration systems rotted in the mismatch between the international systems of states and the complex set of factors governing human spatial mobility; and the micro analysis of irregular migrants. Accordingly, the development of irregular migration is rooted in the structural mismatch between the social and political conditions for migration.

Kanko and Teller (2014) argued that for irregular migration to take place 'there must be a mismatch between the demand for entry, embedded in the international labour market, and the supply of entry slots, determined by the political systems' (2014, NP).

In Africa, sending or source countries of irregular migrants are experiencing difficult political, social, economic, and environmental conditions that offer little opportunities for their existing growing young population that are pushed to migrate to access those same opportunities in other destinations. They are influenced by existing information available on social media that provides a false perception of quick financial returns in destination countries, without understanding the legal requirements a migrant must have in destination countries for them to be economically active. Further, there is false illustration that the money earned is not subject to taxation or that the cost

254 Linda Adhiambo Oucho

of living in those destination countries is far more affordable than in their countries of origin. Hence, the risk of failure by a migrant is not considered.

Thus, migrants who fail to achieve their goal in the destination country, are unaware of the laws related to legal migration, are victims of a crime such as trafficking as well as choose to become undocumented because they do not meet the migration criteria required by certain groups put many at risk and become irregular in a country. The conditions in the home country, mostly linked to economic, political especially in African countries, push people into migrating in other destinations with limited or lack of information on the legal processes of migrating in a safe, orderly, and regular fashion, but in response to a culture of migration that has been created over decades of trade and circular migration. Former trade routes have become migration corridors used by smugglers to facilitate the migration of persons to different destinations. Existing political systems today in relation to migration have developed a sovereign stand where the nation states are protecting the needs of their people above those of migrants as such; the supply of people migrating to those destinations is exceeding the demand (Koser, 2005). The perception that irregular migrants threaten the sovereignty and security of states is a misconception as the idea that migrants will flood countries of destination is wrong as the numbers that migrate is not as big as it is reported in comparison to the location population. However, media images create an aspect of fear of invasion and global discussions on migration such as that by the United States fuel the idea of invasion which supersedes facts and evidence.

The development of legal mechanisms to limit flows of certain individuals has been a result of responding to the irregular patterns of migration as different countries adopt different approaches to responding to irregular migration. These strategies include (International Organisation for Migration, 2016):

- Regularization/amnesties
- Opening legal channels
- Voluntary returns (e.g. assisted voluntary return and repatriation of IOM)
- Readmission
- Information campaigns
- Border controls
- Expulsion/deportations

The question is how effective these strategies have been in reducing/curbing irregular flows and whether these strategies are merely diverting irregular migration into a more precarious position to deal with nationally, regionally, and globally.

Reality of irregular migration patterns in East Africa

Within East and the Horn of Africa, there are mixed migration trends with many states in the region registering as origin, transit, and destination routes of irregular migrants as illustrated in Table 13.1:

Table 13.1 Drivers of source, transit and destination countries of irregular migration

Countries	Origin	Transit	Destination	Push factors
Djibouti		X		Economic factors
Eritrea	X			Obligatory national service Political Oppression Economic Factors
Ethiopia	X	X	X	Socio-economic factors Ethnic tensions Environmental factors
Kenya	X	X	X	Economic factors
Somalia	X	X	X	Conflict and chronic insecurity Economic factors Environmental factors
South Sudan	X	X	X	Conflict Economic Factors Lack of infrastructural and social services Food insecurity
Sudan	X	X	X	Conflict Economic factors
Uganda	X			Demographic factors Economic factors Environmental factors

Source: (Marchand et al., 2017).

The conditions in many of the source countries are similar as drivers include economic, political, social, and environmental factors that may be linked with the lack of political will to address these challenges in some of these countries. In countries such as Somalia, the existence of insecurity caused by al Shabab activities pushes many to consider migration for security purposes. Source countries include, Kenya, Eritrea, Somalia, South Sudan, Uganda, Ethiopia, and Sudan. Djibouti is the only country that is a transit country because of its convenient location between Africa and the Middle East. Primarily, Ethiopians and, to a small extent, Somalians in Somaliland use this route to migrate irregularly to the Gulf States. From East and the Horn of Africa, there are four primary irregular migration corridors:

- **Northern Route (Central Mediterranean Route):** Migrants from the East and Horn of Africa pass through Sudan to North African countries such as Egypt and other countries where border management is weak, such as Libya to access Italy via the Mediterranean. The rising numbers of migrants bound for North Africa have increased the demand for more smugglers, thereby creating new employment opportunities along the migration corridors.
- **Sinai Route (via Egypt into Israel):** Migrants destined for Israel via this route often fell victim to human trafficking or organ smuggling rings along the route. Over the years the number of migrants using this route has lowered due to the restrictive migration policies being implemented

in the Sinai–Israeli border. Often, migrants bound for this route were primarily from Somalia and Eritrea

- **Eastern Route:** This route was for migrants bound for the Gulf States via Yemen and popularly used by Somali and Ethiopian migrants. The exist ports included Obock in Djibouti and Bossaso in Somalia, with migrants often bound for Saudi Arabia. Saudi Arabia's response to the increasing number of irregular migrants was to develop a policy that required migrants to regularize or face deportation. The mass deportation of irregular migrants has meant countries such as Ethiopia have to explore a policy that reintegrates the returnees back into the country while at the same time explore strategies for reducing the irregular pathways adopted by their nationals

- **Southern Route:** Popularly used by Ethiopian and Somali migrants migrating through transit countries (Kenya, Tanzania, Malawi, Zambia, Zimbabwe, and Mozambique) both on land and via sea depending on the amount paid to a smuggler. Although there are reports on this southern route, it tends to be underreported and under-focused because the irregular pathways are moving away from Gulf States and Europe. Countries with weak migration border management systems such as Malawi, Zimbabwe, and Mozambique have eased transfers for many migrants bound for South Africa (Marchand et al., 2017).

Akinboade (2014) observed that there are various reasons why irregular migration continues to persist in the East African Community (EAC) despite efforts by non-governmental organizations and nationals government to eliminate it. These reasons include difficult living conditions, high unemployment rates, conflicts and wars due to political instability, lack of reliable data on irregular migration flows to control it, trafficking and smuggling networks that appear to be organized between officials, and inadequate policies to harmonize all the countries and address the issue. What's more, Masabo (2015) noted that women are particularly vulnerable to irregular migration. He claimed that due to gender norms and male-biased admission policies women face more challenges connected to irregular migration than men.

It is difficult to document details and information concerning irregular migration because of its clandestine nature. All too often, countries estimate the number of irregular migrants with evidence of those who have been arrested and detained with reports on the flows and the migration corridors used by irregular migrants. With limited data, governments are unable to develop laws and regulations that manage this type of migration.

Within East Africa, the Mixed Migration Centre (MMC, formerly Regional Mixed Migration Secretariat) has attempted to not only document flows of migration including irregular pathways but also identify hot spots where corruptive practices and high risks in security have been identified. Through the Mixed Migration Monitoring Mechanism Initiative known as 4Mi, they conducted a smuggler survey by the MMC in East Africa and

Yemen region, reporting on data from June 2017 to September 2018, from Egypt, Kenya, Somaliland and, South Africa. They identified 219 smugglers of which 215 were male and 14 female with an average age of the smugglers was 36.23%. The smugglers interviewed stated that this was their primary source of funding with an average profit of $2,900 per month. While 62% of the other smugglers identified themselves as business owners, 11% identified themselves as within the service industry and 8% as civil servants and other occupations. The roles of smugglers varied from providing accommodation, transporting migrants across border points to liaising with authorities to guarantee safe passage. Given that the relationship between smuggler and migrant is a business transition, one smuggler saw it as an opportunity for both as one will gain some source of income and the other gains access to the destination country (Mixed Migration Centre, 2018).

The MMC platform, though does not reflect all the conditions on the ground, provides a snapshot of how different types of migration patterns take place, gives a sense of whether policy is working as well as identifies gaps in the system for countries to respond to, in terms of drivers of migration and also protection of migrants especially those who fall victim to human trafficking. Responses to human trafficking and migrant smuggling have been outlined through policies and frameworks guided by international and regional conventions that allow member states to shape their responses based on their context.

Policies, frameworks, and conventions on irregular migration

The establishment of the OAU was significant for Africa as the beginning of the conversation related to regional and continental integration for the economic benefit of the continent. In 1975, the Economic Community of West African States (ECOWAS) was one of the first RECs that developed a regional policy that allowed for Free Movement of Persons in 1979. In Southern Africa, elements of apartheid remained strong until the 1990s which had a significant impact on mobility of persons, but after apartheid, migrants were attracted to South Africa due to the opportunities it provided, leading to increased flows to the country, both regular and irregular. In Eastern Africa, countries that have experienced relative stability since independence have been Kenya and Tanzania, with neighbouring states experiencing political shifts that forcibly displaced large populations of people hosted in neighbouring countries.

The current state of migration through the media lens create a perspective of a continent on the move due to instability, bad economic conditions, conflict among others, that has led a significant population of African nationals to move in search of better opportunities. Indeed, people are moving with push factors related to the conditions within a country linked to economic, social, political, and environmental. Reports of increasing migrant deaths along the Mediterranean seas, and the under-reported deaths of those transiting the Saharan desert from East and West Africa via North Africa, have become the story of irregular migration in Africa. The reality is some of these migrants are using common migration corridors that may allow them to move from one region to another, governed by the agreements set by the REC; however, the way in which they access the countries is classified as illegal as they have not undergone the formal documentation process that allows them to be present in a country, and thus classified as illegal or irregular. The existing literature looks at irregular migration for those bound for European destination, and when looking at irregular migration within the continent itself, the literature is not as dominant.

Within Eastern Africa, there are certain countries that have developed policy responses to irregular migration (Table 13.2).

These national policies are influenced by the regional/continental frameworks and conventions related to migration that may have informed the design of these policies in order for them to be inclusive of all aspects of migrating and develop a formal strategy of addressing irregular migration.

At the African Union level, the following treaties and conventions capture aspects of all forms of migration, including irregular migration. These frameworks, policies, and conventions aimed to ensure the right tools are in place to create a conducive environment for member states' citizens to live and work in a safe and stable environment and reduce the need to out-migrate out of necessity.

- 1991 Treaty Establishing the African Economic Community (Abuja Treaty)
- Migration Policy Framework of Africa (2018)
- African Common Position on Migration and Development
- 1969 Convention Governing specific Aspects of Refugee Problems in Africa
- 2004 AU Plan of Action on Employment Promotion and Poverty Alleviation
- 2009 AU Convention for the Protection and Assistance of Internally Displaced Persons in Africa (Kampala Convention)
- 2009 Minimum Integration Programme
- 2009 AUC Initiative Against Trafficking (AU–COMMIT)
- 2009 AU Minimum Integration Programme
- 2012 AU Plan of action on Boosting Intra-African Trade
- 2017 AU African Continental Free Trade Area
- Joint Labour Migration programme
- AU Border Programme
- 2018 AU Free Movement Protocol

The **1991 Treaty Establishing the African Economic Community (Abuja Treaty)** led to the existence of RECs where they promoted free

Table 13.2 Policies and laws in selected countries on irregular migration

Country	Policy/law
Kenya	Citizenship and Immigration Act 2011
	Kenya Citizens and Foreign Nationals Management Service Act
	The Refugee Act 2006 and associated; Refugee (Reception, Registration and Adjudication) Regulation 2009
	Security Laws (Amendment) Act 2014
	Counter-trafficking in Persons Act 2010
	National Plan of Action to Counter Human Trafficking (2013–2017)
	Constitution
	The Prevention, Protection and Assistance to Internally Displaced Persons and Affected Communities (IDP Act)
	The Penal Code
	The Sexual Offences Act 2006
	The Children's Act 2001
South Sudan	Refugee Act 2012
	Passports and Immigration Act
	Action plan to Eliminate the Recruitment and Use of Child Soldiers 2016
	National Action Plan against Trafficking
	Directorate for Child Protection
	South Sudan's Penal Code Act 2008
	South Sudan's Child Act 2008
Uganda[1]	Prevention of Trafficking in Persons Act 2009
	Aliens (Registration and Control Act) 1985
	The Uganda Citizenship and Immigration Control Act 2000-
	Refugee Act 2006
	The Employment Act 2006
	Constitution of the Republic of Uganda 1995
	Registration of Persons Act 2015
Rwanda[2]	National Migration Policy and Strategies
	Constitution of the Republic of Rwanda
	Organic Law No.30/2008 Relating to Rwandan Nationality
	Law No. 13/2009 Regulating Labour in Rwanda
	Law No.04/2011 on Immigration and Emigration in Rwanda
	Law No.13/2014 Relating to Refugees
Tanzania	Constitution of Tanzania 1977
	Tanzania Immigration Act 1995; Immigration Amendment Act 2015
	Tanzania Citizenship Act 1995
	Refugees Act 1998
	Anti-trafficking in Persons Act 2008
	Non-Citizens (Employment Regulation) Act 2015

Marchand et al. (2017)[1] Maastricht Graduate School of Governance (2017);[2] (African Centre for Migration and Society & Samuel Hall, 2018).

movement pf people under Article 43 of the treaty. In response to this, the AU developed a framework that would assist RECs with design and implementation of the strategy through the Migration Policy Framework of Africa (MPFA)

The **Migration Policy Framework of Africa** (MPFA) came into existence in 2006 when member states developed it as a guiding document to assist on RECs and member states to understand their migration flows. It was recently revised in 2018 as very few countries had mainstreamed the framework at REC and national levels (AU, 2017). The comprehensive framework outlines objectives and strategies on how to address the different migration flows with regard to economic, social, and environmental issues among others and includes a strategy on how to address irregular migration. It also outlined a ten-year action plan that guides the AU approach to supporting member states to identify their migration issues, develop policies of strategies to addressing the problem, and identify ways that the member states can implement the strategies or policies that they design. So far, only the Intergovernmental Authority on Development (IGAD) is the only REC to have developed a regional migration policy framework and is in the process of implementing it. Within the framework they have outlined strategies for addressing human trafficking and migrant smuggling and administering the return, re-admission, and reintegration with guidance from international and regional instruments. ECOWAS and Community of Sahel-Saharan States (CEN-SAD), however, have implemented the free movement protocol facilitating migration between member states without a regional migration policy framework.

The **African Common Position on Migration and Development** adopted in 2006 developed 11 priorities for migration policies and recommendations for stakeholders operating at a national, regional, and international level. The rest of the legal frameworks outlined above were providing guidance to member states on the formal agreement of managing mixed migrant groups as well as conditions within their country to reduce the risks of migrating out of necessity.

In Eastern Africa, the following legal instruments, plans, projects, and discussions have been adopted and taken place to address irregular migration, previous and current (Marchand et al., 2017: 94–95):

- Inter-Governmental Authority for Development
  - IGAD Regional Migration Policy Framework 2012
    - IGAD Migration Action Plan
    - IGAD Regional Consultative Process (IGAD-RCP) 2008

- East African. Community
  - Treaty for the Establishment of the East African Community 1999
    - Protocol on the Establishment of the EAC Common Market
    - East African Labour Migration Policy Framework (draft)

- Regional Committee on Mixed Migration for Horn of Africa, Yemen[3]
- Joint Border Administration between Kenya, Djibouti, Sudan, South Sudan and Somalia
- Joint Border Operations with South Sudan, Uganda and negotiations with Ethiopia
- East African Police Chiefs Cooperation Organisation (EAPCO)[4]

- UNODC Indian Ocean Forum on Maritime Crime[5]
- UNODC Strengthening Criminal Justice responses to Trafficking in Persons and Smuggling of Migrants in Ethiopia and Djibouti
- Strategy and regional Plan of Action on Smuggling and Trafficking from the East and Horn of Africa (2012)
- Global Initiative on Protection at Sea led by UNHCR – two-year project
- Horn of Africa Initiative on Human Trafficking and Smuggling of Migrants for the AU (2014)
- First Regional Anti-Human Trafficking Conference in Eastern Africa 2007
- Live, Learn and Play Safe Regional Initiative (2015–2016)
- Tripartite Agreement between Kenya, Ethiopia and Tanzania on Irregular Migration

Although the IGAD has a number of migration-related frameworks in place, the biggest challenge it faces is implementing the free movement of persons which is active in ECOWAS dating as far back as 1979 through the Free Movement Protocol. The limitations affecting free movement in EAC and IGAD are the conflicting policies on migration which the GCM may not be in a position to resolve. Once these overlapping and conflicting policies are addressed and an overall regional free movement strategy is adopted, the guiding principles provided in GCM can be used to strengthen the approach.

Most of these activities predate the Global Compact process, illustrating interest and political will to address irregular migration in the region. It becomes a question of how the compact fits into the already existing agenda or activities at national, regional, and continental levels. The Global Compact was a result of a long-term discussion of migration between global states and since it was included as one of the SDGs, it can become the focus of many countries on ways to address especially the negative impacts of migration, one of which include irregular migration as well as strengthening existing policies and practices related to migration governance.

Strategies to addressing irregular migration

The dynamism of irregular migration makes it difficult to develop a one-stop solution to curb, reduce, or eradicate it. The idea that a policy or framework that can be used to guide national and/or regional processes to prevent irregular migration from occurring is quite a daunting task especially in many African countries. Developed countries have tried to create legal pathways for migration through the guest worker programmes (Bracero Programme between the United States and Mexico; Germany's guest worker programme) that targeted specific migrants working within a specific sector. However, the unintended result of the programme was chain migration where migrants facilitated the migration of their household members.

The current tier programme adopted in countries such as Canada, Australia, and the UK is being used as a process of identifying skilled migrants that would contribute to the development of the economy. The GCM has advocated for the need to create more legal pathways to migration; however, it must also create a solution or strategy to some of the direct and indirect impacts of these legal pathways to migration from source, transit to destination countries. This, however, continues to limit low-skilled workers with intentions to migrate as they may not meet the selection criteria outlined in the tier programmes. The realities of also creating such a programme in many African countries may not be achievable if the resources, capacity, and policies/laws are not in place or operational.

A recent United Nations Development Programme report (2019) argued that for irregular migration to be reduced or curbed, there needs to be a 'transformative development' within Africa creating opportunities within the continent. This includes making economies inclusive by engaging the youth who are instrumental in shaping the future economies of Africa today. Further, countries should tackle constraints to structural transformation, that is, engaging with regional and international actors as partners in trade and development. Hence, the idea of the African Continental Free Trade Area Agreement (2018) would be a useful tool to strengthen relationships between member states in a region and continent on a mutual understanding of trade among others. They also advocate for the need to develop more legal pathways to migration to reduce irregular pathways. Looking at the services provided by low-skilled and unskilled labour and how they develop the economies of destination and sending countries could be key to reducing the need to explore irregular pathways to migrate, but this depends on how information is shared in the source countries of migrants. For existing irregular migrants, destination countries would need to regularize undocumented migrants. Oucho and Odipo (2017) proposed that there should be inter-state and interregional cooperation to manage all forms of migration. Discussing within the context of regional integration in EAC, the recommendations have implications for irregular migration as if countries adopt clear objectives, exchange best practices, and work towards a coordinated programme on migration while including the contributions of civil society actors, member states may be in a better position to address irregular migration regionally. In addition, by strengthening border management in terms of technology and infrastructure, capacities of border officials, among others, to identify cases of irregular migration should be an ongoing process that each African state has to develop in order to address cases of irregular migration at the borders. This requires collaboration and shared responsibilities between countries sharing borders.

The strategies outlined in GCM can assist African states that are signatories to understand their migrant population, which is highly dependent on data which identifies trends, while at the same time informing the formulation of policies and strategies that are subject to regular changes through time. At a continental level, the African Union Commission advocates for the creation of regional migration policy frameworks that is guided by the recently updated Migration Policy Framework for Africa (MPFA) to help member states understand their different migration flows, including irregular migration. This process requires also that Regional Economic Commissions develop a regional response to migration which will help member states of REC to find a collective response to addressing irregular migration within their region. Limitations to this process have been related to roles, responsibilities, and resources available for member states as if member states are using different border management equipment or are not equally sharing the responsibility of manning porous borders, irregular migration is likely to continue. Good relations between member states is also key as there is sharing of responsibilities in managing irregular migration flows that are encountered at their borders which requires regular social dialogue that can establish effective and efficient bilateral agreements that can be used as migration governance tools to facilitate safe, regular, and orderly labour migration between countries (United Nations, 2017).

Hence, although developing legal pathways to migration may be a solution for countries in the global north, within Africa, some countries need to understand their mixed migration patterns through data and research; identify gaps in policy, resources, and capacities; and develop solutions to address those gaps, including developing a budgeting system for migration governance, thereby building a foundation where the idea of free movement of persons, goods, and services as well as creating a conducive environment for trade is possible. The strategies to addressing irregular migration should be reviewed over time through established monitoring and evaluations practices adopted by government ministries and departments to be able to respond to the dynamism that defines irregular migration.

Mainstreaming the GCM into national and regional approaches

GCM is a result of a six-year engagement across the globe to identify the challenges experienced at a national, regional, continental, and global level when it comes to migration through the GFMD process. The final nonbinding document, which reaffirms the New York Declaration for Refugees and Migrants, outlined objectives and strategies for creating an environment where migration can be safe, orderly, and regular guided by the principles that ensure a people-centred approach, with international cooperation, while ensuring national sovereignty, rule of law, and due process. At the same time, ensure that sustainable development takes place while respecting the human rights of all migrants regardless of migrant status, being gender responsible and child sensitive at all times. Furthermore, member states would adopt a whole of government and whole of society approach allowing engagement from the top and bottom on migration issues.

Out of the 23 objectives outlined in the compact, only eight have discussed irregular migration (Figure 13.2).

•Objective 2 (18): Minimize the adverse drivers and structural factors that compel people to leave their country of origin	•Objective 3 (19e): Provide accurate and timely information at all stages of migration	•Objective 7 (23h & i): Address and reduce vulnerabilities in migration
•Objective 9 (25c & f): Strengthen the transnational response to smuggling of migrants	•Objective 10 (26c): Prevent, combat and eradicate trafficking in persons in the context of international migration	•Object 11 (27f): •Manage borders in an integrated, secure and coordinated manner
	•Objective 15 (31b): Provide access to basic services for migrants	•Objective 23 (39b): Strengthen international cooperation and global partnerships for safe, orderly and regular migration.

Figure 13.2 8 Objectives of the GCM related to Irregular Migration.
Source: United Nations General Assembly (2018)

Mainstreaming GCM on irregular migration into practice has to take into account the regional and national aspects. At a regional level, the existing tools, frameworks, and conventions provided by the Africa Union and contextualized by the RECs would need to assess what is missing in their existing framework to address irregular migration. In this case in East Africa, some member states are members of three RECs: IGAD, COMESA, and EAC. As mentioned, IGAD already has a migration policy framework in place, which already highlights strategies for addressing the primary forms of irregular migration that takes place in and around member states. As illustrated in Figure 13.2 above, there are some strategies in place that match what has been outlined in the GCM. However, this is a regional approach to addressing transnational responses to irregular migration. When narrowed down to member states, some, not all, countries have existing legal instruments used to address cases of irregular migration, i.e. counter trafficking laws, immigration, and citizenship laws, in which different forms of irregular migration are embedded. A review of the existing laws at the national level to determine how they address irregular migration, and how case law can identify gaps in the policy in practice, needs to be undertaken to ensure that when a case is brought forward, an existing law that has not effectively mainstreamed migration may be used to build a case.

Data and knowledge generation is key as it identifies changes in trend. The data and information give a perspective of the scale of the flow, the drivers, and the impact in source, transit, and destination countries. This also provides information for awareness raising from grassroots level (a bottom-up approach), as well as formulating policies that address irregular migration at source, transit, and destination countries and agreements of strengthening transnational responses to smuggling of migrants and human trafficking, among others, that affect the region. Interestingly, the IGAD Regional Migration Policy Framework (RMPF) states on migrant smuggling that smuggled migrants will be treated as 'victims of a crime rather than criminals' (Inter-Governmental Authority on Development, 2012: 32), which differs from GCM. Given the complexity of irregular migration and the thin line between migrant smuggling and human trafficking, defining migrant smuggling as a crime is dependent on the evidence and the process of legal procedures, which also depend on the country dealing with human trafficking/migrant smuggling cases. Within IGAD, they have outlined a commitment to not only strengthen the dialogue on irregular migration among member states but also 'reinforce and encourage joint cross border patrols between IGAD member states and between the latter and Member State of neighbouring REC levels' (Inter-Governmental Authority on Development, 2012: 32). This approach is also adopted as a strategy for human trafficking and aligns with objective 11 of the GCM.

There is already evidence that some steps have been taken within Eastern Africa that are mainstreaming into practices some elements of the GCM. Innovative technology is currently being used to map out migration corridors to North Africa, Middle East, and, to a certain extent, Southern Africa through the 4Mi platform. The MMC 4Mi platform collects data along migration corridors of migrants from the Horn of Africa bound for different destinations; however, the data are not comprehensive. Data on irregular migration can assist key stakeholders to understand how irregular migration is changing with the external and internal factors affecting migrants with different demographic profiles. Member states in Eastern Africa, especially those that may be source/transit countries, may not have documented the irregular migration corridors, and there may be a need to adopt, develop, or strengthen research methods that allow countries to capture data or conducting research on irregular migration from the source. In this day and age of technology, irregular migration is slowly becoming a digitized process where information sharing is easier and faster, while at the same time it can be used to connect with families left behind creating information stream. Zijlstra and Liempt (2017) argued that smugglers are using social media platforms to advertise their services while at the same time providing information to potential migrants soliciting services from smugglers. Access to reliable information can change the relationship dynamics of the smuggler and the migrant, as it provides the migrant with more agency which some still are solely dependent on the information provided by the smuggler.

The use of technology, thus, would have an adverse impact on how to address the structural factors as if not all structural factors are known, as they are evolving with technological changes. This also requires that source countries address those factors that drive people to migrate and consider irregular pathways. Political will and an interest in understanding mixed migration flows at a national and decentralized level are key. The need to have accurate and timely information depends on the resources available at source, transit, and destination countries. At present, the existing data is usually generated in developed countries who are able to identify undocumented migrants with the deportation data they collect. However, it is unclear whether the countries receiving the deportees is recorded once they return. The interest on data has been on transit and destination countries only.

In April 2019, the governments of Kenya, Ethiopia, and Tanzania signed a tripartite agreement to address irregular migration through their countries. Studies have identified Ethiopia as a main source country with nationals migrating through Kenya, Tanzania, Malawi, and Mozambique to access South Africa. The discussions led to agreements in line with GCM, which include:

- Harmonization of anti-trafficking and smuggling laws between the three countries.
- Sensitization of irregular migration among the diaspora, countries of origin, and the risks involved.
- Ensure the human rights of migrants are upheld.
- Providing access to irregular migrants in prison (International Organisation for Migration, 2019).

Implementation remains a challenge in many countries, especially in response to irregular flows, which are riddled with lack or limited resources and capacity to implement some of the strategies. Further clarity as to whether the resources are lacking or need to be strengthened needs to be assessed as part of capacity building but also it is a question of whether migration in general is key to the political agenda. That is, addressing the negative impacts of migration through active practices and engagement with Member States while exploring opportunities of creating regular pathways for migration for the benefit of development. For countries to reduce irregular migration from, through, and to their countries, the challenges need to be stemmed from the sources which requires certain practices to take place to make countries conducive to live in and less likely to consider outmigration as a necessity.

Looking ahead, the African Union is advocating for free movement through the *Protocol to the Treaty Establishing the African Economic Community Relating to the Free Movement of Persons, Right of Residence and Right of Establishment* (African Union, 2018) and *Agreement Establishing the Continental Free Trade Area* (African Union, 2019). Questions have been raised as to whether by opening the borders for regular migration and trade to occur it will reduce some forms of irregular migration, i.e. migrant smuggling and undocumented migrants, but increase other forms such as human trafficking across borders (African Centre for Migration and Society & Samuel Hall, 2018).

Questions on protecting the sovereignty of their states have been raised alongside some security risks associated with criminal activities. Part of the AU agenda is to undertake consultative processes to ensure that member states understand how the protocol works and how it can be implemented at regional and national levels, including addressing the key concerns regarding security. At the national level, countries that have a thorough understanding of mixed migrating flows in their country will be in a better position to create policies or strategies that govern migration within, to, and from the country; however, there is a need to decentralize the process in order for district or county governments to be able to understand how to implement the policy at a decentralized level as recipients of migrants.

Conclusion

Irregular migration is a complicated issue that many countries face that changes in response to the mechanisms put in place by countries and regions. There is no single solution that can stop or curb irregular migration, but there are systems and strategies that can be developed in partnership with member states to curb or reduce irregular migration at the country of origin and protect the rights of migrants at risk of human trafficking along the migration corridor. To reduce the need to migrate, member states would need to take an active approach to addressing structural issues within their country and adopt a transformative agenda that is inclusive and responsive to the growing young population that we see across Africa today. A key element that countries in Eastern Africa should focus on is reducing inequalities within the countries. To address these inequalities, countries would need to review and mainstream migration into the national development plans/agendas and develop initiatives that are aimed at reducing inequalities.

To be able to effectively address the issue of irregular migration, Eastern African governmental laws and policies at the national level need to be strengthened to ensure that countries are able to persecute the right perpetrators. The existing legal instruments in place in East Africa and some of the dialogue as well as practices taking place in the region illustrate a political will to address irregular migration in the region. Although many of the local instruments pre-date GCM, they already include within them some aspects that take care of irregular migration in the region. GCM provides global strategies to address different forms of migration across the globe, including irregular migration, and signatories are not bound to the agreement but simply can use it to guide some of the processes and procedures that they may already have in place but need to be strengthened using the tool. Not all strategies provided may apply as different regions and countries experience different forms of migration and may not have the resources and/or capacity to handle such flows. GCM, therefore, can help to strengthen existing policies in place related to irregular migration and help countries to align some of their approaches and strategies with SDGs.

One of the major challenges countries experience is beyond the formulation of policy or strategies, but the implementation process which depends on resources (human and financial) as well as capacities and skills of those that have a migration governance role. There are different stakeholders that need to be part of the discussion to identify duplication of efforts and bottlenecks in governance of irregular migration. In addition, the capacities of government personnel need to be strengthened to better respond effectively and distinguish different forms of irregular migration. This, in part, helps to promote partnerships between states and share the responsibility of reducing the risks faced by migrants taking up irregular pathways to migration. East African countries would need to regularly monitor and evaluate some of the policies in practice and understand the migration corridors frequented by irregular migrants, determine why they continue to remain key corridors, and identify how mechanisms put in place divert or create alternative corridors. Adopting strategies such as the 4Mi can be useful for identifying some numbers, creating a demographic profile of the migrant which can determine if it has changed as well as identify how existing policies can be strengthened.

Currently, East African member states have been using GCM and MPFA along with other related instruments to strengthen existing systems related to irregular migration which requires evidence to identify changes in flows, trends, and demographics, among others. Creating an effective system that takes stock of the knowledge and data on irregular migration from a variety of sources and services providers is required that will help member states to identify trends and flows. Such a system will take time to strengthen as it will respond to the dynamic nature of irregular migration. Adopting a community-based information-generating approach can lead to rich data given that they are source and host locations for some of the irregular migrants. Creating engagement platforms at a decentralized level is key as community members know their population are would provide a rich source of qualitative information from recruitment practices of traffickers as well as profile the mobile population from their communities. A bottom-up approach will be resourceful for the policy design, revision, and implementation as it will identify whether some of the stated strategies are being practiced as well as the limitations of the practices. Thus, an information-gathering system through the local chiefs or leaders and awareness information should be focused more at a decentralized level. A similar practice of having a human trafficking or migrant smuggling annual report shared with government and non-government stakeholders helps as a monitoring and evaluation tool that assesses how well the country is doing in addressing irregular migration. Furthermore, focus on capacity building should also be extended to different stakeholders that come in contact with irregular migration directly or indirectly and not limited to only law enforcement. This ensures that different players are involved in addressing irregular migration at different sectors.

The reality is that GCM is already part of existing policies and frameworks at AU and REC levels, and it is a question of what aspects are missing in the existing documentation and whether the guidance provided fits the regional context on irregular migration. Fundamentally, the ultimate test on whether the GCM is an effective and efficient tool to responding to irregular migration in East Africa lies in the practical implementation at member state level as well as regionally.

Notes

1 Anti-government protests that engulfed North African countries such as Tunisia, Libya, and Egypt that led to the collapse of governments in the respective countries.
2 Burundi, Comoros, Djibouti, Ethiopia, Kenya, Rwanda, Seychelles, South Sudan, Sudan, Tanzania, and Uganda.
3 Includes East African countries such as Kenya and Ethiopia.
4 Members include Djibouti, Eritrea, Ethiopia, Kenya, Somalia, and Uganda.
5 Members: Djibouti, Ethiopia, Uganda, Yemen, Kenya, and Somalia (Puntland).

Works Cited

African Centre for Migration Studies & Samuel Hall, (2018). *Free and safe movement in east Africa - Research to promote people's safe and unencumbered movement across international borders.* New York: Open Society Foundations.

African Development Bank, (2019). *East Africa Economic Outlook 2019: Macroeconomic developments and prospects.* Abidjan: African Development Bank.

Akinboade, O. A., (2014). A Review of the Status, Challenges and Innovations Regarding Temporary Immigration of Labour in the Regional Economic Areas of Africa. *Journal of International Migration and Integration,* 15, 27–47.

African Union, (2018). *Protocol to the Treaty Establishing the African Economic Community Relating to the Free Movement of Persons, Right of Residence and Right of Establishment.* [Online]. Retrieved from https://au.int/sites/default/files/treaties/36403-treaty-protocol_on_free_movement_of_persons_in_africa_e.pdf (Accessed 13 May 2019).

African Union, (2019). *Agreement Establishing the African Continental Free Trade Area.* [Online]. Retrieved from https://au.int/sites/default/files/treaties/36437-treaty-consolidated_text_on_cfta_-_en.pdf (Accessed 13 May 2019).

Cvajner, M., & Sciortino, G. (2010a). Theorizing Irregular Migration: The Control of Spatial Mobility in Differentiated Societies. *European Journal of Social Theory,* 13(3), 389–404.

Cvajner, M., & Sciortino, G. (2010b). A Tale of Networks and Policies: Prolegomena to an Analysis of Irregular Migration Careers and their Developmental Paths. *Population, Space and Place,* 16, 213–225.

Flahaux, M. L., & De Haas, H., (2016). African Migration: Trends, Patterns, Drivers. *Comparative Migration Studies,* 4(1), 1–25.

Inter-Governmental Authority on Development, (2012). *IGAD Regional Migration Policy Framework.* Djibouti: Inter-Governmental Authority on Development.

International Organisation for Migration, (2016). *Irregular Migration.* [Online]. Retrieved from https://www.unitar.org/ny/sites/unitar.org.ny/files/IML_Irregular%20migration.pdf (Accessed 13 May 2019).

International Organisation for Migration, (2019). *Tanzania, Ethiopia, Kenya Agree on Roadmap for Addressing Irregular Migration.* [Online]. Retrieved from https://www. iom.int/news/tanzania-ethiopia-kenya-agree-roadmap-addressing-irregular-migration (Accessed 13 May 2019).

Kanko, T., & Teller, T. (2014). Irregular migration in Sub-Saharan Africa: Causes and consequences of young adult migration from Southern Ethiopia to South Africa. Princeton conference paper. Available at http://paa2014.Princeton.edu/papers/140147.

Karagueuzian, C., & Verdier-Chouchane, A., (2014). Taking Africa's Irregular Migrants into Account: Trends, Challenges and Policy Options. *Chief Economist Complex,* 5(1), 1–15.

Koser, K., (2005). *Irregular Migration, State Security and Human Security,* Global Commission on International Migration. Retrieved from https://www.iom.int/jahia/webdav/site/myjahiasite/shared/shared/mainsite/policy_and_research/gcim/tp/TP5.pdf.

Marchand, K., Reinold, J., & Dias e Silva, R., (2017). *Study on Migration Routes in the East and Horn of Africa.* Maastricht: Maastricht Graduate School of Governance.

Masabo, J., (2015). *Unblocking the Barriers: Making the EAC Regime Beneficial to Female Migrant Workers.* Oxford: University of Dar es Salaam.

Maastricht Graduate School of Governance, (2017). *Uganda Migration Profile: Study on Migration Routes in the East and Horn of Africa.* Maastricht: Maastricht Graduate School of Governance.

Mixed Migration Centre, (2018). *Mixed Migration in East Africa and Yemen -4Mi Snapshot - Smuggler Survey.* [Online]. Retrieved from http://www.mixedmigration.org/wp-content/uploads/2018/10/tr-ea-1809.pdf (Accessed 14 May 2019).

Ogu, P. I., (2017). Africa's Irregular Migration to Europe: A Re-Enactment of the Transatlantic Slave Trade. *Journal of Global Research in Education and Social Science,* 10(2), 49–69.

Oucho, J. O., & Odipo, G. (2017). Prospects for free movement of particular persons in the East African Community: The feasibility and dilemmas of integration in *Migration, Free Movement and Regional Integration,* 119. Edited by Nita, S., Pécoud, A., Lombaerde, P. D., Neyts, K., & Gartland, J. UNESCO Publishing.

Sahan Institute and Inter-Governmental Authority on Development, (2016). *Human Trafficking and Smuggling on the Horn of Africa - Central Mediterranean Route.* Nairobi: SAHAN and IGAD.

United Nations, (2017). *Irregular Migration and Regular Pathways, Including Decent Work, Labour Mobility, Recognition of Skills and Qualifications and Other Relevant Measures.* New York: United Nations.

United Nations Conference on Trade and Development, (2018). *Economic Development in Africa Report 2018.* New York: United Nations Conference on Trade and Development.

United Nations Development Programme, (2019). *Scaling Fences: Voices of Irregular African Migrants to Europe.* Geneva: United Nations Development Programme.

United Nations General Assembly, (2016). *New York Declaration for Refugees and Migrants.* New York: United Nations General Assembly.

United Nations General Assembly (2019). *Global Compact for Safe, Orderly and Regular Migration.* New York: United Nations General Assembly

Zijlstra, J., & Liempt, I. V., (2017). Smart (phone) Travelling: Understanding the Use and Impact of Mobile Technology on Irregular Migration Journeys. *International Journal for Migration and Border Studies,* 3(2/3), 174–191.

14 Sub-Saharan migration in transit countries

The case of Morocco

Fouzi Mourji, Claire Ricard and Macoura Doumbia

Introduction

International migration involves people or groups of people who leave their country in order to settle temporarily or permanently in another country.

Since the origin of mankind, people have moved in search of better living conditions. Currently, migratory movements affect all countries. Thus, according to United Nations statistics, the number of international migrants is estimated at 272 million in 2019 with an upward trend, an increase of 51 million since 2010 (United Nations, Department of Economic and Social Affairs, Population Division [2019]). International migrants are estimated at 3.5% of the world population, compared to 2.8% in 2000. Moreover, most of these migrants move between countries in the same region. Indeed, the majority of international migrants from sub-Saharan Africa (89%), East and South-East Asia (83%), Latin America and the Caribbean (73%), and Central and South Asia (63%) originated from the region in which they resided. In contrast, international migrants living in North America (98%), Oceania (88%), and North Africa and Western Asia (59%) were born outside their region of residence. Taking the case of Morocco, the number of sub-Saharan migrants is estimated at 700,000 in 2019 (Driss El Ghazouani, 2019). The migratory flows from sub-Saharan Africa (hereinafter SSA) to the countries of North Africa began to intensify in the early 1990s and became significant during the following decade (Bredeloup & Pliez, 2005).

The case of Morocco is interesting because until 2008, it was mainly a country of transit for migrants whose objective was to reach Europe. But due to the economic crisis affecting those countries and also the increasingly difficult conditions of access, many migrants abandoned that objective and decided to remain permanently in Morocco. Accordingly, after having been only a country of departure, then one of departure and transit, it became equally a country of settlement.

The object of this chapter is to analyse the characteristics and behaviour of the SSA migrant population in Morocco. We base this on data from a survey conducted between October 2015 and January 2016, with 877 male and female migrants:[2] (a) in Casablanca-Mohamédia, an urban area that is inherently attractive for the employment possibilities it offers;[*] (b) in Rabat-Salé, which although to a lesser extent offers comparable opportunities; and c) in Tangiers, which is a transit city *par excellence*, lying only 15 kilometres from the European coast and thus attracts the most determined candidates.

The first section examines the social and occupational integration of this population in Morocco. These questions are crucial because, on the one hand, they embody the main reason impelling migrants to undertake this adventure: a search for better living conditions, facilitated by access to a job. Thus, apart from migrants' relations with the Moroccan population, we test the hypothesis of an eventual downgrading of migrants on the Moroccan labour market. More precisely, does being a migrant increase one's propensity to occupy a job whose required qualification is inferior to that corresponding to his/her education level? We treat this question via a triple analysis: determinants of the downgrading of qualifications by comparison with those affecting Moroccans, and finally by comparison with the migrants' situation in their countries of departure. The findings of this section make it possible to understand the variations to which migrants' aspirations are subject.

Finally, we look at the interdependence between the social integration of migrants and their integration on the labour market.

Entry of SSA migrants onto Morocco's labour market: questions of downgrading and meeting requirements

We study here the quality of migrants' entry into the Moroccan labour market. Given problems of under-employment and downgrading on the market, we examine first why the migrant's entry onto the labour market deteriorates following his/her migration. Secondly, we look at the downgrading of migrants, comparing the reasons for downgrading of both migrants and Moroccans. Our findings show that the length of residence, the migrant's origin, level of education, and place of residence influence the level of his/her entry. Comparison of the degree of downgrading of the two populations displays reasons for downgrading peculiar to Moroccans and other reasons specific to migrants.

As noted above, until 2008 Morocco was mainly a transit country for SSA migrants seeking to reach Europe. But faced with increasingly difficult conditions of access, more and more migrants have abandoned that goal and decided to remain permanently in Morocco, hoping for the best possible entry here.

The success of these migrants in Morocco depends largely on the quality of their entry onto the labour market. On the other hand, at first view the Moroccan labour market does not seem to facilitate entry, given problems of downgrading and under-employment due to three market characteristics. According to the Haut Commissariat au Plan (2018), (*Full report on the*

---

[*] This characteristic has likewise held with regard to internal migration in Morocco since the 1920s, when it was decided to make Casablanca-Mohamédia the country's largest port and economic capital.

adequacy of employment and training on the Moroccan labour market), the labour market is characterized by a lack of inclusion due to insufficient integration of young people and women. It turns out that only 23.6% of women participate in the labour market Mourji (2017) explains the reasons for this low rate).

Also, the labour market is characterized by **slow creation of jobs**, below the rate of growth of the working-age population. In 2017, the Moroccan labour market displayed 4.2% growth of unemployment, against 0.8% job growth. The third characteristic is the **precarious quality of jobs and preponderance of the informal sector**. This is shown by workers' affiliation or lack thereof of social security. In 2015, close to 80% of the active population worked informally. This implies general precariousness on the Moroccan labour market.

Several empirical studies have looked at the determinants of migrants' job entry. For example, Dumont and Monso (2007) finds that immigrants' rate of employment is inferior to that of natives in many OECD member countries. She finds many reasons for this. The first is the level of education. However this represents only a small part of the difference in employment rates between the two populations. The second reason might be the level of qualification. Although higher qualifications favour better access to the labour market, employment rates between immigrants and natives are different practically in all OECD countries. These studies (Dumont and Liebig, 2005; Dumont and Monso, 2007) thus conclude that education levels have only a small impact on immigrants' entry to the labour market in the host country. Moreover, findings of another study (Battu and Sloane, 2002) explain immigrants' high exposure to downgrading because of the obstacles of recognition of diplomas obtained outside the host country. For example, in the Shanghai's classification, the value of a master's degree changes between countries. Accordingly, if universities in the migrant's home country are less highly regarded, and he/she moves to a country with better universities, his/her diploma will automatically not be as highly regarded as that of a native. In this context, Friedberg (2000) compares the returns to human capital in Israel and abroad. He finds that returns to human capital obtained abroad are inferior to those acquired in Israel. Returns to national education are estimated at 8.8%, while those to education abroad are estimated at 7.6%. Friedberg explains this gap by the low value placed on immigrants' human capital. Accordingly, we imagine that a migrant's country of origin may act negatively on his/her integration in the host country's labour market. It is important to mention that, according to Dumont and Monso's (2007) study, recent immigrants fall among the persons most affected by downgrading. According to a survey of the rate of downgrading of persons born abroad as a function of their period of stay, the data show the rate declining with the length of residence (*Survey of European Union Labor Forces, 2003–2004*). However, it must not be forgotten that length of stay may mask cohort effects in terms of the level of education and country of origin. Thanks to Massey et al. (1994), we know that emigration from a country takes place in waves. At first it is those who are better off and most educated who migrate. Subsequently, migration is democratized and less qualified individuals arrive on the host country labour market. This phenomenon arises in the absence of a policy of 'select migration' in the receiving country. In that case, different cohorts tend not to be downgraded because they have been chosen to enter the labour market. If despite select immigration and long presence in the host country migrants are still downgraded, it is because there were hidden factors causing a discrepancy between training and employment. As a result, length of stay plays a key role in downgrading migrants.

Moreover, Dumont and Monso (2007) mentions that the lack of specific skills in the host country increases downgrading of migrants. These skills may be acquired by comprehension of the host country's language. Such comprehension may reduce downgrading because it allows migrants to develop their skills on the labour market.

In this context we pose the following question: what is the level of job entry of SSA migrants in Morocco, and what are its determinants?

We will use data from a survey carried out by Laboratoire de Statistique Appliquée à l'Analyse et la Recherche en Économie (LASAARE) between September and December 2015 on the topic, « *characteristics, aspirations and behavior of immigrants in Morocco* ». The questionnaires were administered to 1,453 migrants in Casablanca, Salé, Mohammedia, Rabat and Tangiers. It should be noted that, to our knowledge, this study is the first one to examine the job entry of sub-Saharan migrants to Morocco, especially by making a comparison with the entry of natives.

To begin with, the study will examine causes of deterioration of the migrants' activity. A second part will analyse the downgrading of migrants in comparison with that experienced by Moroccans.

Deterioration of the type of activity

In this study we are interested in the deterioration of the migrant's activity. We look at if the migrant was occupied in his/her country of origin and has become unemployed in Morocco. This variable will allow us to appreciate the migrant's job in Morocco relatively to the one he had in the host country. It is a dichotomous variable, taking the value 1 if the migrant has experienced deterioration of his/her activity and 0 if not. Analysis of this variable shows that 64.88% of migrants have seen their job situation deteriorate after arriving in Morocco.

Regarding migrants' activity in their country of origin, more than half (58.70%) were employed, while 29.28% were still studying in their country of origin. Among these, only 7.6% were unemployed. The high percentage of migrants employed in their country of origin (close to 59%) is directly connected with the foregoing argument that the first condition for emigration is ability to raise money. Regarding policies that could be implemented to influence the behaviour of candidates for emigration, one aspect to consider is working conditions and its evaluation in the countries of departure. Moreover, analysis of migrants' occupational status in their country of origin shows that 51.33% were self-employed. In other words, half were entrepreneurs, owners of their means of production and self-employed. Migrants describing themselves as wage-paid represent only 16.14% of the migrant population.

The migrant's length of residence seems to reduce significantly the probability of job deterioration (Table A.1, Appendix 1). The longer the migrant lives in Morocco, the more he increases his/her chances of not being either unemployed or a beggar. The table shows that one additional year of residence in Morocco diminishes the risk of job deterioration from 3.1 to 3.3%.

Integration into the Moroccan labour market

This section focuses on the determinants of the occupational integration of migrants. Here the status of the migrant is taken into account. We want to know whether the migrant has experienced an improvement in his or her professional situation by going on the Moroccan labour market. First, the idea is to study the determinants of the professional integration of migrants.

Analysis of findings

This section aims to find out whether the migrant is more likely to be professionally integrated in Morocco than in his/her country of origin. This will thus enable us to find the determinants that facilitate the professional integration of the migrant in Morocco. Results of the study can be found in Table A.2 (Appendix 2). To be specific, we are interested only in the professional integration of migrants who were unemployed in their country of origin.

The first factor influencing the integration of sub-Saharans in Morocco is gender. Its influence is quite significant (10%). Indeed, the fact of being a woman increases the probability between 23.4% and 24.1% that a female migrant who is unemployed in her country of origin is an employed worker in Morocco compared to an unemployed male migrant in his/her country of origin. This can be explained by the ease of integration into the labour market of female migrants who have more job opportunities in sectors which are gendered and still employ more female than male such as home care services and catering. For instance, Moroccan families prefer to hire sub-Saharan women from French-speaking countries as domestic helpers so that they can teach their children French.

Moreover, the level of education approximated by the number of years of study positively influences the probability of professional integration of sub-Saharan women in Morocco. Indeed, completing an additional year of study increases (between 4.8% and 10%) the probability that an unemployed person in his/her country of origin is an employed worker in Morocco. The higher the level of education, the better it gives a good signal about the migrant's qualifications and skills. Therefore, a migrant with a high level of education has a great facility to integrate professionally into the Moroccan labour market.

Residence status has a significant negative marginal effect (between 32.5% and 33.6%) on the probability of an unemployed person having a job once in Morocco. Indeed, a migrant in transit has a limited duration of stay that does not allow him/her to integrate into the labour market. Moreover, it is important to note that transit migrants who already have the necessary financial means will not spend their time looking for a job.

The determinants of the integration of sub-Saharans migrants who were unemployed in their country of origin are gender, education level, and residence status.

The quality of integration: explaining the downgrading of sub-Saharan migrants in Morocco

The literature on downgrading generally distinguishes between a so-called 'horizontal' downgrading and a so-called 'vertical' downgrading. The first type refers to the mismatch between an individual's field of study and employment, while the second is defined by the notion of overeducation, i.e. working in a job that requires a lower level of education than the individual possesses.

In order to complete Section titled 'Social integration of SSA migrants in Morocco' of the study, we are interested in the quality of the professional integration of migrants. We are interested only in horizontal downgrading as measured by the level of adequacy between the training and the job held by the migrant.

Analysis of findings

Beyond unemployment, 'downgrading' can be another form of under-utilization of human skills on the labour market. It is the result of the poor match between training and employment. We decided to measure the level of downgrading of migrants on the Moroccan labour market based on the level of adequacy between training and the job held by the migrant. From our results (Table A.3, Appendix 3), after applying an ordered logit model, some interesting elements emerge that could determine the level of downgrading of this part of the labour force in Morocco.

The study reveals that the length of residence of the migrant increases the probability of perfect adequacy between 1.6% and 2.3%. A migrant who has lived in Morocco for an additional year has a higher chance of having a job that is a perfect match for his or her education (estimated between 1.6% and 2.3%). This would be explained by the fact that the longer the migrant resides in Morocco, the more time he or she has to build up a reliable professional network that would allow him or her to have information on job opportunities that are more in line with his or her qualifications.

Moreover, the second factor influencing the quality of professional integration is the level of education approximated by the number of years of study. A migrant who has completed an additional year of education has between 3.7% and 4.5% higher chance of not being downgraded. This shows that the level of education has an enormous impact on the downgrading of sub-Saharan Africans in Morocco. The level of education gives employers an idea of the migrant's actual skills. Moreover, diplomas gives a signal on the skills of the job seeker. Indeed, according to the signal theory (Spence, 1973), diplomas, representing the level of education, are considered as a method of selection on the labour market. The diploma obtained allows employers to have an idea of the migrant's qualifications.

Moreover, residence status impacts the quality of integration into the labour market. Choosing Morocco as a transit country and not as a country of residence significantly reduces the probability of a perfect match (models 4 and 5 in Table A.3 in Appendix 3). Indeed, migrants in transit are between 13.3% and 14.2% less likely to have a perfectly matched job compared to a resident migrant. For a temporary migrant it might be preferable to have a job that is not a good match for her/his skills, rather than devoting time to having her/his skills recognized in a country that is not her/his final destination. Therefore, they are encouraged to accept all job opportunities that are presented to them, even those that do not match their training. The objective of this type of migrant is to have the maximum income before departure, even if this would imply a downgrading.

Finally, the migrant's place of residence affects the downgrading of the migrant. Living in the periphery reduces the probability of adequacy and therefore increases the probability of downgrading. Its marginal effect is strongly significant at 1%. A migrant who lives in the periphery is 42.7% less likely to have a job that is perfectly suited to his or her training compared to a migrant who lives in the city centre (model 5 in Table A.3 in the appendix). Proximity to the labour market reduces the informational asymmetry regarding available job opportunities. Also, it would be difficult for the migrant to find a job on the periphery since most of the tertiary sector activities are located in the city centre. However, this result is to be considered with caution. It is important to note that there may be an endogeneity bias following the use of this variable. This bias is due to the problem of reverse causality. Living in the periphery could cause a mismatch between the migrant's employment and training. A downgrading could also be the reason why the migrant chooses to live in the periphery because housing is cheaper there compared to the city centre. In this case, the downgrading could create a loss of income for the migrant who would be forced to live on the periphery for lack of financial means.

This study shows thus that the main determinants of migrant downgrading are length of residence, place of residence, level of education, and being a transit migrant.

Comparative study of the downgrading of SSA and Moroccan migrants

In a parallel study, Kabboul and Eddari (2018) analysed why Moroccans face downgrading.

In their sample, 36.11% of active Moroccan diploma holders suffer from downgrading, against 73.68% for migrants with university degrees. In other words, migrants suffer more from downgrading than natives.

We push forward this analysis by comparing the reasons why Moroccans are downgraded with those affecting migrants. To begin with, gender has no influence on downgrading of either Moroccans or migrants. In other words, gender is not a cause of downgrading of the active population on the Moroccan labour market.

The study also finds that residential location does influence the probability of Moroccans being downgraded. Those living in rural areas run a higher risk of downgrading than urban dwellers. The latter have a better chance of finding jobs in urban areas that correspond to their diplomas. This corresponds to what we found with migrants. It seems that downgrading has some common causes for both Moroccans and migrants.

Moreover, length of holding a job reduces a Moroccan's risk of downgrading. According to Glaude and Jarousse (1988), poor matching, which can be a cause of downgrading, disappears after a certain period. Thus, the longer an individual holds a job, the better the chance that it will eventually match his/her skills. We also found that migrants residing longer in Morocco have a lower risk of downgrading. Given the connection between the migrant's length of residence and length of holding his/her job, duration is clearly a relevant variable in explaining downgrading for either population.

In summary, some causes of downgrading on the Moroccan labour market affect both natives and migrants. Those peculiar to migration include where the migrant obtained his/her diploma, and whether he/she is in transit. In any case, SSA migrants have suffered more downgrading than Moroccans. These additional difficulties are connected with certain forms of discrimination that migrants may face upon recruitment. Accordingly, in the following section we look at the social integration of SSA migrants in Morocco. We build on the hypothesis that social integration and integration on the job market are interdependent. A migrant who is well integrated socially probably has a better chance of finding a job. Likewise, a migrant who is working may well find it easier to integrate in the Moroccan population.

Social integration of SSA migrants in Morocco

The previous section highlighted that Moroccans and migrants from SSA face difficulties in integrating properly into the labour market. Migrants from SSA seem to face greater difficulties, notably because of the discrimination they face. According to LASAARE's survey in Casablanca regarding Moroccans' perception of migrants from SSA, 72.02% of respondents think that migrants face discrimination in hiring. This tendency holds as well with migrants,[3] 84.04% of whom believe they face discrimination. Moreover, 36.84% of Moroccan employers and independents report having refused a position to an SSA migrant.

Discrimination against SSA migrants in Morocco is present not only on the labour market. Even though 55.56% of Moroccans would be willing to join an association that supports migrants and 61.13% are favourable to a directive designed to regularize migrants' administrative situation, Moroccans and migrants agree in saying that, on average, SSA migrants are less well treated in Morocco. Of Moroccans surveyed, 68.78%, against 86.96% of migrants, stated that migrants in general are less well treated than locals. Thus, only 26.91% of migrants feel themselves integrated in Morocco, while few Moroccans think that a majority of migrants are excluded.

We would like to understand why migrants from SSA are so poorly integrated into Moroccan society. In order to measure the openness of one of the communities to the other, we use two questions from the questionnaires administered to migrants and Moroccans, in the surveys conducted by LA-SAARE. In each questionnaire, one question is asked about the respondent's opinion about marriage between members of the two communities,[4] and another question about having close friends within the other group.[5] Regarding marriage between Moroccans and migrants from SSA, 45.95% of Moroccans disapprove while 44.36% of migrants approve. Thus, migrants seem to be relatively ready to integrate, but Moroccans give less the impression of wanting to mix the communities. Another question asked to both populations may be interpreted as an indicator of more or less significant tolerance: «Have you rubbed shoulders with migrants from SSA? »/ « Do you frequently associate with Moroccans? (Often, moderately, never) ». We also use a variable indicating whether Moroccans think migrants are useful or not to the country's economy to measure their degree of openness to migrants.

Drawing on the literature on the integration of migrants in host societies, we hypothesize that the social integration of migrants is closely linked to their integration into the labour market. Indeed, according to Mayda (2004), people who feel they are competing with migrants on the labour market may tend more towards a negative view of immigration.

On the other hand, by working together, the two communities can get to know each other better. Voci and Hewstone (2003) and Van Oudenhoven et al. (1998) stipulate that negative attitudes of one group towards another are caused by lack of knowledge about that group. Thus, Dubourg and Souk-Aloun (2016) have found that more information would significantly improve Moroccans' perception of migrants. The cost of information is lower when one shares social, demographic, and cultural characteristics with someone. That is the *similarity attraction* hypothesis of Byrne (1971).

We therefore first look at to what extent the situation of Moroccans on the labour market influences their degree of tolerance towards migrants from SSA. Second, we will observe whether Moroccans and SSA migrants are present in the same segments of the labour market. If this is the case, this could possibly explain the distrust some Moroccans may have towards SSA migrants.

Situation on the labour market and tolerance towards migrants

Close to half of Moroccans consider that the arrival of SSA migrants has a negative impact on Morocco. Three-quarters of these justify their response on economic grounds: migrants increase Moroccans' unemployment. The 34.34% who think migrants are useful to Morocco give as their main reason the creation of wealth thanks to increased manpower.[6] Here too the justification is economic. It is thus interesting to check the responses as a function of the respondents' activity.

Applying a Chi^2 test of independence to the interdependence of variables arising from the questions « Do you think the coming of people from SSA is ... » and « The situation in your profession », it turns out that the relation between the two variables is not significant ($Chi^2(12) = 14.23$; $p = 0.286$). The relation between the respondent's area of activity and his/her opinion on migrants' usefulness to Morocco is also not significant ($Chi^2(22) = 29.5062$; $p = 0.131$). Thus, the situation in the profession and the area of activity have no effect on one's thinking whether or not migrants are 'useful' to Morocco.

We apply the same method to interdependence of the following variables: « Increased unemployment » (separating people having responded that migrants have a negative impact on Morocco because they increase Moroccan unemployment, from those having cited other reasons to support a negative impact), and « Situation in the profession », we once again find no significant connection ($Chi^2(6) = 2.6359$; $p = 0.853$). The same occurs when we use the branch of activity where the Moroccan respondent works: the $Chi^2(11)$ rises to 7.7813 and the p-value to 0.733. Thus, the situation in the profession and branch of activity of Moroccans does not seem to influence their degree of openness towards SSA migrants. Nevertheless, tolerance[7] on the part of both migrants and Moroccans is closely tied to the type of activity. Among Moroccans, students are the most tolerant, while those not working and in retirement are the least tolerant. Among migrants, students are the most tolerant, while inactive and unemployed people are least tolerant.

According to our multivariate analysis, seasonality of activity influences tolerance towards migrants. The Moroccan respondent may blame migrants for his/her precarious situation when his/her work's seasonality leads him to have a lower opportunity to associate with them, thus lessening the probability of making friends. Moreover, an individual holding a seasonal job will more likely not favour a mixed marriage than a Moroccan holding a stable job. The individual's precarious situation may be perceived as the result of immigration. A seasonal worker may also feel himself more threatened by migrants who are content with a short-term job when Morocco figures only as a transit country.

Since unemployment and seasonality of employment degrade the mutual tolerance between Moroccans and migrants from SSA in Morocco, it is conceivable that individuals facing issues to enter the labour market may blame the other community for their difficulties. In the next section, we then observe whether SSA migrants and Moroccans are indeed competing in the labour market.

Competition on the labour market

We are interested in knowing whether migrants and Moroccans are competing on the labour market. On the one hand, if Moroccans and migrants are present in the same segments of the labour market, then they can be brought together and develop friendships (Voci & Hewstone, 2003; Van Oudenhoven et al., 1998). On the other hand, Moroccans may feel that they are in competition with migrants if they are applying for the same types of jobs (Esses et al., 2002; Mayda, 2004).

Upon introducing, into a multivariate analysis of the determinants of Moroccans' tolerance, the variable indicating whether they are informed about migrants, it turns out that having such information makes Moroccans more tolerant by reducing prejudice. Moreover, this variable is quite robust since tests have proven that it is not endogenous. Thus, having information about migrants makes it possible to accept them as friends or at least associate with them. It also causes greater openness towards mixed marriage. In other words, information asymmetry is an important factor and has a cost with regard to tolerance. It is less costly to integrate migrants in one's environment if one knows their culture, their way of life, and the conditions of migration. By rubbing shoulders on the labour market, migrants and Moroccans could then accept each other more easily. However, our data suggest that SSA migrants and Moroccans are rarely present in the same segments of the labour market.

The majority of Moroccans surveyed describe themselves as wage-earners (53.05%), but are in competition with only 17.60% of migrants surveyed. Most of the latter belong to the category 'self-employed' (41.02%), which represents only 18.31% of Moroccans surveyed. The heaviest competition occurs between Moroccans and migrants who have never attended school and do not describe themselves as wage-earners.

Looking at the sector of activity, competition between Moroccans and migrants is more nuanced. For example, 54.4% of migrants work in the services sector, against 46.93% of Moroccans. Since these two proportions are close, it might seem that migrants and Moroccans have a strong chance of competing on this labour market. However, the largest share of migrants (37.39%) work in the informal service sector, while Moroccans are more present in the formal service sector (37.28%). This formal/informal dichotomy is particularly present in commerce. It is especially in informal industry and crafts that competition is the most important, since about 3% of the two populations are present there.

Thus, according to the models presented by Mayda (2004), Moroccans working in industry and crafts should be the most resistant to the arrival of migrants since they are the ones that would suffer the most from competition. However, as a rule, competition between migrants and Moroccans on the labour market is not very noticeable. According to our data, the two population are not found in the same segments of the labour market.

Finally, economic variables may explain opinions on the question of marriage between SSA migrants and Moroccans. Thus, the precarious nature of one's job has an influence on Moroccans' opinion on mixed marriage. In this case, Moroccans may feel threatened by the presence of SSA migrants in the labour market, even though our data indicate that the two populations are not present in the same market segments. There are also non-economic characteristics that determine the openness of Moroccans to SSA migrants. Moroccans are more or less friends with migrants as a function of their age, gender, their perception of migrants, information they have about them, and the presence or not of migrants in their neighbourhood.

General conclusion

In Section titled 'Entry of SSA migrants onto Morocco's labour market: questions of downgrading and meeting requirements', the analysis of the Moroccan labour market identified the risk of under-employment in the kingdom as well as the reasons for under-employment of SSA migrants.

Several variables explain the level of SSA migrants' job integration in Morocco. Length of residence, the migrant's origin, level of education, gender, understanding of *darija*, and status as a refugee determine the level of downgrading of the type of occupation following migration. Except for the level of education, these variables all relate specifically to migration. Some of them decrease the risk of downgrading (length of residence, level of education, being female, speaking *darija,* and originating from a francophone country), while others increase it (living with Moroccans or being a refugee).

Variables such as length and place of residence, place of obtaining a diploma, and being a migrant in transit in Morocco determine the level of downgrading in Morocco, in particular for migrants holding a diploma. With regard to the professional downgrading of migrants, there are several factors.

In addition to these findings, comparison of the level of downgrading of the two populations show interesting patterns. First, our results show that migrants have a higher likelihood to be downgraded than Moroccans. Second, we have found that factors such as place and length of residence are common determinants of the probability of being downgraded to both populations. However, determinants specific to migrants are the country where the diploma was obtained, and the fact of being in transit.

The study shows that both migrants and Moroccans suffer downgrading on the labour market. One of Morocco's greatest challenges is thus to better integrate university graduates into the labour market. To this end, a new national employment strategy was launched in 2015 and should last until 2025.

Migrants' human capital would be a major asset for the Moroccan economy if it manages to absorb it into productive employment. However, migrants seem to encounter more difficulties than Moroccans in integrating themselves in the labour market. These additional difficulties may be connected to certain forms of discrimination which migrants face during the recruitment process.

To explain this discrimination, Section titled 'Social integration of SSA migrants in Morocco' looked at the determinants of tolerance of both Moroccans and migrants. Our findings indicate that the situation on the labour market does not influence tolerance on the part of either population. In other words, few individuals attribute their labour market problems to individuals of the other community. It is more the socio-demographic characteristics of the two populations that influence their level of tolerance towards the other one. The UNDP's 2009 *Human Development Report* reached the same conclusions while looking at a global scale. Subsequently, to better integrate SSA migrants in the Moroccan population, it is necessary to promote contacts between the two populations, especially at the neighbourhood level. This will allow exchanging more information from one community to the other reduce information asymmetry between the two groups which will increase their tolerance levels, respectively.

This chapter on integration of migrants in transit countries is particularly related to SDG 8 relative to decent work and economic growth and SDG 10, reduce inequalities. A better integration of migrants into the labour market of transit and host countries means a better access to good jobs and an opportunity for a stable source of income. That would have positive effects on remittances but also help reduce possible inequalities between migrants and natives. There is room to improve the situation of SSA migrants in Morocco in terms of jobs and social integration. Regularizing the migrants' situation would thus help them perform better on the labour market, while expanding the diffusion of information from one population to the other would make for greater social cohesion.

Acknowledgements

We are grateful to Clive Gray, a former Institute Fellow at the Harvard Institute for International Development, for the translation and for his careful reading of an earlier version of this chapter and for his suggestions for improvement.

Notes

1 But for the questionnaire, we have used a « household approach », giving us information on 1,453 individuals.
2 But for the questionnaire, we have used a « household approach », giving us information on 1,453 individuals.
3 According to LASAARE's survey of 1,453 SSA migrants, interviewed in Rabat, Tangiers, and Casablanca regarding their characteristics, aspirations, and behaviour.

4 « What do you think in general of marriage between Moroccans and people from sub-Saharan Africa? » The variable relating to this question in the survey of Moroccans takes the value 0 if the interviewee is unfavourable to marriage between the two communities, 1 if he is favourable only if the migrant is Muslim, and 2 if he is favourable to mixed marriage. In the survey of SSA migrants the variable takes the value 1 if the interviewee is against mixed marriage, 2 if he is not against, 3 if he is for, and 4 if he has no opinion.

5 « Do you have close friends among migrants? » / « Do you have close friends among Moroccans? ». These variables take the value 1 if an interviewee has close friends in the other community, 0 otherwise.

6 Thinking that migrants are useful to Morocco seems also to be a sign of openness to integration of a migrant in one's family circle, since this variable has a significant positive impact on Moroccans' tolerance of SSA migrants.

7 We measure tolerance on the basis of an index built from three variables resulting from the questions mentioned above: Do you have close friends in the other community? what do you think of mixed marriage? Do you rub shoulders with people of the other community?

Bibliography

Battu, H. and Sloane, P. J., To What Extent are Ethnic Minorities in Britain Over-Educated?. International Journal of Manpower, 2002, vol. 23, no. 3, pp. 192–208.

Bredeloup, S. and Pliez, O., Migrations entre les deux rives du Sahara. Autrepart-Bondy Paris-, 2005, vol. 36, p. 3.

Byrne, D., The attraction paradigm. New York: Academic Press, 1971.

Driss El Ghazouani, A., Growing Destination for Sub-Saharan Africans, Morocco Wrestles with Immigrant Integration, Migration Policy Institute (MPI), July 2019.

Dubourg, M. and Souk-Aloun, C., Etude sur la perception des Marocains vis-à-vis des migrants d'Afrique Subsaharienne, Approche Microéconométrique sur la base d'une enquête réalisée à Casablanca, LASAARE working paper and essay presented at CERDI, 2016.

Dumont, J. C. and Monso, O., Adéquation entre formation et emploi: un défi pour les immigrés et les pays d'accueil, deuxième partie. Perspectives des migrations internationales, 2007, pp. 141–170.

Dumont, J-C. and Liebig, T., Labour market integration of immigrant women: Overview and recent trends. Migrant Women and the Labour Market: Diversity and Challenges. Brussels: OECD and European Commission, 2005.

Esses, V. M., Dovidio, J. F., & Hodson, G. "Public attitudes toward immigration in the United States and Canada in response to the September 11, 2001 "Attack on America"." *Analyses of Social Issues and Public Policy*, 2002, vol. 2, no. 1, pp. 69–85.

Friedberg, R. M., You can't take it with you? Immigrant assimilation and the portability of human capital. *Journal of Labor Economics*, 2000, vol. 18, no. 2, pp. 221–251.

Kabboul, G. and Eddari, M., Essay: L'analyse de la qualité de l'insertion professionnelle sur le marché du travail marocain: La question du déclassement, 2018.

Glaude, M. and Jarousse, J-P., L'horizon des jeunes salariés dans leur entreprise. Economie and statistique, 1988, vol. 211, no. 1, pp. 23–41.

Haut-Commissariat au Plan (HCP), L'adéquation entre formation et emploi au Maroc (complete report, 2018). file:///C:/Users/mlm105542/Downloads/L%E2%80%99ad%C3%A9quation%20entre%20formation%20et%20emploi%20au%20Maroc,%20Rapport%20complet%20(Version%20Fr).pdf

Massey, D. S., Goldring, L. and Durand, J., Continuities in transnational migration: An analysis of nineteen Mexican communities. American Journal of Sociology, 1994, vol. 99, no. 6, pp. 1492–1533.

Mayda, A. M., Who is against immigration? A cross-country investigation of individual attitudes toward immigrants. The Review of Economics and Statistics, 2004, vol. 88, no. 3, pp. 510–530.

Mourji, F. and Ezzrari, A., "Economic analysis of the situation of women in Morocco," In *Women's inheritance: a multidisciplinary perspective on inheritance in Morocco*, Benchekroun, S. (Eds.), Casablanca: Editions Empreintes, 2017

Spence, M., Job market signaling. The Quarterly Journal of Economics, 1973, vol 87, pp. 355–374.

United Nations, Department of Economic and Social Affairs, Population Division (2019). International Migrant Stock 2019. (United Nations database, POP/DB/ MIG/Stock/Rev.2019).

Van Oudenhoven, J. P., Prins, K. S. and Buunk, B. P., Attitudes of minority and majority members towards adaptation of immigrants. European Journal of Social Psychology, 1998, vol. 28, pp. 995–1013.

Voci, A. and Hewstone, M., Intergroup contact and prejudice toward immigrants in Italy: The mediational role of anxiety and the moderational role of salience. Group Processes and Intergroup Relations, 2003, vol. 6, no. 1, pp. 37–54.

Appendices

Methodology and tables

Appendix 1

Degradation of the type of activity

To look at the determinants of activity downgrading for migrants in Morocco, we estimate the following binary logit model:

$$Prob(degradation\ i = 1) = \Lambda \begin{pmatrix} \alpha + \beta\ duration\ of\ stay_i + \gamma\ age_i + \delta woman_i + \\ \eta\ years\ of\ scholling_i + \rho university\ degree_i + \\ \tau darija_i + \omega live\ with\ moroccan_i + \\ \varphi distant\ french\ speaking\ country_i + \\ \theta Senegal_i + \mu English - speaking\ country_i + \\ \vartheta\ near\ french - speaking\ country_i + \\ \pi\ moroccan\ TV_i + \sigma refugee_i + \varepsilon \end{pmatrix} \tag{1}$$

Where the dependent variable 'degradation of the type of activity' is a dichotomous or two-modality (0 or 1) qualitative variable. Duration of stay is the number of years a migrant has stayed in Morocco. Other determinants include age, gender, or number of years of schooling. The model also includes a variable taking into account if the migrant holds a university degree; if he speaks Darija (darija), the Moroccan dialect Arabic; live with a Moroccan (live with Moroccan), is from a distant French-speaking country; or from Senegal. If the migrant is from an English-speaking country; or a near French-speaking country; if he/she has Moroccan friends or watch Moroccan TV; he/she is a refugee.

Table A.1 Determinants of activity downgrading for migrants in Morocco: binary logit

Downgrading	Model 1	Model 2	Model 3	Model 4	Model 5	Model 6
Duration of stay	−0.032★★★	−0.031★★★	−0.032★★★	−0.032★★★	−0.033★★★	−0.031★★★
	(−4.38)	(−4.30)	(−4.32)	(−4.28)	(−4.32)	(−4.23)
Age 15–24 y.o.	−0.068★	−0.067★	−0.067★	−0.059★	−0.056	−0.060★
	(−2.34)	(−2.33)	(−2.32)	(−2.03)	(−1.91)	(−2.07)
Age 25–44 y.o.	Ref.	Ref.	Ref.	Ref.	Ref.	Ref.
Age 45–64 y.o.	0.025	0.031	0.025	−0.027	−0.020	−0.026
	(0.29)	(0.35)	(0.28)	(−0.33)	(−0.24)	(−0.31)
Female	−0.064★	−0.066★	−0.063	−0.058	−0.057	−0.060
	(−1.98)	(−2.06)	(−1.94)	(−1.77)	(−1.74)	(−1.86)
Years of schooling	−0.009★★★	−0.009★★	−0.009★★★	−0.009★★★	−0.009★★	−0.009★★★
	(−3.45)	(−3.24)	(−3.47)	(−3.35)	(−3.16)	(−3.29)
University degree	0.037	0.040	0.037	0.043	0.039	0.042
	(0.81)	(0.89)	(0.81)	(0.92)	(0.85)	(0.92)
Darija	−0.122★	−0.115	−0.125★	−0.117		−0.120
	(−1.97)	(−1.83)	(−2.00)	(−1.90)		(−1.94)
Live with Moroccan	0.068★	0.066	0.067★		0.050	0.053
	(2.02)	(1.95)	(2.01)		(1.40)	(1.48)
Distant French-speaking country	−0.126★★★	−0.126★★★	−0.126★★★	−0.150★★★	−0.143★★★	−0.143★★★
	(−4.51)	(−4.50)	(−4.48)	(−5.39)	(−4.99)	(−4.98)
Senegal	−0.381★★★	−0.376★★★	−0.381★★★	−0.364★★★	−0.371★★★	−0.362★★★
	(−6.17)	(−6.07)	(−6.16)	(−5.96)	(−6.03)	(−5.92)
English-speaking country	Ref.	Ref.	Ref.	Ref.	Ref.	Ref.
Near French-speaking country	−0.124★	−0.130★★	−0.124★	−0.117★	−0.112★	−0.113★
	(−2.47)	(−2.61)	(−2.47)	(−2.32)	(−2.22)	(−2.27)
Moroccan friends		−0.051				
		(−1.64)				
Moroccan TV			0.014			
			(0.36)			
Refugee				0.120★★★	0.118★★★	0.116★★★
				(3.60)	(3.47)	(3.45)
Observations	777	777	774	768	768	768

Note: Z statistics in parentheses. P-values ★★★ 1%, ★★5%, ★10%.

Appendix 2

Vocational integration of migrants

The methodology lies on the following binary logit:

$$Prob\left(Statut_i = 1\right) = \Lambda \begin{pmatrix} \alpha + \beta \, duration \, of \, stay_i + \\ \delta \, woman_i + \rho \, university \, degree_i + \\ \eta \, years \, of \, schooling_i + \tau \, darija_i + \\ \omega \, french \, speaking \ \ country_i + \\ \varphi \, migrant\_transit_i - \\ \theta \, periphery\_housing_i + \varepsilon \end{pmatrix} \quad (2)$$

The dependent variable Statut takes the value 0 if the migrant was unemployed in his country of origin and is still unemployed in Morocco and 1 if he has become his active worker. Explanatory variables include the duration of stay, gender, level of education of the migrant (university degree and years of schooling); if the migrant speaks darija or if he is from a French-speaking country; if he/she is in transit or live in a periphery housing.

Table A.2 Determinants of the professional integration of the unemployed (in the country of origin) in Morocco: binary logit model

Statut	Model 1	Model 2	Model 3	Model 4	Model 5
Duration of stay	−0.01	−0.007	−0.006	−0.008	−0.004
	(0.0140)	(0.0136)	(0.0134)	(0.00417)	(0.00451)
Woman	0.217★	0.224 ★	0.216★	0.234★	0.241★
	(0.254)	(0.261)	(0.291)	(0.355)	(0.346)
University degree	0.01	0.02	0.095	0.03	0.06
	(0.101)	(0.105)	(0.124)	(0.0373)	(0.0521)
Years of schooling	0.049 ★	0.048★		0.106★★	0.109 ★★★
	(0.0288)	(0.0287)		(0.0165)	(0.0168)
Darija		−0.055	−0.134	−0.05	−0.078
		(0.141)	(0.179)	(0.0801)	(0.0916)
French-speaking country			−0.126	−0.043	−0.057
			(0.0931)	(0.0440)	(0.0420)
English-speaking country	Ref	Ref	Ref	Ref	Ref
Transit migrant				0.325★★★	0.336★★★
				(0.0779)	(0.0758)
Periphery housing					0 (omitted)
Observations	59	59	57	56	52

Note: Robust standard errors in parentheses ***p<0.01, **p<0.05, *p<0.1.

Appendix 3

Quality of vocational integration

We estimate the following ordered logit model:

$$y_i = 0 \quad si \quad 0 < y_i^* \leq s_1 \tag{3}$$

$$y_i = 1 \quad si \quad s_1 < y_i^* \leq s_2 \tag{4}$$

$$y_i = 2 \quad si \quad s_2 < y_i^* \leq s_3 \tag{5}$$

$$Prob\left(adequation_i = 0\right) = \Phi\left(\begin{array}{l} S_1 - \beta length_i - \delta gender_i - \eta schooling\_duration_i - \\ \tau darja_i - \omega french\_speaking\_country_i - \\ \varphi migrant\_transit_i - \theta periphery\_housing_i \end{array}\right)$$
$$- \Phi\left(\begin{array}{l} -\beta length_i - \delta gender_i - \eta schooling\_duration_i - \\ \tau darja_i - \omega french\_speaking\_country_i - \\ \varphi migrant\_transit_i - \theta periphery\_housing_i \end{array}\right) \tag{6}$$

The dependent variable is a qualitative ordered polytomic variable with three alternative values : 1 if he or she thinks that his/her job does not correspond to his/her skills at all, 2 if he or she thinks that his/her job fits moderately his/her skills and 3 if the migrant thinks that his/her job fits perfectly his/her skills. Explanatory variables are the same as in Equation 2.

In the following equations, xi and zi are the same explaining variable than the ones used in the first equation:

$$Prob\left(adequation_i = 1\right) = \Phi\left(s_2 - \beta x_i - \kappa z_i\right) - \Phi\left(s_1 - \beta x_i - \kappa z_i\right) \tag{7}$$

$$Prob\left(adequation_i = 2\right) = \Phi\left(s_3 - \beta x_i - \kappa z_i\right) - \Phi\left(s_2 - \beta x_i - \kappa z_i\right) \tag{8}$$

Table A.3 Adequacy between training and employment: ordered logit

	Model 1	Model 2	Model 3	Model 4	Model 5
Duration of stay	0.021★★★	0.023★★★	0.022★★★	0.019★★	0.016★★
	(0.007)	(0.008)	(0.008)	(0.008)	(0.008)
Woman	−0.073	−0.07	−0.104	−0.088	−0.056
	(0.087)	(0.089)	(0.096)	(0.097)	(0.087)
University degree	−0.095★	−0.087	−0.074	−0.071	−0.107★
	(0.057)	(0.058)	(0.061)	(0.061)	(0.061)
Years of schooling	0.041★★	0.04★★	0.045★★	0.038★	0.037★
	(0.019)	(0.02)	(0.021)	(0.021)	(0.021)
Darija		−0.101	−0.076	−0.085	−0.037
		(0.076)	(0.085)	(0.084)	(0.098)
French-speaking country			−0.018	−0.037	−0.085
			(0.064)	(0.064)	(0.066)
English-speaking country	Ref	Ref	Ref	Ref	Ref
Transit migrant				−0.133★★	−0.142★★
				(0.0643)	(0.0658)
Periphery housing					−0.427★★★
					(0.148)
Observations	151	151	143	143	139

Robust standard errors in parentheses. ★★★ p<0.01, ★★ p<0.05, ★ p<0.1.

15 Conclusion

Maty Konte and Linguère Mously Mbaye

Over the last decades, both migration and remittance flows have not only shown an ever-going increase but have also revealed to be a potential source of development in Africa. Even though their implications are formally recognized in some SDGs, migration and remittances may indirectly affect many other SDG targets as well. There is a need to research and inform their cross-cutting nature, as they should strongly be considered for policymaking and monitoring towards the accomplishment of SDGs. In an attempt to close this gap, the chapters in this book have addressed some of the developmental opportunities, as well as challenges, related to migration and remittances in Africa. More precisely, the contributors have explored issues on the relationship between migration, through remittances, and topics such as innovation, economic transformation, trade, household welfare, youth employment, education and knowledge, corruption and political violence, gender equality, and women's empowerment as well as issues related to the management of migration flows. Moreover, the contributions have shed light on the primary threats that mitigate the achievements of SDGs in achieving responsive migration policies and positive individual welfare outcomes. Authors of the chapters have contributed to the existing literature and thoroughly discuss the link between their findings and the SDGs.

Summary of key findings

Part I investigates the relationship between migration, remittances, and the African economic transformation through three chapters. In Chapter 2, Vanore investigates the conceptual and empirical linkages between migration and trade. Through this chapter, the author motivates that facilitating intra-continental migration could greatly support businesses to acquire the necessary knowledge and skills contributing to the innovation of products and processes, technological upgrading, and productivity through diversification. Moreover, this chapter provides insights on how easing migration and circularity may stimulate the development of business and scientific networks among migrants and non-migrants. Lastly, the author also shows how export and import flows could be supported by the private sector, for which the development can be facilitated by migrant resources, such as social, human, and financial capital. Mbaye and Tani, in Chapter 3, explore the relationship between innovation and short-term labour mobility in Africa. The authors provide empirical evidence that short-term mobility, proxied by tourist arrivals per capita, is associated with higher innovation activity in Africa, through the exchange and formation of productive knowledge. Their findings support the idea that in addition to other factors such as R&D, foreign direct investments, and trade, short-term mobility can also be an effective channel for economic development Nevertheless, the authors shows that this relationship can be mitigated by the quality of governance, which can be both an obstacle to mobility and innovation.

In Chapter 4, Oucho explores the multifaceted dynamics of internal migration patterns and flows of youth, examining the motivations, policy, and operational contexts as well as the lived experiences of youth migrating in search for employment, entrepreneurship, and other economic opportunities in Kenya. The chapter outlines the potential avenues that county and national governmental bodies can pursue policies that support and generate adequate opportunities decent employment for internally migrating youth towards inclusive economic growth and achieve SDG Goal 11 in order to make cities and human settlements inclusive, safe, sustainable, and resilient to large flows of youth migration. The chapter also concludes with a robust discussion of the potential limitations that government could face while managing youth internal migration flows, highlighting policy implementation gaps that stem from a lack of understanding of youth migration profiles. Chapter 5 examines the effects of remittance costs on welfare in sub-Saharan African (SSA) region, which is recognized as being one of the most expensive corridors across the globe, exceeding international averages and SDG-determined targets for remittance costs. The findings in this chapter provide evidence of a negative effect of cost of remittance transactions on household consumption level. The results add support to the United Nations–led initiative to sustainably reduce the cost of sending remittances as a means of engendering positive welfare outcomes for SSA countries which experience high levels of economic growth stagnation, poverty, and other multidimensional deprivations.

Part II explores the relationship between migration, remittances, and education and knowledge in Africa through three chapters. Chapter 6, by Cebotari, uses longitudinal data to investigate the effect of migration and remittances on child development in Ghana. The findings show that children whose parents migrated either internally or internationally, and receive both monetary and in-kind remittances, are more likely to experience higher levels of school enjoyment and educational outcomes. As advanced by the chapter, remittances are crucial for migration to have a positive impact on education, since the findings revealed that the absence of remittances may negatively impact the education of children, and more particularly for girls. In addition to this implication, the school enjoyment of girls is more negatively affected in case parents migrate internally and send in-kind remittances, as well as their educational outcomes when no remittances are received. Mueller, in Chapter 7, examines how diaspora members involved in a Dutch diaspora programme transferred knowledge in countries of origin. Through case examples based on Sierra Leone and Somaliland, the author demonstrated that two types of knowledge transfer – formal trainings and closely working together with diaspora experts – contribute to capacity building as well as to the introduction of new procedures in the host institutions.

In Chapter 8, Setrana and Arhin-Sam investigate the impact of skilled return migrants on Ghana's development. The authors employed secondary sources including administrative reports from public and private bodies as well as collected primary data based on qualitative evidence from 15 return migrants. This chapter shows that these returnees can be a source of development by transferring skills and knowledge, which can subsequently create employment in origin countries. However, the chapter also points the importance of policies facilitating the inclusion of capital brought by the returnees for Africa's development. The findings encourage governments and private stakeholders to broaden their focus towards the potential benefits of social remittances by supporting safe and responsible migration back to their home countries from the diaspora. Developing countries can stand to benefit from the subsequent 'brain gain' when migration policies create an enabling environment for returning migrants to contribute to the physical and intellectual economy of the country.

In Chapter 9 Fourmy examines the relationship between mobile money and the welfare and education of internal remittance recipient households in Kenya. The introduction of mobile money in Kenya in 2007 influenced, not provided, a cheaper means of transmitting internal remittances, but it also made it faster and safer to transfer money to recipient households. Using an instrumented household fixed effects model on a household-level panel data survey, Fourmy finds evidence that mobile money has a direct positive effect of mobile on the welfare of recipient households through the maximization of receipts driven by the growth in count, regularity, and value of remittance receipts within the country. Mobile money also has an indirect impact on the welfare of remittance receipts' household welfare through a higher allocation of expenditures towards education in the long run

Part III consists of three chapters that explore the implication of migration and remittances with regard to corruption and conflict and vice versa. In Chapter 10, Konte and Ndubuisi explore empirically the relationship between remittances and corruption using the Afrobarometer surveys for 36 African countries. On the one hand, the findings show that remittance-receiving individuals living in countries with higher level of remittances are more likely to pay bribes to access public goods and services than non-receivers and respondents from countries with lower level of remittances. However, this positive effect of remittances on corruption tends to be lessened in the presence of higher control of corruption at the national level. On the other hand, individuals living in countries with a higher number of migrants residing in

OECD countries are less likely to pay bribe. Therefore, this finding suggests that social remittances, such as anti-corruption attitudes, may be shared with the ones staying in countries of origin, consequently having a negative impact on the level of corruption.

In Chapter 11, Merkle, Alberola, Reinold, and Siegel analyse both how corruption plays a role in the home country in shaping the migration path and how it continues to be important throughout the journey. The authors found that corruption comes into play whenever legal options for migration are limited and is constant throughout all stages of the migration process of several migrant groups. In addition to this finding, the chapter shows that women, and especially those who are travelling alone, are vulnerable to atypical forms of corruption compared to men, such as sexual extortion. Furthermore, the chapter reveals that women are not only participants in corrupt exchanges but are also commodified as the means of exchange for groups of migrants when crossing borders.

Ouedraogo and Soureouema, in Chapter 12, investigate the relationship between remittances and electoral violence in Africa. The empirical analysis uses the individual-level Afrobarometer surveys covering 30 African countries as well as supplementary data on precipitation and rainfall, employing an instrumental variable approach to addresses issues of endogeneity within the empirical analysis. The authors present robust evidence that financial remittances have a strong negative effect on electoral violence across the African region. Contrary to several claims that suggest that remittances increase the incidence and intensity of local electoral conflicts, the findings convincingly demonstrate that by economically supporting families within receiving countries, remittances promote peace through support of democratic institutions and improvements in human development.

Part IV on the challenges in the management of migration flows in Africa contains two chapters. Chapter 13, by Oucho, provides foresights on the implementation of the Global Compact on Migration (GCM) to address irregular migration in the Eastern African region.

The author argue that GCM should be used to guide the implementation of processes and procedures with regard to migration flows, and although some processes and procedures may already be in place in some countries, this framework should still be considered to strengthen them. Furthermore, the chapter advances that different stakeholders should be involved in the formulation of policies and strategies, in order to understand migration dynamics through better knowledge and data sharing. In Chapter 14, Mourji, Ricard, and Doumbia give a detailed description of migration issues in Morocco, a country that is experiencing transformation in the migration process, going from a departure country, to a transit country and now becoming a destination country. Their findings show that sub-Saharan African migrants face difficulties in terms of integration in the Moroccan job market. They also face a risk of being 'professionally' downgraded. These issues can be explained by various factors, including the length of residence, level of education, being female, speaking darija (the local language), being from a francophone country, being integrated in the Moroccan society, or having the status of refugee.

Relevance of key findings to SDGs

Through this book, findings of several chapters can be related to SDG 1, 'No poverty'. While Chapter 13 is directly related to Target 10.7 on facilitating orderly, safe, regular, and responsible migration, this chapter is also indirectly related to Targets 1.1 and 1.2, which aim to eradicate extreme poverty and reduce poverty according to national definitions. In fact, through the implementation of processes and procedures with regard to migration flows, this can subsequently increase the impact of migration on poverty reduction for both host countries and migrants themselves (Hagen-Zanker et al., 2017). Furthermore, the improvement of regular channels addressed through the chapter facilitates migrants to be legally recognized in destination countries. Therefore, this implication points to Target 1.4, which seeks to ensure that all men and women, in particular the poor and the vulnerable, have equal rights to economic resources, basic social services, ownership and control of various forms of property as well as appropriate new technologies that enhance access to economic opportunities.

Target 1.5 aims to decrease the exposure of the poor and vulnerable to extreme events, such as economic, social, and environmental shocks. As advanced by the literature, remittances can be viewed as an informal insurance, which act as a safety net to households in event of negative shocks (Lucas & Stark, 1985; Yang, 2011). However, the effectiveness of this insurance mechanism may be disrupted by remitting channels that are costly, by hindering the volume of remittance funds and subsequently their impact on welfare, as exposed in Chapter 5. The results of Chapter 5 also demonstrate how the disproportionally high cost of remittances in resource-limited sub-Saharan African countries has a negative impact on household consumption per capita of receiving countries as one of the welfare indicators. This has a direct implication on SDG 1 through Targets 1.1 and 1.2 which relate to reduction of national poverty. As the cost of remittances are increasingly reduced by innovative internet-based technologies, this chapter and Chapter 9 support Target 1.4 which seeks to enhance access to economic rights through new cost-reducing technology such as mobile money and financial services such as alternative transfer mechanisms from banks and higher degrees of competition between remittance service providers.

In addition to supporting Target 10.C, aiming to reduce by 2030, 'to less than 3 per cent the transaction costs of migrant remittances and eliminate remittance corridors with costs higher than 5 per cent', the issue addressed in Chapter 5 may impede the impact not only of remittances on the achievement of Target 1.5, but also of SDG 2, 'Zero hunger', through Target 2.1, which intends to end hunger and ensure access by all people to safe, nutritious, and sufficient food all-year round. Target 3.4 of SDG 3, 'Good health and well-being', seeks to promote mental health and well-being for all at all ages. In Chapter 11, the authors stress the importance of achieving Target 10.7, as irregular migrants may face challenges in their journey that impact negatively their health. More precisely, this chapter shows that experiences with corruption and consequences of non-payment in irregular channels have serious consequences for the short-, medium-, and long-term physical and mental health of male and female migrants. In the same vein, the issue of irregular migration addressed in Chapters 11 and 13, which limits the access to basic services such as health coverage for migrants using these channels, is linked to Target 3.8 that seeks to achieve universal health coverage access to quality essential health-care services.

This book has devoted a central focus on SDG 4, 'Quality of education', in Part III, which explores the relationship of migration with education and knowledge in Africa. First, the findings in Chapter 6 about the positive effect of remittances on educational outcomes can be linked to Target 4.1, which aims to ensure children have access to equitable and quality education leading to relevant and effective learning outcomes. Moreover, the results exposed in the chapter provide more evidence that point to gender differences, for which girls tend to be more negatively affected. These issues posit challenges in complying with Target 4.5, which seeks to eliminate gender disparities in education and ensure equal access to all levels of education. Chapter 9 also offers direct evidence towards the importance of achieving Target 4.1. Through the increased efficiency of mobile money use in transmitting internal remittances (via enhanced maximization of receipts), recipient households are able to allocate greater expenses towards education in the long run. If this investment is turned into quality education, the use of mobile money in remittance transfers would thus contribute to Target 4.1.

Second, the findings in Chapter 7 related to knowledge transfer from diaspora members through formal trainings in higher education institutions point to Target 4.C, which promotes the supply of qualified teachers, such as through international cooperation for teacher training in developing countries. Based on the assumption that diaspora skill sets are well aligned with country of origin development needs, and skill transfer programmes are well executed, this can be linked to the objective of Target 4. 7, which ensures that all learners acquire the knowledge and skills needed to promote sustainable development. Third, the findings exposed in Chapter 8 with regard to the contribution of returnees can be associated with Target 4.4, which encourages the increase of youth and adults who have relevant skills, including technical and vocational skills, subsequently improving employment, decent jobs, and entrepreneurship in origin countries.

Chapter 11 also provides several implications regarding the vulnerability of women employing irregular channels, which can be linked to SDG 5, 'Gender equality'. As documented by this chapter, women are exposed to sexual extortion, in addition to more typical forms of corruption that are experienced by men. Furthermore, women from highly patriarchal societies are found to travel with little financial resources and are therefore often more vulnerable to sextortion and abuse. These issues can be recognized as harmful for the accomplishment of Target 5.1, which aims to eradicate all forms of discrimination against all women and girls. These practices can also have indirect implications for other SDGs, such as SDGs 2, 3, and 6 on 'clean water and sanitation'. For instance, the authors report female migrants in prisons having to engage in sexual acts for food, health services, and water. In addition, the chapter reveals that women are also commodified as the means of exchange for groups of migrants when crossing borders. Thus, this finding provides insights on Target 5.2, which seeks to end all forms of violence against all women and girls in the public and private spheres, such as trafficking and sexual and other types of exploitation. These vulnerabilities faced by women through irregular channels emphasize even more the importance of the Target 10.7 that encourages the facilitation of orderly, safe, regular, and responsible migration and mobility of people.

This book has provided some lessons for people who are interested in SDGs 8, 'Decent work and economic growth', and 9, 'Industry, innovation and infrastructure', which have been addressed directly or indirectly through different chapters. The linkages between migration and trade in Chapter 2 can be directly linked to Target 8.2, which aims to achieve higher levels of economic productivity through diversification, technological upgrading, and innovation. Findings in Chapter 4 are directly linked with the achievement of Target 8.6 which supports the substantial reduction of unemployed youth. By better understanding the internal migration of youth, governments can better craft coherent policies that support youth-based employment initiatives (towards decent jobs and entrepreneurship) which can leverage the drive and talent of incoming young people. By streamlining youth-centric issues into national labour and migration policies, countries can reduce youth employment driven by internal migration.

Moreover, the findings in Chapter 2 related to the development of business and scientific networks can be linked to several targets included in SDG 9, 'Industry, innovation and infrastructure'. For instance, this mechanism complies with Target 9.3, which promotes the increased access of small-scale industrial and other enterprises to financial services. In addition, this finding can be associated with Target 9.4, which seeks to upgrade infrastructure and industries to make them sustainable, through resource-use efficiency and greater adoption of clean and environmentally technologies and processes. Through Targets 9.3 and 9.4, migration can be linked to Target 9.A, which aims to facilitate sustainable and resilient infrastructure development through enhanced financial, technological, and technical support to African countries. Furthermore, findings in Chapter 3 can also support the achievement of targets included in SDG 9, such as Target 9.A.

Because innovation is greatly stimulated by the transfer of skills, knowledge, and technology, Chapters 7 and 8 in Part III also provide implications regarding SDG 9. For instance, the skills and knowledge transferred by diaspora members and returnees can be regarded as a strong source of innovation in African countries. Additionally, Chapter 8 shows that skilled migrants may have the ability to generate employment at return, which contributes to the wellbeing of the returnees themselves and the country's youth, as well as generating income through taxes for the country's economy. Therefore, these findings can be associated with several SDG 8 targets, such as 8.3, 8.5, and 8.6, which commonly aim to increase productivity and reduce unemployment through job creation. Based on the insights related to SDGs 8 and 9, these add support to the importance of facilitating mobility through safe, orderly, regular, and responsible migration through better migration policies, as stated in Target 10.7. Findings in Chapter 6 in Part III can also be linked to SDG 9, and more particularly to Target 9.C, which promotes the access to information and communications technology. In fact, the author argues that besides remittances, parents who migrated engage with new media environments and technologies of communication to keep an active parenting, foster intimate ties, and help with childcare. Consequently, the achievement of Target 9.C would allow parent migrant to stay engaged in the decision-making of children, such as decisions related to schooling, which relates indirectly to SDG 4.

SDG Goal 10 focuses on the reduction of inequality within and among countries with Target 10.7 focusing specifically on the importance of facilitating and ensuring safe, regular, and responsible migration and mobility of people. The evidence generated in Chapter 3 directly supports the direct achievement of this target as short-term movements of migrants carry technological innovations which enhance economic growth. The author contends that the advancement of free movement of people across the continent, through the erosion of border-based barriers, can facilitate knowledge exchanges that foster innovation. The short-term labour mobility also has a positive indirect impact on poverty reduction (Goal 1) through economic growth, ensures quality education (Goal 4), promotes productive employment and decent work (Goal 8), and promotes peace, justice, and strong institutions (Goal 16). Chapter 9 offers indirect support for the accomplishment of Target 10.C which, as mentioned before, supports the reduction to less than 3% the transaction costs of migrant remittances and eliminates remittance corridors with costs higher than 5%. While the improved efficiency of mobile money has had a positive, direct impact on recipient households' welfare, international remittance channels are still expensive and slow in processing transfers. The author contends that it is not only cost that determines the efficiency of transfer—international remittance systems must also improve on speed and ease of use in order to achieve Target 10.C.

SDG 11, 'Sustainable cities and communities', seeks to make cities and human developments inclusive, safe, resilient, and sustainable by addressing issues of housing, transport, urbanization, regional development, and the environment. Based on the insights of Chapter 4, the results support the importance of achieving SDG Targets 11.1 and 11.3 where governments are encouraged to provide adequate and safe dwelling spaces as many rural youth migrate to urban spaces where they live in sub-par housing facilities, often in slums, and suffer from exorbitant pricing rates of basic housing services such as water and sanitation. Achieving Targets 11.1 and 11.3 would shift the motives for youth to leave the country to secure a better social environment. Targets 11.6 and 11.B support the attention towards the environmental landscape of urban areas towards which many Kenyan youth internally migrate in search for promising economic opportunities. The chapter highlights how young people suffer from degraded air and water quality as urban cities buckle under the pressure of an increased population without the adequate waste and chemical management systems along their life-cycle. This has a negative impact on both the environmental sustainability of cities and the health of city youth dwellers. Clearly, the need for adequate city planning by Kenyan national and sub-national bodies is key in order to achieve SDG 11 on sustainable cities and communities.

As advanced by the literature, institutional quality does play an important role not only in driving migration but also in determining the effects of remittances in Africa (Adams & Klobodu, 2016; Chitambara, 2019). Therefore, several chapters in this book have provided insights related to SDG 16, 'Peace and justice strong institutions', which promotes peace, justice, and strong institutions. Among this SDG, Target 16.5 seeks to reduce corruption and bribery in all their forms. Findings exposed in Chapter 10 relate to the positive impact of financial remittances on corruption could thus be harmful for the accomplishment of that target. On the contrary, social remittances by migrants residing in OECD countries support positively the accomplishment of Target 16.5. Through this social remittances channel, Chapter 10 also provides evidence that diaspora members can contribute positively to the enhancement of institutions, such as illustrated in the case example in Somaliland. In addition to the ones exposed in Chapter 12 concerning the reduced electoral violence, these findings thus provide insights for Targets 16.1 and 16.4, which aim to reduce all forms of violence and illicit financial and arms flows.

Chapter 11 on vulnerabilities of irregular migrants can also be associated with different targets included in SDG 16. For instance, the authors reinforce that corruption becomes relevant whenever legal options for migration are limited, and that corruption is constant throughout all stages of the migration process for many migrants, which stress even more the importance of Target 16.5. Targets 16.1 and 16.2, for which the latter refers to eradicating the abuse, exploitation, trafficking, and all forms of violence, can also be associated with this chapter. Moreover, this chapter can be associated with Target 16.6, which promotes the development of effective, accountable, and transparent institutions. In fact, the authors in this chapter illustrate that the distinction between state and non-state actors asking for payments is blurred in many transit countries. Additionally, the chapter reports that experiences with corruption and severe violence incurred by state and non-state actors may also explain why many migrants are scared of authorities upon arrival in Europe.

Chapter 13 provides some guidance on the implementation of planned and well-managed migration policies, connecting some aspects of SDG 16, in order to facilitate orderly, safe, regular, and responsible migration and mobility of people, as motivated in Target 10.7. For instance, the author encourages the involvement of different stakeholders in order to understand migration dynamics and, consequently, engage in appropriate policies to address irregular migration. In addition to support Target 16.6, this implication can be linked to Target 16.7, which seeks to ensure responsive, inclusive, participatory, and representative decision-making at all levels.

Along with this need to involve different actors at different levels to address irregular migration, the guidance provided in Chapter 13 can be associated with many targets in SDG 17, 'Partnerships to achieve the goal', which calls for partnerships in order to achieve the sustainable goals. This chapter invites Eastern African countries to create an efficient system of taking stock of the knowledge and data on irregular migration from a variety of sources and services providers, including community-based information, which reveals to be rich given that they are source and host locations for some of the irregular migrants. This points to Targets 17.16 and 17.17, which promote multi-stakeholder partnerships that mobilize and share knowledge, expertise, strategic, technology, and financial resources. Along with these targets, the author encourages practices that report human trafficking or migrant smuggling, which help to monitor and evaluate how well a country addresses irregular migration.

In this book, several chapters provide evidence on remittances as a source of development, and especially when they are facilitated through efficient channels as encouraged by Target 10.C, as demonstrated in Chapter 8. Therefore, remittances should be strongly considered in Target 17.3, which promotes the use of additional financial resources from multiple sources. For instance, findings in Chapters 8 and 9 imply that achieving this target through an increase in remittances could help to attaining SDGs 16 and 4, respectively. However, Chapter 10 recalls that anti-corruption policies related to Target 16.5 should be considered for the success of Target 17.3.

Besides remittances, Chapter 2 advances that migrant resources, including social, human, and financial capital, can support development within the private sector through both investment and philanthropy, which is not only linked to Target 17.3 but also indirectly to Target 17.11, which aims to increase the exports of developing countries. In Chapters 7 and 8, the authors stress the importance of the existence of an environment facilitating the contribution of diaspora members and returnees to the development in the countries of origin. This contribution can be facilitated to the achievement of Targets 17.5, 17.6, 17.7, 17.8, and 17.9, which commonly aim to promote investment, to encourage regional and international cooperation facilitating science, knowledge and technology sharing, and to enhance the international support for implementing effective and targeted capacity building.

Through these chapters, and their relevance to SDGs, it can be further advanced that migrants may face challenges and barriers throughout each step of their journey, which may subsequently impede the impact of migration on development in Africa. Therefore, certain SDGs and SDG targets reveal to be crucial to tackle these challenges and barriers. As mentioned earlier, Target 10.7 on facilitating orderly, safe, regular, and responsible migration can be recognized as a central element for facilitating the positive impact of migration on development in Africa. Through the accomplishment of this target, vulnerable people willing to migrate would not be constrained to transit through irregular channels. As a consequence, the implementation planned and well-managed migration policies could be beneficial towards the achievement of several SDG targets that were negatively affected by irregular migration, such as SDG 1, 2, 3, 5, and 6. Furthermore, facilitating migration, as well as return migration, could facilitate even more the transfer of knowledge and skills as motivated by some chapters, which could consequently stimulate the impact of migration on SDGs 4, 8, 9, and 16. The latter, SDG 16, also revealed to be important in determining not only migration itself but also the impact of migration and remittances in origin countries. As argued multiple times across this book, the achievement of SDG 16 remains central for remittances to have a positive impact in origin countries. Afterwards, Target 17.3 should be promoted along with Target 10.C, in order to maximize the welfare impact of remittances, as well as the accomplishment of SDGs in Africa.

References

Adams, S., & Klobodu, E. K. M. (2016). Remittances, regime durability and economic growth in Sub-Saharan Africa (SSA). *Economic Analysis and Policy, 50*, 1–8.

Chitambara, P. (2019). Remittances, institutions and growth in Africa. *International Migration 57*(5), 56–70.

Hagen-Zanker, J., Vidal, E. M., & Sturge, G. (2017). Social protection, migration and the 2030 Agenda for Sustainable Development. Retrieved from https://doc. rero.ch/record/308981/files/24-10._ODI_Socialprotection.pdf

Lucas, R. E., & Stark, O. (1985). Motivations to remit: Evidence from Botswana. *Journal of Political Economy, 93*(5), 901–918.

Yang, D. (2011). Migrant Remittances. *Journal of Economic Perspectives, 25*(3), 129–152.

Index

Note: Page numbers followed by "n" refer to notes.

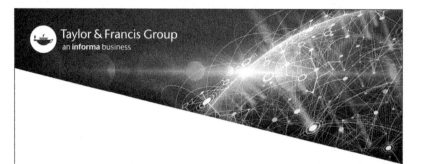

Printed in the United States
By Bookmasters